# .NET Wireless
# Programming

# .NET Wireless Programming

Mark Ridgeway

SYBEX

San Francisco · London

Associate Publisher: Richard Mills
Acquisitions and Developmental Editor: Denise Santoro Lincoln
Editors: Brianne Hope Agatep, Susan Berge, Jim Gabbert, Joseph Webb
Production Editor: Leslie E.H. Light
Technical Editors: Robert (Bob) Laberge and Srdjan Vujosevic
Graphic Illustrator: Tony Jonick
Electronic Publishing Specialist: Judy Fung
Proofreaders: Laurie O'Connell, Yariv Rabinovitch
Indexer: Jack Lewis
Cover Designer: Carol Gorska/Gorska Design
Cover Photographer: Tony Stone

Library of Congress Card Number: 2001096242

ISBN: 0-7821-2975-7

*To the two most important people in my life:*
*my wife, Marian, and our son, Tyler.*

# Acknowledgements

Many people have contributed to this book along the way. To the good people at Sybex, thank you for your ideas, support, and guidance. In particular, thank you to Denise Santoro Lincoln, who originally suggested the book and got the whole project off the ground. Thank you also to Leslie Light and Brianne Agatep, who have guided the project through to completion, gently repaired my many grammatical mistakes, and helped entire paragraphs make sense. I must also thank Joe Webb, Jim Gabbert, and Susan Berge from Sybex for doing some of the editorial work on various chapters.

I would also like to thank the various people who have lent their technical expertise in suggesting things I have overlooked, picking up any errors, and making sure that what I have written about will actually work. In particular: Bob LaBerge, Srdjan Vujosevic, and Michael Bruce—I would be in trouble without you!

I must also thank the many people at Microsoft who helped out with advice, suggestions, and technical support at various points along the way. And a big thank you to the various members of the mobile/wireless developers community—a rapidly growing brood who are always willing to help each other out with ideas, suggestions, and specialized knowledge.

Finally, I must thank my family for their love, tolerance, and support. I wouldn't have gotten there without you.

# Contents at a Glance

# Contents

# Introduction

The lights in the crowded theatre had dimmed and the spotlight was focused on the Microsoft evangelists doing their thing on the stage. I had settled a little into my seat amongst the audience and closed my eyes, waiting for the third coffee of the day to kick in. All of a sudden, I heard the guy in a suit next to me straighten up in his seat and mutter, "Amazing!" It was his first introduction to the power of mobile, wireless technologies, and he instantly reminded me (who had been playing with the technology for the past 18 months) of just how serendipitous that experience can be.

Imagine all your data, all your applications, and all your work available simultaneously from a cell phone, a laptop, and a desktop computer. Imagine that your cell phone can be used as a pocket or handheld PC. Access your organization's Intranet and obtain information from the Internet anytime, any place.

The Microsoft evangelists demonstrated an e-commerce system where they placed an order over the Internet and then used a wireless Pocket PC to process the order at the warehouse level. A confirmation of the order was sent to the client's cell phone by the system.

The system just seemed to make so much sense that the guy in the suit muttered to himself, "Why aren't we doing this now?" Around the whole theatre, this sense of excitement rose as the rest of the demonstration unfolded. Never mind how all of this was supposed to work—most of these people were playing at the management level and when they get excited by an idea they expect to be able to point to others and say, "Make it happen."

But Microsoft did not leave us hanging; they then introduced the next generation technology that could help build a total end-to-end solution. Microsoft is by no means the first to offer powerful tools for developing mobile, wireless applications. However, their .NET technologies offer possibilities for cross-platform solutions that extend the notion of computing far beyond where we are today.

With this simple demonstration, Microsoft had succeeded in inspiring another generation of management with a vision of the long-term, strategic possibilities for their IT budgets.

And for those of us who love to play at the cutting edge of technology, we thrive on new ideas and exploring new possibilities, and we are more than happy to be the ones that are told to "make it happen."

If you haven't been here before, welcome to the world of wireless and mobile connectivity. This book that you hold in your hands now is about how to create interactive and dynamic applications for the Mobile Internet using some of the new tools being developed by Microsoft, specifically, Microsoft's Mobile Internet Toolkit and Visual Studio .NET.

The areas of wireless computing and mobile applications have grown rapidly over the last five years, and it is expected that by the year 2005, the majority of Internet users will be able to access the Web from a mobile device.

This creates enormous opportunities for developers wishing to get in on the "ground floor" of a new technology and opens up exciting possibilities for how people will do business and communicate in the early part of the 21$^{st}$ century.

Microsoft sees mobile technology as a key part of its integrated .NET strategy. The company no longer views different technologies and platforms as being distinct entities that operate independently from each other. Working with Microsoft's mobile technologies means that we also work with back-end database technologies, desktop application development, Web design, distributed application architecture, ASP technologies, and content and service provision.

To borrow a phrase that is almost irritatingly popular at Microsoft sponsored events: "This stuff is amazingly cool!"

I even heard the guy in the suit say it. Enjoy the ride!

Mark Ridgeway, December 2001.

## Key Terminology

The term *wireless* can be applied to a wide range of scenarios where computers are connected by something other than wires. Examples include infrared, radio, and microwave. Wireless can be used to connect the whole spectrum of digital devices, including desktop computers, laptops, palmtops, PDAs, and mobile phones.

*Mobile device* usually refers to any digital device that is small enough to be easily carried around and possessing its own power supply. This includes laptop computers, PDAs, palmtops, and mobile phones.

For our purposes, we are interested in wireless, mobile devices of the pocket-sized variety, such as PDAs, palmtops, and mobile phones.

We also need to distinguish between online and embedded applications. The development of embedded applications that exist and run on the device itself is very different from applications that exist online and are accessed by some form of browser software.

The purpose of this book is to illustrate the building of online sites and applications.

Finally, we need to distinguish between the Internet and the Mobile Internet. Internet sites are mainly built using HTML (Hypertext Markup Language) and are designed for viewing on conventional computer screens. On the other hand, Mobile Internet sites may or may not be built using HTML—more likely WML (Wireless Markup Language)—and are designed for viewing on very small, limited screens.

## What Is the Mobile Internet Toolkit?

As part of its .NET development framework, Microsoft has introduced the Mobile Internet Toolkit.

With the Mobile Internet Toolkit, Microsoft offers mobile developers a "write once, run anywhere" approach. This is coupled to a drag-and-drop development environment powered by the developer's own language of choice.

Currently the mobile world is populated by a growing multitude of devices, each with their own idiosyncrasies and individual interpretations of the protocols they support. There are also a number of competing standards. This has resulted in a situation where a developer, looking to create a widely accessible mobile application or site, needs to write a lot of extra code and often multiple versions of the same site. Tools have been released by a number of companies to help developers cope with this problem, and Microsoft has entered this rapidly expanding market with its Mobile Internet Toolkit.

Microsoft has created a development/deployment environment that simplifies things significantly. The developer is able to create their application or site using a combination of graphical tools and their preferred language (i.e., Visual Basic, C++, C#, etc.). The deployment aspect of the package then automatically takes care of all the presentation problems. It identifies the particular device and generates appropriate code (whether it be WML, HTML, etc.) so that the site/application can be presented on that device.

The mobile developer, using the Mobile Internet Toolkit, no longer needs to have a detailed understanding of the various mobile languages or keep up with the particular requirements of the growing list of mobile devices. This enables developers to concentrate on designing the business logic aspect of their applications and producing meaningful content for their sites.

In addition to the .NET development tools, Microsoft has developed an entire end-to-end approach for mobile development and deployment. This includes the following packages:

- Microsoft Mobile Information 2001 Server
- Microsoft Mobile Explorer (Web browser for mobile devices)
- Stinger (software platform for mobile phones)

- Pocket Internet Explorer and Pocket Office applications for pocket PCs
- Content and services, including MSN Mobile

The company is also conducting ongoing development into related technologies such as smart cards, location-based services, and speech technologies.

## Who Should Read This Book?

First, answer these questions:

- Are you interested in the exciting world of the Mobile Internet? Have you heard about the possibilities of mobile applications and wonder whether they have a place in your organization?
- Are you a developer currently using Microsoft tools for application and/or Web development? Are you looking for a way to expand your horizons and leverage your skills across to mobile applications?
- Do you currently design sites for the Mobile Web and are you interested in whether Microsoft offers a more powerful and/or simpler solution?
- Have you dabbled a little bit with Web design, maybe had a little exposure to scripting languages such as VBScript, and want to find out more about building sites for mobile devices?
- Are you a student or a teacher looking for information and projects to build for the Mobile Web?

You do not need to have a detailed understanding of Visual Basic to read this book, although it would help if you had some understanding of programming. The beauty of .NET is that developers are able to use their preferred language to build their applications. All the examples in this book are fully explained and can be easily rewritten into other computer languages.

## Tools Required

To work with .NET and the Mobile Internet Toolkit, you will need to have a few tools:

**Software**   You will need the following:

- A copy of Microsoft's Visual Studio .NET including the .NET Framework and the Mobile Internet Toolkit. These may be obtained separately or as part of the Visual Studio .NET package.

- Emulators for various mobile devices are either provided as stand-alone entities or included in the SDKs released by various companies. These tools allow developers to test code for a particular device on their own computer without having to go out and buy that device. The following are good starting points:
  - Mobile Explorer from Microsoft (worth getting as part of the Microsoft Mobile Explorer Content Toolkit)
  - The UP.Browser (`http://www.openwave.com`)
  - The Nokia browser (`http://forum.nokia.com/main.html`)
- Your computer should be running (in either their Professional, Server, or Advanced Server guises) Microsoft Windows NT 4, 2000, or XP (each with latest service packs). Note that NT 4 Workstation is only supported for client-side development. You will also need a copy of Microsoft's Web server, IIS 5.0, and Internet Explorer 6 or up.

**TIP**   The Mobile Internet Toolkit and Microsoft Mobile Explorer Content Toolkit can be obtained directly from Microsoft at `http://msdn.microsoft.com/downloads`.

**Hardware**   You will need the following:

- A computer powerful enough to run your particular mix of software and operating system. The minimum recommended specifications for Visual Studio .NET are 450 MHz Pentium II class processor or above, 64MB RAM, and 3GB of installation space available on the hard drive. Recommended specs are 733 MHz Pentium III class processor, 128MB RAM, and 3GB hard drive.
- A mobile device capable of accessing the Internet (such as a WAP-enabled mobile phone) is useful for viewing and testing your applications in "the wild."

**Production Systems**   For application deployment, a server requires the following software:

- Microsoft .NET Framework
- The Mobile Internet Controls Runtime component of the Mobile Internet Toolkit

## More Information

Sybex has published all the code used in this book on their Website at `www.sybex.com/`. Search for this book using the title, author, or the ISBN number (2975), and click the Downloads button. Once you have accepted the license agreement, you'll be able to download any of the code listed in this book.

As with any code published on a Website, be careful when copying and pasting as extra line breaks can sometimes occur that cause your application to go pear shaped!

A list of developer sites has been included in Appendix C, "Internet References." Many of these sites run excellent e-mail lists where people can discuss these technologies and share problems and solutions. Microsoft runs its own Mobile Internet Toolkit SDK newsgroup at `http://microsoft.public.dotnet.framework.aspnet.mobile` which can be accessed through `http://msdn.microsoft.com/newsgroups`.

## Some Final Points

This book has been written using the beta and release-candidate versions of the Mobile Internet Toolkit and Visual Studio .NET. Inevitably, there will be some differences between these and the final release versions of these packages. I have attempted to anticipate a number of these differences and to point them out where they are likely to occur.

Many of the lines of code included in this book are simply too long for the page widths! I have indicated line breaks in code listings with the following ➥ symbol.

Enjoy the book. I hope you find it a valuable resource as you explore the exciting new world of wireless and mobile connectivity!

# Part I

# Microsoft .NET: The Overview

# CHAPTER 1

# What Is .NET?

- The .NET Framework

- Visual Studio .NET

- SOAP (Simple Object Access Protocol)

- About the Mobile Internet Toolkit

At the end of the chapter, readers can expect to have achieved a basic understanding of the following:

- What Microsoft is hoping to achieve with .NET
- The distributed nature of .NET and the role of new developments such as XML Web Services
- The role of individual aspects of .NET, particularly relevant to this book such as the .NET Framework, Visual Studio .NET, SOAP, and the Mobile Internet Toolkit

Before we launch into a study of the Mobile Internet Toolkit portion of .NET, it is a good idea to have an understanding of the entire .NET package.

In this chapter we will have a look at a broad outline of .NET, some of its key components and how the Mobile Internet Toolkit fits into the total package.

Microsoft defines .NET as being a five-part strategy consisting of the following:

- The .NET Framework and Visual Studio .NET developer tools
- Server infrastructure—Microsoft's various server packages
- Building Block Services such as portable user identification (Passport)
- Devices—software products covering a range of different devices
- User experiences—applications such as Office and services such as MSN

Later in this chapter, we will cover the .NET Framework and Visual Studio .NET package. We will also investigate some of the other key .NET components. In Chapter 2, "Microsoft's End-to-End Mobile Strategy," we will have a more detailed look at server infrastructure, devices, and some of the building block services and user experiences.

Essentially, .NET represents an integrated approach to software development, deployment, and usage. Developers no longer need to build applications and services just for a mobile platform, a Pocket PC platform, or a desktop platform. Each of these is seen as a greater part of the whole with users able to seamlessly transfer data between the platforms. A single application might work across these platforms—for example, a messaging system that communicates delivery instructions from warehouse PCs (personal computers) to the delivery drivers' mobile phones via a server. The information entered into the PC might come directly from a dedicated wireless mobile barcode reader.

.NET is also firmly based on a distributed computing model. Applications can be assembled from components or XML Web Services that exist on different machines. XML (eXtensible Markup Language) is the language used to communicate between these XML Web Services, and Microsoft sees it as the "glue" that makes .NET work. XML Web Services may be either software components or resources such as data libraries.

XML Web Services rely on SOAP (Simple Object Access Protocol) to transmit and receive data and commands within a distributed system. This protocol describes how the data and commands should be represented using XML. There are a number of other services and technologies associated with the use of SOAP that are described in the "SOAP" section later in this chapter.

As an application may consist of a number of XML Web Services accessing a number of other XML Web Services, which could be spread over a large number of machines potentially across the planet, execution sequences can become a problem. Not everything will necessarily happen in the correct order. In these scenarios, .NET allows for the synchronous (in sequence) or asynchronous (out of sequence) execution of the various functions. This needs to be specified in the code during design, but it means that applications won't sit there churning away to themselves, waiting for something to come down the pipe, and locking the user out of doing something else on their machine. Figure 1.1 illustrates how an application built around XML Web Services might look.

**FIGURE 1.1:**

Sample application using XML Web Services

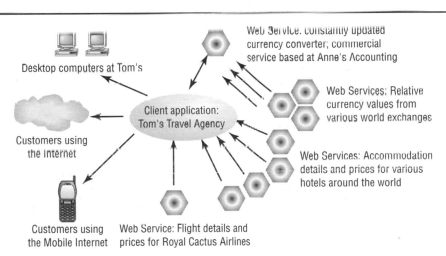

Tom's Travel Agency (TTA) is able to give up-to-the-minute quotes on travel costs using a Web Service-driven application. This application makes use of a currency converter Web Service provided by Anne's Accounting. This application draws on other Web Services to give hourly updated figures. Anne charges users (such as TTA) for accessing this service. TTA also accesses flight details and prices from their preferred airline and accommodation costs from a range of worldwide hotels using Web Services. TTA provides the information to customers from the desktop computers at the agency, over the Internet, and over the Mobile Internet.

## The .NET Framework

The .NET framework is the main environment for building, deploying, and using XML Web Services. It consists of the following:

- The Common Language Runtime (CLR), the platform's execution engine; code written for .NET runs under its control

- The Framework classes

- ASP.NET (Active Server Pages for .NET)

Code is written using ASP.NET. Developers are able to use any .NET Framework-compatible language to write their applications and can access all elements of the .NET Framework from their code. Compatible languages include those shipping with .NET such as Visual Basic .NET, C++ and C# (pronounced "C Sharp") as well as a range of third-party languages such as Eiffel that have compilers developed to target the .NET common language runtime.

WYSIWYG (What You See Is What You Get) tools, such as Visual Studio .NET, work seamlessly with ASP.NET and developers can use a forms-based approach to build Web applications similar to how they may have used more traditional tools such as Visual Basic to build conventional applications in the past. Microsoft refers to these as *Web Forms*.

## Visual Studio .NET

Visual Studio .NET is the principal development tool for .NET. It integrates the formerly separate Microsoft development platforms (such as Visual Basic, Visual FoxPro, Visual C++, as well as the new C#) into a single IDE (Integrated Development Environment). You can build the majority of your applications in Visual Studio .NET, whether it be a traditional application, a distributed application based on XML Web Services, an XML Web Service or COM component, or a Website.

It also provides the IDE for building mobile sites and applications using the Mobile Internet Toolkit.

As illustrated in Figure 1.2, programmers can open Visual Studio .NET, and choose the type of project they wish to build (such as a Windows application or XML Web Service) and the language they wish to build it in. You can even change languages within a project where necessary or use a non-Microsoft language (such as Eiffel).

**FIGURE 1.2:**

Developers have the choice of project type and language in Visual Studio .NET.

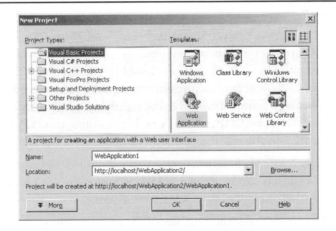

In addition, Microsoft has included a new language in Visual Studio .NET, C#. This language is designed to bring a simpler, more RAD (Rapid Application Development) approach to the world of C/C++ programming. It is object-oriented, is type-safe, and offers automatic garbage collection. As you can see in Figure 1.3, if you have previously used any of the Microsoft visual development tools, the new Visual Studio .NET interface is very familiar.

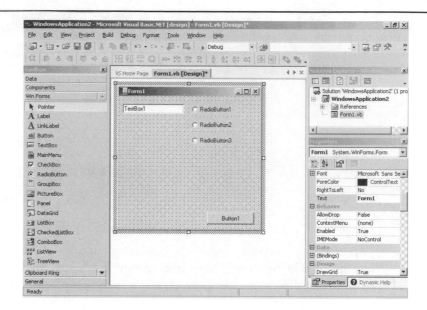

## SOAP

SOAP (Simple Object Access Protocol) is a lightweight protocol for exchanging data in a distributed heterogeneous environment. It provides a set of rules (or grammar for XML) about how data and commands should be represented. In the past, distributed computing has run aground because the objects required are unable to be accessed through the firewalls and security protocols set up (quite rightly!) around many networks. SOAP now allows these objects to transmit their data or receive commands via Port 80 (the HTTP port that any network administrator wishing to use the Internet would normally leave open).

New XML Web Services are set up with SOAP already incorporated into them. Existing COM objects can be given a SOAP "wrapper" (using Visual Studio .NET) that enables them to be used as a distributed XML Web Service.

Microsoft has other members of the SOAP "family" that work alongside the protocol to help make it possible for developers to actually find and use available XML Web Services in their applications:

**WSDL**    Another XML "grammar" (set of rules for XML) is WSDL (Web Service Description Language). WSDL is used to expose the capabilities of an XML Web Service. For example, we might have an XML Web Service that has some function called "calculate" that requires three variables $a$, $b$, and $c$. We would talk to the XML Web Service using WSDL to find out about this function and what its requirements were.

**Disco**    Disco, which is short for SOAP Discovery, is used to locate descriptions for XML Web Services. When an XML Web Service is created, a file with the extension `.disco` is also generated. This file enables the WSDL description files for a particular site to be automatically located when someone wishes to make use of the XML Web Services in a distributed application. (This assumes that the owner of the site is willing to allow the use of his or her XML Web Services in some other distributed application!)

**UDDI**    UDDI (Universal Description, Discovery, and Integration) is a directory service to provide the location of a whole range of XML Web Services. They are categorized into various types of information and services. For more information, see `http://www.uddi.org/`.

## The Mobile Internet Toolkit

The Mobile Internet Toolkit is all about developers being able to write a single site or application for the mobile Internet that is viewable on any device irrespective of its individual idiosyncrasies, platform, supported protocols, languages dial tone, case color, etc.

In principle, we could write a single site viewable on the "big screen" Internet as well as the mobile Internet using this "write once, present anywhere" approach. In practice however, we need to keep our desktop Internet sites and mobile Internet sites as separate entities unless we are intent on wishing unsatisfactory browsing experiences on our site visitors! It may be at some point in the future that the two may begin to converge, but at the moment they are two quite separate mediums in the way they are used and the information they can convey.

Mobile applications are built in ASP.NET using a special set of mobile controls. The controls are added to a Mobile Web Form (which is a particular type of ASP.NET Web Form) and then coded "behind" using the development language of choice. We will be using Visual Basic .NET in this book.

The Mobile Internet Toolkit SDK consists of a set of server-side mobile controls, the Mobile Web Forms Designer, a tutorial, and relevant documentation. It is included as part of the Visual Studio .NET package. Although it is possible to write the code for the Mobile Internet Toolkit using any text editor (such as Notepad), it is a lot simpler to graphically build the mobile site or application using Visual Studio's standardized IDE.

If you are particularly keen to hand write applications using a standard text editor, the Mobile Web Forms are saved with the same `.aspx` file extension used now for all ASP.NET Web Forms. (Note: this is different from the old `.asp` extension used for Active Server Pages pre-.NET.) The "code behind" needs to be saved in a file using the extension of the language that you have used (`.vb` for Visual Basic and `.cs` for C#). This then needs to be compiled, which can be done from the command line, but I'll let you chase up the appropriate Microsoft documentation on how to do it yourself! It then needs to be placed in a "bin" directory inside the directory containing the Mobile Form. This can then be opened via your Web server as will be explained later in Chapter 4, "An Example of Mobile Technology: WAP and WML."

As the mobile environment is a rapidly expanding and changing field, the Mobile Internet Toolkit has been designed to support a wide range of platforms and devices. It is also extensible and allows for the further inclusion of new devices as they are developed.

Applications and sites built using .NET can be tested using "real devices" or emulators such as the Mobile Explorer emulator or the Openwave emulator (as illustrated in Figure 1.4).

**FIGURE 1.4:**

The UP.Simulator, an example of Openwave's mobile emulator

Image of UP.SDK courtesy Openwave Systems, Inc.

Mobile applications are usually built-in "decks" of "cards" with each card representing the Internet equivalent of a page. Each deck is in fact a single page of code, so in HTML terms, it would be like writing your entire Website onto a single page of code and only using a section of the code to represent each page of the site. The Mobile Internet Toolkit allows this to happen by permitting developers to place multiple form controls onto a single Mobile Form Web page. As controls are added to the forms on the page, each control has a `runat=server` attribute declared to ensure that they are executed as server-side code.

The result is a streamlined development environment with drag-and-drop controls onto a single form (or multiple forms if you wish). The business logic and content can then be added in the traditional "code behind" approach used with Microsoft development tools. Developers already schooled in ASP.NET have very little to learn before they begin developing sites and applications for the mobile Internet. The adaptive rendering of the Mobile Internet Toolkit handles device detection and appropriate presentation of the code for any mobile device.

## Summary

Microsoft's .NET brings together a range of development tools, platform software, and services under one integrated umbrella. The developer can now create user-centric applications that are designed to work across a particular environment rather than just on a particular platform. Developers are able to use the tools and languages of their choice within the single IDE of Visual Studio.NET. At the wider level, XML Web Services and their associated protocols open up the real possibilities of building and using distributed applications across the Internet. The strong mobile focus of .NET and the creation of a set of dedicated tools simplify development in this area and help to ensure that any software solution is able to be equipped with mobile capability where appropriate.

# CHAPTER 2

# Microsoft's End-to-End Mobile Strategy

- Understanding Microsoft's Mobile Strategy

- Working with Components of Microsoft's Mobile Strategy

The purpose of this chapter is to introduce Microsoft's strategy for mobile devices and to investigate some of its key components. By the end of the chapter, the reader can expect to have some understanding of Microsoft's philosophy in this area, which is designed to target each aspect of mobile application development and delivery. Microsoft is working closely with hardware manufacturers to jointly produce products (such as mobile phones and handheld computers) that run its software on its operating systems. These products, in turn, are linked very closely with other products (such as servers) also running on and using Microsoft software. Lastly, Microsoft is also working at the service end to create and provide a range of both free-to-air and commercial (paying) services available over the Internet to the full range of devices and platforms capable of accessing the Web.

Readers will also be taken through various individual examples of Microsoft's strategy with a view to developing a closer understanding of how it all fits together. The examples include the following:

**Stinger**    Microsoft's mobile phone platform.

**Microsoft Mobile Explorer**    Microsoft's Internet browser for mobile devices.

**Microsoft Mobile Information 2001 Server**    Server platform specifically developed for mobile devices.

**Pocket PC**    PDA style mobile devices.

**Handheld PC**    Small, portable computers.

**Windows Embedded Operating Systems**    Various flavors of embedded operating systems developed by Microsoft to run mobile and industrial devices.

**My Internet**    An example of a commercial service being developed and offered by Microsoft over the Internet.

## Understanding Microsoft's Mobile Strategy

Microsoft's strategy for mobile technology goes far beyond just a development platform. It also includes platform software for mobile devices, applications, server software and services such as e-mail notification. Microsoft is also committed to ongoing research and development in the field. Figure 2.1 is a screen shot of the emulator for Microsoft Mobile Explorer that forms one plank of this strategy.

FIGURE 2.1:

The Mobile Explorer
Emulator

FIGURE 2.1:

The Mobile Explorer
Emulator

In Microsoft's vision and strategy documentation for mobile technology, "Microsoft Vision and Strategies for Mobile Technology," Microsoft says its strategy is "to extend, connect, and innovate." This documentation can be found at http://microsoft.com/business/mobility/vision.asp The company expands these key words with the following descriptions:

- "To *extend* the communication and collaboration potential of the more than 80 million users of MSN, MSN Hotmail, Microsoft Outlook, and Microsoft Exchange Server."

- "To *connect* users to the information they want, when and how they want it."

- "To *innovate* towards a new synergy among the platforms, applications, and tools of the computing and wireless industries."

Note that the italics are mine.

The company's aim is to seamlessly connect people to their data and information irrespective of the device they are using. It has identified four categories of wireless players that it is targeting with various services and technologies:

- Content and service providers

- Device manufacturers

- Carriers or network operators
- Computing/software technologists

The technological developments and services that Microsoft is promoting to these groups include the following:

**Content and services**    MSN Mobile service, which offers things such as mobile browser support for Hotmail.

**Software platforms and applications**    For mobile devices, this includes the operating systems, embedded applications, and development environments for these devices.

**Server software**    Includes mobile support in existing server platforms (such as Exchange 2000) and the development of new platforms (such as Mobile Information 2001 Server).

**New technologies**    On-going investment in new technologies (such as various flavours of speech-related software), location-based services, and smart-card technology.

Microsoft has also set up a number of partnership deals with key mobile players such as Ericsson and Samsung. It is involved with the consortium guiding the emerging standard of Bluetooth and maintains relationships with key organizations such as the WAP Forum. (The Bluetooth standard and the role of the WAP Forum are described in Chapter 3, "Wireless Overview.")

## Components of Microsoft's Mobile Strategy

The remainder of this chapter treats some of the key components of the strategy in more detail. We'll look at several of the mobile devices that Microsoft has developed platforms for, such as the Stinger mobile phone and the Pocket and Handheld PCs. We'll investigate the mobile-specific server software the company has developed and the Microsoft Mobile Explorer microbrowser. We'll also take a look at the Windows embedded operating systems and an Internet-based service, My Internet. Figure 2.2 illustrates the various roles played by the components in Microsoft's mobile strategy.

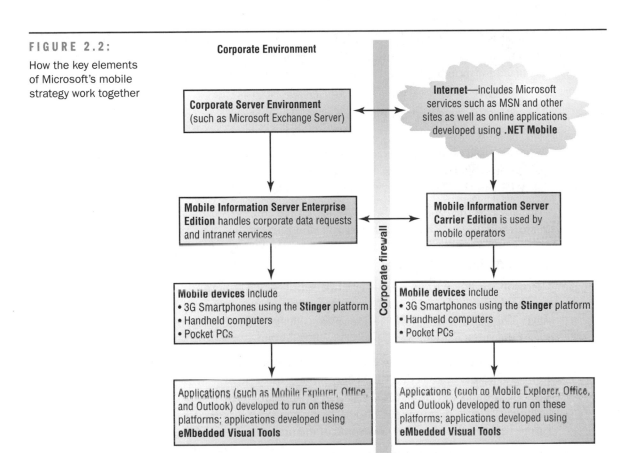

**FIGURE 2.2:**

How the key elements of Microsoft's mobile strategy work together

**Corporate Environment**

**Corporate Server Environment** (such as Microsoft Exchange Server)

**Internet**—includes Microsoft services such as MSN and other sites as well as online applications developed using **.NET Mobile**

**Mobile Information Server Enterprise Edition** handles corporate data requests and intranet services

**Mobile Information Server Carrier Edition** is used by mobile operators

**Corporate firewall**

**Mobile devices** Include
• 3G Smartphones using the **Stinger** platform
• Handheld computers
• Pocket PCs

**Mobile devices** include
• 3G Smartphones using the **Stinger** platform
• Handheld computers
• Pocket PCs

Applications (such as Mobile Explorer, Office, and Outlook) developed to run on these platforms; applications developed using **eMbedded Visual Tools**

Applications (such as Mobile Explorer, Office, and Outlook) developed to run on these platforms; applications developed using **eMbedded Visual Tools**

## Stinger Mobile Phone

Stinger is Microsoft's software platform for third-generation (3G) mobile phones. Microsoft uses the term "smartphone" to describe Stinger's capabilities and likens it to bringing the power of a PDA to a phone. It is designed to take advantage of broadband wireless 2.5G and 3G networks.

It is expected that third-generation phone technology will offer a full range of multimedia and data services including full motion video, e-mail, and location-based services. Stinger has been designed to give Microsoft a leading edge into this market with a platform that will support these services and, by its existence, encourage their deployment.

Stinger is based on the Windows CE 3.0 environment and therefore offers a high level of compatibility with other versions of Windows and their applications. It has been especially optimized for mobile phones to reduce battery load, reduce memory requirements, and offer real-time processing.

Microsoft has worked in conjunction with a number of other companies including Sendo and Samsung to develop the hardware for the platform.

Stinger-based phones have color screens, use Mobile IE to browse both WAP- and HTML-enabled sites, offer secure access to corporate data, have e-mail and PIM functionality, and can play MP3 and Windows Media audio files. Examples include the Z100 Smartphone from Sendo.

Stinger is at the forefront of the recent trend to add PDA capability to cell phones and to create a convergence between these two technologies.

## Microsoft Mobile Explorer

Microsoft Mobile Explorer 3.0 is a lightweight browser (microbrowser) designed for the mobile phone platform. It currently supports content written in HTML, cHTML, and WAP. This gives it an advantage over most other mobile phone browsers that support only one of the three popular formats.

Developers can test with the Mobile Explorer emulator on a standard computer. The only limitation at this stage is that the host computer must be running either Windows NT, 2000, or XP to support the emulator. As with most emulators, the Mobile Explorer emulator offers a range of "skins" to mimic the phones being emulated. Figure 2.1 illustrates the default skin for the package. Figure 2.3 shows some of the other skins available.

**FIGURE 2.3:**

The various flavors of Microsoft Mobile Explorer. A selection of phone "skins" are bundled with the emulator.

With a view to the developing e-commerce opportunities across the mobile platform, Mobile Explorer also offers full end-to-end security. It supports both SSL 3.0 (Secure Socket Layer 3.0) and the WAP 1.2.1 specification that includes the WTLS (Wireless Transport Layer Security) security specification.

Mobile Explorer 3.0 also supports push specifications for both WAP and SMS (Short Messaging Service). There have been some fears over the appropriateness of push technology with mobile devices. Some scenarios that have been painted include your phone ringing constantly as you walk past various commercial outlets. However, the way that push has been implemented means that you are unlikely to receive any content without having given prior consent to that particular provider.

The microbrowser also offers a wide range of graphics support across various formats. It is designed to provide access to e-mail, personal information, and data at either the personal or corporate level.

Samsung is one of the leading proponents of Mobile Explorer with their SGH-N350 being one of the first phones to be equipped with version 3.0 of the microbrowser.

## Microsoft Mobile Information 2001 Server

As part of its .NET server family, Microsoft has developed a mobile applications server designed to deliver secure and real-time services for mobile devices. The server comes in two flavors:

- Enterprise
- Carrier

The Enterprise version is designed for the corporate climate and would work closely with other corporate servers (such as Exchange) to provide wireless users with access to data, e-mail, and various intranet services. It is optimized for high-performance connections and the high level of security that occurs within the corporate firewall.

The Carrier edition, on the other hand, is developed for use by mobile operators and allows them to offer mobile servers to both business customers and the general public. Mobile data services can be rapidly deployed across a single platform and differentiated for consumers or corporate customers. Traditional desktop-based Internet services (such as MSN or Hotmail) can be accessed via the Carrier edition.

An organization could use the two versions together to provide mobile intranet services within the organization using the Enterprise version and wider Mobile Internet coverage using the Carrier version.

The server is designed to support a wide range of mobile specifications including WAP, HTML, and HDML. Additionally, Microsoft Outlook has been integrated into the server package in the form of Outlook Mobile Access. This application is designed to link with PIM applications and data on Microsoft Exchange servers. This fits into the end-to-end, seamless philosophy where users will have complete control over their PIM data, whether from a desktop computer or mobile device.

## Pocket PC

Pocket PCs are similar devices to the popular Palm Pilot series. The key difference (apart from manufacturer!) is that they run the Microsoft Windows CE operating system and support a series of Microsoft applications (such as Mobile Office).

The devices are produced by a number of manufacturers—for example, the Cassiopeia series by Casio (see Figure 2.4). At the time of writing, the Pocket PCs typically have a color display, 16 or 32MB of RAM, and anything up to a 206MHz, 32-bit processor. A variety of processor types may be employed in the devices, including MIPS, ARM, SH3/4, and PowerPC.

**FIGURE 2.4:**

The Cassiopeia
Pocket PC

There is a wide range of applications currently available for the Pocket PC. Microsoft applications include Word, Excel, Outlook 2000, Pocket IE, Pocket Money, and Media Player. Wireless connectivity is normally available as an option on these devices.

## Handheld PC

Handheld PCs are a step up from Pocket PCs in size and functionality, although they run the same Windows CE operating system. (Although the latest package, Handheld PC 2000, does not support the Common Executable Format [CEF] as found in the Pocket PCs.) In appearance, they look like a small laptop computer and offer larger screen sizes (half-size VGA, full-size VGA, and Super VGA screens) than a Pocket PC. (The Pocket PC is limited to a quarter VGA size, 320 × 240) They also may possess a keyboard and offer the same stylus-operated, touch screens found in the Pockets.

Wireless connectivity can be managed using appropriate PC cards within a wireless LAN, the CDPD paging network (AT&T Wireless), or via the use of a cell phone as a modem. The connection to the cell phone may be either by direct cable link to the phone or a wireless Bluetooth connection to a suitably enabled phone.

The Internet browser included in the Handheld PC 2000 release is the equivalent of the desktop version of Internet Explorer version 4.0 and supports HTML 4.0, XML/XSL, and DHTML.

## Windows-Embedded Operating Systems

Microsoft currently offers two embedded operating systems: Windows CE 3.0 and Windows NT Embedded. It has also announced the next generation of its embedded systems, codenamed "Talisker" and "Whistler Embedded." It is important to note that embedded operating systems aren't just used in mobile devices (such as the Pocket PC) but are used across a whole range of dedicated devices that require a fast, real-time system (such as appliances and commercial equipment).

Windows CE is the principal Microsoft OS employed in mobile devices, and it is similar in many ways to Windows NT, except that it lacks the full range of functionality of NT and it supports a range of processors. It includes Microsoft's Common Executable Format (CEF), which allows applications to be written without specifying a particular processor. This eases the burden for developers writing applications for the Pocket PC market.

Applications are written using the eMbedded Visual Tools 3 toolkit, which is currently available as a free download from Microsoft. (Go to www.microsoft.com/mobile and click the Download link.) The kit includes a compiler, debugger, samples, documentation, and a Pocket PC emulator. The emulator is illustrated in Figure 2.5 and running a form written using Visual Tools in Figure 2.7.

The Pocket PC
emulator

As with the Mobile Explorer emulator, you will need to use either Windows NT, Windows 2000 or XP for it to run; however, the rest of the development tools work fine under Windows 95/98/Me. Developers have the choice of writing applications using Visual Basic or C++. See Figure 2.6 for an example of the IDE. Mainstream Visual Basic developers will find it a very familiar environment.

The VB IDE in
eMbedded Visual
Tools. Visual Basic
developers will find
themselves in familiar
territory.

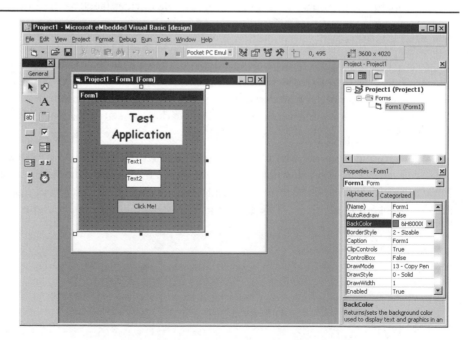

FIGURE 2.7:

The Pocket PC emulator running the form illustrated in Figure 2.6

Microsoft has also announced plans to produce a version of .NET for the embedded platform, known as .NET Compact.

## My Internet

My Internet is an example of the range of online services being provided and developed by Microsoft. Although not specifically targeted at Mobile Internet Toolkit users, it is one of the end-user services that can be accessed as part of the .NET initiative. It is built around a set of XML Web Services.

My Internet builds on the existing Passport user authentication system to allow an individual to build an online profile and data bank that can be used across a whole range of services from online transactions to personal communications. Thus, the individual user will not have to remember a variety of different username/password combinations to access various sites or bank and credit details to make transactions. My Internet will also store personal information (such as time/task management details), application settings, URL bookmarks, device settings, and contacts. This means that a user can log into their My Internet account from anywhere in the world and have this information at their fingertips. The user also gives My Internet explicit permission to give certain aspects of this information to organizations when appropriate—for example, credit card details when making a purchase.

My Internet can also combine with information from other accounts to only show what is relevant—for example, someone making a theater booking would only be shown those seats that are available and match their own predetermined preferences.

My Internet is designed to be a commercial service. Microsoft intends to charge users, developers and service operators for its use, although pricing has not yet been announced.

## Summary

Microsoft has concentrated on covering all aspects of the mobile market from operating systems and embedded applications on the mobile devices currently available, through the server software for delivering online services, as well as the online services themselves. By integrating all these aspects underneath the .NET umbrella, the company has ensured that mobile services become an integral part of any large distributed development. In the service area, the company is seeking to create a user-pays approach, which, if successful, will have long term consequences not only for how we do business on the Internet but also on the nature of projects that developers will be working on in the future.

# PART II

# Mobile Wireless Technologies

# CHAPTER 3

# Wireless Overview

- The Mobile Internet

- The "G" factors

- Current services

- WAP (Wireless Application Protocol)

- i-Mode

- HDML (Handheld Device Markup Language)

- SMS (Short Message Service)

- Bluetooth

With this chapter we will develop an overview of some of the main technologies currently employed in the delivery of the Mobile Internet. At the end of the chapter, you should have some level of understanding as to the following:

- Possibilities for the use of the Mobile Internet and the range of services that a user can reasonably expect when subscribing to a Mobile Internet service.

- An understanding of where we are with carrier technologies in terms of speed and capability, and where we expect to be in a few years time.

- The key Mobile Internet services currently available (WAP, i-Mode, HDML), their history, their strengths and weaknesses, and the underlying technologies that drive them.

- The role of SMS as a competing or parallel service and a brief description of a major development in wireless technology—Bluetooth—which is likely to impact the type of devices that are wirelessly connected and the ways in which we use them.

## The Mobile Internet

The Mobile Internet Toolkit allows a developer the luxury of creating an application for the Mobile Internet with little or no understanding of the mobile medium. I think most developers would agree that this is potentially a dangerous practice and that understanding your technology base is a key prerequisite for any serious designer! In particular, the Mobile Internet is composed of a range of competing technologies. Many of these technologies are still relatively immature and subject to fairly constant and substantial change. Designing for the Mobile Internet also carries its own unique challenges. Screen sizes are small, current transmission rates are slow, memory limitations may apply (depending on the device), and many devices offer a limited keyboard. Although this book is primarily about using Microsoft's Mobile Internet Toolkit, the next few chapters are devoted to giving a broad understanding of the Mobile Internet and the associated wireless technologies.

There is a range of technologies currently employed across the Mobile Internet. In this chapter, I will discuss some of the possibilities for the Mobile Internet and give a brief introduction to each of the key technologies.

Before we begin building applications and sites, we should consider what is the actual use of the Mobile Internet? Who are the people who are likely to use it and what are those people likely to use it for? Let's consider a couple of possibilities:

**The Sales Representative**    As a sales representative, spending large amounts of your time "on the road," one of your most valuable tools is your Stinger-based mobile phone. With this device, you are constantly connected to your organization's database. You can check the latest prices and availability of your products, check your online appointment book, place orders, and track the progress of your client's orders through the company's system. Text messages can be sent directly to your phone via SMS (Short Message Service); you have access to your e-mail and can browse the Internet using Microsoft Mobile Explorer (MME). Although in the past you could obtain much of this information with a phone call, it was awkward. It also took someone else away from their normal responsibilities to handle your requests. The consequence was that you normally only sought this information when you absolutely had to. Mistakes were made and, on occasions, orders lost. These days, clients expect you to have the latest information at your fingertips, and your Stinger-based phone enables this.

Your phone also enables you to do your banking, pay bills, and make some online purchases. Push services that you subscribe to for your favorite stores ensure that their latest special deals are communicated directly to you. At lunch, when you grab a bite to eat, you can sit in the park and listen to some of your favorite music either as MP3s or on the radio using your phone. It may also be possible to watch television. At the end of the day, you can use your phone to access your home computer and instruct it to turn the heating on. You may also receive a message from your home computer during the day to advise you that the heating has been left on and asking you if you wish to have it turned off!

The larger screen on the Stinger, combined with location-based services, enables you to display a map giving your location and best available route to your next appointment. If traffic flow information is publicly available, then this information can be optimized even further. Using the same location-based service, you can identify where the closest fast food outlet of your choice is on the way home.

And of course, if you also feel the urge to talk to someone, you can also use the phone to ring that person up!

All the technology exists for this scenario, although its availability and degree of implementation may vary widely. The possibilities that exist for the future of wireless are boundless.

**The Writer**    For example, as a writer, I could be dictating this chapter to my computer via a Bluetooth-enabled headset (pictured in Figure 3.1) while I am outside indulging in my passion for gardening. Using the same headset, I could then instruct the computer to e-mail the completed text to my publisher. I might then access my phone from the headset and ring the publisher to discuss some aspects of the text.

Again, these technologies already exist. It is possible to purchase a Bluetooth-enabled mobile phone that can be accessed from a headset. Unfortunately, I still have to type this text at the keyboard and my speech recognition software stubbornly refuses to recognize my Australian accent with the necessary degree of reliability!

For the remainder of this chapter, we will explore the various mobile, wireless technologies (such as Bluetooth) that are available.

Ericsson T28
phone with Bluetooth
headset

Image courtesy of Ericsson

## The "G" Factors!

If you have paid some attention to mobile and wireless press releases recently, it is likely that you will have encountered references to 2G, 2.5G, and 3G networks. The actual particulars of the underlying technologies attached to these are beyond the scope of this book, but suffice to say that as time goes by, we can expect wireless services to become faster and more efficient.

So called first-generation technology is based on analog radio technology. Second generation (2G) is based on digital technology and caters to both voice and data services. This is where many services are at the moment. 2.5G is an interim step that lifts the performance of 2G. It is based on GPRS (General Packet Radio Service) technology. This offers the cost advantages of a packet-based service and speeds of around 50kbps. Third generation (3G) is packet-based technology that promises the speed and capacity to support multimedia and video streaming. Anticipated data transfer rates vary according to individual implementations, but 3Mbps to 5Mbps are typical of long-term expectations. It also offers "always on" capability.

Current technologies restrict mobile access to speeds much less than that available over the "standard" Internet (9600bps is typical). Various companies and organizations are currently vying to introduce 3G networks. Competing standards and various legislative barriers are slowing down this introduction, and progress varies from country to country and region to region. However, it is likely that over the next few years we can expect some dramatic improvements in the bandwidth available for mobile applications.

## Current Services

As a current Mobile Internet user, what services can you reasonably expect to be provided? What you can expect for your money varies according to the particular technology that you are using. A number of the technologies described in this chapter are not really the Mobile Internet as such. I have included them here, not because we will be necessarily doing anything with them in .NET, but because they are related (and in the case of SMS, competing) technologies that are very relevant to wireless technology today. In particular, SMS is messaging technology that allows text-based, peer-to-peer messaging between devices. Bluetooth is a technology that enables your phone to communicate directly with other devices within a fairly close range of it (for example, your desktop computer).

However, WAP, i-Mode, and HDML are truly Mobile Internet technologies. What can we expect to do with them?

- We can expect to access appropriately enabled sites on the Internet, whether static or dynamic, such as daily news sites.

- We can expect to send and receive e-mail.

- We can use the technology to use online applications such as currency converters, PIMs (Personal Information Managers), or to access our company databases.

- We should be able to play interactive, online games.

- We can engage in e-commerce activities such as banking, managing subscriptions, and purchasing items.

- We can view images, albeit not terribly high-quality ones.

- We will have location-based services that customize content depending on where we are.

- Push services will be available that can automatically update us with desired information.

- At some point in the future, we can reasonably expect to be able to view online multimedia content, download and listen to music, view high-quality graphics (and possibly transmit them), and engage in other bandwidth-intensive activity as the wireless networks move to 3G.

## WAP (Wireless Application Protocol)

WAP has become the de facto standard for wireless access to the Internet. It was developed by a consortium of industry players in response to the fragmented attempts to establish a standard that have characterized the wireless industry over the last decade or so. The consortium became known as the WAP Forum and its original members were AT&T Wireless Services, Nokia, Motorola, Ericsson, and Unwired Planet (now Openwave). They originally announced the WAP initiative in June 1997 and version 1.0 of the WAP standard was published in May 1998. This was then declared obsolete early in 1999 (fortunately before any WAP deployments reached the market!) and replaced by version 1.1 in May 1999. Although version 1.2 was released in December 1999 (and updated to 1.2.1 in June 2000) a vast number of mobile phones have shipped with browsers based on version 1.1. Implementation of version 1.2 has been very patchy (despite some major advancements such as support for push) and with recent announcements regarding version 2.0 having a different technology base, many developers tend to play it safe and code for 1.1.

By 2001, the membership of the WAP Forum had grown to over 600 with representatives from right across the industry. Their website at `www.wapforum.org` contains the latest news and developments as well as the most recent specifications for WAP.

In keeping with modern network design, WAP has a layered architecture (see Figure 3.2). However, unlike other standards, WAP layers not only provide services to the immediate layer above them, but also directly to applications and services. This enables an application to access only those services required without the overhead of working down through the other layers.

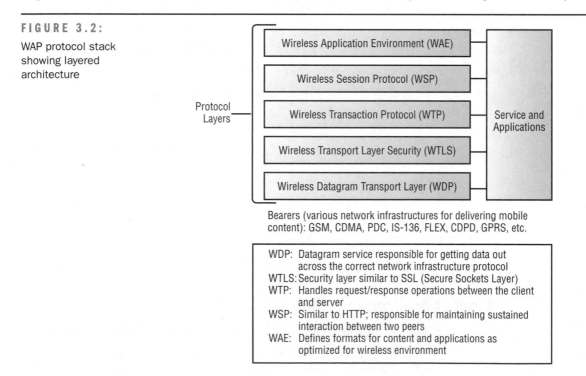

**FIGURE 3.2:**

WAP protocol stack showing layered architecture

Application development within WAP is handled using WML (Wireless Markup Language). WML is derived from XML (Extensible Markup Language) and is also strongly influenced by HTML and HDML (Handheld Device Markup Language), an earlier wireless language developed by Openwave.

Internet content and applications written using WML are developed as "decks" and "cards" rather than the "pages" found in the HTML world. A deck is essentially a single page of code, which may contain a number of cards. Each card represents a screen as displayed on a mobile device.

WAP can handle images (utilizing a special form of bitmap known as *wbmp*) and has its own scripting language (WMLScript) for client-side dynamic applications. However, some devices support other image formats such as GIF, and WMLScript is not universally supported. WAP content can be hosted on a server as WML files or using some form of server-side technology such as ASP (Active Server Pages). Though Microsoft-based technologies are proving very popular in providing dynamic content and hosting WAP sites in the WAP world, many developers also opt for Java- and Apache-(web server) based solutions.

WAP continues to grow in popularity as the preferred model for mobile delivery due to the fact that it is specifically optimized for the wireless medium. Competing technologies (such as HTML) lack this level of optimization. For example, content delivered from a server to a mobile device must pass through a WAP gateway before it can be converted into an acceptable format for viewing on a WAP browser. Because of the limited bandwidth and memory capability of most mobile devices, WAP content is compiled at the gateway and sent through to the device as binary content. This results in a smaller file being sent to the device with associated performance advantages. See Figure 3.3 for a diagrammatic representation of this.

**FIGURE 3.3:**

A logical view of how WAP devices access WML content on the Internet

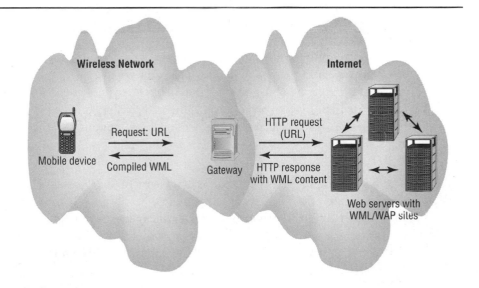

WAP is also compatible with the wider HTTP-based Internet. Although a wireless network may be constructed as "pure" WAP (totally based on the WAP protocol stack), in practice a lot of content has to be sourced over the Internet. Thus a WAP gateway is able to generate an HTTP request to source wireless content stored on a WWW server. From a developer's perspective, it means that we can create our WAP sites (using WML) and post them to a standard ISP (Internet Service Provider) that offers web hosting. As long as the ISP has their MIME types set up correctly, a WAP-enabled phone can access the sites. Many organizations have set up wireless versions of their sites alongside their existing WWW sites. The site checks HTTP header content to identify the device and preferred protocol of the visiting client and directs it the appropriate version of the site.

Some developers and site operators precompile their WML (into WMLC) at the server end. This offers some advantages in speed (as the content can pass straight through the gateway without having to be compiled) and reliability (content size can be more strictly controlled). However, as it adds an extra level of complexity (and is often quite unnecessary), it is not a common practice.

Currently, version 2 of the WAP specification has been released. This represents a technology shift for WAP, as it includes XHTML as one of its markup languages. XHTML is similar in syntax to HTML. The exact impact of this on the WML language is not entirely clear yet, although early announcements indicate that the new specification is backward compatible. One of the key advantages of shifting to XHTML is that it is more closely aligned with cHTML (compact HTML) than WML. cHTML is the language used for i-Mode (which will be discussed next).

## i-Mode

i-Mode is a proprietary technology owned by NTT DoCoMo, a Japanese cell phone operator. It has proven enormously popular in Japan. This popularity is probably due to DoCoMo's aggressive marketing of the product, and their clever implementation has resulted in a wireless service that (for the consumer) is cheap and reliable. It is a constantly connected, packet-based service and consumers are charged for the amount of data they consume rather than the amount of time they are connected (connection-time is the way most current WAP services are billed).

Although initially restricted to Japan and parts of Southeast Asia, i-Mode is currently migrating into other markets. The technology was originally introduced in February 1999 and is based on Japan's Personal Digital Cellular standards (PDC), which are incompatible with anywhere else in the world. However, DoCoMo worked with other companies such as Ericsson to jointly develop a 3G standard, known as Wideband Code Division Multiple

Access (W-CDMA), for mobile phones. This has been recognized by the relevant peak bodies as one of the global standards for 3G systems and has paved the way for i-Mode to enter other markets.

i-Mode has some clear advantages over other technologies (such as WAP) in that it uses cHTML (a subset of HTML) as its development language and its governing organization, DoCoMo, is amongst the early adopters of 3G technology. Developers have only a small learning curve to build i-Mode sites, and users have the advantage of speed and price over 2G services. (WAP, on the other hand, has the advantages of being an open specification, is already widely used, and with the shift to XHTML is likely to nullify any language advantages that i-Mode possesses.) It will be interesting to see what impact, if any, i-Mode has on the global wireless scene over the next few years.

As previously stated, cHTML (or compact HTML) is a subset of HTML. Developers creating i-Mode sites, essentially create HTML sites, but are restricted to a certain range of tags and need to follow certain rules. cHTML doesn't employ tables or frames, and images need to be in GIF format. DoCoMo offers two versions of cHTML. The second version supports some additional tags such as the dreaded <BLINK>, which can be viewed on some of their newer phones. See Table 3.1 for the list of HTML tags used in version 1.0 of cHTML. Table 3.2 contains the additional tags included in version 2.0. Although i-Mode doesn't currently support a scripting language, DoCoMo has formed an alliance with Sun Microsystems that is likely to see Java eventually incorporated into i-Mode phones.

**TABLE 3.1:** Support Tags for cHTML (i-Mode compatible) 1.0

| Tag | Function | Tag | Function |
|---|---|---|---|
| <!-- → | Codes comment | HTML | Designates the page as an HTML document |
| A | Designates a link | IMG | Inserts an image |
| BASE | Designates base URL for relative paths | INPUT | Designates the type of data entry device in a form |
| BLOCKQUOTE | Creates a text block | LI | Creates a list item |
| BODY | Designates content section of page | MENU | Creates a menu list |
| BR | Creates a line break | OL | Creates a numbered list |
| CENTER | Center aligns text | OPTION | Designates selected (initial) value |
| DIR | Creates a list of menus or directories (used with LI tag) | P | Designates a block of text |
| DL,DT,DD | Lists tags | PLAINTEXT | Displays a text file exactly as entered |

*Continued on next page*

**TABLE 3.1 CONTINUED:**   Support Tags for cHTML (i-Mode compatible) 1.0

| Tag | Function | Tag | Function |
|-----|----------|-----|----------|
| DIV | Designates alignment (left, center, right) | PRE | Displays a file exactly as entered |
| FORM | Designates a data input area | SELECT | Creates a menu in a form |
| HEAD | Designates the header area of the page | TEXTAREA | Creates a multiline text box in a form for data entry |
| H | Designates size and alignment of header | TITLE | Generates the title of the page |
| HR | Creates a horizontal line | UL | Creates an unordered list |

**TABLE 3.2:**   Additional Tags Supported by cHTML (i-Mode compatible) 2.0

| Tag | Function |
|-----|----------|
| BLINK | Causes text to flash on and off |
| FONT | Defines some text attributes |
| MARQUEE | Generates a moving text effect |
| META | Enables additional control over the page properties |

As with "normal" HTML, various attributes may be applicable to each tag. These can be obtained from the DoCoMo website (www.nttdocomo.com/).

cHTML is also equipped with a large range of standard icons that can be used in online applications. Guidelines are supplied for maximum GIF sizes ($94 \times 72$ dots), data volume per page (maximum 5KB, recommended less than 2KB), display sizes (six lines of eight full-width characters) and so on. The relevant information can be downloaded from the DoCoMo website. Information relevant to particular devices is also available from the site and, compared to WAP, the development process, particularly for an existing HTML programmer, is comparatively painless.

DoCoMo also exercises a lot of control over the content of i-Mode-enabled sites. In order to register for inclusion in the official i-Mode menu, content has to be submitted to DoCoMo for approval and must meet certain stringent standards of quality and good taste. Apart from these requirements, setting up an i-Mode site is little different from setting up any regular HTML site.

An i-Mode-enabled phone is very similar to a standard cell phone and versions are manufactured by a number of companies apart from DoCoMo (which, however remains Japan's leading cell phone manufacturer). The main distinguishing feature of an i-Mode phone is the four-point navigation button at the center of the phone. This gives single click access to i-Mode and allows the user to navigate the on-screen pointer. The phones are installed with a micro-browser that usually has a title bar of icons providing links to various services at the top of the screen.

As with WAP, cHTML content must pass through a gateway before making its way to the mobile phone. DoCoMo currently provides the gateway for their users in Japan. Some commercial gateways available outside Japan (such as m-WorldGate by Logica) now offer cHTML support. See Figure 3.4 for an overview of how an i-Mode system accesses the Internet.

From a client perspective, current versions of Microsoft's Mobile Explorer now support cHTML.

**FIGURE 3.4:**
Accessing the Internet via i-Mode

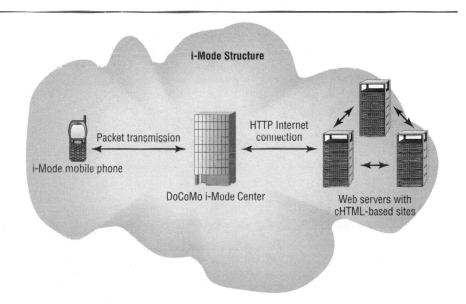

## HDML

Openwave created HDML (Handheld Device Markup Language) back in the days when the company was still known as Unwired Planet. It was an early attempt to produce a Mobile Internet standard. HDML combined with HDTP (Handheld Device Transport Protocol) and a micro-browser to form a complete package to support web access from mobile phones. Openwave ultimately went on to help develop the WAP standard as a founding member of the WAP Forum and many of the features of HDML/HDTP reappeared in WAP/WML.

HDML was (and continues to be) particularly popular in the United States, and a number of mobile sites exist that are still coded in this format. Mobile services in this format were generally written specifically for phones running the UP.Browser 3.*x* and earlier. It is essentially a subscriber service, with users registered with an UP.Link server to take full advantage of the services offered. The specification was restricted to phones running versions of the UP.Browser, and with the arrival of WAP, Openwave began to phase out the standard and provide a migration path to the more widely used WAP/WML.

Services written in HDML continue to run on UP.Browser 4.*x* versions as long as they are operating via networks that run UP.Link Server 4.1 (and later). The UP.Link servers provide a translation service from HDML to WML (see Figure 3.5). A number of features supported by the later HDML 3.0 were not included in WML 1.1. For example, push services existed on HDML 3.0 but were not introduced into WAP until version 1.2. As a consequence, Openwave provided a number of "extensions" to WML 1.1, available in their UP.Browser 4.*x*, to facilitate the migration path. This caused some confusion for developers who happily used the (very useful) extensions in their WML-based sites, only to find that they didn't work on phones such as Nokia.

As with WAP, HDML content is fed through a gateway to be encoded. The HDTP protocol stack is optimized for wireless/mobile delivery. For developers looking to migrate their applications and services from HDML to WML, Openwave has extensive documentation on their website at `http://developer.phone.com/`.

**FIGURE 3.5:**

The UP.Link platform

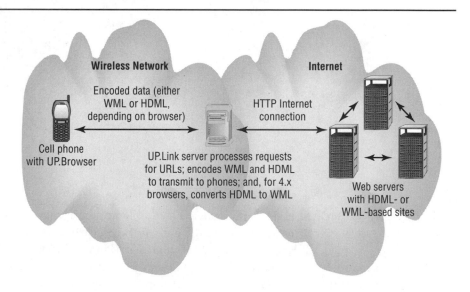

# SMS

SMS (Short Message Service) has been to the general mobile community what i-Mode has been to the Japanese market. It is the e-mail of wireless technology—it has been an enormous success and has continued to grow and expand in popularity since its introduction.

Strictly speaking, we won't cover SMS at any depth in this book. We will not be building SMS applications with the Mobile Internet Toolkit any time soon. However, it is an important component of the mobile spectrum, often forms one of the cornerstones of mobile solutions and it is useful for us as developers to have some understanding of what it is and how it works as we are bound to bump up against it at some stage if we are writing applications in this area.

SMS is built on GSM (Global System for Mobile communications) technology, which has meant that it has not been as common in America as it has been throughout Europe and parts of Asia. It was first introduced in the early 90s (the first message is believed to have been sent in 1992) with the introduction of the GSM Phase 1 standard and allows users to send text messages to each other over their mobile phones.

At first glance, one may ask *so what?* Surely it would be easier to use a phone as it was intended to be used and simply talk to your contact rather than laboriously type out a message on the fairly limited phone keypad! There are a number of key reasons why it has been so popular:

- A message can be up to 160 characters long.

- It is very cheap; a 160-character message is the rough equivalent of a one-second voice call in cost (although this does vary between providers).

- Messages do not have to be responded to straight away—they can be stored in the phone indefinitely.

- Messages can be sent and received in situations where a voice call is inappropriate (such as in a meeting).

- SMS can be linked to various other services and can directly use their formats, such as e-mail or fax.

- SMS messages can be broadcast to large groups of recipients at once.

- SMS messages can be automated (such as automatic notification each time you receive a new e-mail).

A number of enhancements have been made to simplify the problems attached to typing messages over a phone pad. Predictive text input enables the phone to use a built-in dictionary to predict the word being typed based on the first few letters. (Similar to the autocomplete feature that appears in a lot of Microsoft software.) There has also been a whole subset of abbreviations and acronyms built up among regular SMS users to compact quite complex messages down to a few letters.

As it is based on GSM, SMS is transmitted at 9600bps. With the advent of 3G technologies, this is likely to improve dramatically and also enable SMS to be available in areas that do not use GSM. (CDMA and TDMA, which are largely used in the U.S., only allow very limited SMS capabilities.)

SMS messages can be sent from a client device or can be automatically generated at a server in response to some precondition. The messages are sent over the Internet to an SMS center which strips off the HTTP header content and forwards it to the intended recipient. (See Figure 3.6 for a diagrammatic representation of this.) Various gateway and server packages are available from a number of solution providers. Further information can be obtained from either of the following:

- The SMS section of the AnyWhereYouGo Website at www.AnyWhereYouGo.com.

- GSM world at www.gsmworld.com/technology/sms.html.

**FIGURE 3.6:**

Outline of SMS message transmission

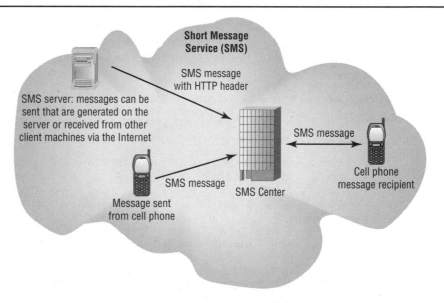

SMS is not only used for personal communications. With its broadcast capabilities, it has been used as the basis for various push-type services. Examples include the following:

- Businesses updating their people "in the field" (such as sales reps) with latest information, prices, etc.

- Telecommunications companies advising their account holders of latest deals (such as cheap long distance rates during certain hours over a certain period)

- Large outdoor concerts where patrons have given their cell phone numbers on entry and are regularly updated through the event as to which bands are about to play on which stage

SMS can also be used to obtain regular updates such as sports results or the weather. In these types of examples, it becomes a direct competitor to Mobile Internet services that may attempt to provide the same type of information whether on a lookup basis or using a push scenario. With current technology, the Internet option is far more expensive and it won't be until 3G arrives that the two will be more comparable.

## Bluetooth

As with SMS, Bluetooth is not strictly a technology we should be spending too much time on here, because it is unlikely that we will be writing Bluetooth applications with the Mobile Internet Toolkit. Bluetooth is embedded technology that is usually written in C++. However, it is quite likely that at some time in the near future we will write applications and services for devices that are Bluetooth enabled, and we may design our applications to take advantage of Bluetooth capabilities.

Bluetooth technology is designed to create short range wireless connectivity between separate devices. It currently operates on the ISM (Industrial, Scientific, and Medical) band of 2.45GHz, which is more or less globally available. The wireless LAN standard, 802.11, also shares this bandwidth (along with microwave ovens—more on this later!). Bluetooth has a limited bandwidth, 1Mbps, and limited range, 30m, although there have been some moves to lift the bandwidth to 2Mbps. Most importantly for mobile devices, Bluetooth has a very low power requirement.

Bluetooth uses a Time-Division Duplex scheme (TDD) to achieve a full duplex data rate of about 700Kbps. Stability within a noisy radio environment is achieved through a frequency hopping approach which enables the Bluetooth module to avoid interference from other signals. It starts at 2.402GHz and can make up to 79 "hops" in 1MHz increments to 2.480GHz. It can hop at up to 1600 hops/s. Data transmission is packet based and security is implemented at the hardware layer with the option of three levels of security.

The Bluetooth radio is built into a microchip, enabling it to be placed into devices where space is at a premium. It supports both point-to-point and point-to-multipoint connections, where up to seven devices can be controlled from the one master. These so-called "piconets" can be linked together into flexible configurations of "scatternets," allowing relatively easy scalability of Bluetooth networks.

Some concerns over the Bluetooth standard have centered on its use in the same band as the wireless networking standard, 802.11, and as microwave ovens. Bluetooth has been structured to operate in a "noisy" wireless environment and tests have shown that it operates alongside 802.11 with only marginal performance drops. Safety concerns have been expressed over the microwave issue as it is at this frequency that microwaves boil water, and having a Bluetooth headset pumping out water-boiling radiation in close proximity to one's brain has made a few people concerned! However, Bluetooth proponents assure us that the power levels of Bluetooth are so low that they would have little if any effect on the temperature of our brains. With the issue of the microwave oven interfering with the Bluetooth device, it has been pointed out that if your oven is leaking radiation at this level, then you have much bigger problems than your headset not working!

Bluetooth is designed to enable devices to communicate directly with each other. For example, a smartcard or electronic wallet could be used to make payments via Bluetooth instead of having to physically swipe the card. (Anybody who has been stuck in a gas station with a barely functioning card that has to be swiped 20 or 30 times to register would see the benefit of this!) So-called "smart appliances" (such as the annoyingly diet conscious "smart fridge," that can automatically update your shopping list on the computer or the "smart car" that decides when it is "due" for a tune-up and books its own servicing) have all made the rounds of the popular press. However, if the technology does take off, it is likely that we will see it incorporated into many everyday appliances, performing mundane, behind-the-scenes tasks.

As with WAP, a consortium of major industry players, including such heavyweights as Ericsson, IBM, Nokia, Intel, and Microsoft, has developed the technology. As with WAP, developing a specification is one thing, achieving consistent implementation is another. Bluetooth has been plagued by various players doing it their own way, and this has resulted in some embarrassing moments for the embryonic technology. However, commercial products are beginning to appear, such as the Ericsson Bluetooth headset (refer to Figure 3.1) and Bluetooth-enabled cards for the PC. See Figure 3.7 for some proposed Bluetooth solutions.

It remains to be seen how successful Bluetooth will be once it finally begins to impact the market. Currently, 802.11 is well established and provides a greater bandwidth, but it also has a much greater power drain and requires some form of central master unit. Some commentators have noted that it has already claimed large segments of the potential Bluetooth market and has the capability to claim more.

**Bluetooth Services**

Pocket PC uses file
transfer via Bluetooth
to communicate
with desktop PC

Bluetooth provides
wireless connection
to existing LAN

Pocket PC

Desktop PC

Local area
network (LAN)

Synchronization:
PIM information is
synchronized between
the cell phone, the
Pocket PC, and the
desktop PC

"Ultimate" headset can
be used to communicate
through the phone or
operate the computer
by voice commands

Three-in-one Phone can act as:
1. Normal cell phone with
   voice and data services
2. Handset extension or
   walkie-talkie for another phone
3. Cordless phone in home or office,
   incurring normal fixed-line charges

Internet bridge exists
between mobile phone
and Pocket PC, allowing
the phone to act as a
modem for the Pocket PC

## Summary

The mobile wireless landscape is currently very diverse with not only a range of industry
players but also a number of standards jockeying for position. Much of the technology is
immature and, in some cases, too many expectations have been placed on it. In the case of
WAP, it could be argued that rolling out the standard before packet-based services became
widely available was premature and has done more harm than good by damaging the public
perception of the technology. Wireless has also been caught in the backlash to the technology sector that occurred post-Y2K and the dot-com crash in 2000, as it was the rising star
at the time and an easy target.

However, wireless continues to grow steadily in usage and improve in technology. Wireless
LAN solutions (based on 802.11) are no longer unusual, and industry magazines are now
beginning to run wireless technology comparisons as part of their staple fare (a sure sign that
wireless has "arrived"). Mobile devices, such as Pocket PC, are growing rapidly in popularity
(and in capability) and it seems that everybody has a cell phone these days. Mobile phone

companies are releasing phones with increasingly PDA-type functionality and convergence is rapidly occurring between these devices. Wireless connectivity is moving from a "luxury extra" to simply part of the package with handheld devices, and most mobile phones now ship with a micro-browser and some sort of web connectivity. 3G bandwidth has been auctioned around the world and various industry players are now advertising heavily for developers in this area.

DoCoMo has moved its services out of Japan and is looking to introduce i-Mode to Europe. WAP is looking to become more developer-friendly with a shift in its markup language to XHTML. This shift will also see a convergence and greater compatibility between the two competing technologies. In the next chapter, we will look at one of these technologies (WAP) in greater detail and see how applications are created using the WML language and how existing Microsoft technologies can be used to turn simple static sites into true client/server driven applications.

# CHAPTER 4

# An Example of Mobile Technology: WAP and WML

- Getting started: Tools of the trade

- Setting up: MIME types and servers

- Introducing WML

- Working with images in WAP

- Serving dynamic WML using ASP

- Using advanced WAP: push technology, user identification, and location-based services

- Overcoming some implementation issues

**D**esigning Mobile Internet sites is an area of computing that can be very confusing, even for experienced developers. This is largely due to the number of varying standards and the lack of maturity of the technology involved. The Mobile Internet Toolkit is designed to help the developer avoid many of these problems by taking care of them "behind the scenes." However, as a developer starting afresh in the mobile world, it is useful to have a basic level of understanding of the structure of the technology and some of the peculiarities associated with using it.

If you are an experienced wireless developer, you can probably afford to either skip or just skim through this chapter. If you are new to wireless, take some time to get a basic understanding of one of the main technologies currently employed in the wireless world. In particular, it will help put the next chapter on Mobile Internet design into perspective.

The purpose of this chapter is to introduce the reader to the basics of using WAP/WML to create Mobile Internet sites and applications. By the end of the chapter, we will have done the following:

- Introduced the basic tools required to write and view mobile sites.
- Covered the fundamentals of the WML language (at a very basic level).
- Introduced the use of Microsoft technologies such as Visual Basic and ASP (Active Server Pages) to create dynamic, server-side applications.
- Explored some of the issues associated with creating mobile sites and applications.

I do not plan on giving a comprehensive coverage of WML in this book. There is a range of references on the subject, both on the Net and available in text. Have a look at any of the key developer sites:

- AnyWhereYouGo at `www.AnyWhereYouGo.com`.
- Wap Forum at `www.wapforum.com`.
- Nokia at `http://forum.nokia.com/main.html`.
- Ericsson at `www.ericsson.com/developerszone/`.
- Openwave at `http://developer.phone.com/`.
- Or the following books:
  - *Getting Started with WAP and WML* by Huw Evans and Paul Ashworth (Sybex, 2001).
  - *WAP Integration: Professional Developer's Guide* by Robert Laberge and Srdjan Vujosevic (John Wiley & Sons, 2001).

These sites (and book) all contain tutorials, white papers, and references that will give you a far more detailed understanding of the technology than I will be covering here.

## Getting Started: Tools of the Trade

WML pages can be written using any plain text editor. I find Microsoft's Notepad to be ideal. There are many far more advanced third-party development tools and middleware solutions available, but that's why we are going to be using Microsoft's Mobile Internet Toolkit!

Along with Notepad, you will also need an emulator or two (or three or four!) to view your results. You are going to need these emulators later on, anyway, for use with the Mobile Internet Toolkit, so it is a good idea to get them downloaded and configured now. It is also a means by which we can become familiar with their use before things get too complicated.

Mobile phone emulators are software packages that run on your desktop computer and mimic the activities and functions of the phones they are modeled on. A huge range is available, but the key ones to have are probably the UP, the Nokia, the Ericsson, and the Microsoft Mobile Explorer (MME). These can be obtained from the relevant Websites (although in some cases you are required to register with the site to obtain them). If you expect to have significant usage of your site by a particular phone type not covered here, it is always a good idea to check if an emulator exists for that phone and obtain it.

**NOTE**    The Ericsson emulator will probably require you to have a gateway installed on your machine to view Mobile Web Forms (with the `.aspx` extension) delivered by your server. A demo version of the Ericsson gateway can be downloaded from their Website, but you will need to partition your hard drive into separate C and D drives to run it. This can be done when installing Windows 2000 or later using a dynamic partitioning tool such as PowerQuest's Partition Magic.

Many of the emulators are available with a full SDK (Software Development Kit). These are useful as they provide a lot of additional documentation and support.

**NOTE**    Microsoft offers a version of MME, called the Microsoft Mobile Explorer Content Toolkit, that can be run within Visual Studio .NET. This can be obtained from their download site at `http://msdn.microsoft.com/downloads`.

Emulators vary considerably in the way they work, look, and feel as well as how well they mimic the real device. Many sad experiences have shown that it doesn't matter whose emulator you are using, there are always differences between what happens "on screen" and what happens "in the wild!" This is not always the emulator's fault. Irrespective of platform, most wireless content needs to pass through a gateway and is modified to some extent between being sent from the server on the Internet and received by your phone. And gateways vary....! A site that works perfectly well on a particular phone using a certain browser via one carrier (and associated gateway) can go all pear shaped when viewed on the same phone, same browser, but with a different carrier.

**NOTE**    Mobile phone browsers are often referred to as *microbrowsers* although I will tend to stick with the term *browser* in this book.

The classic solution has been to "dumb down" sites and applications. By writing them for the lowest common denominator, only using tags known to work everywhere, developers can produce sites that are more or less guaranteed to work everywhere in a largely boring and uninteresting way. Either that or use the approach of writing multiple versions of the same site and employing some sophisticated device and protocol detection procedures that are not always guaranteed to work. This has led to the rise of middleware solutions that offer device detection and appropriate display according to capability based on one version of the site. Microsoft's Mobile Internet Toolkit is a sophisticated version of these solutions that enables development and presentation across the mobile spectrum as well as seamless integration with the desktop environment. However, for our purposes in this chapter, we are going to employ the dumb-down method (and see why, for some applications, it is not such a bad alternative after all).

For the purposes of this book, I will be generally using the UP.Browser as my emulator of choice (see Figure 4.1). I like this particular emulator as it is not based on Java (and doesn't bring my machine to a grinding halt whenever I start it up!), and it contains a very informative compiler, which is relatively easy to check for and identify errors with. Normally, I like to test across a range of emulators, so I will also reference the Nokia and MME emulators.

**FIGURE 4.1:**

The UP.Browser emulator and compiler

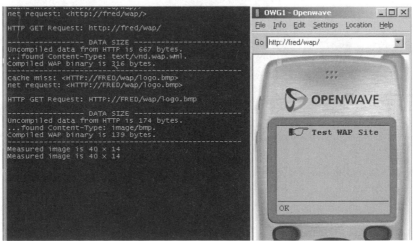

Image of UP.SDK courtesy Openwave Systems, Inc.

It is worth noting that to be truly useful, an emulator must contain its own compiler, so that you can compile and view your content directly off your machine. Many people, new to wireless, wonder whether they need their own gateway to test applications. This is not normally necessary with the UP and Nokia toolkits as they ship with their own gateways and perform all the necessary compiling and communication with Web servers (refer to the earlier note about the Ericsson emulator). Microsoft Mobile Explorer and the Ericsson emulator both have their own compilers and can view "straight" WML pages without a gateway while the version of MME in the Microsoft Mobile Explorer Content Toolkit for Visual Studio .NET can view content within Visual Studio that is being developed using the Mobile Internet Toolkit.

Installing the SDKs is usually a straightforward process. Extract the downloaded files and keep clicking the Next button until the process is finished. The only things to watch out for are that the Nokia and Ericsson SDKs require fairly recent versions of Java to run properly (appropriate warnings and links are placed on their download sites) and MME isn't compatible with versions of Windows 9x—you will need NT, 2000, or XP.

For the purpose of viewing sites, you will not need anything beyond the emulator for straight WML content. However, as later in the chapter we will be looking at some ASP, you will need a Web server. You can use either PWS (Personal Web Server) or IIS (Internet Information Server) from Microsoft. These servers are normally available on your operating system CD if they are not already installed on your machine.

To install one of these servers, select Start ➤ Control Panel (or, for Windows 2000 users, Start ➤ Settings ➤ Control Panel). From the Control Panel dialog box, select Add/Remove Programs. From the Add/Remove Programs Properties dialog box, select the Windows Setup tab (or Add/Remove Windows Components in Windows 2000), choose Internet Tools (IIS in Windows 2000), and follow the prompts.

**TIP**     PWS can be downloaded for free from the Microsoft Website at www.microsoft.com. It is contained in the NT Option Pack.

## Setting Up: MIME Types and Servers

If you wish to have the wireless content delivered through your Web server, you will need to establish the appropriate MIME types on your machine. If you have already installed the Mobile Internet Toolkit, this will have been taken care of for you. However, if you wish to do it manually, the procedure varies a bit depending on which Web server you are using.

## PWS

As we will be using IIS later for .NET, I will concentrate my examples around it. However, PWS is a fairly simple thing to set up and use, and for those who wish to use it at this stage, I'll run through it briefly here.

There are a couple of different versions of PWS. One has a Web-based interface; the other has the standard application-style interface. I will cover the application-style interface here. (I use version 4.02 of PWS with WAP and found it to work well. Some of the other versions have been reported to cause problems.) If PWS is installed on your machine, you can normally expect an icon to appear in the system tray at the bottom-right corner of the taskbar (Windows 9x). An active version of PWS will appear as in Figure 4.2.

**FIGURE 4.2:**

PWS icon on the taskbar

PWS in the System Tray

If PWS has been deactivated it will appear in the System Tray as in Figure 4.3.

**FIGURE 4.3:**

Inactive PWS icon on the taskbar

PWS (disabled) in the System Tray

**WARNING**   It is often a good idea when not directly using PWS to have it stopped, as it does leave a potential security hole in your machine that could be exploited by any roaming hackers that might stumble over your IP address while you are connected to the Internet. Alternatively (or "as well"), install one of the personal firewall products that are available such as ZoneAlarm. Note that Windows XP ships with its own personal firewall preinstalled.

Double-clicking the taskbar icon should bring up PWS. If for some reason the icon is not present, try Start ➤ Programs ➤ Accessories ➤ Internet Tools ➤ Personal Web Server ➤ Personal Web Manager. The screen should appear as in Figure 4.4.

FIGURE 4.4:

The main screen of
the PWS Interface

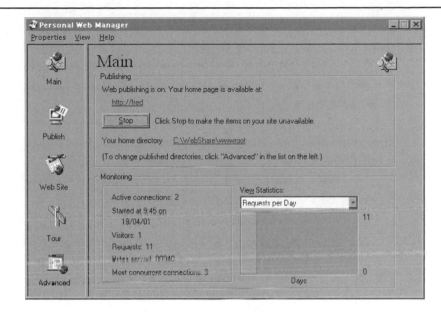

Under the Properties menu, you will find a menu item to toggle the system tray icon for
PWS. On the left panel, there are links to the other PWS control panels (all four of them!). The
Publish, Web Site, and Tour control panels are fairly irrelevant to what we want to do here, but
under the Advanced panel, we can set up virtual directories, exercise some control over their
properties, and set the default document types that are served by PWS (see Figure 4.5).

FIGURE 4.5:

The PWS Advanced
control panel

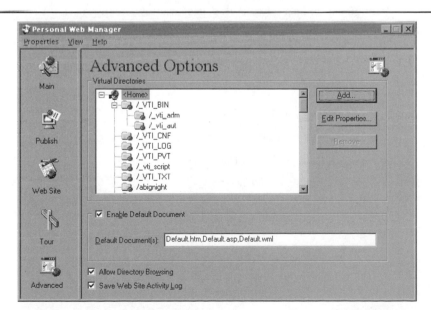

To create a new *virtual directory* (virtual directories are the directories that are accessed through your web server and are created by taking an existing directory on your machine that you wish to be available over the Internet and turning it into a virtual directory), click the Add button. Browse to, or type a path to, the directory you wish to make available through the server, give it an appropriate name that it will be accessed by (it may be its existing name), and click the OK button.

To set PWS so that it will serve `default.wml` or `index.wml` as default documents, add these after a comma to the default document text box. It is also a good idea to add `default.asp` if it is not already there.

To access your sites via PWS (or IIS for that matter), open your Web browser and use the following URL:

```
http://localhost/mysitename.html
```

Even using just `http://localhost` should produce a result as PWS creates a default Website at this location. Alternatively, if you have given your computer a name (i.e., esmerelda), typing the URL `http://esmerelda` or `http://esmerelda/mysitename.html` should have the same effect. The Main panel gives the location of the default Website (normally `c:\WebShare\wwwroot`).

---

**NOTE**    Note that the default Website home directory for IIS is normally `c:\Inetpub\wwwroot`.

## Setting MIME Types in PWS

MIME (Multipurpose Internet Mail Extensions) types for PWS (the file extensions that it recognizes and serves as Web pages) are not actually set in the service itself (as they are for IIS). Open a window from your desktop, double-clicking the My Computer icon will do. Select View ➤ Folder Options, and then from the File Types tab and choose New Type.

In the Add New File Types dialog box, select the following MIME types:

| MIME Type | Extension |
| --- | --- |
| text/vnd.wap.wml | .wml |
| image/vnd.wap.wbmp | .wbmp |
| text/vnd.wap.wmlscript | .wmls |
| application/vnd.wap.wmlc | .wmlc |
| application/vnd.wap.wmlscriptc | .wmlsc |

## Testing PWS

You can test that PWS is behaving as it should by opening Notepad and typing out the ASP scrip contained in Listing 4.1.

**Listing 4.1          Test ASP Page**

```
<html>
<head>
<title>Test asp</title>
<head>
<body>
<center>
<h1>Test asp Page</h1><p>
<h2>The time is <%=Time%></h2>
</body>
</html>
```

Use the Save As command and save your script using All Files option (rather than Text Document). Save the file as test.asp.

Save the file to your Web share folder (usually c:\Webshare\WWWROOT). Use your Web browser to call the file (type **http://localhost/test.asp** into the location bar). The page should open with the current time as read from your computer.

## Internet Information Server 5.0 (IIS)

To access IIS (in Win2000), select Start ➣ Programs ➣ Administrative Tools ➣ Internet Services Manager.

This opens up the Microsoft Management Console (MMC) for IIS as seen in Figure 4.6. In the left panel (under the Tree tab) you should find something like *web. If this is collapsed, click on the + (plus sign) to expand it, and it should list default FTP, Web, Administration, and SMTP sites. These sites are also shown in the right panel. The one we are interested in is the Default Web Site, which is probably the most convenient place to put our WAP content. Double-clicking the Default Web Site icon will expand its content into the right panel.

Right-clicking Default Web Site will give a list of options, including the New option that we can use to create virtual directories. The Stop button enables us to stop the service, and clicking properties will open up a much larger range of configuration options (as shown in Figure 4.7) than available under PWS.

**FIGURE 4.6:**

The MMC for IIS
showing the expanded
contents of Default
Website

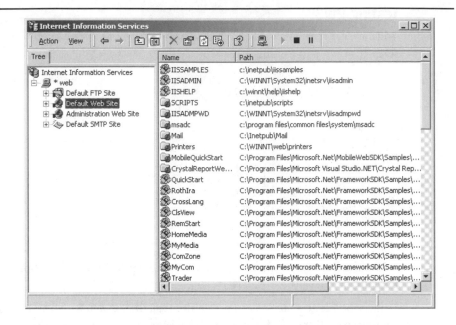

**FIGURE 4.7:**

The Properties
dialog box for
Default Website

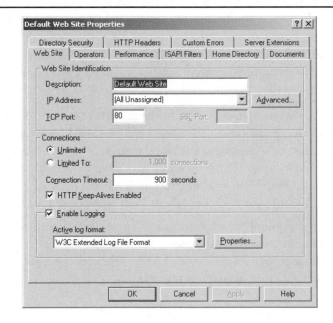

## Setting Up IIS

For our purposes, it is worth having a unique folder for our WAP files. To do so, follow these steps:

1.  Create a new directory somewhere convenient on your computer and label it 'Wap'.

2.  Open up IIS and right-click on the Default Web Site directory in the left window. (You may need to expand the root directory by clicking the + symbol next to that directory.)

3.  Choose New ➤ Virtual Directory.

4.  In the Virtual Directory Creation Wizard, click the Next button and name the Virtual Directory as Wap, then click Next and browse to the location of the Wap directory on your computer.

5.  Make sure that permissions are correctly set—Read and Run Scripts are selected. Click the Next button to complete the wizard.

## Setting MIME Types in IIS

If you have not already installed the Mobile Internet Toolkit, then you will need to set up the MIME types for WAP in IIS. In this example, I will take you through setting the types for an individual directory, but it is possible to set them globally in IIS by following a similar process on the root *web and selecting the Computer MIME Map option as shown in Figure 4.8.

1.  In the MMC for IIS, right-click your new Wap virtual directory and select Properties.

2.  Select the Documents tab, click the Add button, and type **default.wml** in the Default Document Name dialog box. This creates a default start document if we were to go on and build a site.

3.  Select the HTTP Headers tab, and click File Types under MIME Map.

4.  In the dialog box click New Type to enter each of the following MIME types:

| MIME Type | Extension |
| --- | --- |
| text/vnd.wap.wml | .wml |
| image/vnd.wap.wbmp | .wbmp |
| text/vnd.wap.wmlscript | .wmls |
| application/vnd.wap.wmlc | .wmlc |
| application/vnd.wap.wmlscriptc | .wmlsc |

5.  Once finished, click OK and close off the Internet Services Manager.

Enter MIME types
globally in IIS using
the Edit button in the
Computer MIME Maps
section of the *web
Properties dialog box.

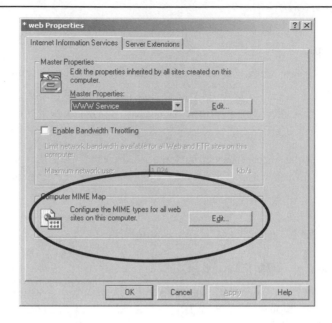

This is only meant to be a very brief introduction to IIS, giving us enough to get started. There are whole books devoted to making the thing run properly and they can be a worthy investment if you are planning to do a lot more than using it to test a few WAP sites or, as can happen, things come unstuck and it begins serving error messages instead of Internet content!

## What Is WML?

WML is based on XML, derives much of its format from HTML and its overall approach to creating content from HDML. Because it looks very similar to HTML (and shares many of the same tags), many developers have fallen into the trap of thinking that it shares the same forgiving nature. Some of the common traps for new players include the following:

- WML is case sensitive.

- WML tags must be closed where required (and most tags have a closing tag), and there is no room for incorrect or "loose" tags.

- Any mistakes will cause the entire deck to be rejected by the compiler and only an error message will be displayed on the client.

- Some tags need to be nested in particular ways.

- WML has an XML-style header that must be present at the start of every deck and formatted in a particular way.
- Certain tags will display very differently on different devices.

You may remember that we discussed earlier how WAP sites are set up as decks and cards. A particular site may consist of one or more decks and each deck may consist of one or more cards. The advantage of this is that, when a call is made to a site, an entire deck of cards is downloaded and stored in cache. When the next card is required, it can be popped from cache rather having to wait for it to download. Although current services are fairly slow compared to the Internet (typically 9,600bps), the data size of the content means that it does in fact load quite quickly by comparison. However, phones are single task devices, and the latency period for someone standing there, holding their phone, waiting for a site to come through can seem very long. The card and deck approach helps to overcome this.

The downside, however, is that cell phones tend to be very reliant on their cache and very reluctant to look anywhere else. This can be a problem for a developer building a dynamic content site that requires a client to keep referring back to it. There are ways to convince a phone not to keep looking at its cache, but they don't always work as they should. We will look at this in more detail later in the chapter.

Let's have a look at a typical "Hello World" style application in WML in Listing 4.2 to get some idea of its structure. Note that this is a single-card deck.

**Listing 4.2**     **"Hello World" Style Example in WML**

```
<?xml version="1.0"?>
<!DOCTYPE wml PUBLIC "-//WAPFORUM//DTD WML 1.1//EN"
➥"http://www.wapforum.org/DTD/wml_1.1.xml">

<wml>
<card>
<p align="center">
<b>Hi There!</b>
</p>
</card>
</wml>
```

The first thing to note is the so-called WAP header:

```
<?xml version="1.0"?>
<!DOCTYPE wml PUBLIC "-//WAPFORUM//DTD WML 1.1//EN"
➥"http://www.wapforum.org/DTD/wml_1.1.xml">
```

Although often called the WAP header, this is technically the *XML document prologue*. The first line is the *XML declaration*, which indicates that the rest of the document conforms to version 1.0 of the XML specification. The next line has been wrapped on this page. It should always be on one line (although it may be wrapped). Essentially it tells the recipient where to go to look for the WML specification. This information is contained in the DTD (Document Type Definition), which is a construct used extensively in XML to create a *schema* (a set of rules for custom markup languages, such as WML, that have been created using XML). Notice that this one lives at the Wap Forum, but it may be possible to source your DTD from elsewhere (although not always a good idea!).

**NOTE**     It is often a good idea to leave a line between the WAP header and the rest of the code as some devices can have problems without the additional blank line.

The remainder of this code almost looks like HTML with the `<wml>` tags substituting for `<html>`, and `<card>` substituting for `<body>`. As in HTML, the `<p>` tag denotes a body of text with a "center" attribute to align it. The `<b>` tag is a (bold) text formatting tag.

Many of these similarities exist with other tags in WML, and in many ways they make the learning curve for experienced HTML programmers less severe. However, there are some key differences, even in this small piece of code. It is case sensitive, and if we had deleted any of the closing tags (such as `</p>` or `</b>`), the code would have failed.

To view this using your emulator, open up Notepad and type out the code exactly as written in the "Hello World" example. Use the Save As command, and save your script as All Files (rather than Text Document). Save the file as `test.wml` in your Wap directory created earlier. Open up the UP.Browser by selecting Start Menu ➤ Programs ➤ UPSDK ➤ UP.Simulator.

It is worth taking a look at some of the accompanying documentation while you're there. The UP.Browser will open in two windows. The first window is the mobile phone simulator, and the second window gives the report from the compiler. Navigating to sites is achieved by typing the address in the location bar on the phone simulator and hitting the Enter key. Type `http://localhost/Wap/test.wml`, and then press Enter. Your phone simulator should look something like Figure 4.9.

**TIP**     You can also view straight WML pages directly by typing in your local path (for example, `file://c:/intepub/wwwroot/Wap/test.wml`). You will not be able to view any ASP pages using this method.

**FIGURE 4.9:**

"Hello World" example
in UP.Browser

Image of UP.SDK courtesy Openwave Systems, Inc.

If you run into any problems with the code sample, have a look at the Phone Information window. It will usually give an error report that identifies where the problem lies. Clicking on the Info menu on the phone simulator also give access to a range of useful information, which you can then view in the compiler window. Figure 4.10 gives an example of an error report where the closing tag </wml> was left out.

**FIGURE 4.10:**

Example error report
from the UP compiler

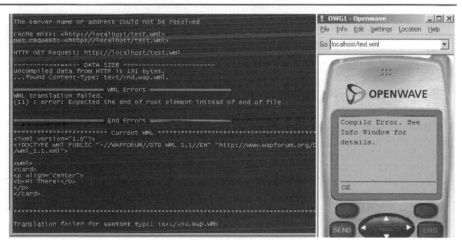

Image of UP.SDK courtesy Openwave Systems, Inc.

Here is a quick run through of the contents of the report illustrated in Figure 4.10:

- Cache miss indicates the page wasn't stored in cache and the device is going elsewhere to get the request, which is indicated by the Request and Get lines.

- Data size gives the size of the uncompiled data. A successful result would have given us a compiled data size as well. The MIME type is identified as WML.

- An error is reported including the nature of the error (unterminated root element; i.e., no </wml> tag) and the line number (11) in which it appears.

- The rest of the report consists of the successful WML that made it through the compiler.

**TIP**    If you are working with WML files in the UP.Browser and you are doing a lot of debugging, press the F9 and/or F12 keys between attempts. F9 forces a reload, and F12 clears the contents of the cache.

## Simple WML

Let us have a look at some simple examples of how sites can be constructed using WML. In the first example we will build a slightly more sophisticated deck than we constructed previously and we will demonstrate how to navigate between cards. The code for a typical (and very simple) two-card deck might appear as shown in Listing 4.3:

**Listing 4.3**        **Basic Two-Card Deck**

```
<?xml version="1.0"?>
<!DOCTYPE wml PUBLIC "-//WAPFORUM//DTD WML 1.1//EN"
➥"http://www.wapforum.org/DTD/wml_1.1.xml">

<wml>
<card id="c1">
<p align="center">
<b>Welcome to My WAP Site</b>
<br/>
Next card:-<br/>
<a href="#c2">Go!</a>
</p>
</card>

<card id="c2">
<do type="prev" label="Back">
```

```
<prev/></do>
<p align="center">
<b>My WAP Site</b>
<br/>
This is the second card
</p>
</card>
</wml>
```

A few things you should note in this listing are the following:

- Give each card a unique identification as an attribute in the card tag (`<card id="c1">`). Make sure that you always include those inverted commas!

- Create links using an `<a>` tag (as in HTML) and use this tag to navigate between cards.

- The `<br/>` is an example of a tag that does not require a closing tag. It has the same role as it has in HTML, creating a line break, but note where the slash appears in it. Many people fall into the trap of using the HTML version, `<br>`, or pacing the slash as you would in HTML, `</br>`. Consider the following code:

```
<do type="prev" label="Back">
<prev/></do>
```

These lines create what is known as a *soft key* on the phone. There is generally a left soft key and a right soft key. They are programmable on-screen keys (that are accessed from the keypad on the phone) that the developer can assign specific functions to in the application (may vary from card to card). Generally, they are used for navigation.

Try this code in your UP.Browser and have a play with it. (Copy it to Notepad and save it as `twocard.wml` in your Wap directory.) If you have access to the Nokia SDK, open it in the Nokia emulator as well. You will immediately see a difference in the way the two browsers are handling the soft key on the second card. I have also shown the output from the two browsers in Figure 4.11 and Figure 4.12. This is a simple example of how even very simple code may be interpreted differently between devices.

**WARNING** Even different phones running the same browser may display sites quite differently. For example, the Mitsubishi T250 shows four lines on the display, whereas some other species of phone running exactly the same browser (both make and version) display only three.

FIGURE 4.11:

The Two Card example in the UP.Browser

Image of UP.SDK courtesy Openwave Systems, Inc.

FIGURE 4.12:

The Two Card example in the Nokia emulator

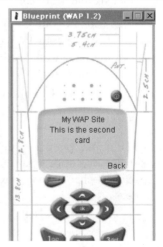

The <a> tag can also be used to navigate between decks and between sites as with the "normal" Internet. Listing 4.4 is an example of where this tag has been used to create a link to the popular wireless developer's site AnyWhereYouGo.

**Listing 4.4          Simple Link Example**

```
<?xml version="1.0"?>
<!DOCTYPE wml PUBLIC "-//WAPFORUM//DTD WML 1.1//EN"
➥ "http://www.wapforum.org/DTD/wml_1.1.xml">

<wml>
<card>
<p align="center">
<b>Link Card</b>
<br/>
<a href="http://www.anywhereyougo.com">AnyWhereYouGo</a>
</p>
</card>
</wml>
```

Using this model, a list of links can be easily built up (using a line break between each link). WML also supports simple tables, and lists are often presented in this manner. Another popular way of representing lists of links is to use the "option onpick" approach. (I won't go into this here—suffice to say it exists and creates a numbered list.) But here we run into the problem of whether or not to dumb down our approach. For example, option onpicks represent fairly basic WML, but are displayed and handled quite differently between the UP.Browser and the Nokia. Although it is a very basic list construct, it is often safer to go with manually creating the list as previously described.

Despite the vagaries of the various implementations, the language is quite powerful and offers the developer the opportunity to use client-side variables, controls (such as data entry fields), timer functions that can be used to automatically trigger events (such as navigation to another card), and a moderate level of text and layout control. The developer can also exercise some control over caching, introduce simple images, create links that automatically dial set phone numbers, and manage security (using WTLS).

In Listing 4.5 we will see how a simple template can be used to set some common properties of a multi-card deck.

**Listing 4.5          Simple Template Example**

```
<?xml version="1.0"?>
<!DOCTYPE wml PUBLIC "-//WAPFORUM//DTD WML 1.1//EN"
➥ "http://www.wapforum.org/DTD/wml_1.1.xml">
```

```
<wml>
<template>
<do type="prev" label="Back">
<prev/></do>
</template>

<card id="c1">
<p align="center">
<b>Welcome to My WAP Site</b>
<br/>
Next card:-<br/>
<a href="#c2">Go!</a>
</p>
</card>

<card id="c2">
<p align="center">
<b>My WAP Site</b>
<br/>
This is the second card
<br/>
Next card:-<br/>
<a href="#c3">Go!</a>
</p>
</card>

<card id="c3">
<p align="center">
<b>My WAP Site</b>
<br/>
This is the third card
</p>
</card>
</wml>
```

In this example, we use the following code to construct a template that is used on all cards:

```
<template>
<do type="prev" label="Back">
<prev/></do>
</template>
```

In this case, the template specified the role of one of the soft keys as a Back or Previous button. Again, it will look slightly different between the Nokia and UP emulators.

## Working with Images in WAP

Images in WAP are, by necessity, very basic. This may change with the introduction of 3G technologies, but currently we work mainly with very simple black and white pictures using the WBMP format.

Although the WBMP probably has the widest support currently amongst mobile devices, it is not the only image format used. The UP.Browser version 3.0 and below supports BMP images, MME supports a range of image types, i-Mode supports GIFs, and the new range of 3G-enabled phones will encourage wider image type support. The Mobile Internet Toolkit is able to detect the client device and choose the appropriate image type to be used, but as a developer, you will need to make multiple image formats of the same image available.

Other limitations also apply, such as the size of the image, which should be restricted to less than $150 \times 150$ pixels (this will still be too large for some device screens). The file size of the image needs to be less than 1461 bytes due to WAP memory limitations (more precisely, 1461 minus the minimum amount of WML tags required to define the image). As not all phones can display graphics, the alt property in the <img> tag (which is similar to its HTML counterpart and used to display images) must be used to give a text alternative label if the image does not show.

A range of methods exists for creating WBMPs, including plug-ins for existing graphics packages such as Adobe Photoshop, JASC Paint Shop Pro, and Macromedia Fireworks. There are also some online conversion services that will convert your GIFs, JPGs, and BMPs to WBMPs (for example, at www.teraflops.com/wbmp/). WBMP galleries have also been created where images can be downloaded from the Internet.

**TIP**    A free WBMP clipart gallery can be found at http://hicon.nl/cgi-bin/library/clipart/clipart.pl.

Stand-alone editing tools for creating WBMPs have also been developed. WebCab.de has an online image creator at http://webcab.de/woe.htm.

At this stage, WAP does not directly support animated images such as animated GIFs. It is possible to program simple animations using the phone cache to hold two or three simple images and then employing the timer tag to flick through the images, generating an animated effect.

## Serving Dynamic WML Using ASP

Although WAP currently is fairly limited as a presentation-style medium along the lines of the desktop Internet, it really shines in the area of providing instant up-to-the-minute information. To do this successfully requires work at the server end (and also in the actual gathering of current content, but that's another story), where constantly updated information can be made instantly available.

Microsoft technologies (such as ASP) combined with languages (such as Visual Basic) provide an excellent (although not the only) solution to generating this type of content. Linking the WAP site to the corporate database can provide instant updates on pricing and stock availability for customers and sales teams alike. Direct purchases can be made over the phone using WAP, e-mail and other text or voice messages can be received, and latest breaking news can be accessed. Although .NET takes all this several steps further, it is worth a quick look at how these technologies can be employed at a fairly basic level to provide dynamic content, how the process works, and what are some of the pitfalls that can occur.

## Simple ASP

An Active Server Page can easily be used to generate WML content as long as it has a line of code instructing it to send the page with the WML file extension. Take a look at Listing 4.6.

**Listing 4.6**      **"Hello World" Example Using ASP**

```
<%Response.ContentType = "text/vnd.wap.wml"%>
<%Response.Write "<?xml version="&chr(34)&"1.0"&chr(34)&"?>"%>
<!DOCTYPE wml PUBLIC "-//WAPFORUM//DTD WML 1.1//EN"
➥"http://www.wapforum.org/DTD/wml_1.1.xml">

<wml>
<card>
<p align="center">
<b>Hi There!</b>
</p>
</card>
</wml>
```

The first line of code

```
<%Response.ContentType = "text/vnd.wap.wml"%>
```

uses a server-side response object (`Response.ContentType`) to set the file type of the returned page to WML. The script delimiters <% and %> indicate that some scripting instructions are to follow. You use these whenever you execute some VBScript or need to call a variable. The second line of code uses another response object (`response.write`) to specify code that will be written in the page. You will need to use these objects whenever you are specifying WML content to appear in the page that is occurring inside a pair of script delimiters. The remainder of the code is just the straight WML that we wrote for our "Hello World" example.

**TIP**      Note the use of "&chr(34)&" inside the script delimiters. This substitutes for quotation marks (") when working in scripts.

Copy the code sample exactly as above into Notepad and save the file as waptest.asp. Remember to use the Save As command and to use the All Files option. Save it into your Wap directory. Access it using the following URL from your emulator:

```
http://localhost/Wap/waptest.asp
```

You should get the same response in the browser as you did for the original "Hello World" example.

This particular example is a simple static card that doesn't really offer us any advantage over working with straight WML. The next example is a more full-blown demonstration of how WML, ASP, and Visual Basic can be combined. We will build a game that is a version of the old favorite: Rock, Paper, and Scissors. Although this is a text version, the project could easily be modified to use simple images.

---

**NOTE**    We will build the Rock, Paper, and Scissors game again later on using .NET to compare the technologies.

---

Before we look at the code, I'll briefly cover a couple of issues that we will face in this project. One problem for many developers using ASP with WAP is in the implementation of session variables. These variables are kept at the server end and they essentially maintain the identity of the particular user between requests for pages (or cards in this case). In the HTML world, checking a cookie stored temporarily on the client's machine is normally used to indicate ownership of a particular session variable. In the WAP world, cookies have only limited support and the entire process comes unstuck. This project illustrates one work-around for this problem. The project also illustrates a solution for a particular cache problem. The standard way to control cache in WAP is to include a META tag as follows:

```
<meta http-equiv="Cache_Control" content="max-age=0" forua="true"/>
```

This tag is supposed to stop the phone referring to its cache when accessing this card. However, it doesn't always work as reliably as it should and many developers go to great lengths to introduce workarounds, guaranteeing that the phone will always look for updated content.

Copy Listing 4.7 and save it as default.asp in your Wap directory.

**Listing 4.7**        **Rock, Paper, Scissor Code—First Deck (*default.asp*)**

```
<%Response.ContentType = "text/vnd.wap.wml"%>
<%Response.Write "<?xml version="&chr(34)&"1.0"&chr(34)&"?>"%>
<!DOCTYPE wml PUBLIC "-//WAPFORUM//DTD WML 1.1//EN"
➥"http://www.wapforum.org/DTD/wml_1.1.xml">

<wml>
<card id="c1">
<do type="accept">
```

```
<go href="#c2"/>
</do>
<do type="prev" label="Back">
<prev/></do>
<p align="center">
<b>Ready for a Game!?</b>
<br/><br/>
Care for a challenge??
<br/>
Select OK to continue<br/>
</p>
</card>

<card id="c2">
<do type="prev" label="Back">
<prev/></do>
<p align="left" mode="nowrap">

<a href="game.asp?choice=1&amp;you=0&amp;me=0&amp;num=0">Rock beats
➥Scissors</a><br/>
<a href="game.asp?choice=2&amp;you=0&amp;me=0&amp;num=0">Scissors beats
➥Paper</a><br/>
<a href="game.asp?choice=3&amp;you=0&amp;me=0&amp;num=0">Paper beats Rock</a>

</p><p align="left" mode="wrap"><br/>
Which will you choose???
</p>
</card>
</wml>
```

This code is a straightforward implementation of what we have covered so far with the exception that the URLs have been set up to contain some ASP parameters (for example, game.asp?choice=3&amp;you=0&amp;me=0). These are used to pass game control variables back and forth. It is in the next deck that we will be introducing some new stuff. Copy Listing 4.8 and save as game.asp.

⤴ **Listing 4.8**      **Rock, Paper, Scissor Code—Second Deck (*game.asp*)**

```
<% @LANGUAGE="VBSCRIPT" %>
<% 'game.asp
Option Explicit
Response.Expires=0

Dim intResult
Dim strYourName
Dim intMyChoice
Dim strMyName
Dim intMyScore
Dim intYourScore
```

```
Dim intChoice
Dim strText
Dim intGameNum

intMyScore=Request("me")
intYourScore=Request("you")
intChoice=Request("choice")
intGameNum=Request("num")

If intChoice = 1 then
strYourName="rock"
ElseIf intChoice=2 then
strYourName="scissors"
ElseIf intChoice=3 then
strYourName="paper"
End If

Randomize
intMyChoice=(Int(Rnd * 3))+1

If intMyChoice = 1 then
strMyName="rock"
ElseIf intMyChoice=2 then
strMyName="scissors"
ElseIf intMyChoice=3 then
strMyName="paper"
End If

Select Case intMyChoice
Case 3 'paper
If intChoice = 2 then
intResult=1 'player wins
ElseIf intChoice = 1 then
intResult=0 'player loses
ElseIf intChoice = 3 then
intResult=2 'player draws
End If
Case 2 'scissors
If intChoice = 2 then
intResult=2 'player draws
ElseIf intChoice = 1 then
intResult=1 'player wins
ElseIf intChoice = 3 then
intResult=0 'player loses
End If
Case 1 'rock
If intChoice = 2 then
intResult=0 'player loses
ElseIf intChoice = 1 then
intResult=2 'player draws
ElseIf intChoice = 3 then
```

```
intResult=1 'player wins
End If
End Select

Select Case intResult
Case 0
strText="I won!!"
intMyScore=intMyScore+1
Case 1
strText="You won!!"
intYourScore=intYourScore+1
Case 2
strText="We drew!!"
End Select

intGameNum=intGameNum+1

Response.Buffer = TRUE
%>

<%Response.ContentType = "text/vnd.wap.wml"%>
<%Response.Write "<?xml version="&chr(34)&"1.0"&chr(34)&"?>"%>
<!DOCTYPE wml PUBLIC "-//WAPFORUM//DTD WML 1.1//EN"
➥"http://www.wapforum.org/DTD/wml_1.1.xml">

<wml>
<head>
<meta http-equiv="Cache_Control" content="max-age=0" forua="true"/>
</head>
<card id="c3">
<do type="accept">
<go href="#c4"/></do>
<do type="prev" label="Back">
<go href="default.asp"/></do>
<p align="center">
<b>Game Results!</b><br/>
<%response.write "You chose "&strYourName%><br/>
<%response.write "I chose "&strMyName%><br/><b>
<%response.write strText%></b><br/>
<%response.write "My score = "&intMyScore&"<br/>"
response.write "Your score = "&intYourScore&"<br/>"
response.write "Game Number = "&intGameNum&"<br/>"%>

</p>
</card>
<card id="c4">
<do type="accept">
<go href="#c3"/></do>
<do type="prev" label="Back">
<go href="default.asp"/></do>
```

```
<p align="center">
<b>Care for another game?</b></p>
<p align="left">
<%Response.write "<a
➥href="+chr(34)+"game.asp?choice=1&amp;you="&intYourScore&"&amp;me="&
➥intMyScore&"&amp;num="&intGameNum&""+chr(34)+">Rock</a><br/>"
Response.write "<a
➥href="+chr(34)+"game.asp?choice=2&amp;you="&intYourScore&"&amp;me="&
➥intMyScore&"&amp;num="&intGameNum&""+chr(34)+">Scissors</a><br/>"
Response.write "<a
➥href="+chr(34)+"game.asp?choice=3&amp;you="&intYourScore&"&amp;me="&
➥intMyScore&"&amp;num="&intGameNum&""+chr(34)+">Paper</a>"%>
<br/>
Make your choice to continue or click "Back" to quit. Click "OK" to
➥check your score.
</p>
</card>
</wml>
```

This generates a simple two-card deck but it also provides the game engine that does all the work! Let's break the code down chunk by chunk.

First, declare the scripting language as VBScript and declare all variables. (Use Option Explicit to ensure that no undeclared variables creep through.)

```
<% @LANGUAGE="VBSCRIPT" %>
<% 'game.asp
Option Explicit
Response.Expires=0

Dim IntResult 'outcome of the game - 0=player loses, 1=player wins, 2=drawn game
Dim strYourName 'the name of player choice ie: rock, paper or scissors
Dim intMyChoice 'the numerical value of the computer's choice
Dim strMyName 'the name of the computers choice
Dim intMyScore 'the computer's score
Dim intYourScore 'the player's score
Dim intChoice 'the numerical value of the player's choice
Dim strText 'a string variable to hold a text message on the state of the game
Dim intGameNum 'the number of games played
```

The next code snippet reads the game variable values from the ASP parameters passed through from the previous card.

```
intMyScore=Request("me")
intYourScore=Request("you")
intChoice=Request("choice")
intGameNum=Request("num")
```

This code reads the parameters passed back and forth between the phone and the server. By constantly updating these parameters, and passing them back and forth we can avoid having to use session variables to keep track of scores and number of games played. The intGameNum parameter serves two purposes: It keeps track of the number of games and provides a workaround for an odd caching problem that no amount of fiddling with the various cache control properties seems to have any effect on!

The following code snippet assigns some names to the numbers passed, which represent the choices the player has made. We could have just as easily passed the names back and forth, which would have simplified the code a bit.

```
If intChoice = 1 then
strYourName="rock"
ElseIf intChoice=2 then
strYourName="scissors"
ElseIf intChoice=3 then
strYourName="paper"
End If
```

The following is a standard VB code snippet for generating a random number from 1 to 3:

```
Randomize
intMyChoice=(Int(Rnd * 3))+1
```

This next code assigns a name to the numerical choice made by the computer:

```
If intMyChoice = 1 then
strMyName="rock"
ElseIf intMyChoice=2 then
strMyName="scissors"
ElseIf intMyChoice=3 then
strMyName="paper"
End If
```

The following is the actual game engine. It uses a select case statement to reach a decision as to which player has won the bout and returns a value in the intResult variable.

```
Select Case intMyChoice
Case 3 'paper
If intChoice = 2 then
intResult=1 'player wins
ElseIf intChoice = 1 then
intResult=0 'player loses
ElseIf intChoice = 3 then
intResult=2 'player draws
End If
Case 2 'scissors
If intChoice = 2 then
intResult=2 'player draws
```

```
ElseIf intChoice = 1 then
intResult=1 'player wins
ElseIf intChoice = 3 then
intResult=0 'player loses
End If
Case 1 'rock
If intChoice = 2 then
intResult=0 'player loses
ElseIf intChoice = 1 then
intResult=2 'player draws
ElseIf intChoice = 3 then
intResult=1 'player wins
End If
End Select
```

The following code uses the intResult variable to determine the appropriate text response to give to the game:

```
Select Case intResult
Case 0
strText="I won!!"
intMyScore=intMyScore+1
Case 1
strText="You won!!"
intYourScore=intYourScore+1
Case 2
strText="We drew!!"
End Select
```

This code snippet increments the game number:

```
intGameNum=intGameNum+1
```

The following code snippet ensures that all code is processed before anything is sent back to the phone and closes off the code segment.

```
Response.Buffer = TRUE
%>
```

These are the standard WAP headers set up to be accommodated in an ASP page. Note the necessity for the `Response.ContentType` to tell the ASP page to send the response as WML and the use of the escape character &chr34& instead of quotation markswithin the `Response.Write`.

```
<%Response.ContentType = "text/vnd.wap.wml"%>
<%Response.Write "<?xml version="&chr(34)&"1.0"&chr(34)&"?>"%>
<!DOCTYPE wml PUBLIC "-//WAPFORUM//DTD WML 1.1//EN"
➥ "http://www.wapforum.org/DTD/wml_1.1.xml">
```

Next, is standard WML code to set up the cards. The cache control is important, as you want the phone to keep looking back to the server for updates. However, it doesn't quite cover every base; hence the need for the `intGameNum` parameter that ensures that the ASP call is always different each time it is made and prevents the thing looking back to the phone's cache.

```
<wml>
<head>
<meta http-equiv="Cache_Control" content="max-age=0" forua="true"/>
</head>
<card id="c3">
<do type="accept">
<go href="#c4"/></do>
<do type="prev" label="Back">
<go href="default.asp"/></do>
<p align="center">
<b>Game Results!</b><br/>
```

Next, we use `response.writes` (contained within the script delimiters) to send the latest value of the various game variables back to the phone. On the first three lines I've put each of the `response.writes` inside their own script delimiter (`<%...%>`). This can help with setting up this type of code and makes it easier to debug, but the following three lines set between one set of delimiters reduces the load on your server and can ultimately improve performance in a heavily loaded environment (although realistically it will make zilch difference here!).

```
<%response.write "You chose "&strYourName%><br/>
<%response.write "I chose "&strMyName%><br/><b>
<%response.write strText%></b><br/>
<%response.write "My score = "&intMyScore&"<br/>"
response.write "Your score = "&intYourScore&"<br/>"
response.write "Game Number = "&intGameNum&"<br/>"%>
```

Of note in the following code snippet is the contents of the `response.writes`. These illustrate how the hrefs can be constructed with the appropriate ASP parameters contained in them. These parameters hold the values of the game variables. In the HTML world, we would probably use session variables to hold these values back at the server. However, support for session variables is inconsistent in WAP, and it's not safe to construct applications (that are expected to have wide appeal) based on them.

In applications where security of these values may be an issue or complexity makes it impractical to pass them around, it is possible to set up a database to hold the values and generate a unique ID that is valid for that particular connection and can be passed back and forth as an ASP parameter.

The remainder of the code is similar to what we've already covered. It completes the deck and provides the hrefs to continue playing the game:

```
</p>
</card>
```

```
<card id="c4">
<do type="accept">
<go href="#c3"/></do>
<do type="prev" label="Back">
<go href="default.asp"/></do>
<p align="center">
<b>Care for another game?</b></p>
<p align="left">
<%Response.write "<a
➥href="+chr(34)+"game.asp?choice=1&amp;you="&intYourScore&"&amp;me="&
➥intMyScore&"&amp;num="&intGameNum&""+chr(34)+">Rock</a><br/>"
Response.write "<a
➥href="+chr(34)+"game.asp?choice=2&amp;you="&intYourScore&"&amp;me="&
➥intMyScore&"&amp;num="&intGameNum&""+chr(34)+">Scissors</a><br/>"
Response.write "<a
➥href="+chr(34)+"game.asp?choice=3&amp;you="&intYourScore&"&amp;me="&
➥intMyScore&"&amp;num="&intGameNum&""+chr(34)+">Paper</a>"%>
<br/>
Make your choice to continue or click "Back" to quit. Click "OK" to
➥check your score.
</p>
</card>
</wml>
```

To run the game, type `http://localhost/Wap/default.wml` in the location bar of your emulator and press Enter.

## Using Advanced WAP

WAP is capable of a lot more than we have the opportunity to investigate here. There are uniquely mobile-related capabilities that either already exist or are being built into the platform. (Many of these capabilities are also shared across other mobile platforms as well.) This section provides provide a quick overview (from a WAP perspective) of some of the services that we can expect to be part of a mature wireless platform.

### Push Technology

Push technology enables site owners to directly transmit their content to a client without having to wait for an initial request from that client. It's not only a wonderful opportunity for advertisers, but from the user's perspective, it represents the ability to automatically receive the latest information without having to go looking for it.

The big fear with push technology has always been the privacy invasion issue. The way this technology has been implemented across the Mobile Internet has been to make it available for organizations to push content only to registered users who have explicitly requested the service. Using this service, I can automatically receive latest specials from some of my favorite stores, latest sport results and weather forecasts, and daily viewing times from my local cinema. If I wish to delete a service, I can.

Although push has been available in HDML and i-Mode for some time, it has only been available in WAP since version 1.2 and has been fairly patchily implemented. Many developers have turned to using either e-mail or SMS as a push solution. The Nokia 2.0 SDK offers quite a lot of information and support for push.

## User Identification

For technology such as push to be successful, it is important to be able to identify the user. Additionally, a number of governments have placed a requirement on mobile phone operators that by some future deadline, for the purpose of emergencies, an individual's identity and location must be able to be pinpointed from their mobile phone.

This type of information has the potential to be obtained from the HTTP headers transmitted by the phone and gateway. It is possible to read the contents of these headers (see "Protocol and Device Detection" in the next section, "Overcoming Some Implementation Issues"). Most of the headers are standard HTTP headers. However, there are some additional extensions to the standard that may be generated by the device or gateway. These lines in the header area are ones that start with X or x. Two new headers were defined for the WAP 1.2 standard. These were X-MSISDN and X-Infinite-ClientID. The gateway can be configured to send either of the two headers, depending on who it is forwarding information to. The X-MSISDN specifies the phone's telephone number, while the X-Infinite-ClientID provides a unique identifier that can be used to maintain a session but keeps the phone number hidden, protecting the user's privacy.

## Location-Based Services

Location-based services enable a service to target either the approximate or exact location of the cell phone user. They are potentially very powerful in terms of location-based targeted advertising (your phone rings with a message from the fast-food store that you are passing), emergency services, traffic information, street directory–based services, billing services (your cell phone calls are cheaper within a particular zone), etc.

Although a little limited at the moment, there is no doubt that as the mobile technology improves (with the introduction of 3G) so will location-based services. Currently under 2G, in a GSM network, location can be pinpointed to the particular base station being used by the phone and even to within a certain distance from that base station.

## WML Script

WML Script enables client-side scripting on the mobile device, similar to the way that JavaScript or VBScript are used in the HTML world to write applications that are downloaded and executed on the client device. The difference is that WML Script is quite limited in comparison, and cards must be completely written using WML Script. Unlike HTML documents, you cannot embed a slice of WML Script within a WML deck. It is similar in many ways to Java Script and can be used to write applications such as currency converters or mortgage calculators. However, it is not fully implemented on all devices, and it is often far quicker and more reliable (particularly in the current technological climate) to carry out this type of processing on the server side. Tutorials on WML Script exist on many developer sites.

## Overcoming Some Implementation Issues

There is an enormous range of implementation issues that the developer faces when working in this area. Some of them, such as session variables and cache control I have covered earlier. Most problems are due to the lack of maturity of the technology—it is still very new—and will be resolved over time. However, we still have to deal with these problems in the interim.

The main thing is not to panic. Also be aware that new problems (or old ones with a new name) seem to pop up all the time. Joining a news group or e-mail list is an excellent way of putting you in touch with people who may have encountered the problem before and are able to offer some solutions or people who may be able to offer some advice and suggestions on a new breed of difficulty. Accessing these lists is not difficult and generally the people are friendly and all too willing to help. Most of the large developer sites offer some form of discussion forums. It is simply a case of registering and participating at a level that you feel comfortable with.

Most of the problems that occur can usually be fixed or worked around with a bit of lateral thinking. I have included a couple more common problem areas in this section and some of the fixes that can be employed.

## Redirects

Often it is necessary to send a user somewhere else. This may occur when detecting the device they are using or after having processed some input from the user and responding appropriately. Redirecting a user to another deck, card, or site in WAP should be straightforward (after all, it is in HTML), using the `Response.Redirect` object, but like all things wireless, it trips up when least expected. Fortunately, part of the problem (a big part) is easily fixed.

WAP is supposed to support relative URLs—where the address of the target is given in relation to the current location (i.e., `/Wap2/nextpage.wml`) rather than the absolute address (i.e., `http://localhost/Wap/Wap2/nextpage.wml`). However, many gateways seem to have rather patchy support for redirects that use relative URLs. Some refuse to find the target directory, others send the client there, but the client's device is left not knowing where it is, which causes problem with the next relative URL.

The solution, when using redirects, is to use absolute addresses on the redirection. This will solve a lot of the problems, but not all of them. Some developers advocate not using redirects at all if you can possibly help it. Others use absolute addresses for absolutely everything, but this can be a problem if you have to shift directories around. I tend to think that the answer lies somewhere in the middle.

If you give the user a link to click (with an absolute address) after they have been redirected, the phone will again "know" where it is supposed to be and the rest of the site can then rely on relative addresses. The trick is to force the user to click that particular link or set of links. A little bit of care with site design can solve most of these problems.

Sample code for a redirect might look something like the following:

```
<%Response.Redirect "http://localhost/Wap/Wap2/nextpage.wml"%>
```

Once in the `nextpage.wml`, we could code all the href's and navigation buttons out of it using absolute addresses. Alternatively, the card could be on a timer, which, after some period, automatically triggers an href to another card.

## Protocol and Device Detection

Many site developers want to create a WAP site that integrates with an existing HTML site. They also want to use an existing domain name rather than having a separate one for the wireless site. In other words, if I access `www.siteofinterest.com` with my Web browser, I get the HTML version. If I type the same URL into my Openwave-based cell phone, I get the WAP version.

Again, in theory and on paper, it is fairly straightforward. We can read the contents of the HTTP header to identify the device type and content desired, then make sure that we redirect the client accordingly (allowing for our redirection issues discussed previously).

Later on, this will all be taken care of by .NET. Part of the advantage of using the Mobile Internet Toolkit is that it handles the device and protocol detection for us. However, it is worth taking a quick look at how the process works, if only to get some understanding of what we will be missing out on. (And you never know, at some stage down the track you may have to install a quick fix until Microsoft releases a latest update to detect some new device that has just hit the market!)

The following code snippet uses ASP and Visual Basic to detect whether a device is capable of receiving WAP by looking in the HTTP_ACCEPT header and redirecting accordingly:

```
<%Response.Buffer = True
httpAccept=LCase(Request.ServerVariables("HTTP_ACCEPT"))
if Instr(httpAccept,"wap") then
Response.Redirect "http://www.my_site/my_wap_site.wml" : Response.Flush
➡: Response.End
else Response.Redirect "http://www.my_site/wy_web_site.html"
End If
%>
```

Variations on this code can be added as the default page (default.asp) to a Website and enable basic protocol detection and appropriate redirection. If you need to make as little impact as possible on an existing site and keep all the meta tags etc. intact, you might use Listing 4.9:

**Listing 4.9    Protocol Detection Code (*Default.asp*)**

```
<% @LANGUAGE="VBSCRIPT" %>

<% Option Explicit
Dim httpAccept

Response.Buffer = True
httpAccept=LCase(Request.ServerVariables("HTTP_ACCEPT"))
if Instr(httpAccept,"wap") then
Response.Redirect "http://www.my_site/my_wap_site.wml" : Response.Flush
➡: Response.End
End If
%>
<html>
<head>
<META HTTP-EQUIV="REFRESH" CONTENT="0;
➡URL=http://www.my_site/my_web_site.html.">
<title>My_Web_Site</title>
<META name="useful description" content="search engine type
➡description">
<META name="keywords" content="useful search engine type identifiers">
</head>
</html>
```

**WARNING**   Note that this protocol detection will only work for HTML or WML devices; it won't work for an HDML-only device. Nor will it distinguish between a large screen–HTML device or a small screen–HTML device—you will need to use actual device detection for that.

You can do a lot more than simply detect the acceptable protocol; it is also possible to use the USER_AGENT out of the HTTP header to detect the actual device type being used, employing a similar approach as above. This approach combined with information on that device can allow you to tailor your site specifically for that client. Of course, with the large number of different devices available, you can end up with an awful lot of if...then statements or a fairly complicated Case statement. User agent profiles are available from a number of sources. These are lists that, depending on the source, give us a thorough list of devices and their capabilities. An example of one can be found at http://internetalchemy.org/wap/ualist .phtml.

## Summary

We do not need sophisticated programming tools to create Mobile Internet sites. Knowledge of WML and a basic text editor is sufficient. However, due particularly to the lack of maturity of the technology and the diversity of devices and platforms available, sites either need to be extremely simple in design or constructed in multiple versions to be successfully delivered using basic tools.

Middleware solutions such as the Mobile Internet Toolkit give the developer the opportunity to create sophisticated sites that are capable of meeting the needs of the wide range of devices in use without the need for "dumbing down" the sites or creating multiple copies.

Developers can make use of device emulators to gather some idea of how their applications will look in practice. These emulators run on the development computers but don't always completely reflect the true behavior of the devices they emulate. They do, however, offer the developer the opportunity to test new applications across a wide range of devices without the cost (and often impracticality) of using multiple real devices. However, it is still a good idea to have a couple of real devices on hand to test the applications in addition to testing them on the emulators. Another testing option is to make use of one of the online testing facilities that exist. These will test your site for compatibility against a range of devices and for WAP standards compliance. The WAP Forum (www.wapforum.com) keeps a list of online testing facilities that they recommend.

Currently, server-side processing solutions offer the best alternative in most dynamic situations because they cater for the limited memory and processing power of many mobile devices. The Mobile Internet is ideally suited for the delivery of dynamic, constantly updated content, and this is well supported by the range of mature server-side technologies currently available.

Finally, while WML is not a difficult language to learn, it is far less forgiving than HTML and offers a range of features that are unique to the mobile world. In later chapters, we will compare the WML generated by .NET with what we have covered here to gain some understanding of how the Mobile Internet Toolkit actually works "under the hood."

# CHAPTER 5

# Designing for the Mobile Web

- Ensuring appropriate content for mobile sites

- Designing applications: twelve tips

- Considering technical aspects

- Looking at the coexistence of Mobile and Web

In this chapter we will investigate some of the things that developers should take into account when designing and building sites for the Mobile Internet. Although the Mobile Internet Toolkit takes care of much of the design and presentation aspects for us, there is still a range of considerations that we need to be aware of.

By the end of the chapter, the reader should have a basic understanding of how to structure content for appropriate presentation on mobile sites and some of the key differences that exist between mobile and desktop-targeted sites. We will cover many of the technical limitations, such as maximum file size and screen size limitations. We will also look at some of the ways that we can structure our Web and desktop sites to share content but not place unnecessary limitations on each other.

## Appropriate Content for Mobile Sites

We can do a lot with desktop-targeted Websites. We can use them for large impressive presentations. We can load them down with complex images, media, and animations. Many of the former restrictions (such as low bandwidth, the inherent limitations of HTML, and significant browser variations) are no longer applicable to the same extent that they were a few years ago. Web-based applications that dynamically link us to databases, e-commerce functionality, and server-side processing have added a whole new dimension to what the Web is all about and how we use it. The one thing we really can't do with the Internet is to roll it up and shove it in our back pocket. Immediacy, for the Internet, still depends largely on our ability to sit at a desktop computer. (Yes, I know there *is* such a thing as laptop computers *and* they can be wirelessly connected, but it's still not quite the same as true instant-access portability.)

Mobile devices such as cell phones offer the back-pocket portability, but try loading the average Website onto one of these devices and we start exploring new dimensions of futility. Quite apart from waiting several (agonizingly slow) minutes for the Website to load at current mobile data rates, it is quite impossible to intelligently render the complete contents of a 15" high-resolution monitor onto a 1.5" low-resolution display. Clearly, we would need to make some changes.

Some early developers (and commentators) thought that these changes simply involved removing the image content from a Website and devolving the layouts back to device-rendered content (rather than specifying layout with frames, tables, etc.). The results were often unsatisfactory, and critics of the Mobile Internet were quick to focus on these efforts as evidence of the absurdity of "surfing the Net with a mobile phone."

The secret to developing successful mobile sites is to make use of the strengths inherent in the concept of Mobile Internet. The mobile site needs to cater to how people are likely to be viewing the site and under what conditions. It is important to ask questions such as the following:

- What sort of information is someone after when they access my site using a mobile phone?

- Are people likely to be on the move when they access my site or will they be stationary?

- Will they be out in public or in private?

- Will somebody accessing my site have time available or is it only going to be a quick visit?

Remember, cell phones are *mobile* devices. People use them on the train, sitting in airports, at the football game, and walking down the street. If I am sitting at my desk, am I more likely to use my computer to access the Internet or my telephone? (I would probably—well, definitely—use my computer. However, I have seen mobile sites that seem to have been developed on the belief that I would use my phone!)

The Mobile Internet offers the user the opportunity to get instant knowledge gratification. (*I want to know what the latest winning Lotto numbers are, and I need to know them now.*) The Mobile Internet gives me that possibility. I can have instant weather updates. I can find the nearest specialty antique shop in a strange city. I can find out who has the best deals on high-quality running shoes and what are the latest cattle prices. Need to know the latest news headlines? They're only a WAP away!

Notice, that I have only mentioned headlines. Ever tried to read a long complex article on a screen, 15 characters wide and 3 lines deep? In the past, some news services have obviously thought we could, but thankfully they seemed to have now worked through this one. Figure 5.1 shows an attempt to present the contents of this section on a mobile phone; I have only illustrated three screens, but I'm sure you get the idea. It is tedious to manipulate and difficult to read.

**FIGURE 5.1:**
Large block of text displayed on a cell phone

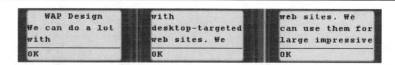

However, the situation is steadily getting better. The technology is improving and new devices have larger, better screens and are more PDA-like in their functionality. But this kind of back-pocket mobility will always mean "small" and, to a degree, limited. So, with all this in mind, welcome to the world of Mobile Internet design!

Ultimately, content that works on the Mobile Internet is content that is informative, update-able, and concise. Weather reports and sports scores are ideal examples. See Figure 5.2 for a weather forecast example. The two-page match report is probably better left for the Website or newspaper article, but the headlines and perhaps first paragraph or summary might have a place. See Figure 5.3 for an example of how a news report might be summarized for mobile purposes.

**FIGURE 5.2:**

View of a weather forecast application from the Nokia toolkit

**FIGURE 5.3:**

Sample news report in the UP.Browser

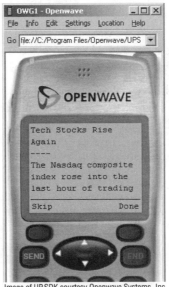

Image of UP.SDK courtesy Openwave Systems, Inc.

The unique nature of the phone can also be exploited. Remember that it can also be used to call people. Rather than try to include lengthy product descriptions on your mobile site, include a linked phone number to a real person who can extol your product's virtues to a potential customer. Include links that will automatically e-mail information to the customer.

From the corporate perspective, a cell phone has the potential to act as a remote mobile terminal for the organization's backend computers. Sales personnel (and clients) can access latest prices and availability. The progress of orders can be tracked from packing to billing to shipping. PIMs can be accessed and managed remotely, and messaging services can be established.

The Mobile Internet offers countless possibilities for content delivery, but it is important for the designer to get out of the headset of "desktop Internet" and think mobile and efficient.

If you are developing using the WML language, many of the developer sites offer comprehensive style guides that explore the appropriate context in which to use each tag and the specific differences that exist in the way that content is delivered between various devices. In particular, excellent guides can be obtained from Openwave at `http://developer.phone.com/`.

In the rest of this chapter I have briefly described a range of key topics to consider when designing for the Mobile Internet. I have put these into the context of using the Mobile Internet Toolkit, which will take care of a lot of the presentation aspects for you anyway. As with most design, there are no hard and fast rules, but there are guidelines that are useful to follow, and often it is simply a matter of common sense.

## Twelve Tips for Application Design

The following tips are general guidelines for designing online mobile applications:

1. Know what your user is hoping to achieve by using your application. Discover why, when, and where they would use it. Knowing your user will dictate much of the application design elements for you.

2. Scale the application down to core functionality. Avoid bells and whistles. This will speed up content delivery to your users and make it easier for them to use your application for what they want.

3. Personalize your application. Keeping a user's personal settings and preferences will make it easier for them to use (and reuse) the application.

4. Avoid making your users enter too much text. This is helped by allowing your users to set personal preferences and making careful use of menus.

5. Make your application easy to navigate. Clearly label links and allow users to step through your application in a logical fashion. Include Back soft-keys that enable users to backtrack through your application.

6. Use the deck and card approach where appropriate to maximize the use of local cache. This can be achieved in the Mobile Internet Toolkit by using multiple Mobile Web Forms on one page. Take care in your use of cache with dynamic applications that rely on current information.

7. Because of the limited nature of phone displays, it is permissible to move your users through a number of cards. Enable your users to drill down so as not to have to display too much information on any one card. However, balance this by avoiding burying important information too deep. Users should be able to access their information easily and quickly. A common scenario is to allow users to create their own personalized menu that they can use to directly access what they need.

8. Use a "one task per card" approach rather than having users complete multiple inputs on the one form. Minimize the number of cards by combining the acknowledgement of successful entry of the previous task with the next task to be completed on the one card. Give your users a final verification card, and allow your user to change values if necessary.

9. Manage your errors. Try to ensure that any mistakes made by the user are picked up and immediately rectified. Look for ways to minimize user error. Construct your code to trap any application errors back at the server and transmit meaningful messages and options to your users. Many error messages, left untrapped, will result in an HTML message being sent to the phone—in the case of a WAP browser, this will produce another error—frustrating your user further.

10. Strive for a consistent look and feel to your application. This is often achieved in Web applications by using common backgrounds and images (to achieve the "look"), but consistent functionality (the "feel") is just as important and achievable in mobile applications.

11. Keep the responses from your application short and succinct. If you are providing information that is text/content heavy, give your user an outline and the option to either connect to the full article or have it e-mailed or delivered in some other form.

12. Test, test, and test again. Run your application through as many as possible versions of the devices that are likely to use it. Never take it for granted that if it works well on one device that the experience will be the same on another. Look for feedback from your users. What do they find difficult? What works well? What needs changing?

Taking this checklist into account when building our applications won't guarantee a perfect application every time, but it will go a long way towards helping us build user-friendly, mobile applications. The following example demonstrates how we can use the checklist to set up an "on paper" model for an application that provides an entertainment directory service for visitors to the mythical city of Megapolis.

## Example Application: The Megapolis Civic Entertainment Guide

In our application we want to be able to provide visitors (and residents) to our fair city with a current entertainment guide. Users should be able to log onto the guide using some form of ID and password, which gives them access to their list of preferences. From there they can identify what's on and where. The site is noncommercial (run as a tourism service by the Megapolis Council), so we do not need any revenue-raising components. It should allow people to set up new accounts and use the site anonymously if necessary. It should also include information on latest main events that may be happening.

**Tip 1: Identify your users.**   Users will consist of visitors to the city and existing residents. Visitors may be new to the city, occasional visitors, or regular visitors. Typically they would use the service from their mobile device and could be using it while traveling into the city or from somewhere in the city when considering where else to go. They are using it to quickly identify entertainment options available to them including times, costs, locations, etc.

**Tip 2: Scale down the application.**   The application will consist of the following:

- A search mechanism for entertainment venues under particular headings.
- A user setup, login, and preference-setting facility.

**Tip 3: Personalize your Application.**   Users can set up a personal profile that offers direct links to items that they specify in preferences. For example, a user might specify that they only want locations of French and Italian restaurants.

**Tip 4: Avoid making users enter too much text.**   The search engine can respond to only a few letters. Use menus where applicable.

**Tip 5: Include clear navigation.**   All cards should be set up with clear links. Back buttons should always be available.

**Tip 6: Use the card and deck approach.**   As this application depends on current information, we need to ensure that the cache is cleared between uses.

**Tips 7 and 8: Use the card and deck structure.**   See Figures 5.2 and 5.3 for how the card structure is constructed.

**Tip 9: Manage errors.**   To be handled in the code for the site.

**Tip 10: Ensure site consistency.**   Each card carries either site name or personal reference and is clearly linked to the next and previous card. Clearly indicate where the card is in site hierarchy.

**Tip 11: Make sure content is succinct.**   Limit content to addresses and menu items.

**Tip 12: Perform tests.**   A comprehensive testing plan needs to be drawn up and implemented.

Because this is not a real application, some of these steps are handled very briefly here. However, it is sufficient to give an overview of how the checklist can be applied. Figures 5.4 and 5.5 give an overview of the card and deck structure for such a site.

FIGURE 5.4:

Overview of functional structure of the Megapolis application

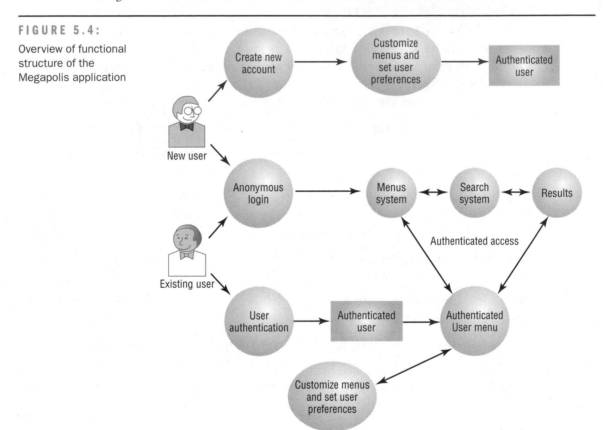

The data-flow diagram in Figure 5.4 essentially dictates the card and deck structure illustrated in Figure 5.5.

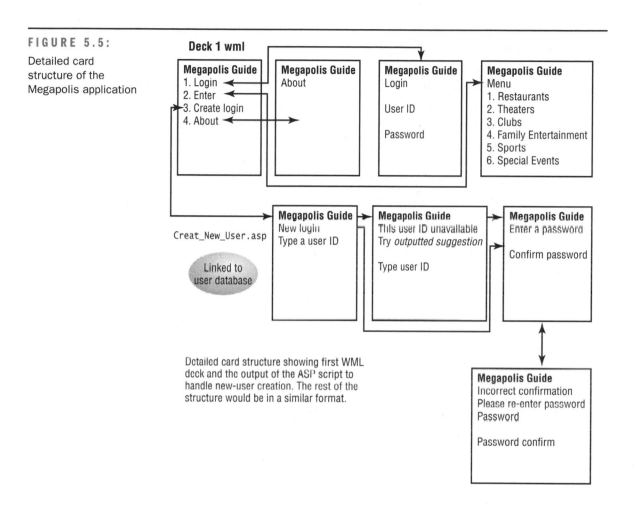

Detailed card structure of the Megapolis application

**Deck 1 wml**

**Megapolis Guide**
1. Login
2. Enter
3. Create login
4. About

**Megapolis Guide**
About

**Megapolis Guide**
Login

User ID

Password

**Megapolis Guide**
Menu
1. Restaurants
2. Theaters
3. Clubs
4. Family Entertainment
5. Sports
6. Special Events

Creat_New_User.asp

Linked to user database

**Megapolis Guide**
New login
Type a user ID

**Megapolis Guide**
This user ID unavailable
Try *outputted suggestion*

Type user ID

**Megapolis Guide**
Enter a password

Confirm password

Detailed card structure showing first WML deck and the output of the ASP script to handle new-user creation. The rest of the structure would be in a similar format.

**Megapolis Guide**
Incorrect confirmation
Please re-enter password
Password

Password confirm

# Technical Aspects to Consider

There is a range of technical aspects that apply to designing for the Mobile Internet. Fortunately, by using the Mobile Internet Toolkit, we avoid dealing with many of them. Most style guides for this area will recommend that you customize your sites individually for specific devices (or ranges of devices) to maximize the user experience of your site. This can become quite tedious without some form of middleware solution to manage it. In terms of .NET, we need to consider what the Mobile Internet Toolkit will construct as an appropriate response from our site for a particular device and whether that response is what we actually want to be sent.

We can handle some of this in advance by taking into account some of the generic properties of the devices we expect to be using our site when building the application. It is much easier, of course, if we are building a corporate application that will be used by a known range of devices. It is made more difficult where we are producing an application for general consumption and the range of devices that may access it is numerous.

Some of the broad specifications for mobile phones (WAP) accessing the Mobile Internet that concern us when using the Mobile Internet Toolkit are listed in Table 5.1.

**TABLE 5.1:** Specification Ranges for WAP-Enabled Mobile Phones

| Specification | Typical Range |
| --- | --- |
| Connection speed | 9,600bps up to whatever will be achieved using 3G (anticipated 5Mbps, although it could be a long time before we see this!). |
| Characters per line | Typically targeted at 15 characters per line. Some phones are as few as 12 characters per line; some are many more as they can proportionally scale their fonts. |
| Number of display lines | Typically 3 or 4 lines. Some as few as 2 lines, others are developing screens of small PDA dimensions and are comparatively very large. |
| Text display | Maximum about 800 characters per card. (Always try to wrap your text.) |
| Images | WBMP format.<br>Nokia: 96 × 44 pixels. Images wider than 96 pixels are cropped on the right. Can be scrolled vertically.<br>Openwave: 40 pixels max width. Can be scrolled vertically. |
| Caching | TTL (time to live)<br>Nokia: Default is 1 day.<br>Openwave: Default is 30 days. |
| Cookies | Support is dependent on the particular browser/gateway combination. Safest to assume that cookies are not supported and build applications accordingly. |
| Maximum deck size (compiled) | Varies from device to device. Typical range between 1,000 and 8,000 bytes of compiled WML. The compiler in the UP.Browser will give the compiled size of a deck. Note that limitations also apply to GET and POST that are also device specific. |
| Recommended deck size (compiled) | Due to the latency currently experienced over mobile networks and the single tasking nature of phones, the recommended maximum size for a compiled deck is no more than 500 bytes. |

Separate specifications exist for phones equipped with the MME browser, i-Mode devices, Stinger phones, and of course, Pocket PCs and Handheld PCs. These can be accessed from the relevant Websites. Microsoft has detailed information on its mobile platforms in the mobile section of its Website at www.microsoft.com/mobile/.

Although we do not need to necessarily limit ourselves by these specifications when designing with the Mobile Internet Toolkit, it is worth bearing them in mind, and we should build our applications knowing that they will be scaled back to fit these requirements.

## Mobile and Web: Can They Coexist?

Many organizations that are looking to maintain a strong Web presence are considering not only a desktop-style Website but also a mobile Website. One of the commonly asked questions is *How can I present my Website on mobile phones?*

Often, there is the assumption that the solution is simply a case of applying some form of technology to an existing HTML-based Website that will automatically (also painlessly and reliably) turn it into a WML-based WAP site. Certainly there is technology available that does this. HTML to WML converters exist, but their capabilities vary widely, depending on the nature of the site they are converting and the individual converters themselves. Most developers working in the wireless arena are reluctant to recommend them. (Although the cynical might argue that the wireless developers are merely protecting their jobs!) They are normally based on some form of XSLT (Extensible Style Language Transformation).

As we have seen earlier, the basic nature of the desktop Internet and the Mobile Internet can be very different. Simply removing images and formatting does not necessarily make a Website suitable for presenting over the Mobile Web. The fundamental differences that exist between the two mediums mean that, at least for the moment, it is probably better to run two different sites—one aimed at the desktop and the other at the mobile user. As we saw in the previous chapter, it is possible to run two sites together, and using appropriate device detection, point the user to the site they need to use. Figures 5.6 and 5.7 respectively show desktop and mobile versions of my Website. These are both accessed from the same URL and rely on protocol detection to deliver the appropriate site.

There is a problem with the way I have set these Websites up. If someone accesses the site using a mobile browser that supports HTML, they will be redirected to the desktop site. This site has been optimized in terms of usage for someone sitting in the relative comfort of his or her desk with a computer and a reasonable amount of time. However, if they access the site using a Pocket PC while walking down the street, they will get this site rather than the one optimized for the mobile user.

**FIGURE 5.6:**

HTML (desktop) version of Ridge's Website

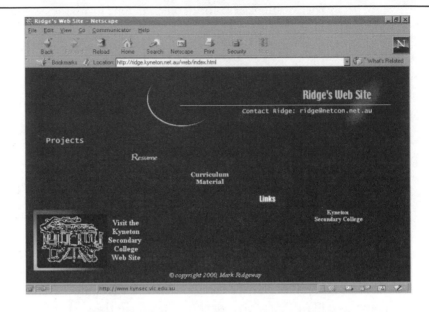

**FIGURE 5.7:**

WML (mobile) version of Ridge' Website

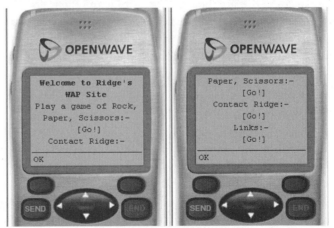

Image of UP.SDK courtesy Openwave Systems, Inc.

I could get around this by using fairly comprehensive device detection coupled with protocol detection, but I am not always guaranteed a satisfactory result. And what happens with the Mobile Internet Toolkit, which will deliver either WML or HTML on demand and is supposed to look after device detection for me? Often it seems that as one problem is solved, a new device and a new issue comes along! Many large commercial sites have sidestepped these issues by setting up their mobile site under a variation on their domain name. For example, I might name my sites www.mysite-web.com and www.mysite-wap.com.

To access Yahoo! over the Internet go to www.yahoo.com. From a WAP phone, you need to use wap.yahoo.com. Yahoo! also has an HTML mobile-optimized site at mobile.yahoo.com.

Whether I use separate URLs or appropriate redirection to enable the visitor to get the appropriate version of the site is a separate issue than how I build the distinct sites. Although the two sites might be quite different in presentation and functionality, they would share a lot of information and processing in common. Both sites can access the same information stored in the same databases and use the same components to carry out key processing. Indeed this is desirable, as it avoids doubling up in entering information and creating the business logic for the sites. Figure 5.8 illustrates how this might be setup.

**FIGURE 5.8:**

Schematic of how Web and Mobile sites can share common components and database

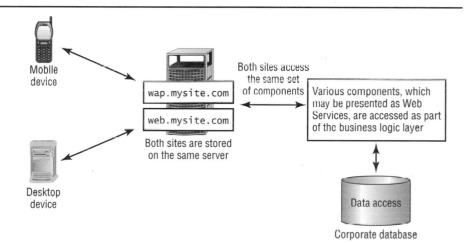

## Summary

When building mobile sites, it is worth remembering that people do not use mobile devices to browse the Internet or surf the Web—at least not at the moment. Mobile users are after concise and current information that they can access easily. I once saw a quote from Phillips Publishing, Inc., on AnywhereYouGo.com that summed this up nicely: Mobile "customers want simplicity, not miniature Web."

We should not be trying to replicate our Websites on mobile devices but focus on delivering key and relevant services that are simple and intuitive to use. When building mobile sites with .NET, we can focus on the usability and relevance of our sites without being unnecessarily distracted by having to meet the different technical requirements of the various devices that are being produced. However, it is worth having a basic understanding of these requirements, as ultimately it will help us build better applications.

Although we can jointly access information and components when it comes to running our mobile applications with our Websites, it is worth keeping these sites separate. Desktop and mobile are too fundamentally different at the moment to try and produce a sophisticated site that will do both. (I imagine that the Mobile Internet Toolkit could be used to generate some simple brochure-style sites that work in both mediums.) Whether we choose to use separate URLs for these sites or employ device and protocol detection to make an intelligent decision about which site should be presented is going to depend largely on the nature of the site, what exists already, and how we expect visitors to use the site.

# PART III

# Introducing .NET Mobile

# CHAPTER 6

# Getting Started with the Mobile Internet Toolkit

- Checking the system requirements

- Introducing the Microsoft Mobile Internet Toolkit

- Working with the Microsoft Mobile Explorer Content Toolkit

- Exploring supported devices

- Getting started using the IDE and the "Hello World" example

- Building a simple deck

- Using code behind to build a simple application

This chapter introduces the basics of setting up and working with the Microsoft Mobile Internet Toolkit. We will create some introductory applications, view them in our emulators, and compare the code generated by the toolkit with the kind of code that we wrote back in Chapter 4, "An Example of Mobile Technology: WAP and WML" for our simple WAP (WML) applications.

By the end of the chapter, you should have an understanding of how to install and run both the Mobile Internet Designer in Visual Studio .NET and the Mobile Explorer Content Toolkit, which provides a Mobile Explorer Emulator that runs within the Visual Studio .NET–integrated environment.

## Checking System Requirements

The system requirements for the Mobile Internet Toolkit are the same as required for Visual Studio .NET discussed in the Introduction for this book. To run the Mobile Internet Designer (the Visual Studio component of the Mobile Internet Toolkit), you will need to run one of the following operating systems:

- Windows 2000 Professional SP2
- Windows 2000 Server SP2
- Windows 2000 Advanced Server SP2
- Windows XP Server 32 bit
- Windows NT 4.0 Workstation (supported only for client-side development) SP6

Your computer will also need to run IIS 5.0 and Internet Explorer 6.0. Hardware requirements for Visual Studio .NET include the following:

- Minimum 450MHz Pentium II processor—anything less and it runs agonizingly slow
- Minimum 64MB RAM (128MB is *a lot* better)
- 3GB of available hard drive space (Microsoft recommendation)
- Microsoft specifies a CD-ROM (and, presumably, a monitor, keyboard, and mouse!)

Once installed, the Mobile Internet Toolkit will only take up a further 2.5MB of hard drive space. The Microsoft Mobile Explorer Content Toolkit (which provides an MME emulator for Visual Studio .NET) requires 10MB of hard drive space for installation.

## Introducing the Microsoft Mobile Internet Toolkit

The Microsoft Mobile Internet Toolkit is a variation of ASP.NET that has been both customized and optimized for mobile Web applications. The Mobile Web Forms Designer, which provides developers with a graphical interface for building applications, is included in Microsoft Visual Studio .NET. However, developers who prefer a slightly more intrepid approach to their projects are still able to lovingly handcraft their code with only a text editor and command-line compiler as accompaniment.

For the purpose of this book, I will assume that you are expecting to use Visual Studio .NET and have a copy loaded and functioning correctly upon your computer. You may also have some experience with working with ASP.NET to create Web applications. If so, you will find building .NET mobile applications a very similar experience. See Figure 6.1 for a look at the Visual Studio .NET Mobile Web Forms Designer.

FIGURE 6.1:

Visual Studio .NET
Mobile Web Forms
Designer

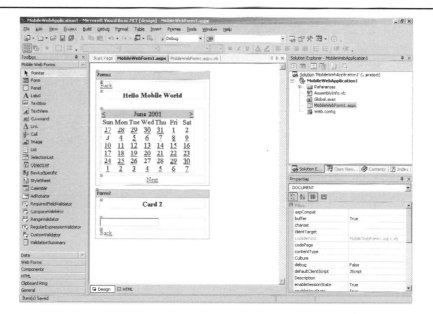

## Obtaining the Toolkit

The kit may be downloaded from the Microsoft download site at `http://msdn.microsoft.com/downloads`. The file is approximately 4.0MB and can be found in the SDK section. If the toolkit has been included with your copy of Visual Studio .NET, then open up Windows Explorer and navigate to Program Files ➢ Microsoft Visual Studio .NET ➢ Visual Studio SDKs ➢ Mobile Internet Toolkit. Installation involves double-clicking the `MobileIT.msi` file and following the prompts.

## Toolkit Contents

The Microsoft Mobile Internet Toolkit contains the following:

**Mobile Internet controls Runtime**    A set of controls that can be dropped onto a Mobile Web Form to generate appropriate content for the specific device accessing them.

**Mobile Internet Designer**    Development interface that integrates into Visual Studio .NET for building mobile applications.

**Device capabilities**    For mobile devices.

**Device Adaptor Code**    Code that enables support for new devices to be added through the extensibility model.

**QuickStart Tutorial**    A useful tutorial provided by Microsoft that introduces how to use the toolkit.

**Documentation**    Language and technical reference.

## Toolkit Overview

Building a .NET mobile application essentially consists of creating a Mobile Web Form, which is in fact a specialized ASP.NET Web Form page. This is a text file saved with the .aspx extension (and can be just as easily written in Notepad).

Note that ASP.NET should not be confused with the more traditional ASP (Active Server Pages) technology that many of us would be familiar with when using Microsoft products to build dynamic Web pages. ASP uses the .asp extension and is very different from the newer ASP.NET. Although ASP pages cannot easily be directly converted (generally speaking) to ASP.NET, the two technologies can coexist on the same server and run side by side. This is covered in a little more detail in Chapter 8, "A Deeper Look at the Mobile Internet Toolkit and VB .NET."

**NOTE**    Be aware that some key differences, such as difficulties using page level tracing to debug mobile applications, exist between ASP.NET and Mobile Web Forms.

Using the Mobile Web Forms Designer, various mobile controls can be dragged onto this form. These controls are capable of exposing a device independent object model containing properties, methods, and events. Double-clicking the controls in the design phase gives access to the code behind the form, which can be used to add additional functionality to the controls and to the application. This code is eventually compiled and stored in a bin directory, which is normally in the same directory as the Mobile Forms we create. We will be mainly using VB .NET for our "code behind." Figure 6.2 illustrates a directory listing for a simple 'Mobile' application. The `Mobile.aspx` file is the Mobile Web Form, and the compiled code for the controls on this form is stored in the bin directory.

FIGURE 6.2:

Sample Directory

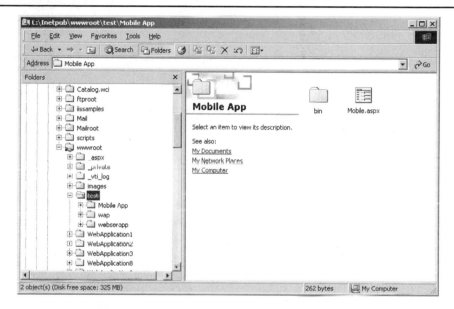

We can also take a more distributed approach to our applications and make use of XML Web Services to provide additional functionality. These XML Web Services may be located on our own machine, the local network, or elsewhere on the Internet. We will be looking later at how to create a simple Web Service and make use of it from our mobile (or, for that matter, non-mobile) applications.

We can also use COM objects to provide access to code in a slightly less public manner than XML Web Services. These have been traditionally used in ASP programming to separate the so-called business logic from the presentation layer in a Web-based application. ASP pages tended to mix the business of building the Web page in with the code that carried out whatever functionality the application required. Separating this functionality out and compiling it as a COM object in its own right offered advantages across the board in terms of performance, security, reusability, upgrade ability, and general reliability. The same applies to our mobile applications.

As stated earlier, a Mobile Web Form Page may contain multiple forms, which mimics the card and deck approach that is popular with many mobile development platforms. The Mobile Web Form Page is a more limited design vehicle than the Web Form environment included in Visual Studio .NET. Controls can only be added one at a time down the form;

the designer doesn't have the luxury of placing the control exactly where he or she expects it to appear in the live application. The order of controls on the form can also be important—for example, we will see later in this chapter how the placement of links and their order in relation to other controls determines whether they will be rendered as a list of HREFs or as Option Onpicks in the final application.

Although multiple forms and Mobile Web Pages can be used to mimic the card and deck approach favored in WAP and HDML, it is not an exact fit. ASP.NET delivers each form, one at a time, to the client on request, not all together as a collection of forms from the one page as happens with a collection of cards on a single WML page or deck.

## The Microsoft Mobile Explorer Content Toolkit

Installing the Microsoft Mobile Explorer Content Toolkit creates a copy of Microsoft Mobile Explorer (MME) that runs within Visual Studio .NET. Content can be viewed from the local machine, the Internet, or the Mobile Internet. Multiple "skins" are offered with the installation, giving the developer the opportunity to test the appearance of applications on a range of devices. One advantage of using the toolkit is that MME can be set as the default browser for any given project. Figure 6.3 illustrates a sample application at design time and running in the integrated MME browser.

**FIGURE 6.3:**

Visual Studio .NET with the MME Content Toolkit installed

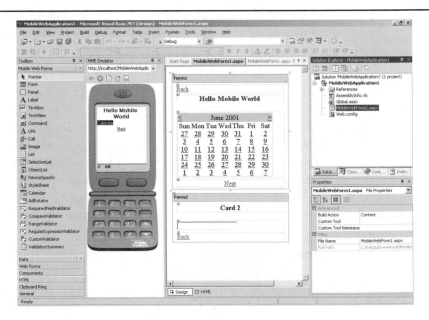

## Obtaining the Toolkit

The kit may be downloaded from the Microsoft download site at `http://msdn.microsoft.com/downloads`. It is less than a 2.5MB download. Installation involves opening the EXE file and following the prompts. A folder named Microsoft Mobile Explorer Content Toolkit is created in the Program Files directory (assuming that you have followed the default install).

## Using the Toolkit with Visual Studio .NET

Once the toolkit is installed, MME can be operated from the Mobile Explorer Browser menu, which is available under the View menu in Visual Studio .NET. Options include the following:

**Show Browser**　Brings the browser up if it is not activated.

**Show Log**　Gives information on the current activity of the browser.

**Back**　Navigates to the previously displayed page.

**Home**　Returns user to the Home page.

**Device**　Offers choice of device skin.

These options are also available from the toolbar below the address bar in the emulator itself. You can access the sites by typing the URLs in the address bar and hitting the Enter key. Onscreen links may be accessed directly using the mouse, or the phone environment can be simulated by clicking the onscreen buttons on the emulator. (Only the buttons down the right side of the keypad and the two under the screen actually do anything.) The following lists the button activity:

**Buttons under the screen**　The following buttons are present:

> **Left softkey**　Carries out action listed on the left of the status bar (directly below screen and above buttons).

> **Right softkey**　Carries out action that may be listed on the right of the status bar.

**Keypad buttons**　Use the following buttons from the keypad:

> **Green phone**　Goes to the information page for Mobile Explorer.

> **Red phone**　Stops current page from loading or returns user to previous page (if nothing is loading).

> **Up arrow**　Scrolls up the screen.

> **Down arrow**　Scrolls down the screen.

The device may be either activated only when required from the Visual Studio .NET's View menu or set as the default browser option for that particular project. Right-clicking on the Web Form in the Design window offers the option to View in Browser. Normally this would be either Internet Explorer or the Visual Studio .NET's internal version of IE. To set MME as the default, select Browse With from the File menu, choose Microsoft Mobile Explorer, and click Set as Default.

If for any reason, MME doesn't appear as an option in the Browse With window, it can be located in the Microsoft Mobile Explorer Toolkit folder (in Program Files) using the Add Browser option from the Browse With window. Once in the Toolkit folder, choose the cdkmbrvs.exe file and when prompted give it a more meaningful name, such as Microsoft Mobile Explorer.

It's also possible to use the toolkit with normal Web projects, except that here you will need to right-click on the Web application project in the Solution Explorer and choose the Properties option. Under Configuration Properties, deselect the Always Use Internet Explorer when Debugging Web Pages option. You will not need to do these steps for mobile Web projects.

Although MME is a handy tool to have as the default browser in Visual Studio .NET, I would normally have the Openwave and Nokia emulators running as well. This is particularly important, because currently the vast majority of Internet-enabled phones (outside of Japan) use one or the other or close relatives or versions of these browsers. I have illustrated this in Figure 6.4.

**FIGURE 6.4:**

Sample mobile Web application shown at design time and running in three separate emulators (Nokia, MME, and Openwave)

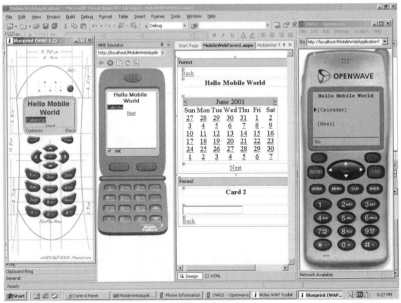

Image of UP.SDK courtesy Openwave Systems, Inc.

## Supported Devices

It is intended that, as new devices appear on the market, support will be made available in the toolkit on an ongoing basis. It is also possible for the developer to create his or her own extensions to the device support base within individual applications.

At the time of writing (Beta 2), Microsoft had tested the following devices and emulators (to a greater or lesser extent) with the Mobile Internet Toolkit:

**Devices**

Mitsubishi T250

Nokia 7110

Pocket PC with Microsoft Pocket Internet Explorer version 4.5

Ericsson R380

Microsoft Internet Explorer 5.5

Microsoft Internet Explorer 6.0

Mitsubishi D502i

NEC N502i

Nokia 6210

Palm VIIx

Palm V

Panasonic P502i

RIM Blackberry 950

RIM Blackberry 957

Samsung 850

Siemens S-35i

Sprint Touchpoint phone

**Emulators**

Microsoft Mobile Explorer version 2.01

Pocket PC with Microsoft Pocket Internet Explorer version 4.0

(Openwave) Phone.com UP.SDK 4.1 emulator with generic skin

(Openwave) Phone.com UP.SDK 3.2 for WML emulator with Mitsubishi T250 skin

DoCoMo 502

This list had grown considerably by the time that the RC version of the Mobile Internet Toolkit was released. It's also worth noting that individual devices may still require some extra code massaging to render your applications correctly. Keep an eye on the Microsoft documentation for any identified problems and suggested fixes.

**TIP**    Microsoft recommends that, where possible, device displays should be set fit to screen when viewing pages rendered by the toolkit.

## Getting Started

Let's start with a Microsoft Mobile Internet Toolkit version of the "Hello World" type application we first looked at back in Listing 4.2 from Chapter 4. Open up Visual Studio .NET and click the New Project option. See Figure 6.5.

**FIGURE 6.5:**

Step 1 of creating a mobile Web application

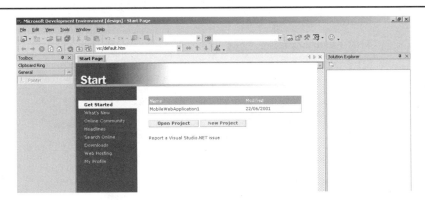

In the New Project dialog box, choose Visual Basic Projects from the Project Type options and Mobile Web Application from the Templates options. As the name that you give the application becomes its URL, it is a good idea to choose a name other than the default MobileWebApplication*N*. Long names can become a pain when typing URLs later on. For this project we'll call it Mobile1. If you wish to save your project to a location other than the default, now is the time to choose it. I usually tend to stick with the default, particularly for small projects; I always know where to find them, and I don't have to get into any unnecessary arguments with Visual Studio .NET about where they should be! See Figure 6.6.

FIGURE 6.6:

Step 2 involves
the New Project
dialog box.

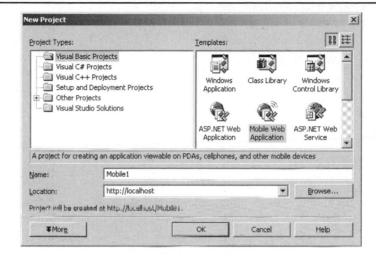

. If all went according to plan, your screen should look something like Figure 6.7. You may
need to add or remove some windows with the View menu and resize others. As there is not
much actual layout design involved with the toolkit and the controls are simply placed one
after the other down the mobile Web form, I tend to keep this area fairly narrow—only as
wide as the controls.

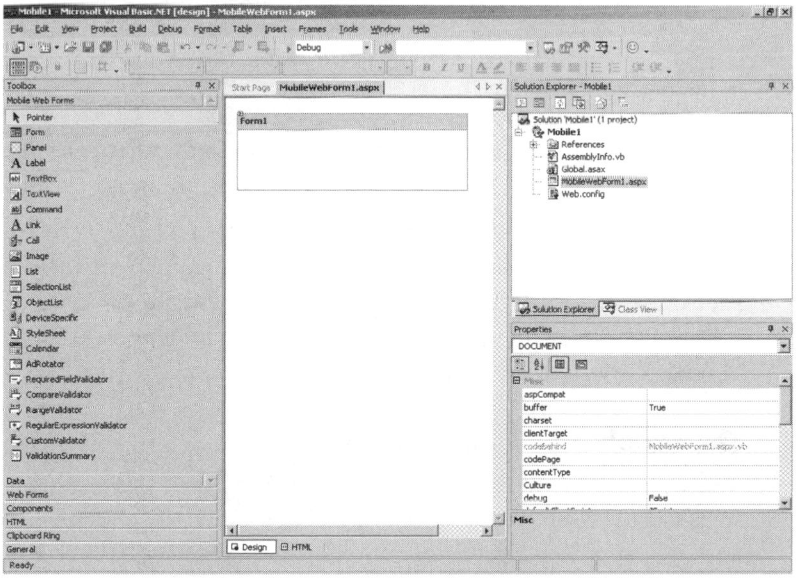

FIGURE 6.7:

Step3 involves the
Mobile Web Form
Designer with Toolbox,
Solution Explorer, and
the Properties window.

The window on the left contains the Toolbox, which includes the traditional runtime controls that we can drag and drop to our forms and some additional features such as the Clipboard Ring, which are described in the next section on the Toolbox. The middle window contains the Mobile Web Forms Designer where we define our Mobile Web Forms, add controls, and do all (well most) of our coding. The window on the right contains the Solution Explorer, which lists the various components of our application and the Properties window where we can define many of the properties that apply to the particular controls we are using.

## The Toolbox

The Toolbox contains the runtime controls available with the toolkit. Many of these controls would be very familiar to anyone used to working with Microsoft development environments. Some controls (such as PhoneCall and DeviceSpecific) are unique to the Mobile Toolkit, while others are either quite different when used as mobile controls or have experienced some changes under the shift to .NET. An example of this is the Label control, which now has a `Text` property in line with the TextBox control rather than the `Caption` property found in earlier versions of VB.

To use a control from the Toolbox, select the control and drag it to the MobileWebForm. This is a slightly different process for those used to earlier incarnations of Microsoft's IDE.

---

**WARNING**   You have to be a little careful as well that you don't accidentally click into the Web Forms controls in the Toolbox and try and start dropping non-mobile components onto your forms. A warning message will occur, but it can be a little disconcerting the first time it happens.

---

Data controls are grouped under the Data section of the Toolbox. It is also worth browsing the controls available under the HTML and Web Forms categories (not that we are really likely to use them for our mobile applications).

Another useful addition to the Toolbox is the Clipboard Ring, which can be used to store multiple code snippets as you work. Simply highlight what you wish to copy, drag it to the Clipboard Ring; and when you wish to reuse it, drag it from the ring back to your code. If you wish to remove it from the ring, right-click on the reference and choose Delete.

## The Mobile Web Form Designer

The central window contains the Mobile Web Form Designer. A new project opens in default with a single form on the Mobile Web Page and in the Design View. You can generate the card and deck approach by creating more forms on the Mobile Web Page. Controls are created on the form by clicking and dragging from the Toolbox. As mentioned earlier, controls are placed sequentially down the form and cannot be resized or located in specific parts of the form as can occur with Web Forms. To illustrate this, Figure 6.8 shows two forms with a succession of Label controls added to Form 1 and a number of Command Button controls added to Form 2.

**FIGURE 6.8:**

Example of two forms with multiple controls

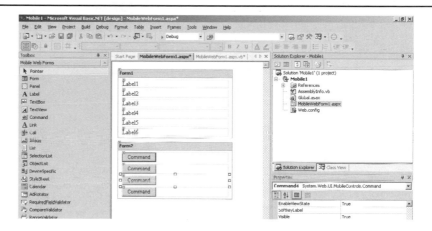

To get back to our project, drag a (single) Label control to Form 1. Double-click the control or the form itself to show the code behind (see Figure 6.9). This is where we get to work with our Visual Basic (although not in this example). Above the Class and Method windows at the top of the Code Behind window, you will see a set of tabs. Choosing the MobileWebForm1.aspx tab will take us back to the Design View. Alternatively, we could click on the View Designer button in the traditional View Object position at the top of the Solution Explorer window. We can return to the code by choosing the MobileWebForm1.aspx.vb* tab, double-clicking the form or controls, or clicking the View Code button next to the View Designer button. Well, we cannot say that Microsoft doesn't give us lots of options!

The other aspect of the form we need to consider is the code of the actual ASPX page itself. This is what we would be writing if we were building this project using Notepad rather than the Mobile Web Forms Designer. Right-click the form in Design View and choose the View HTML Source option. See Figure 6.9. We can edit this code directly from here if we wish or right-click and select View Design or click on the Design tab in the bottom left corner of the window to return to Design View. (Clicking the HTML tab will take us back to the ASPX code.)

HTML View of our
ASPX page

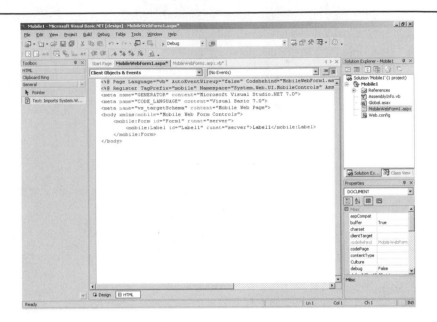

## The Properties Window

The Properties window is little changed except in appearance from what most Microsoft developers have become used to over the years. Its default organization is now Categories rather than Alphabetical, and it still seems to need more screen space than it actually gets.

Clicking on the Label control in our Design window will bring up the properties for Label in the Properties window. Note that a number of properties carry a Not Set tag as their default value. This setting leaves the exact rendering of the control up to the individual device. In the case of our label, set the following properties in Table 6.1:

**TABLE 6.1:** Property Settings for Label Control

| Property | Value |
| --- | --- |
| Alignment | Left |
| Text | Hi There |
| Wrapping | Wrap |
| StyleReference | Title |

When working with mobile devices and in doubt about wrapping, be sure to wrap! Click somewhere on the form other than the Label control and set the Alignment and Wrapping properties for the form to Left and Wrap respectively.

Your screen should now look like Figure 6.10. It's probably a good idea to save about now! Click the Save All icon on the standard toolbar. (It looks like a stack of floppy disks, and it is next to the traditional Save icon.)

**FIGURE 6.10:**

Hello World application in Design View

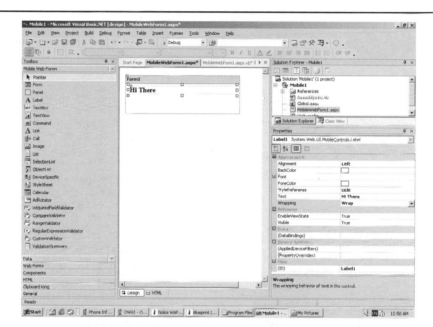

## Testing the Application with the Emulators

Now, we are going to view our application in our emulators. Right-click the form and choose View in Browser. If you have successfully set up MME, the browser should come up and, after a moment, connect to the server and display the form. Choose the Openwave emulator by opening UP.SDK ➤ UP.Simulator from the Start ➤ Programs menu and type the following URL into the Address window and then press Enter.

```
http://localhostMobile1/MobileWebForm.aspx
```

Minimize the Phone Information window for the moment and your screen should look something like Figure 6.11.

**FIGURE 6.11:**

Hello World
application displayed
in the emulators

Image of UP.SDK courtesy Openwave Systems, Inc.

Pull up the Phone Information window for the Openwave (UP) emulator. From the Phone window itself, choose Source from the Info menu. This will display the source code as received by the UP.Browser (see Figure 6.12). As you can see, it is pretty much the same WML code that we wrote for this application back in Chapter 4 (Listing 4.2).

**FIGURE 6.12:**

Hello World source
code as received by
the UP.Browser

```
HTTP GET Request: http://localhost/Mobile1/MobileWebForm1.aspx
Checking for URL 'localhost/Mobile1/MobileWebForm1.aspx' in Whitelist
         not found

---------------------- DATA SIZE ----------------------
Uncompiled data from HTTP is 272 bytes.
...found Content-Type: text/vnd.wap.wml.
Compiled WAP binary is 81 bytes.


******************** Current WML ********************
<?xml version='1.0'?>
<!DOCTYPE wml PUBLIC '-//WAPFORUM//DTD WML 1.1//EN' 'http://www.wapforum.org/DTD
/wml_1.1.xml'><wml><head>
<meta http-equiv="Cache-Control" content="max-age=0" />
</head>


<card id="Form1">
<p><big><b>Hi There</b></big><br/>
</p></card></wml>
****************************************************
```

Image of UP.SDK courtesy Openwave Systems, Inc.

When quitting the UP Emulator, always exit from the Phone window. Earlier versions generated an error if you tried to exit from the Phone Information window, although this appears to have been fixed for version 4.1.

Return to the Visual Studio .NET IDE and right-click on the form in Design View and choose View HTML Source. Have a look at the tags for the Form and Label controls within the Body section of the code. I have reproduced this code in Listing 6.1. The properties that we have defined for these controls are now specified within these tags. These properties can be edited directly in this window, and indeed, some properties that we will need to specify for our applications later on will have to be done here.

**Listing 6.1**          **Code from the HTML Source View for Hello World Application**

```
<%@ Register TagPrefix="mobile"
➥ Namespace="System.Web.UI.MobileControls"
➥ Assembly="System.Web.Mobile, Version=1.0.3300.0, Culture=neutral,
➥ PublicKeyToken=b03f5f7f11d50a3a" %>
<%@ Page Language="vb" AutoEventWireup="false"
➥ Codebehind="MobileWebForm1.aspx.vb"
➥ Inherits="Mobile1.MobileWebForm1" %>
<meta name="GENERATOR" content="Microsoft Visual Studio.NET 7.0">
<meta name="CODE_LANGUAGE" content="Visual Basic 7.0">
<meta name="vs_targetSchema"
➥ content="http://schemas.microsoft.com/Mobile/Page">
<body Xmlns:mobile="http://schemas.microsoft.com/Mobile/WebForm">
   <mobile:Form id="Form1" runat="server" Wrapping="Wrap"
➥ Alignment="Left">
      <mobile:Label id="Label1" runat="server" Wrapping="Wrap"
➥ Alignment="Left" StyleReference="title">Hi There</mobile:Label>
   </mobile:Form>
</body>
```

It is also worth noting that the runat attributes for these control tags are normally set to Server.

## Building a Simple Two-Card Deck

For our next introductory application we will build a simple two-card deck and use it to illustrate both navigation between cards and the importance of the order of control placement in the Mobile Internet Toolkit.

Create a new mobile project (called Mobile2) using Visual Basic. Create a second form in the designer and add Label and Link controls as depicted in Figure 6.13.

**FIGURE 6.13:**

Control layout for the "Simple Two-Card Deck" project

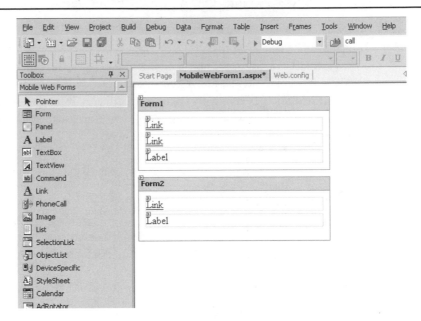

For the controls in Form1 set the following properties listed in Table 6.2:

**TABLE 6.2:** Property Settings for the Controls in Form1

| Control | Property | Value |
|---|---|---|
| Link1 | Text | A Link to Somewhere |
| | SoftKeyLabel | <empty> |
| | Visible | True |
| | NavigateURL | <empty> |
| Link2 | Text | Next Card |
| | SoftKeyLabel | <empty> |
| | Visible | True |
| | NavigateURL | #Form2 |
| Label1 | Alignment | Center |
| | StyleReference | Title |
| | Text | Simple Deck |

By placing Links 1 and 2 above Label1 on the form we ensure that Link1 and Link2 are rendered as HREFs rather than Option Onpicks in the Openwave browser.

Link1 is a dummy link for the purpose of the example. Later on we will make it more functional and insert a real address into the NavigateURL property. Link2 provides the link to Form2.

To set up Form2, set the property values as in Table 6.3.

**TABLE 6.3:** Property Settings for the Controls in Form2

| Control | Property | Value |
| --- | --- | --- |
| Link3 | Text | Back |
|  | SoftKeyLabel | <empty> |
|  | Visible | False |
|  | NavigateURL | #Form1 |
| Label2 | Text | Card 2 |

In this Form, we have kept Link3 inactive for the moment, but it will eventually act as a Back softkey. Click Save All and pull up the Openwave (UP) browser. Type in the following URL:

```
http://localhost/Mobile2/MobileWebForm1.aspx
```

Your two cards should appear as in Figure 6.14. Notice that in Form2 a Back softkey should appear at the bottom of the screen.

Back in Visual Studio .NET, right-click Form1 and select View in Browser. In the MME emulator, you will notice that we cannot click and highlight A Link to Somewhere at all unless it has an address entered into its NavigateURL property. Select the properties for Link1 and add the setting #Form2 to the NavigateURL property. Refresh MME and click through to the next card. Notice that we have no Back softkey or access to the link that we entered into Link3. We need to use the Back arrow on the MME toolbar to return to the first card.

Let's play a little further with our links in the application. Move the two links below the Label control on Form1, save everything, and refresh both the Openwave browser (F9) and MME (from the toolbar). MME should look essentially the same (apart from the transposed links and label), but the Openwave browser should now show its links as Option Onpicks. See Figure 6.15 for the code and Figure 6.16 for the screenshot of the browser.

FIGURE 6.14:

FIGURE 6.14:

The simple two-card
deck as it appears in
the Openwave browser

Image of UP.SDK courtesy Openwave Systems, Inc.

FIGURE 6.15:

WML generated for
Openwave browser
showing links as
Option Onpicks

```
/wml_1.1.xml'><wml><head>
<meta http-equiv="Cache-Control" content="max-age=0" />
</head>

<card id="Form1">
<p></p><p align="center"><big><b>Simple Deck</b></big></p><p align="left"><br/>
<do type="accept" label="Go"><go href="MobileWebForm1.aspx?__ufps=63129681688008
9872" method="post"><postfield name="__EVENTTARGET" value="Form1" /><postfield n
ame="__EVENTARGUMENT" value="$(Form1)" /></go></do><select name="Form1"><option
onpick="#Form2">A Link to Somewhere</option><option onpick="#Form2">Next Card</o
ption></select></p></card>

<card id="Form2">
<p><do type="accept" label="Back"><go href="#Form1" /></do>Card 2<br/>
</p></card></wml>
**********************************************************************************

cache hit: {
                <http://localhost/Mobile2/MobileWebForm1.aspx>
          }
cache hit: {
                <http://localhost/Mobile2/MobileWebForm1.aspx>
          }
```

Image of UP.SDK courtesy Openwave Systems, Inc.

FIGURE 6.16:

Screenshot showing
the Openwave browser
with Option Onpicks

Image of UP.SDK courtesy Openwave Systems, Inc.

In the Openwave browser, Option Onpicks are far nicer than simple HREFs. However, they are not always the best way to go, and to give the user a Back option, we have to include it as one of the URL choices. They can also be fiddly in the Nokia environment, although, thankfully, it doesn't appear as if the Mobile Internet Toolkit generates them for Nokia.

NOTE    Note that the Nokia has by default a Back right softkey. Our current setup with Card 2 (once the link is made active by setting the Visible property to True) contains the slightly absurd situation of the Nokia of having both right and left softkeys labeled as Back.

Returning to our design environment, select the properties for Link4 on Form2. Change the Text property from Back to Card 1, the SoftKeyLabel to Back, and the Visible property to True. Save and refresh the Openwave browser (by pressing F9).

Click through to Card 2. The link should now appear in the window as [Card 1], but the content of the left softkey should be different. Highlight the link (it has an arrow next to it) to give the softkey the label of Back that we entered into the links properties. In Visual Studio, delete the SoftKeyLabel property for Link3 and return to the Openwave browser. Use the up and down buttons on the browser to deselect the link. It should now show the softkey label as the text property of the link (Card 1).

Delete the link entirely. Save and refresh the browser. We now have the default Back soft-key in the bottom left of the screen. The Nokia (if you are using it) has only its single default Back softkey, and MME has no onscreen navigation at all (although we can still use the Back button on the toolbar).

This might seem all rather trivial, but it demonstrates that even at this fairly basic level, there are differences in how our applications are going to present. It's worth knowing what they are in advance, and it's worth testing as much as possible to ensure that what we are building isn't going to come back to bite us in some horrible fashion in the near future. Of particular interest is that, by virtue of their placement on the form, the relative positions of the links determine whether the Openwave browser uses HREFs or Option Onpicks to render its links.

## Using Code Behind

In this project we will build a simple application that illustrates the use of the code-behind feature in designing mobile applications with the Mobile Internet Toolkit.

Create a new project and name it Mobile3. Drag a Label and Command control onto the form in Design View (see Figure 6.17).

**FIGURE 6.17:**

Control layout for the "Simple Code Behind" project

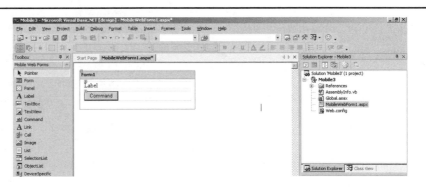

Set the text property of the label (Label1) to "Hi There!" and the text property of the command button (Command1) to "Click Me." Double-click the command button to enter the code behind. Add the code in Listing 6.2 to the subroutine.

**Listing 6.2**      **Code for the *Command1_Click* subroutine in the Simple Code Behind Project**

```
Private Sub Command1_Click(ByVal sender As System.Object, ByVal e As
➡ System.EventArgs) Handles Command1.Click
        Label1.Text = "Hi Mobile World"
        End Sub
```

This is a straightforward and very typical "Hello World" style application that sets the `Text` property of `Label1` in response to the `Click` event of `Command1`.

**TIP**   Don't forget to compile your code before we leave this screen. Click the `Build` command under the Build menu. This is important, as code behind requires a design time compile for it to be available to the project. The ASPX code can be simply saved, as it is not compiled until run time.

An Output window will appear in the bottom of your screen displaying the progress and eventual success (or otherwise!) of your build (see Figure 6.18).

**FIGURE 6.18:**

Visual Studio .NFT showing the Output window after a successful build

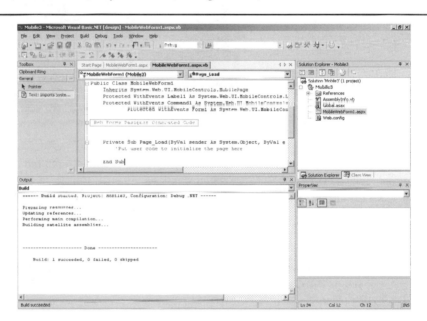

Close the Ouput window to recover some screen space, and click back to the Design View of your form (using either the View Designer button on the Solution Explorer or the `MobileWebForm1.aspx` tab at the top of the Mobile Web Page).

Save the project and fire it up in the Openwave browser using the `http://localhost/Mobile3/MobileWebForm1.aspx` URL. The command button appears in the browser as a link. Click the link to change the text message from "Hi There" to "Hi Mobile World." See Figure 6.19 for the expected output.

FIGURE 6.19:

Expected output for
the "Simple Code
Behind" project

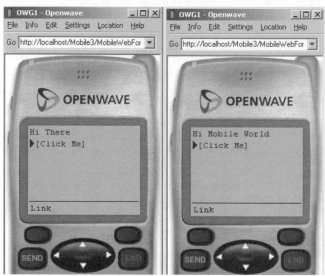

Image of UP.SDK courtesy Openwave Systems, Inc.

**NOTE**     Although this application will run in the Nokia browser, repeated clicks on the command
link will generate Cookie Expired warnings because the Nokia browser does not support
cookies. We will see in Chapter 8 how to manage session state without cookies.

Finally, it is worth noting that we could also have built this simple application using similar
code but only using the HTML View window.

Open a new project as Mobile4 and recreate the form, the label, and the command button from Mobile3. Open the Mobile Web Form in HTML View and add the code from
Listing 6.3.

**Listing 6.3**     **HTML Code for Simple Code Behind Project Running Only as an ASPX Page**

```
<%@ Register TagPrefix="mobile"
➥ Namespace="System.Web.UI.MobileControls"
➥ Assembly="System.Web.Mobile, Version=1.0.3300.0, Culture=neutral,
➥ PublicKeyToken=b03f5f7f11d50a3a" %>
<%@ Page Language="vb" AutoEventWireup="false"
➥ Codebehind="MobileWebForm1.aspx.vb"
➥ Inherits="Mobile4.MobileWebForm1" %>
<meta name="GENERATOR" content="Microsoft Visual Studio.NET 7.0">
<meta name="CODE_LANGUAGE" content="Visual Basic 7.0">
<meta name="vs_targetSchema"
➥ content="http://schemas.microsoft.com/Mobile/Page">
```

```
<script runat="server" language="VB">
   Protected sub Command1_Click(sender As Object, e As EventArgs)
      Label1.text = "Hi Mobile World"
         End Sub
</script>

<body Xmlns:mobile="http://schemas.microsoft.com/Mobile/WebForm">

   <mobile:Form id="Form1" runat="server">
      <mobile:Label id="Label1" runat="server">Hi
➡ There</mobile:Label>
      <mobile:Command id="Command1" runat="server"
➡ OnClick=" Command1_Click ">Click Me</mobile:Command>
   </mobile:Form>
</body>
```

The main difference here is the addition of the following script, which contains the code we previously used in the code behind:

```
<script runat="server" language="VB">
   Protected sub Command1_Click (sender As Object, e As EventArgs)
      Label1.text = "Hi Mobile World"
         End Sub
</script>
```

Save the project and open it using the Openwave emulator. The output should be identical to that of Mobile3.

## Summary

Although the Mobile Internet Toolkit offers clear advantages for developers, we still need to be aware of the variations introduced by the range of client devices and configurations available. We need to remember to test our applications in as many configurations as possible and be conscious that even simple applications may give unexpected results when rendered across different devices.

Despite this, the Mobile Internet Toolkit offers a fast and effective method to develop mobile applications. The Mobile Designer, coupled with Visual Studio .NET, is easy to use and can be configured to give instant feedback on the progress of a development using the MME Content Toolkit. Other emulators and devices can run in conjunction with the toolkit and can also be used for ongoing testing.

The real test for an application is an "in the wild" test on a real phone. This is relatively easy to do if your mobile phone is already set up for WAP and your computer has a dial-up or direct line to the Internet. (Those of us developing behind secure corporate firewalls need not apply!) Connect your computer to the Internet and identify its IP address. If you have a dial-up connection, type **ipconfig** in a command window (Start ➤ Run, then type **cmd**) for Windows NT and 2000 machines. From your WAP phone, access your application URL using your IP address as the first part of the URL (for example, `http://255.255.255.1/` `mobile3/MobileWebForm1.aspx`). Yes, I know it's tedious, but think of the adventure!

Finally, be aware that there are some options when developing mobile sites with the Toolkit. For smaller applications and when performance is less of an issue, it may make more sense to code everything directly onto the ASPX page, rather than using the code-behind environment.

# CHAPTER 7

# The Runtime Controls

- Introducing the control categories

- Container controls

- Standard controls

- List controls

- Validation controls

- Special controls

**W**e build applications in the Mobile Internet Toolkit by making use of a range of tools known as the runtime controls. These include components such as text boxes, command buttons, validation tools, and data connectivity tools. We can copy a selection of controls to a Mobile Web Page, set various properties on the controls, and then build their functionality either by coding direct to the ASPX page or into code behind. In this chapter we will be taking a look at each of the following runtime controls that ship with the Mobile Internet Toolkit:

*Form*  Acts as a container for other controls and models a card within the WAP environment.

*Panel*  Provides a mechanism for organizing controls in a form and assigning common properties.

*AdRotator*  Can be used to rotate advertisements or images in an application and can also be used to render different images for different devices.

*Calendar*  Provides calendar functions for mobile devices.

*Command*  Posts input from UI (User Input) elements back to the server.

*Image*  Enables images to be displayed on mobile devices.

*Label*  Provides a mechanism for presenting text on a form.

*Link*  Creates links to other forms, decks, and sites.

*PhoneCall*  Can be used to automatically call or display phone numbers.

*TextBox*  Acts as a data input mechanism for an application.

*TextView*  Displays arbitrary amounts of text with optional markup tags.

*List*  Renders a list of items.

*ObjectList*  Used for interacting with data sources.

*SelectionList*  Extends the basic List control to include a wider base of user interaction.

*CompareVaildator*  Compares one control to another.

*CustomValidator*  Allows for custom development of validation requirements.

*RangeValidator*  Validates that the values of another control are within a set range.

*RegularExpressionValidator*  Validates that the contents of another control match a specific expression.

*RequiredFieldValidator*  Validates that the value of another control is different to its original value.

*ValidationSummary*    Displays a summary of validation errors that have occurred when a form has been rendered.

*DeviceSpecific*    Allows a choice to be specified where multiple alternatives exist for particular content types.

*StyleSheet*    Used to organize styles that will be applied to other controls.

Specifically, we will look at the controls as they appear in the Mobile Internet Designer in Visual Studio .NET. These are not always identical to the controls as they are found in the Mobile Internet Toolkit—for example, they may not share the full range of properties in all cases.

The Help files for Visual Studio .NET contain detailed documentation for all the controls. Rather than reproduce it in this chapter, I will focus on the some of the key elements of each control and, where appropriate, worked examples of their usage.

**TIP**    To find the documentation on the Mobile Internet Toolkit Controls in Visual Studio .NET, choose Contents from the Help menu. Expand Visual Studio .NET in the Contents window, expand SDK's and Tools ➢ Visual Studio SDK ➢ Mobile Internet Toolkit ➢ Mobile Internet Controls Runtime, and choose Inside the Mobile Internet Controls Runtime. Scroll down to the bottom of that page to view a series of links to each of the runtime controls.

**TIP**    To locate the documentation on the controls as they appear in the Mobile Internet Designer, expand Mobile Internet Designer in the Mobile Internet Toolkit section in the Contents window, and choose the Using Mobile Internet Controls in the Designer option.

## Introducing the Control Categories

Each of the controls is a member of System.Web.UI.MobileControls and Microsoft classifies the runtime controls into the following five main groups based on function:

**Container controls**    Organizes content.

**Standard controls**    Displays, enters, or links to information. Includes the Command control to activate events.

**List controls**    Displays lists.

**Validation controls**    Validates the contents of other controls.

**Special controls**    Handles essentially anything not covered by the previous categories!

Table 7.1 shows the various controls grouped in their broad categories.

**TABLE 7.1:** Categories of the Mobile Internet Controls

| Category | Controls |
| --- | --- |
| Container | Form |
| | Panel |
| Standard | AdRotator |
| | Calendar |
| | Command |
| | Image |
| | Label |
| | Link |
| | PhoneCall |
| | TextBox |
| | TextView |
| List | List |
| | ObjectList |
| | SelectionList |
| Validation | CompareValidator |
| | CustomValidator |
| | RangeValidator |
| | RegularExpressionValidator |
| | RequiredFieldValidator |
| | ValidationSummary |
| Special | DeviceSpecific |
| | StyleSheet |

Many of the controls are very similar to their counterparts in ASP.NET. For a really detailed understanding of the controls we need to look at the class specifications, an overview of which is available in Appendix A, "Class Listing for the Mobile Internet Toolkit." Each of the controls is addressed alphabetically within their categories, although this is not the order of how they appear in the Toolbox in the Mobile Internet Designer.

> **TIP** One useful aspect of many of the controls is that they possess a `PropertyOverride` element that can be used to set device-specific options for particular devices. I have given a detailed example of this for the Image control in the "Image Control" section later in this chapter.

**TIP** A number of controls also support Templating Options. These enable us to edit the templates for particular controls for specific devices. When we apply this at the Form or Panel level, we need to use the DeviceSpecific control, which is introduced in the "Special Controls" section later in this chapter.

As working examples of how the controls work, we will build four "dummy" applications (Mobile5, Mobile6, Mobile7, and Mobile8) to illustrate the controls from four of the five broad categories: Container, Standard, Validation, and Special. The fifth category, the list controls, is covered in more detail in Chapter 9, "Data Access with the Mobile Internet Toolkit, Part 1 (List Controls)."

## Container Controls

These include the two main controls used to organize content on your Mobile Web Form: the Form and Panel controls.

### The Form Control

A Mobile Web Form page must contain at least one Form control. Forms can contain all other controls except other forms or style sheets (which need to be placed directly on the page). Where tab order between controls is supported, the tab order is defined by either the order they appear on the page or, in cases where the controls are generated dynamically, by the order in which they are added to the page.

As seen earlier, we can place multiple forms on a page to simulate a WAP deck where each form represents a card of the deck. The first form on the page is the first form to be presented to a user, although this default can be changed programmatically. The advantage of using multiple forms on the one page is twofold: It reduces the number of pages used in the application, which in turn improves application performance, and it enables a logical flow to be developed within the application design where forms sharing a particular aspect of the application can be grouped together on the one page. However, we do need to remember that ASP.NET serves up the page one form (or card) at a time unlike a traditional WAP deck where all the cards on a deck are delivered to the client together. This in turn alters some of the design considerations we may make when designing with the Mobile Internet Toolkit as opposed to a more "traditional" approach to WAP design. When building with the Toolkit (as with any Mobile Internet application) we also need to keep a close eye on the compiled size of the application, which we can do using the Phone Information window of the Openwave SDK. As discussed in Chapter 5, "Designing for the Mobile Web," the minimum for some devices is as low as a 1,000 bytes and, due to latency times, a recommended working maximum of 500 to 600 bytes is often quoted.

Text can be typed directly into the form, and various appearance properties such as background and text colors can be set . These properties will only be rendered by devices that can support them.

To test this, open a new project and call it Mobile5. In the blank form, set its `BackColor` property to Yellow and its `ForeColor` property to Blue. Type the following line of text:

**Why have we been using label controls?**

Save the project and then open it using Internet Explorer. It should be rendered in all its glory. Open the same project in the Openwave browser or MME, however, and we are back to the old black and white display.

---

**NOTE**     Microsoft refers to text typed directly on the form as *literal text*. Within HTML View, this text can be given some basic formatting using the <a> (link), <b> (bold text), <br/> (line break), <i> (italic), and <p> (paragraph) tags. Literal text can also be used in the Panel and FormView controls.

---

Using the DeviceSpecific control, a form can be customized based on the capabilities of the device for which it is rendered by using property overrides or templating. We will investigate this further when we take a look at the DeviceSpecific control in the "Special Controls" section later in this chapter.

## The Panel Control

The Panel control is used to apply styles across a group of controls. It can also supply information about how controls should be paginated at runtime. It must be placed within a `Form` or another Panel control and can contain all other controls except for a `Stylesheet` or a `Form`.

As with a Form control, a DeviceSpecific control can be added to a Panel control to provide facility for templating and property overrides. Text can be typed directly into a `Panel` and various other properties such as colors can be set. For an example of using a Panel, add a Panel to the Mobile5 project and drag a couple of Label controls onto it. Drag a third Label control below the Panel.

Select the `StyleReference` property for the `Panel` and set it to Title. You will notice that the text immediately becomes bold in both the `inpanel` `Labels`. Set the `Alignment` property to Center. The text in the panel `Labels` is also centered. Note that the `Form` `Backcolor` property of yellow is also reflected in the `Panel`. However, we can overcome this by giving the `Panel` a different `Backcolor`.

Now all we need is mobile phones that can actually see this stuff. (Give them time!) Figure 7.1 shows a screenshot of Mobile5 in its development so far.

FIGURE 7.1:

Using a Panel control
to set styles for
multiple controls

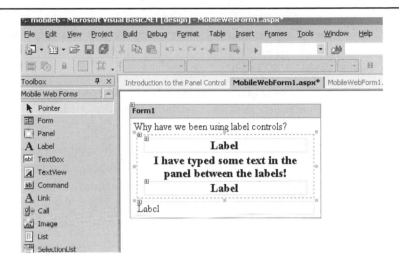

Save and view in your emulator if you need any further convincing.

## Standard Controls

Many of these controls would be familiar to users of previous versions of the Microsoft Visual
Studio family of development tools. However, in this environment, the various behaviors of
these controls can vary from what we are used to and their property set is in some cases quite
different. Don't just assume that just because you have used a particular control a million
times before that it will be the same here—you have been warned!

**TIP** Right-clicking any property in the Properties box for a given control displays a Description
option in the context menu. Selecting this option displays a brief description of the
selected property below the Properties box.

### The AdRotator Control

The AdRotator control can be used to generate a cycle of advertisements for a site. Certain
advertisements can be given more weighting than others, and custom code can be written to
cycle through images. The control links to an XML file that contains the addresses of the
images and the relevant links that make up the advertisements. It can also be used in conjunction with the DeviceSpecific element to choose appropriate image formats for individual devices.

To set up an example of how the AdRotator works, first we will need to get a couple of images and place them somewhere convenient to access. The Openwave folder includes a set of icons (BMPs) in the UPSDK41 folder. The default location is C:\Program Files\ Openwave\UPSDK41\icons.

For this example, I have chosen icons 100 (a book) and 110 (a camcorder). Copy the images and place them in a folder called Icons directly in C drive (i.e., c:\icons). We will move it again later when we have set up the project.

Copy the XML code from Listing 7.1 into Notepad and save it as Ad1.xml. Make sure that you have All Files selected rather than Text Documents in the Save as Type field. Save it into the Icons directory that we previously created. (I normally use the Desktop for this sort of work, but if we do it this way for those of us working in a multiuser environment, we can all be agreed where the folder is!)

**Listing 7.1      Sample *Ad1.xml* File for *AdRotator* Example**

```xml
<?xml version="1.0"?>
 <Advertisements>
   <Ad>
      <ImageUrl>icons/100.bmp</ImageUrl>
      <MonoImageUrl>icons/100.bmp</MonoImageUrl>
      <NavigateUrl>http://www.mycompany1.com</NavigateUrl>
      <AlternateText>Book</AlternateText>
      <KeywordFilter>book</KeywordFilter>
      <Impressions>80</Impressions>
   </Ad>
   <Ad>
      <ImageUrl>icons/110.bmp</ImageUrl>
      <MonoImageUrl>icons/110.bmp</MonoImageUrl>
      <NavigateUrl>http://www.mycompany2.com</NavigateUrl>
      <AlternateText>Camcorder</AlternateText>
      <KeywordFilter>camcorder</KeywordFilter>
      <Impressions>80</Impressions>
   </Ad>
 </Advertisements>
```

Create a new mobile project (called Mobile6) in Visual Studio and drag an AdRotator control onto the form. Before we go any further, minimize Visual Studio .NET and move the icons directory to c:\Inetpub\wwwroot\Mobile6, assuming you have followed the defaults. Open the icons and move the Ad1.xml file directly into the Mobile6 folder.

Maximize Visual Studio .NET and select the AdRotator control that you placed on the form. In the Properties area select AdvertisementsFile and click the small box with the ellipsis (three dots) that appears in the right side and type **Ad1.xml** in the URL field. Click OK, and save the project.

Open up the Openwave browser and access the project with the following URL:

`http://localhost/Mobile6/MobileWebForm1.aspx`

The browser should open showing one of the images as a link. Refresh the browser a number of times with the F9 key and the image should change at some point (see Figure 7.2).

**FIGURE 7.2:**

Openwave browser showing two different renditions of the AdRotator control from the Mobile6 project

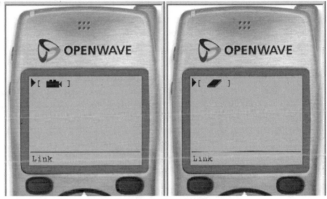

Image of UP.SDK courtesy Openwave Systems, Inc.

**WARNING** This project will not work at all in the Nokia browser because there is no support for BMP images.

Finally, let's take a quick look at the XML in Listing 7.1 to see what it all means and to what extent we can customize it:

- To place more advertisements, we simply add more sets of `<Ad>` ... `</Ad>` tags with appropriate contents.

- The `<ImageUrl>` tags give the location of the appropriate image file for that advert. This is a required tag.

- The `<MonoImageUrl>` tag can be used in conjunction with the `DeviceSpecific` element to set an alternative image for those devices that can only view black and white.

- The `<NavigateURL>` tag is optional, but when it is used it sets the address to which the image is linked.

- The `<AlternativeText>` tag is also optional and provides a text description if the image is unable to be viewed.

- The `<KeywordFilter>` tag is used in conjunction with the `KeywordFilter` property for the AdRotator control and enables advertisements to be filtered into categories.

- The <Impressions> tag sets the relative importance for different advertisements. The higher the number for a particular ad in relation to the others, the more often it is displayed. If all ads have the same value, they get equal weighting.

Using the PropertyOverrides element in the Properties window, we can apply different XML files giving different image types for different devices—assuming that we have developed a detailed set of different images, each specially optimized for particular devices—for the same advertisement. Refer to the section on the Image control to see how we use this element.

## The Calendar Control

The Calendar control adds calendar functionality to our mobile applications. The way it is rendered on the mobile device can vary quite widely from device to device. Drag a copy of the control to the Mobile6 form, save it, and have a look at the application in both Internet Explorer and the Openwave browser. See Figure 7.3 for the two views.

**FIGURE 7.3:**

The Calendar control viewed in IE and the Openwave browser

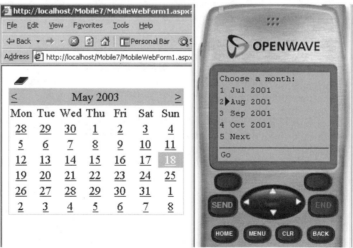

Image of UP.SDK courtesy Openwave Systems, Inc.

The control offers a range of display options (such as defining which is the first day of the week; whether a user can select a single day, week, or month; how a date is formatted; which is the default date displayed; etc.). Refer to Chapter 19, "Morris's Wholesale Fruit & Vege: A Mobile Intranet," for an example of the use of this control.

## The Command Control

As we have seen earlier in Chapter 6, "Getting Started with the Mobile Internet Toolkit," the Command control can be used to post input back to the server and tell it to do something with it.

## The Image Control

The Image control is fairly obviously used to display images. The location of the image is specified in the `ImageUrl` property. As very few images are going to display correctly on all devices, the `PropertyOverrides` property enables us to specify different images for different devices.

We'll illustrate this with the following project. Add an Image control to the form in Mobile6. Find a simple JPEG image from somewhere (grab a legal one from the Internet or clipart, or create one in your image editor of choice) and save it as Image1 into the Icons folder in `c:\Inetpub\wwwroot\Mobile6\icons`.

I have used the PictureTube tool in PaintShopPro to create an image of a plane. Open up the `100.bmp` image used in the `AdRotator` in your Image Editor and save it as a GIF image (`100.gif`).

Back in VisualStudio .NET, select the Image control that you have added to the form and, in the Properties window, set the `ImageURL` to `file:///c:\Inetpub\wwwroot\Mobile6\icons\Image1.jpg`.

Set the `AlternateText` property to JPEG Image. The image should appear in the Image control in Design View. However, if you save the project and attempt to view it with MME, the image will not be shown (unless they have added JPEG support to MME by the time this book goes to press).

Select the Property Overrides control and click the small button (with an ellipsis) that appears. The Image1—Property Overrides dialog box illustrated in Figure 7.4 should appear.

---

**FIGURE 7.4:**

First dialog box when setting Property-Overrides for the Image control

Click the Edit button and, from the Applied Device Filters combo box, choose isMME, click the Add to List button (Figure 7.5), and then click OK.

**FIGURE 7.5:**

Second dialog box when setting Property-Overrides for the Image control

In the Property box that appears (Image1—Property Overrides dialog box), set the ImageURL property to `file:///c:\ Inetpub\wwwroot\Mobile6\icons\100.gif`.

Set the `AlternateText` property to Book Image and click OK (see Figure 7.6).

**FIGURE 7.6:**

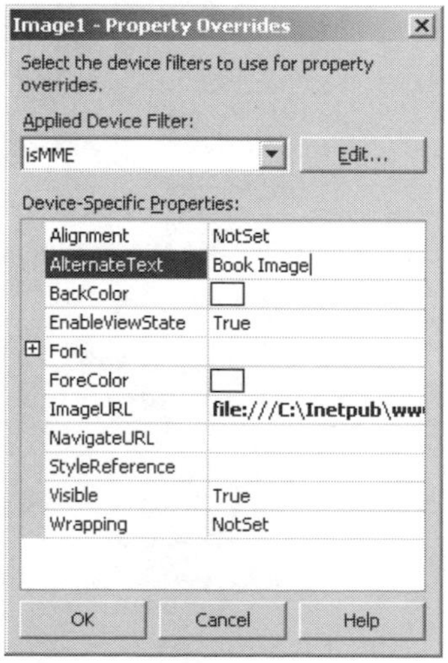

Third dialog box when setting Property-Overrides for the Image control

Save the project and open in the MME browser. The book image should appear on the screen below the other exercises we have done. Open the project in IE and you should see the JPEG image under the other exercises.

Finally, we can also set the `NavigateURL` property to set an image as a link.

## The Label Control

We have already extensively covered the use of the Label control in earlier projects. It's great for displaying short strings of text, but for the big stuff, you're better off using the TextView control.

Generally, we use the Label control for displaying output (such as the Simple Code Behind project). In some of the earlier projects we could have got away with typing the text straight into the Form control.

---

**TIP**  Many mobile controls (such as the Label control) automatically insert a line break after they have been rendered on the client device. These controls offer a `BreakAfter` property that can be set to `False`. Setting the property to `False`, enables the contents of multiple controls (client display permitting) to be rendered on the same line at runtime. However, you will not see the effects of setting the `BreakAfter` property to `False` in the design environment.

## The Link Control

We have also covered use of this control in earlier projects. One additional note is that if we wish to use an image as a link, then we need to use an Image control.

## The PhoneCall Control

One powerful tool when working with WML is the ability to generate a phone number on the user's cell phone that can be used directly. For example, a user browsing my business's site could access the Contact Us card, which would then pop the relevant phone number that could be called directly from the phone without the user having to type it in again. However, as with all things WAP, support for this feature varies widely from device to device.

Microsoft's PhoneCall control takes the agony out of coding for this and also allows for the number to be presented as text with an optional hyperlink for those devices that aren't telephones.

Open up the Mobile6 project, drag a PhoneCall control to the project form, and have a close look at the properties. The following are the key properties:

***PhoneNumber***   The number you want called.

*AlternativeURL*   The address of the hyperlink you wish to be displayed if making a phone call is not an option.

*AlternativeFormat*   This is a little cryptic as it displays {0} {1} (we will discuss it in the next few paragraphs), but this property determines the format of the number for display when the device can't make phone calls.

The {0} {1} in the AlternativeFormat property denotes that the number will be formatted with the contents of the Text and PhoneNumber properties respectively (i.e., Fred Smith 5555555). It can be modified to read something like "Give {0} a call at {1} for information on our new products."

Assuming that the Text property value was Fred Smith and the PhoneNumber property value was 5555555, this would be rendered out as "Give Fred Smith a call at 5555555 for information on our new products."

Of course this doesn't happen on all devices. Internet Explorer and the Nokia browser will display this text, but the Openwave browser and MME both do something different. They essentially display the content of the Text property as a link—selecting the link takes you to a screen with the phone number and a device-generated message to call it.

## The TextBox Control

Text boxes are used for data input. A new feature in Visual Studio .NET is the ability to set password masking in the Properties window. The Size and MaxLength properties need to be set to determine the size of the input filed on the client device and the maximum number of characters allowed (the latter is a feature currently only supported by WML devices).

We can test this by returning to our Mobile5 application and by dragging a text box onto the form and setting the properties as indicated in Table 7.2:

**TABLE 7.2:**  Property Settings for TextBox Control in Mobile5

| Property | Value |
|---|---|
| MaxLength | 8 |
| Password | True |
| Size | 8 |

For the purpose of this demonstration, I have also deleted the initial form text and some of the labels. I have kept one panel Label, given it the text value Password Example, and added the line "Enter Password" directly onto the form below the panel. Save and view in the Openwave browser. Type something into the password field. It should look something like Figure 7.7.

Mobile5 project with
the TextBox control
configured as a
password entry field

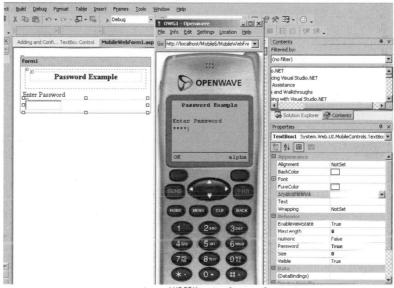

Image of UP.SDK courtesy Openwave Systems, Inc.

**TIP**    Note that when setting passwords, seven seems to be the recommended number of characters for making them hard to crack.

## The TextView Control

Got lots of data to display? Want to format it and include a hyperlink or two? Use a TextView control.

Drag a TextView control onto our Mobile5 project form. For this example I have copied one of the paragraphs out of this chapter, and I will use it in the control. Select the TextView control and, from the Properties window, select the Text property.

Paste your text into the Text property—although you may find it easier to do this directly within the control tags in HTML View. The text can be formatted with a range of basic format tags in HTML View. The options include the following:

- Creating a hyperlink with `<a href="http://www.linktowherever">My Link </a>`
- Bold text with `<b> </b>`
- Line break with `<br/>`
- Italic text with `<i> </i>`
- Paragraph with `<p> </p>`

Figure 7.8 illustrates how the formatting tags can be applied to code in HTML View.

```
<mobile:TextView id="TextView1" runat="server">The Image control is fairly obviously used to display
images. The location of the image is specified in the ImageUrl property.
As very few images are going to display correctly on all devices, the Property Overrides
property enables us to specify different images for different devices.
<br/><b>We'll illustrate this with the following project.</b>
Add an Image control to the form in Mobile6. Find a simple JPEG image from somewhere
(grab one a legal one from the Internet , clipart, or create one in your image editor of choice)
and save it as Image1 into the 'Icons' folder in:
<a href="C:\Inetpub\wwwroot\Mobile6\icons">C:\Inetpub\wwwroot\Mobile6\icons</a>.
I have used the PictureTube tool in PaintShopPro to create an image of a plane.
<br/>Open up the 100.bmp image used in the AdRotator in your Image Editor and save it as a Gif image.
<br/>Back in VisualStudio .NET, select the Image control that you have added to the form and, in the
</mobile:TextView>
</mobile:form>
```

The content should appear in the TextView control in the Design View window of VisualStudio .NET. Save the project and view it in the Openwave browser. You should see the block of text with appropriate formatting and links (see Figure 7.9).

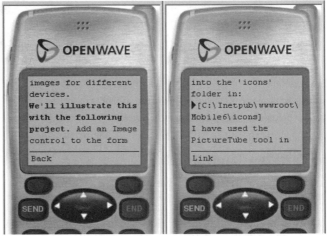

Image of UP.SDK courtesy Openwave Systems, Inc.

## List Controls

The list controls are traditionally used to display data that has either been entered at design time or has been retrieved from a database. There are three list controls provided here that vary in complexity and user interactivity. The List and ObjectList controls also are open to template editing, which I discuss in more detail in the "Special Controls" section later in this chapter.

**NOTE**    We will look at these controls in a lot more detail in Chapter 9.

### The List Control

The List control is the simplest of the List style controls and is used to display a static list of items. It supports data binding. Use the Items property to enter the items for the list. Select the property and click the ellipsis button. In the List1 Properties dialog box that appears, click the Create New Items button and then add your data. Values can be assigned for each item in the Value text box.

The list may be bulleted or numbered using the Decoration property in the main Properties window.

### The ObjectList Control

This is a strictly databound List control. The only way to populate this list is from a data source. The DataSource and Fields properties are used to specify the data source and the fields to be displayed. The TableFields property can be used to present the ObjectList control contents as a table of data.

### The SelectionList Control

If you wish to display items where the use can choose one or more of them, then use this control. It can also be rendered in a range of formats including list boxes, combo boxes, radio buttons, and check boxes. As with the other list controls, SelectionList supports data binding. Be aware that not all the formats will be rendered on all mobile devices.

## Validation Controls

These controls are used to validate data input by your users. They can be easily set up to cover most standard validation requirements and offer quite a bit of flexibility and customization options to the developer.

Each validation control that we place on a form performs only one check, but we can apply multiple validation requirements to a control or range of controls by including more than one validation control.

**TIP**    If you do use multiple validations and wish the output from the controls to be displayed in one part of the page, include a ValidationSummary control with your other validation controls.

**TIP**    If a user leaves an input control blank, the default response from the validation controls is to accept and pass it. If you require a response, such as in the case of a password, include a RequiredField Validator control with your other controls.

There is a great deal more to these controls than I have covered here. Although we will revisit them later in book, it is worth spending quality time with the Microsoft documentation on the topic as this is an area that can really determine how your application interacts with its users.

## The CompareValidator Control

This control is used to check that the value of a particular control matches a specified value or a value in another control on the same form. For example, when having a user set up a new password, you can ask the user to confirm their password and then use this control to ensure that the two entries are the same.

To illustrate this, create a new project and name it Mobile7. Type **Password Validator** in the top of the form and drag two TextBox controls onto the form. Set the following properties for both text boxes as indicated in Table 7.3:

**TABLE 7.3:** Property Settings for the Textboxes in the Password Validator Project

| Property | Value |
| --- | --- |
| MaxLength | 7 |
| Password | True |
| Size | 7 |

Type **Enter Password** directly onto the form above the first text box and **Retype Password** above the second text box. Drag a CompareValidator and a Command control onto the form (see Figure 7.10).

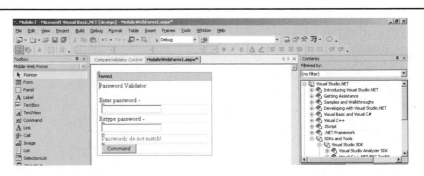

Select the CompareValidator control and set the properties as indicated in Table 7.4:

**TABLE 7.4:** Property Settings for the CompareValidator Control in the Password Validator Project

| Property | Value |
|---|---|
| Display | Static |
| Text | Passwords do not match! |
| ControlToCompare | TextBox1 |
| ControlToValidate | TextBox2 |
| Type | String |

Now, change to HTML View and add the `<script>` section and the `onclick` attribute to the `<mobile:Command>` tag to add some functionality for our command button as shown in Listing 7.2.

**Listing 7.2          Code for HTML View of Password Validator Project, Mobile7**

```
<%@ Register TagPrefix="mobile"
➥ Namespace="System.Web.UI.MobileControls"
➥ Assembly="System.Web.Mobile, Version=1.0.3300.0, Culture=neutral,
➥ PublicKeyToken=b03f5f7f11d50a3a" %>
<%@ Page Language="vb" AutoEventWireup="false"
➥ Codebehind="MobileWebForm1.aspx.vb"
➥ Inherits="Mobile7.MobileWebForm1" %>
<meta name="GENERATOR" content="Microsoft Visual Studio.NET 7.0">
<meta name="CODE_LANGUAGE" content="Visual Basic 7.0">
<meta name="vs_targetSchema"
➥ content="http://schemas.microsoft.com/Mobile/Page">

<script language="VB" runat="server">
   Protected sub Command1_Click(sender As Object, e As EventArgs)
      ActiveForm = Form1
   End Sub
</script>

<body Xmlns:mobile="http://schemas.microsoft.com/Mobile/WebForm">
   <mobile:Form id="Form1" runat="server">
      <P>Password Validator:</P>
      <P>Enter password -
<mobile:TextBox id="TextBox1" runat="server" Password="True"
➥ MaxLength="7" Size="7"></mobile:TextBox>Retype
password -
<mobile:TextBox id="TextBox2" runat="server" Password="True"
➥ MaxLength="7" Size="7"></mobile:TextBox>
<mobile:CompareValidator id="CompareValidator1" runat="server"
➥ ControlToValidate="TextBox2" ControlToCompare="TextBox1"
```

```
➥ ErrorMessage="CompareValidator">Passwords do not
➥ match!</mobile:CompareValidator>
<mobile:Command id="Command1" onclick="Command1_Click"
➥ runat="server">Command</mobile:Command></P>
   </mobile:Form>
</body>
```

The script section to add is reproduced in the following code snippet:

```
<script language="VB" runat="server">
   Protected sub Command1_Click(sender As Object, e As EventArgs)
      ActiveForm = Form1
   End Sub
</script>
```

The `<mobile:Command>` tag needs to be changed from

```
<mobile:Command id="Command1" runat="server">
```

to

```
<mobile:Command id="Command1" onclick="Command1_Click" runat="server">
```

with the addition of the `onclick="Command1_Click"` attribute.

Save the project and open it using the Openwave browser. We haven't put any handlers in this project to take care of a correct password entry—typing the same password shouldn't have any real result but try typing two different passwords. Note that you will need to refresh using the F9 key and then reload the application from the address bar between attempts. You should get the Passwords Do Not Match error message. (You may have to click through twice using the Send button with the Openwave browser.)

The following occurs with the properties that we set:

- The `Display` property determines whether the results of the validation will be displayed. Choose None if you don't wish the results to appear.

- The `Text` property sets the message to be returned if the validation failed.

- The `ControlToCompare` property selects the control that contains the value we wished to check our value against.

- The `ControlToValidate` property identifies the control that we wish to check the contents of.

- `Type` identifies the type of content expected.

You can also use this control to validate the content of a control against a preset value. In this case we would leave the `ControlToCompare` property blank and use the `ValueToCompare` property. For numerical values, we can also set the extent of equality using the `Operator` property.

Although we didn't use one here, if we were using a ValidationSummary control, then we would have needed to add a message to the `ErrorMessage` property. The contents of this property (the default is `CompareValidator`) are also displayed if the `Text` property is empty.

## The CustomValidator Control

The CustomValidator control can be used to create a set of customized validation requirements for an application. Setting up the control is basically the same as for the CompareValidator. The following are key properties to be aware of:

*Display*    Choose Static or Dynamic to display the results of a validation.

*ErrorMessage*    Use if you are including a RequiredFieldValidator control.

*Text*    Displays your error message of choice.

*ControlToValidate*    Nominates the control that you wish to validate.

Drag a copy of the control to the form in our Mobile7 project. Double-click the control on the form to access the `ServerValidate` code in the code behind. This is where we write our custom validation code for the control to be executed at the server. We could also write the code between a set of `<script>` ... `</script>` tags in the HTML View of our ASPX form.

As a simple example, set the properties for the CustomValidator control as shown in Table 7.5.

**TABLE 7.5:** Property Settings for the CustomValidator Control in the Mobile7 Project

| Property | Value |
| --- | --- |
| Display | Static |
| Text | CustomValidator says Wrong! |
| ControlToValidate | TextBox1 |

Double-click the CustomValidate control and copy the contents of Listing 7.3 into the `CustomValidate1_ServerValidate` sub of the code behind.

**Listing 7.3**        **Code Behind for the CustomValidate Control in the Mobile7 Project**

```
Private Sub CustomValidator1_ServerValidate(ByVal source As
➥ System.Object, ByVal args As
➥ System.Web.UI.WebControls.ServerValidateEventArgs) Handles
➥ CustomValidator1.ServerValidate
        If TextBox1.Text = "fred" Then
            args.IsValid() = True
```

```
        Else
            args.IsValid = False
        End If
    End Sub
```

This code sample simply checks whether our password entry in TextBox1 is the string fred. If it is not, then the validation fails. See Figure 7.11 for a screen shot of what happens when we fail both our validation criteria in this project. Remember to compile your code using the Build command before saving and running in the emulator.

**FIGURE 7.11:**

Validation failure in the Mobile7 project

Image of UP.SDK courtesy Openwave Systems, Inc.

Before we go any further, you have probably found this project to be a little buggy and that it doesn't give us any confirmation of correct validation. To fix this, add a second Form control to the project and drag a Label control onto it. Set the Text property of the Label control to read "Validation Confirmed!"

Go to HTML View and add the code from Listing 7.4 to the Command1_Click sub in the <script> section of the code. Delete the existing listing for <script> ... </script>.

**Listing 7.4**  **Modification to *<script>* ... *</script>* Section in the Mobile7 Project**

```
<script language="VB" runat="server">
    Protected sub Command1_Click(sender As Object, e As EventArgs)
      If Page.IsValid
          ActiveForm = Form2
```

```
        Else
            ActiveForm = Form1
        End If
    End Sub
</script>
```

Now when we validate the entry, we should get a Validation Confirmed! message if everything is OK. See Figure 7.12. Note that we still have to click through with the Send button a couple of times to generate the failure messages with the Openwave browser.

**FIGURE 7.12:**

Successful validation in Mobile7!

Image of UP.SDK courtesy Openwave Systems, Inc.

## The RangeValidator Control

The RangeValiator control ensures that user input falls within a preset range of values. The range extremes are set using the `MinimumValue` and `MaximumValue` properties. Other properties (such as `ErrorMessage`, `Text`, `ControlToValidate`, and `Type`) are similar to what we have seen earlier with the validation controls.

In the following example, we will add an Age field to our Mobile7 project and use the `RangeValidator` to ensure that the user is both an adult and likely to be alive.

Drag another TextBox control to the Mobile7 form and add a RangeValidator control underneath it. Above the TextBox and directly onto the form, type **Enter your Age:** (see Figure 7.13 for the control layout).

**FIGURE 7.13:**

Control layout for
RangeValidator
addition to the
Mobile7 project

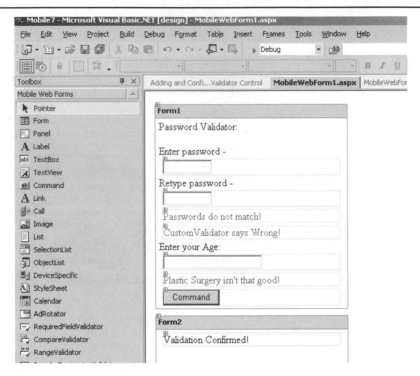

Set the properties of the TextBox and the RangeValidator as shown in Table 7.6.

**TABLE 7.6:** Property Settings for TextBox3 and RangeValidator1 in the Mobile7 Project

| Control | Property | Value |
| --- | --- | --- |
| TextBox3 | Text | <empty> |
| | MaxLength | 3 |
| | Numeric | True |
| | Size | 3 |
| RangeValidator1 | Display | Static |
| | Text | Plastic Surgery isn't that good! |
| | ControlToValidate | TextBox3 |
| | MaximumValue | 150 |
| | MinimumValue | 21 |
| | Type | Integer |

Save the project and run it in the Openwave browser. Play around with entering different correct and incorrect values into the fields. You will notice that the application has started to become a little buggy again—we will fix most of this when we add the ValidationSummary control.

## The RegularExpressionValidator Control

This is used to validate an entry in another control by checking that it follows a set pattern. Again we use properties such as Text and ControlToValidate to set up the control. The ValidationExpression property enables us to validate against set patterns or a custom pattern that we establish ourselves. Click the ellipsis in the ValidationExpression property to open the Regular Expression Editor dialog box (see Figure 7.14). Preset patterns include various international postal codes, U.S. zip codes, Social Security numbers, Internet URLs, and e-mail addresses among others.

**FIGURE 7.14:**

The Regular Expression Editor dialog box in use with the RegularExpression-Validator control

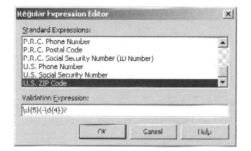

## The RequiredFieldValidator Control

The RequiredFieldValidator control is used to specify fields that must be completed by a user in your applications. As an example, drag the control onto the form in Mobile7. We will use it to ensure that the Age field is completed. (In practice, we would also probably use these controls with our password fields as well.)

Set the Text property to "You must enter your age!" and the ControlToValidate property to TextBox3. Save and test the application in the Openwave browser.

The other property of note here is the InitialValue property. This can be set to whatever the initial value of your control might be. The default is NULL, but you may have set the control to open with some preset value. (In our case, for the Age field, we may have set a default of 21.) Setting the InitialValue property to the same value forces the control to check to see if the preset value in the application has been changed at all and, if so, assumes that a new entry has been made and the field is validated. (Too bad if, in our example, you're a user and your age is 21!)

## The ValidationSummary Control

The ValidationSummary control presents the user with a list of errors that occurred when the form was submitted. To use the control, drag it to the form that you wish to use to display any errors and place it sequentially on the form where you want your error messages to appear.

In our Mobile7 example, create a third form on your page and drag a Label control and ValidationSummary control onto it. Refer to Figure 7.15 for the control layout on the form.

Control layout for the ValidationSummary control addition to the Mobile7 project

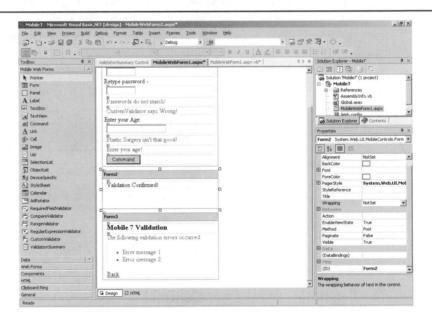

Set the properties as listed in Table 7.7.

**TABLE 7.7:** Property Settings for Form3 in the Mobile7 Project

| Control | Property | Value |
|---|---|---|
| Label2 | StyleReference | Title |
| | Text | Mobile6 Validation |
| ValidationSummary1 | HeaderText | The following validation errors occurred: |
| | FormToValidate | Form1 |

The control creates a link to return the user to the offending form after they have had a chance to read the error messages. The default label is Back, but the BackLabel property can be set to give the link a more meaningful label such as "Return to password entry," if necessary.

Finally, change to HTML View and alter the <script> ... </script> section of code to read as shown in Listing 7.5.

**Listing 7.5**   **Code Changes to the <script> ... </script> Segment for the ValidationSummary Control in Mobile7**

```
<script language="VB" runat="server">
    Protected sub Command1_Click(sender As Object, e As EventArgs)
        If Page.IsValid
            ActiveForm = Form2
        Else
            ActiveForm = Form3
        End If
    End Sub
</script>
```

Note that we have only changed the reference to Form1 in the If/Then/Else statement to read Form3.

Save the project and run it in the Openwave browser. You may wish to change the ErrorMessage property values in the other validation controls used in Form1 to reflect the messages that we placed in the Text properties. It is the contents of the ErrorMessage property values that are reported by the ValidationSummary control. The whole project should run more smoothly now in the Openwave browser and be (relatively!) bug free. See Figure 7.16 for a look at what you should expect.

**FIGURE 7.16:**

The ValidationSummary control in action in the Mobile7 project

Image of UP.SDK courtesy Openwave Systems, Inc.

## Special Controls

The Mobile Internet Toolkit ships with two sets of so-called "special" controls. These include the DeviceSpecific control, which can be used to help target applications for particular devices, and the StyleSheet control, which can be used to define style information for our applications.

## The DeviceSpecific Control

The DeviceSpecific control enables us to use template or property overrides in Form and Panel controls. The other controls offer `PropertyOverrides` as part of their `Property` set, and we have seen with the Image control how we can apply this element. However, to achieve this with a Form or Panel control, we need to drag a DeviceSpecific control onto that particular Form or Panel.

In this example we will set different default text appearance at the form level for different devices (namely the Openwave browser and the MME). Create a new mobile project and name it Mobile8. Drag a DeviceSpecific control to the form. In the Properties box, choose `PropertyOverrides` and click the ellipsis button. In the Device Specific1—PropertyOverrides dialog box, click the Edit button, and then from the Available Device Filters combo box, choose isMME and click the Add to List button. Open the Available Device Filters box again, choose isUP4x, and click the Add to List button again (see Figure 7.17). Click the OK button, and you should be presented with a Property Overrides dialog box, which enables us to set property overrides for individual devices.

**FIGURE 7.17:**

Applied Device Filters dialog box for the DeviceSpecific1 control in the Mobile8 project

In the Property Overrides dialog box, choose isUP4x from the Applied Device Filter combo box and set the `StyleReference` property to Title (see Figure 7.18). Choose isMME from the

Applied Device Filter combo box and set the `StyleReference` property to Subcommand. Click the OK button.

Property Override dialog box for the `DeviceSpecific` control in Mobile8

Above the DeviceSpecific control on the form, directly type **Hello There**. Refer to Figure 7.19 for the form layout.

Form layout for the Mobile8 project

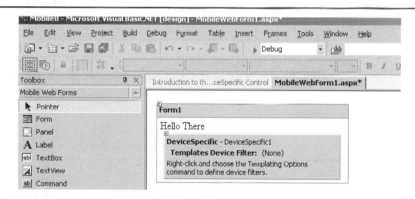

Save the project and view it in the Openwave browser. The text style should be in the bold Title style. If you open the same project in MME, the text should be in the small Subcommand style. If you use another browser, such as the Nokia, the text should be in the default style.

We can also use the control to make use of the templating options. Right-click the Device-Specific control and choose the Templating Options option. We can either edit templates of devices that we have already chosen in the Applied Device Filter list (i.e., UP4x or MME) or add more filters to the list using the edit button and the Applied Device Filters dialog box that was shown in Figure 7.17.

**NOTE**   Templates allow us to customize the way that particular controls render on the particular devices we have chosen from our filter list. For instance, we can customize alternating items in a List or ObjectList control using the `AlternatingItemTemplate`.

If we follow through with our example here, choose the isUP4x filter from the drop-down list and click the Close button. Don't worry about the Markup Schema combo box at this stage; it is related to using IntelliSense in HTML View at design time and has no effect at runtime.

The `TemplateDeviceFilter` property of the DeviceSpecific control should now read isUP4x. Right-click the control and choose the Edit Template option. Choose one of the templates to edit from the drop-down list (the range may be a bit limited for the Form and Panel controls). The chosen template will appear in the DeviceSpecific control in the design view. In this instance, I have chosen the Header and Footer template. We can customize this by typing directly into the box or by dragging a Label control (or Image control) onto it and setting properties. In this instance, I have dragged in a Label control onto the Header area and given it the text value of "Hello Openwave User."

Save the project and open it in MME and Openwave browsers. The Openwave browser should display the message at the top of the screen. The message should not be displayed in MME.

Templates can be edited for a range of controls, although we only need to use the Device-Specific control for `Forms` and `Panels`. For something such as the ObjectList control, we place the control on the form, right-click the control, and the Templating Options and the Edit Template options are directly available. Table 7.8 lists the available templates and what they can be used for.

**TABLE 7.8:** Templating Options Available in the Mobile Internet Toolkit

| Template Name | Control They Are Used in | Purpose |
| --- | --- | --- |
| AlternatingItemTemplate | List, ObjectList | Alternate items |
| ContentTemplate | Panel | Customize device-specific content |
| FooterTemplate | Form, List, ObjectList | Customize footer |
| HeaderTemplate | Form, List, ObjectList | Customize header |
| ItemTemplate | List, ObjectList | Customize all list items |
| ItemDetailsTemplate | ObjectList | Customize list item details |
| SeparatorTemplate | List, ObjectList | Customizing appearance of separators between items in list |

We will revisit templates again in Chapter 11, "Using Styles and Templates in the Mobile Internet Toolkit."

## The StyleSheet Control

The StyleSheet control can only be placed directly onto the `MobileWebForm` page and not into another control (such as a Form or a Panel control). It can define a style for the entire Mobile Web Form and can contain multiple styles that can apply to other controls on the page.

A style sheet can also be used for multiple Mobile Web Forms by using the `ReferencePath` property of `StyleSheet` to point to a ASCX file (user control) that contains the style sheet you wish to use. If you apply styles this way, they won't be applied at design time or be available in the drop-down menu of the `StyleReference` property for other controls. For more information, refer to Chapters 11 and 12.

Drag a StyleSheet control onto the Mobile Web Form for the Mobile8 project. Right-click the control and choose the Edit Styles option from the menu. This opens up the Style Editor dialog box. To set a style, we need to use one of the existing styles from Style Types (top left pane of the Style Editor) or create a new style derived from one of the existing ones. For example, double-click Style in Style Types. This should move a copy of it into the Defined Styles box (top-right pane) called Style1. Double-click it again (or single-click and then click the arrow between the panes) to create a Style2, which we shall edit (see Figure 7.20).

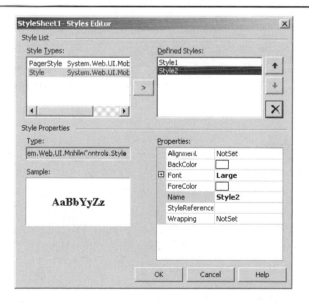

**FIGURE 7.20:**

The Styles Editor dialog box used with the StyleSheet control

Select Style2 and, in the Properties box (bottom-right pane), expand the Font property. Set the Bold property to True and the Size property to Large. Click OK. Select Form1 back in Design View, and in the Properties box choose the StyleReference property. You should now be given the option of Style1 and Style2. Choose Style2, and the "Hello There" text in Form1 should now appear both bold and large! Refer to Figure 7.21.

**WARNING**  Note that we still have device-specific criteria applying here from the previous exercises. That will mean that this style will not appear in either our Openwave or MME browsers at runtime. It does, however, appear in our Nokia browser.

FIGURE 7.21:

Mobile8 with Form1 at design time showing Style2 applied. Note also Style2 as an option in the drop-down box for the StyleReference property.

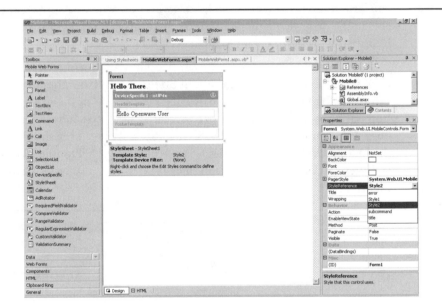

## Summary

We have only scratched the surface of many of the controls here, but the purpose of this chapter is to get us up and running with a basic understanding of this set of tools.

The controls provide us with a rich feature set that automates a lot of the work that we would previously have had to do by hand. We are also given the opportunity to further customize and extend the controls for our target devices. Functionality for the controls can be built at the Property-setting level, the code-behind level, and (in something new for many developers) at the HTML-View level. Developers also have the opportunity to mix and match programming languages when building this functionality. Some of the code might be developed in VB.NET, whereas other sections might use C#.

However, we need to be a little careful that the ease of use of these controls does not lull us into a false sense of security. As we have seen, the controls do render differently across different clients and sometimes the unexpected can occur. I know I keep belaboring this point, but it is vital, as a mobile developer, to know your target devices. The advantage of this with the Mobile Internet Toolkit is that having a good understanding of your target devices really opens up possibilities for tailoring your applications and fully exploiting the power of the toolkit using its device-specific behaviors.

# CHAPTER 8

# A Deeper Look at the Mobile Internet Toolkit and VB .NET

- What's new in Visual Basic .NET?

- How does my code compile under .NET?

- Can I port my existing code over to .NET?

- Contrasting ASP.NET and .NET Mobile Web Forms

- Looking at the `Web.config`, `Global.asax`, and `AssemblyInfo.vb` files

- Debugging your projects

- Handling cookies and state management

- Managing device cache and redirects

- Working with pagination

- Ensuring security with the Mobile Internet Toolkit

In this chapter we explore some of the new features to be found in VB .NET and gain some overview of the structure of applications when they are compiled in .NET. In particular, we will look at some issues such as backward compatibility in relation to VB .NET and previous flavors of Visual Basic.

There are also a number of aspects of working with the Mobile Internet Toolkit that are relevant to most, if not all, projects that we might use it to develop. These include the various configuration files that are automatically created as part of a project—but can then be customized—and other aspects such as debugging, state management, redirects, pagination, and security.

## Components of a .NET Mobile Project

When we first create a new project using the Mobile Internet Toolkit in Visual Studio .NET, a new Mobile Web Form page called MobileWebForm1 is created. MobileWebForm1 forms the basis of our Design View of the project. We drag controls onto this page, directly edit the structure of the page in HTML View, and build functionality for it in the Code Behind View. Of course, we can also build functionality in the HTML View, and the code that we write in the Code Behind View is actually written to somewhere else and then compiled separately.

When we hit the final OK when setting up a new project, the following files are actually created:

*AssemblyInfo.vb*    Contains information about the assembly built by the project.

*Global.asax* and *Global.asax.vb*    ASP.NET application files contain code for responding to application level events.

*MobileWebForm1.aspx*    Is what we see when we open HTML View. It contains declarations for our controls and determines the layout of our application.

*Web.config*    Contains settings specific to the application.

*MobileWebForm1.aspx.vb*    Is our code-behind page where we look after event handling and anything else we have chosen to program into our application (using Visual Basic).

Most of these files are displayed along with other resources and references used by our project in the Solutions Explorer window of the Visual Studio .NET IDE. In this window we can view, add, remove, and rename the listed files.

Let's have a look at the structure of the `MobileWebForm1.aspx` in more detail. Listing 8.1 illustrates the code for two forms: one with a Label control and one with a Command control. The Label control has the properties listed in Table 8.1 set.

**TABLE 8.1:** Property Setting for the Label Control Used in Listing 8.1

| Property | Value |
|---|---|
| Alignment | Center |
| StyleReference | title |
| Text | Hello World |

The Command control has code included in Listing 8.1 to navigate to Form2, and Form2 contains a Label control with its text property set to read Form2.

**Listing 8.1          Code for *MobileWebForm1.aspx***

```
<%@ Register TagPrefix="mobile"
➥ Namespace="System.Web.UI.MobileControls"
➥ Assembly="System.Web.Mobile, Version=1.0.3300.0, Culture-neutral,
➥ PublicKeyToken=b03f5f7f11d50a3a" %>

<%@ Page Language="vb" AutoEventWireup="false"
➥ Codebehind="MobileWebForm1.aspx.vb"
➥ Inherits="Mobile8a.MobileWebForm1" %>

<meta name="GENERATOR" content="Microsoft Visual Studio.NET 7.0">
<meta name="CODE_LANGUAGE" content="Visual Basic 7.0">
<meta name="vs_targetSchema"
➥ content="http://schemas.microsoft.com/Mobile/Page">

<script language="vb" runat="server">
    Protected sub Command1_Click(sender As Object, e As EventArgs)
        ActiveForm = Form2
    End Sub
</script>

<body Xmlns:mobile="http://schemas.microsoft.com/Mobile/WebForm">


    <mobile:Form id="Form1" runat="server">
        <mobile:Label id="Label1" runat="server"
➥ StyleReference="title" Alignment="Center">Hello World</mobile:Label>

        <mobile:Command id="Command1" runat="server"
➥ OnClick="Command1_Click">Command</mobile:Command>
    </mobile:Form>

    <mobile:Form id="Form2" runat="server">
        <mobile:Label id="Label2" runat="server">
➥Form 2</mobile:Label>
    </mobile:Form>
</body>
```

Let us have a detailed look at the various elements of this code listing. Each Mobile Web page must contain the following directives:

```
<%@ Register TagPrefix="mobile"
➥ Namespace="System.Web.UI.MobileControls"
➥ Assembly="System.Web.Mobile, Version=1.0.3300.0, Culture=neutral,
➥ PublicKeyToken=b03f5f7f11d50a3a" %>

<%@ Page Language="vb" AutoEventWireup="false"
➥ Codebehind="MobileWebForm1.aspx.vb"
➥ Inherits="Mobile8a.MobileWebForm1" %>
```

The first directive registers the namespace used for the controls with the `mobile` prefix. If we are creating our ASPX pages directly in an editor such as Notepad, the Version, Culture, and PublicKeyToken attributes are not required. The second directive identifies the language of choice (VB) and the identity of the code-behind class from which it inherits.

The following meta tags are self explanatory. We used the `script` tag in the last chapter to build functionality for our Command button. Inside the `Body` tag we find our individual controls. We begin with the compulsory `Form` tag. Inside the `Form` we have placed two controls. The first is the Label control and its code appears as follows:

```
<mobile:Label id="Label1" runat="server" StyleReference="title"
➥ Alignment="Center">Hello World</mobile:Label>
```

In this we can see where the properties that we declared (`StyleReference`, `Alignment`, and `Text`) are being referenced. The next control is the Command button:

```
<mobile:Command id="Command1" runat="server"
➥ OnClick="Command1_Click">Command</mobile:Command>
```

Here we can see where we specify its response to the `OnClick` event to run our bit of code declared in the script section. We then close off the tag for Form1 and open Form2.

```
</mobile:Form>

    <mobile:Form id="Form2" runat="server">
      <mobile:Label id="Label2" runat="server">
➥Form 2</mobile:Label>
    </mobile:Form>
</body>
```

Form2 contains a single Label control with a specified `Text` property. Finally we close the `Body` tag for the page.

It is easy to see from this example how we can modify our Mobile Web form's behavior by making direct changes to the code and how to create a form from scratch. There are certainly situations where we have to work directly with the code, and in the last chapter, we encountered a couple of them. So it is worth having an understanding of this code, how it works, what it does, and what is required, even if we plan to mainly use the GUI-development environment.

## Exploring Extensibility

The Mobile Internet Toolkit offers a range of extensibility features that can be used to accomplish the following:

- Create new controls from scratch or that take advantage of properties of existing controls
- Write declaratively simple mobile controls
- Combine several controls to form a new control
- Customize a control for individual devices and/or extend its functionality
- Add support for additional new devices to an application using adaptor extensibility

We have already seen how the functionality of controls can be extended using the DeviceSpecific element and control back in Chapter 7, "The Runtime Controls." Later on in the book, we will look at how to create new controls and how to add device adaptors to support new devices with the toolkit.

## What's New in Visual Basic .NET

As much of this book will be about implementing functionality into our applications using Visual Basic .NET, we need to take some time at this stage to look at some of the changes introduced under .NET. I am going to be brief. These changes have been and will be documented in detail in many other resources specializing in the language. However, as there are significant changes under .NET and many people will come to this book with experience in previous versions of VB, it is worth covering some of the major ones here.

First, Visual Basic has finally gotten to the point where it can seriously lay claim to being a fully object-oriented programming language. I know that Microsoft has made the claim with previous releases of the language, and each time it has fallen short. I am sure that there will be purists, raised on Smalltalk or Eiffel, who would disagree with the current claims. However, we now have proper inheritance, polymorphism, overloading, and all the other doodads that developers expect for their object-oriented development.

In practical terms, this doesn't make a huge difference for simple projects, but it does increase its power and scalability when it comes to the large complex stuff. We won't be really dealing explicitly with the OO features here, but if you are serious about VB programming at the enterprise level, take some serious time to find out about these new features and how they can be incorporated into your applications. In particular, when using these features we need to spend a lot more time on the program design and getting it right on paper before we start cutting code. This will be a bit of a shock for many VB developers, as many of us have, over the years, tended to take its RAD features as a given and have the project half built before we give any real thought to its design.

**NOTE** The introduction of .NET sees a whole raft of new acronyms and terminology for us to deal with. Refer to the "How Does My Code Compile Under .NET?" section of this chapter for some of the key definitions.

The following is a broad (and not complete) list of major changes introduced into the language:

- Inclusion of object-oriented features such as Inheritance, Overloading, Overriding, Constructors/Destructors, Shared Members, and Interfaces.

- New data types include the Char (16 bit to store Unicode characters), Short (16 bit; formerly Integer), and Decimal (96-bit signed integer scaled by a variable power 10).

- Structured Exception Handling introduces the Try…Catch…Finally statement to VB, which is very useful for creating robust code.

- With multithreading, applications can now be set up to run various tasks independently of each other, which means that the program no longer has to grind to a halt while some processor-intensive portion of it works its way through to a conclusion.

Visual Basic .NET also supports Web Forms and XML Web Services. There are also a number of structural changes to the language that impact the way that we code and the syntax that we use. Many of these have been introduced to limit bad habits (such as declaring variables on-the-fly inside loops or conditional statements) that some programmers have been allowed to develop with earlier versions of the language. Others have been intended to move VB more into line with other languages. (And some of these had to be put back by Microsoft during the development of the language after general outcry from developers—it seems that people weren't ready for too much change!) Examples of these include the following:

- Obsolete keywords from VB's early days and beyond have been deleted. No longer can we GoSub or On x GoTo…!

- If you wish to load a form, you will need to explicitly instantiate it, rather than using just the old lazy frmMyform.Show.

- We lose the variant data type.

- The integer data type is now 32 bit.

More importantly again is that VB .NET is now a language that is CLS (Common Language Specification) compliant. It possesses and uses a range of the CLS features such as assemblies and namespaces. Assemblies replace type libraries in VB .NET. (We will look at the definitions and some of the significance of these in the next section.) It also means that VB can share classes, objects, and components with other CLS-compliant languages.

In the following example, we will look at setting up structured exception handling in a simple calculator application.

Create a new Windows application in Visual Basic. (We won't go mobile for this!) Drag two TextBoxes, a Command button, and a Label to the form as shown in Figure 8.1. I have also changed the BackColor property of the Label to Window and deleted the text from the two TextBoxes and the Label.

**FIGURE 8.1:**

Form layout for the Simple Calculator project used to illustrate Structured Exception Handling

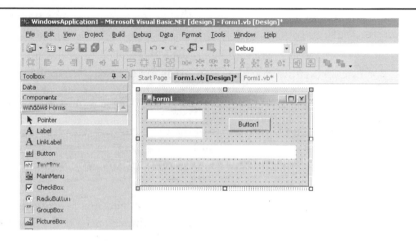

Double-click the Command control to open the Code View. In the Button1_Click sub, type **c = a / b** and press the Enter.

You will notice blue squiggly lines immediately appearing under the three variables. These are there to tell us that something is wrong. Place your mouse over each variable and you will see a message that says that the variable is not declared—and with not an Option Explicit in sight! We cannot do "implicit" declaration of variables anymore; we need to declare them.

Complete the code window so that it resembles Listing 8.2.

**Listing 8.2      Code for Simple Calculator Project without Exception Handling**

```
Public Class Form1
    Inherits System.Windows.Forms.Form

Windows Form Designer generated code "

    Dim a, b, c As Short
    Private Sub Button1_Click(ByVal sender As System.Object, ByVal e As
➥ System.EventArgs) Handles Button1.Click
        Label1.Text=""
        a = TextBox1.Text
```

```
        b = TextBox2.Text
        c = a / b
        Label1.Text = c
    End Sub
End Class
```

This code is obviously open to falling over when in use. We have nothing to determine whether the entry into the two text boxes is in fact an integer and nothing to prevent the b value from being set to 0. Notice that we have used the new type declaration, short, to declare simple integers.

We can test the program by pressing the F5 key, by choosing Start from the Debug menu, or by clicking the little blue Start arrow on the Standard toolbar. To halt the project, press Shift+F5, choose Stop Debugging from the Debug menu, or click the blue Stop Debugging button on the Debug toolbar.

Try entering text into either of the two textboxes or enter a 0 value into the b text box and then pressing the Command button. The program throws an exception and enters debug mode. (Notice that it is not a very good calculator either, as it rounds everything off to whole numbers!)

We can set an exception handler to pick up any errors using the following additions to the Button1_Click sub shown in Listing 8.3. You will need to add a second Label control to the bottom of your form.

**Listing 8.3**    **Code for Simple Calculator Project with Exception Handling**

```
Private Sub Button1_Click(ByVal sender As System.Object, ByVal e As
➥ System.EventArgs) Handles Button1.Click
    Try
     Label1.Text=""
     Label2.Text=""
        a = TextBox1.Text
        b = TextBox2.Text
        c = a / b
    Catch
        Label2.Text = "Something is wrong here!"
    Finally
        Label1.Text = c
    End Try

    End Sub
```

Run the program again and try inserting the b value of 0 or string values into the two text boxes. You should get error messages accompanying a c value of 0. Our program is no longer shot down when the exception occurs.

To break down what we have done, there are three main components of the handler:

- The Try keyword covers what code we expect to throw the exception.
- We use Catch to determine what happens when the exception is thrown.
- In Finally, we include the code to process once we have worked our way through the previous two code blocks.

As we can see, this is a fairly simple process to set up, but it offers a huge amount of power and flexibility and it is nice to see that it has finally found its way into VB.

The last thing I want to refer to here is the generated code for the Windows Form Designer. This can be explored under Code View by expanding the + next to it (refer to Listing 8.2). Note that although we can now access this code in our standard code editor, we cannot modify it here (at least if we wish our program to still work). We need to use the Windows Form Designer (back in Design View) for this task.

## How Does My Code Compile Under .NET?

Before we look at the compile process for .NET, we need to cover a few key definitions (see Table 8.2).

**TABLE 8.2:** Terms Used in .NET

| Term | Definition |
| --- | --- |
| Assembly | Consists of one or more modules packaged into a unit. Defines the namespace for an application at runtime. |
| CLR | Stands for Common Language Runtime and enables any CLS-compliant language to run on the .NET platform. |
| CLS | Stands for Common Language Specification and is a defined set of language features that enables compatible languages to be interoperable. |
| JIT compiler | Stands for Just In Time and refers to when a compiler converts an IL (Intermediate Language) into machine language as the code is executed at runtime. |
| Managed code | Is code designed to run only under the control of the CLR (i.e., in MSIL). VB.NET and C# produce only managed code. Can still generate unmanaged code from C++ in .NET. |
| Module | Is an individual DLL or EXE file, forms part of an assembly. |
| MSIL | Stands for Microsoft Intermediate Language and is output from .NET language compilers and is the input to JIT compiler. |
| Namespace | Is essentially used during design time to clearly identify all the objects belonging to a particular project. Objects can be referenced between projects by using their respective assembly names and namespaces. |

When we compile our code in .NET, we create an assembly (containing all the EXE, DLL, and additional resource files required for the application) in MSIL (Microsoft Intermediate Language). This is then compiled to machine code by the JIT (Just In Time) compiler as the program is executed. The advantage for developers in the future will be that their programs will run on any platform supporting the CLR. (At the moment this is limited to desktop Windows but is likely to change in the near future—at least for Microsoft operating systems.)

---

**TIP**    So far we have been using the `Build` command under the `Build` menu to compile our mobile projects. Pressing the F5 key (or using any of the other Start options) will also compile our project and automatically open the project in the default browser (running in the debug mode).

---

**TIP**    We can also use the `Start Without Debugging` command under the Debug menu (or Ctrl+F5) to compile our project and open it in the default browser without loading the debugger.

## Can I Port My Existing Code Over to .NET?

There are two aspects that developers might wish to consider here. Many developers may have created mobile applications using VBScript and ASP pages. Can these be easily ported to .NET?

The short answer is no (unfortunately). At the time of writing, Microsoft had no plans for offering an upgrade path (and, given the differences between them, it would be extremely difficult to create any kind of backward compatibility). ASP will continue to be supported by the company, at least for the time being, and the two technologies can coexist on an IIS server. However, there may be some advantage in porting some applications across. Depending on the application, its complexity, and how it has been written, the job could vary widely from fairly simple to incredibly complex. Ultimately, it will depend on individual cases, but I suspect that most .NET applications will be new projects.

The other aspect we need to consider is whether we can port our code from earlier versions of Visual Basic into VB .NET. The answer here is a more qualified sort of. Microsoft provides an upgrade wizard for projects written in VB6. The wizard opens as soon as you try to open a VB6 project in VB .NET. It upgrades as much as it can and then generates a list of To Do's for the developer at the end of the process. At the time of writing, (Beta 2) users had reported mixed success (at best) with the wizard. Microsoft had released a list of recommendations as to how to build projects in VB6 that would have maximum compatibility with VB .NET. This, however, doesn't do much for projects that may have been created pre–VB .NET and even those that have been designed with .NET in mind are not exactly guaranteed a smooth transition.

Probably the safest view to take is that .NET is new technology, a new experience that offers clear advantages over what we have used in the past but forget about backward compatibility and focus on new projects.

## Differences between ASP.NET and .NET Mobile Web Forms

If you have had some experience with using ASP.NET, much of what we have been covering will seem very familiar with a few key differences. In fact, experience with Web Forms can be a bit of a double-edged sword, as everything looks the same (well almost!) but doesn't quite do what you expect it to.

The main differences stem from the fact that Web Forms are targeted into a (comparatively) rich HTML environment where the user interface is a desktop browser. Mobile Web Forms, on the other hand, need to adaptively render for a range of protocols, device-specific behaviors, and browsers.

In their supplied documentation, Microsoft provides detailed comparisons between the two based on both application criteria and individual differences between functionally similar controls. If this is proving to be an area of concern, it is worth reading through the documentation. You can find the documentation in two places. To get to the first place, open Help ➤ Contents. Expand Visual Studio .NET. Choose SDK's and Tools ➤ Visual Studio SDK ➤ Mobile Internet Toolkit ➤ Mobile Internet Designer ➤ Getting Started with the Mobile Internet Designer ➤ Comparing the Mobile Internet Designer with the Web Form Designer. The second reference can be found at Mobile Internet Toolkit ➤ Mobile Internet Controls Runtime ➤ Getting Started ➤ Mobile Web Forms and ASP.NET Compatibility Issues. Microsoft also identifies a handful of compatibility issues between the two. (See the second reference for the list of compatibility issues.)

The principal compatibility issue affecting our mobile applications is the old thorn in mobile design: session state and management. ASP.NET provides rich session-management features that enables the server to identify who belongs to what among the various clients accessing your application at any one time. However, the default position is that this relies on cookies (small text files deposited with the client that can be requested by the server to identify parameters such as session IDs, site preferences. etc.). In the real life of the HTML world, there are a number of people paranoid enough to turn off cookie support on their browser (although these days they are probably a very small minority). In the mobile world, for many of us, we don't even have that luxury as cookie support was never "on" to begin with and our browser, device, or gateway does not necessarily support it.

In the United States, the popularity of the Openwave browser means that a significant number of clients accessing from within the U.S. may have cookie support. But if we wish to step beyond the borders to the rest of the world, where the Nokia and related browsers are huge, cookie support is nonexistent.

However, all is not lost. We saw earlier with the Rock, Paper, Scissor game in Chapter 4, "An Example of Mobile Technology: WAP and WML," how we can mung a URL to support cookieless sessions by writing the session ID into the URL as an ASP parameter. We can specify cookieless sessions with the Mobile Internet Toolkit and later on in this chapter in the "Handling Cookies and State Management" section, we will see how.

Another situation where compatibility issues exist is with error handling and reporting. ASP.NET generates an error page when it encounters an error while processing a request. Applications can be configured to return the default error page or a custom page written by your good self. However, there are limitations to how well some of these default error pages will render on mobile devices and, in some cases, only a device-specific error will be shown and that may not be much use from a debugging perspective. Therefore, Microsoft recommends checking for potential configuration or compilation errors using a desktop Web browser (Internet Explorer).

Finally, ASP.NET provides for Tracing as a useful tool for debugging Web applications. Two levels are provided: page level and application level. Page-level tracing appends information written as HTML to the traced page. and this may fall over in a mobile emulator (i.e., if you are tracing with the Openwave browser). Microsoft therefore recommends using application-level tracing only under these circumstances and that you should inspect it from a desktop Web browser. We will look at tracing later in the chapter in the "Debugging Our Projects" section.

## Looking at the *Web.config*, *Global.asax*, and *AssemblyInfo.vb* Files

When we first create our projects, a number of support files are auto-generated by .NET. These files can then be edited to further tweak and enhance our applications.

### The *Web.config* File

One of the files created when we first start a new mobile project is the `Web.config` file. This is an XML document that contains the configuration settings for our application. We can access this document by double-clicking it in the Solution Explorer. It will appear in the Design window from where it can be edited.

Alternatively, we can find the actual document in the directory created for our project. For example, assuming that you have used the default location for Mobile5 (from the previous chapter), the location of its `Web.config` file would be `c:\Intepub\wwwroot\Mobile5`. We can open and edit the document using a text editor such as Notepad.

We can make changes to configuration settings at runtime. ASP.NET automatically detects any changes that have been made and applies the new settings to resources affected by the changes. This is done dynamically without having to reboot the server.

Listing 8.4 shows the content of the `Web.config` file as it has been automatically generated for a typical mobile application. I have included the full listing here, as we will use various parts of it in later sections of this chapter. You will notice that Microsoft includes descriptive and informative comments on each tag, giving its purpose and configuration options.

**Listing 8.4**         **Typical *Web.config* File for a Mobile Application**

```
<?xml version="1.0" encoding="utf-8" ?>
<configuration>

  <system.web>

    <!-- DYNAMIC DEBUG COMPILATION
         Set compilation debug="true" to enable ASPX debugging.  Otherwise,
setting this value to false will improve runtime performance of this
application.
    -->
    <compilation defaultLanguage="vb" debug="true" />

    <!-- CUSTOM ERROR MESSAGES
         Set customErrors mode="On" or "RemoteOnly" to enable custom error
messages, "Off" to disable. Add <error> tags for each of the errors you want to
handle.
    -->
    <customErrors mode="RemoteOnly" />

    <!-- AUTHENTICATION
         This section sets the authentication policies of the application.
Possible modes are "Windows", "Forms", "Passport" and "None"
    -->
    <authentication mode="Windows" />


    <!-- AUTHORIZATION
         This section sets the authorization policies of the application. You
can allow or deny access to application resources by user or role. Wildcards:
"*" mean everyone, "?" means anonymous(unauthenticated) users.
    -->
    <authorization>
        <allow users="*" /> <!- Allow all users ->
```

```
        <!-- <allow     users="[comma separated list of users]"
                        roles="[comma separated list of roles]"/>
             <deny      users="[comma separated list of users]"
                        roles="[comma separated list of roles]"/>
        -->
   </authorization>

   <!--  APPLICATION-LEVEL TRACE LOGGING
        Application-level tracing enables trace log output for every page
within an application. Set trace enabled="true" to enable application trace
logging.  If pageOutput="true", the trace information will be displayed at the
bottom of each page.  Otherwise, you can view the application trace log by
browsing the "trace.axd" page from your web application root.
        -->
   <trace enabled="false" requestLimit="10" pageOutput="false"
➥ traceMode="SortByTime" localOnly="true" />


   <!--  SESSION STATE SETTINGS
        By default ASP.NET uses cookies to identify which requests belong to a
particular session. If cookies are not available, a session can be tracked by
adding a session identifier to the URL. To disable cookies, set sessionState
cookieless="true".
        -->
   <sessionState
➥ mode="InProc"
➥ stateConnectionString="tcpip=127.0.0.1:42424"
➥ sqlConnectionString="data source=127.0.0.1;
➥user id=sa;password="
➥ cookieless="false"
➥ timeout="20"
➥/>



   <!--  GLOBALIZATION
        This section sets the globalization settings of the application.
   -->
   <globalization requestEncoding="utf-8" responseEncoding="utf-8" />

<!-- FULLY QUALIFY URL FOR REDIRECTS
    Some mobile devices require that the URL for client redirects be fully
qualified.
 -->
<httpRuntime useFullyQualifiedRedirectUrl="true"/>

 <!-- SPECIFY COOKIELESS DATA DICTIONARY TYPE
        This will cause the dictionary contents to appear in the local request url
querystring.
        This is required for forms authentication to work on cookieless devices.
    -->
```

```
    <mobileControls
➥ cookielessDataDictionaryType="System.Web.Mobile.CookielessData"/>
    <deviceFilters>
      <!-- Markup Languages -->
      <filter name="isHTML32"
➥ compare="preferredRenderingType" argument="html32" />
      <filter name="isWML11"
➥ compare="preferredRenderingType" argument="wml11" />
      <filter name="isCHTML10"
➥ compare="preferredRenderingType" argument="chtml10" />

      !-- Device Browsers -->
      <filter name="isGoAmerica" compare="browser"
➥ argument="Go.Web" />
      <filter name="isMME" compare="browser"
➥ argument="Microsoft Mobile Explorer" />
      <filter name="isMyPalm" compare="browser"
➥ argument="MyPalm" />
      <filter name="isPocketIE" compare="browser"
➥ argument="Pocket IE" />
      <filter name="isUP3x" compare="type"
➥ argument="Phone.com 3.x Browser" />
      <filter name="isUP4x" compare="type"
➥ argument="Phone.com 4.x Browser" />

      <!-- Specific Devices -->
      <filter name="isEricssonR380" compare="type"
➥ argument="Ericsson R380" />
      <filter name="isNokia7110" compare="type"
➥ argument="Nokia 7110" />

      <!- Device Capabilities -->
      <filter name="prefersGIF" compare="preferredImageMIME"
➥ argument="image/gif" />
      <filter name="prefersWBMP"
➥ compare="preferredImageMIME" argument="image/vnd.wap.wbmp" />
      <filter name="supportsColor" compare="isColor"
➥ argument="true" />
      <filter name="supportsCookies" compare="cookies"
➥ argument="true" />
      <filter name="supportsJavaScript" compare="javascript"
➥ argument="true" />
      <filter name="supportsVoiceCalls"
➥ compare="canInitiateVoiceCall" argument="true" />
    </deviceFilters>

  </system.web>

</configuration>
```

All the configuration information occurs between the root, <configuration>...</config-uration> and, in turn, the <system.web>...</system.web> tags. Each set of tags (such as <authorization>…<authorization> or <authentication mode="Windows" />) represents a configurations section settings area. You will also notice all the device filters towards the end of the file.

## The *Global.asax/asax.vb* Files

The Global.asax and asax.vb files are another pair of files created when you first generate a new project. Global.asax is normally an optional file in ASP.NET, which is used to hold code for application-level events raised by ASP.NET or by HttpModules. As with the Web.config file, it can be found in the root directory of the application and can be edited directly using Notepad.

When we double-click the Global.asax file in Solution Explorer and choose Code View, it is the Global.asax.vb file that is opened. We can use this file to set application-level events. A copy of the preset code template that is displayed when you open it from Solution Explorer is shown in Listing 8.5.

---

**Listing 8.5**      **Default Code Listing for *Global.asax.vb* File**

```
Imports System.Web
Imports System.Web.SessionState

Public Class Global
    Inherits System.Web.HttpApplication

    Component Designer Generated Code "

    Sub Application_Start(ByVal sender As Object, ByVal e As EventArgs)
        ' Fires when the application is started
    End Sub

    Sub Session_Start(ByVal sender As Object, ByVal e As EventArgs)
        ' Fires when the session is started
    End Sub

    Sub Application_BeginRequest(ByVal sender As Object, ByVal e As
➥ EventArgs)
        ' Fires at the beginning of each request
    End Sub

    Sub Application_AuthenticateRequest(ByVal sender As Object, ByVal e
➥ As EventArgs)
        ' Fires upon attempting to authenticate the use
    End Sub
```

```
    Sub Application_Error(ByVal sender As Object, ByVal e As EventArgs)
        ' Fires when an error occurs
    End Sub

    Sub Session_End(ByVal sender As Object, ByVal e As EventArgs)
        ' Fires when the session ends
    End Sub

    Sub Application_End(ByVal sender As Object, ByVal e As EventArgs)
        ' Fires when the application ends
    End Sub

End Class
```

## The *AssemblyInfo.vb* File

The AssemblyInfo.vb file can also be browsed and edited by double-clicking in the Solution Explorer window. It contains information about your project (assembly) and can either be edited by hand or you can rely on default values as they are internally generated within the project. The default code for a typical mobile project is shown in Listing 8.6. Comments in the code indicate where information about the assembly can be added or modified.

**Listing 8.6**          **Code for *AssemblyInfo.vb* for a Typical Mobile Web Project**

```
Imports System.Reflection
Imports System.Runtime.InteropServices


' General Information about an assembly is controlled through the
➥ following
' set of attributes. Change these attribute values to modify the
➥ information
' associated with an assembly.

' Review the values of the assembly attributes

<Assembly: AssemblyTitle("")>
<Assembly: AssemblyDescription("")>
<Assembly: AssemblyCompany("")>
<Assembly: AssemblyProduct("")>
<Assembly: AssemblyCopyright("")>
<Assembly: AssemblyTrademark("")>
<Assembly: CLSCompliant(True)>

'The following GUID is for the ID of the typelib if this project is exposed to
COM
<Assembly: Guid("507D7BEF-7B58-41D9-9E59-94DFDB2F9006")>
```

```
' Version information for an assembly consists of the following four values:
'
'        Major Version
'        Minor Version
'        Build Number
'        Revision
'
' You can specify all the values or you can default the Build and Revision
Numbers
' by using the '*' as shown below:
```

# <Assembly: AssemblyVersion("1.0.*")> Debugging Our Projects

Given that programming projects rarely go as smoothly as we would like, Microsoft has provided us with a wide range of tools for troubleshooting our projects.

## Dynamic Debugging

Visual Studio .NET has an improved and more informative range of traps for syntax errors; in particular it is now very strict (in VB) on demanding explicitly declared variables. (I know it's not exactly a syntax error, except where you mistype one by mistake. In previous versions of VB, without using Option Explicit, this could be interpreted as a new declaration and lead to all kinds of bother.)

However, we still need to use the full arsenal of debugging tools to pick up problems with our programming logic by enabling us to delve into our programs at runtime to see where things are coming unstuck.

To fully enable dynamic debugging for your application, you need to ensure that ASPX debugging has been enabled. To enable ASPX debugging, go to the Solution Explorer window and double-click the `Web.config` file.

`Web.config` should open in the Design window. To set ASPX debugging we need to alter the debug value in the `<compilation>` tag to read as follows:

```
<compilation defaultLanguage="vb" debug="true" />
```

**WARNING**   XML is case sensitive, so ensure that the `debug="true"` statement is all in lowercase.

It may already have this as a default value; however, to improve runtime performance of your applications, you should set the `debug` value of the `<compilation>` tag to `false`.

We then need to ensure that we have debugging turned on in the Properties box for the page (either click away from your forms in Design View or choose DOCUMENT from the pull-down menu in the Properties box). This allows us to control which Mobile Web Forms are debugged if we have multiple forms in our application.

The debugger allows us to inspect the state of our program at any point and to modify existing or even test new code to see what becomes of that state. We need to manually set the points where we want our program to pause (known as *breakpoints*) before we start the debugger. Most of the debugging tools only work when the program is paused at a breakpoint. Breakpoints are easily added in the Visual Studio .NET IDE by clicking in the narrow panel to the left of the code in the Design View to produce a big red spot (see Figure 8.2).

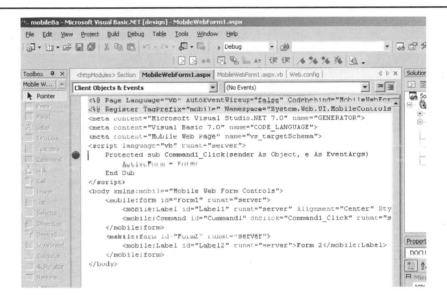

Various breakpoint properties can be set as well, including conditional breaks where the program will break only if certain conditions are met or breaks that occur only once the program has passed through them a set number of times.

Most developers would be very familiar with the debugging tools, and I don't intend to give them detailed coverage here. The basic tools are essentially the same for Visual Studio .NET as the ones we have used in the past. (There may be some confusion for VB programmers trying to find the Immediate window; it is now Ctrl+Alt+I. Ctrl+G now brings up a GoTo *line number* dialog box.). There is a QuickWatch dialog box, Watch window, Local window, and various others.

To debug your application, start it in Debug mode (press the F5 key). Your program should be compiled and start in the default browser. If you are new to debugging, the Immediate window is probably your best friend. Once the program has reached a breakpoint, you can type in the Immediate window to assign new values to variables (type the new value, such as **a=10**, and press Enter, or even write alternative routines and test them). Holding your mouse over various variables within your code will give you their current value.

Choose the Continue option from your Debug menu (or press F5 again) to continue running your code to the next breakpoint. You can also use the Step commands to step through your code line by line. Breakpoints can be added or deleted simply by clicking existing breakpoints in the sidebar to get rid of them or to create new ones. The Debug menu also offers Clear All Breakpoints and Disable All Breakpoints options.

To stop debugging, select the Stop Debugging option from the Debug menu or Toolbar or press Shift+F5 (or click the Exit command box on the running program).

As stated earlier, there is a lot more to debugging, and if you are new to using the tools in this environment, it is worth spending some time with the Microsoft documentation and practicing with the tools.

## Application-Level Tracing

Application tracing enables a trace log output to be generated for every page of an application. It is set in `Web.config`. Identify the `<trace>` tag:

```
<trace enabled="false" requestLimit="10" pageOutput="false"
➥ traceMode="SortByTime" localOnly="true" />
```

And alter it to the following by setting the `enabled` and `pageOutput` properties to `true`:

```
<trace enabled="true" requestLimit="10" pageOutput="true"
➥ traceMode="SortByTime" localOnly="true" />
```

This both begins the trace and sets the output to appear at the bottom of the mobile page, which you will need to view in a Web browser (see Figure 8.3). Leaving this value as 'false' will direct the output to a `trace.axd` file in the application root.

If we have multiple pages in our application we can control which pages are traced by setting the `trace` property to true or false in the DOCUMENT Properties box. (Either click away from your forms in Design View or choose DOCUMENT from the pull-down menu in the Properties box.)

The trace is an extremely informative document, giving you pretty much every detail of the information that has been used to generate the page that you are viewing including HTTP header info and file size information, which is extremely useful when developing for a mobile situation.

---

**WARNING**   Again, disable the trace before you deploy your project!

FIGURE 8.3:

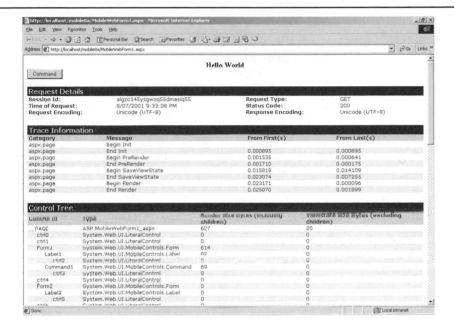

**FIGURE 8.3:**

Half of the trace output for simple mobile Web application. Try viewing this with your phone!

## Custom Error Pages

As mentioned earlier, we can specify custom error pages to appear when certain errors occur rather than relying on the default ones supplied by .NET. This can be a good idea as some of the default pages may not display reliably on some mobile devices and compound the problem at the user end. Although not strictly a debugging issue, identifying the types of errors for which custom pages will be required may well take place during the debugging process, so we will deal with them here.

Custom error pages are built by the developer and then accessed via the Web.config file. The following is the tag to edit within the file:

```
<customErrors mode="RemoteOnly" />
```

The MODE attribute can be set to Off, On, or RemoteOnly. A subtag, <error>, is also used to identify the error code that triggers the custom page. This has the attributes statusCode and redirect.

If mode is set to Off, custom errors are disabled; On means they work, and RemoteOnly specifies that they be shown only to remote clients (the default).

A typical tag might be set up as shown in Listing 8.7.

**Listing 8.7**        *Web.config* Entry for *&lt;customErrors&gt;* Tag

```
<customErrors mode="RemoteOnly">
    <error statusCode="500"
➥redirect="errors/error500MobileWebForm.aspx" />
</customErrors>
```

It is recommended that you build your custom error pages with Mobile Web Forms to take advantage of their adaptive rendering ability. In this example, we would make use of a custom error form presumably stored with a number of similar forms in a subdirectory off the application root named errors. This particular form would be displayed if HTTP Error 500 (Internal Server Error) occurred.

One more element that Microsoft recommends when using custom errors is to add the code in Listing 8.8 to the system.web section of the Web.config file. (This code is also recommended to help solve some problems in managing redirects.) By default, this code is normally present in the Web.config file.

**Listing 8.8**        Addition to *system.web* Section of *Web.config* File to Ensure Correct Operation of Custom Error Pages with WML Devices

```
<system.web>
    <httpRuntime useFullyQualifiedRedirectUrl="true" />
</system.web>
```

## Handling Cookies and State Management

Each time a user accesses a site or an application over the Internet, they are, in effect, making a new request. The server they are dealing with has no idea that they are the same person for whom it handled a previous request perhaps only seconds before and, as far as the user is concerned, they are still trying to have the same conversation. The server sees each request as being unique, individual, and not connected to anything else. This causes some problems for our applications where transactions are not necessarily one off but may need to span a period of time and multiple requests.

In the HTML world, there are various methods for identifying a user and keeping track of relevant information concerning that user and their current session between requests that the user may make. Typically, information is stored for a predetermined period of time in session variables on the server and the user is identified with a particular session by placing cookies on their computer that contain their *session ID*. Cookies also offer the advantage that, once a session is finished, user preferences can be stored in a cookie that may be used if that person visits the site again.

Unfortunately, in the mobile world, this is not quite as straightforward, because cookie support is limited at best.

## Cookies

Unless you are absolutely certain that your application will only be viewed by a range of devices that can support cookies, operating through a gateway that also supports cookies, you should turn *off* cookie support. We do this by editing the Web.config file. Set the <sessionState> tag to cookieless as shown in Listing 8.9.

---

**Listing 8.9**   *<sessionState>* **Tag Set for Cookieless Application**

```
<sessionState
            mode="InProc"
            stateConnectionString="tcpip=127.0.0.1:42424"
            sqlConnectionString="data source=127.0.0.1;
➥user id=sa;password="
            cookieless="true"
            timeout="20"
      ~C/>
```

---

Make sure that you have also not set the <authentication> mode attribute to Cookie (also in Web.config).

---

**WARNING**   We need to ensure that Openwave browsers are able to work under this system as well. They tend to get lost in the redirects. Refer to Listing 8.8 and ensure that a <httpRuntime useFullyQualifiedRedirectUrl="true" /> tag is included and set to true in your Web.config file.

---

We should now be able to configure our projects for use in Nokia browsers. Figure 8.4 shows both the code received by the Nokia (in Element Tree View) and the munged URL in the location bar for a simple project. We can also see in the <go> tags the target URLs with the session ID attached.

This enables us to set up cookieless sessions that allow us to operate an interactive application with a user. It does not however solve the problem of identifying that user once they have finished a particular session and then chosen to come back at some later date. Where security isn't terribly important, cookies allow us to automatically identify a repeat visitor. When we look at building applications later in the book, we will also look at ways around this problem.

FIGURE 8.4:
Code View in the
Nokia browser
showing URLs with
attached session ID
for cookieless session

## Hidden Variables

The Mobile Internet Toolkit uses the HiddenVariables collection to specify hidden variables. These are automatically resubmitted as part of a form submission.

## State Management

Apart from enabling cookieless sessions, ASP.NET provides a range of features for managing state in our mobile applications. From a network administrator's and a manager's viewpoint, one of the most important aspects is a scalable system that works across server farms. From a developer's perspective, we have ViewState, which provides for page and control-level state management.

When ViewState is activated (and there are circumstances where it is better to deactivate it), any property values set for controls in the application are automatically saved as part of the control's state so that multiple requests from the client will effectively see the same page. With Mobile Web Forms, this ViewState is saved as part of the state stack in a user's session on the server.

ViewState can be deactivated for a page by choosing enableViewState from the properties for that document and setting it to false. (Either click away from your forms in Design View or choose DOCUMENT from the pull-down menu in the Properties box.) ViewState can also be deactivated for individual controls. Disabling ViewState may be better when multiple users are accessing the same document; this avoids having multiple copies cached across the server (a copy for each user).

With Mobile Web Forms, the ViewState is not constantly round tripped to the client to save bandwidth (as it is with ASP.NET) and it is possible that if the user has been using the Back softkey to browse his/her cache on the local device, then the ViewState is not in sync with the current page. To sidestep this problem, a history of ViewState information is kept at the server. This history enables the server to return to the point in the ViewState history that the client is posting from. History size can be set, and it needs to be customized for the particular application. The default size is 6, but it can be altered in the Web.config file with the addition of the following tag between the <system.web> and </system.web> tags:

```
<mobileControls sessionStateHistorySize="6" />
```

You will also need to alter the 6 value to whatever is appropriate for your application.

If the device posts back for a session when the ViewState has expired, unless the application is unable to restore ViewState after expiry, an exception is raised to indicate that the ViewState has expired.

## Managing Device Cache and Redirects

Two areas to note are cache control and redirects. The MIT doesn't give us much opportunity to directly manipulate device cache, but it does give us access to some powerful server-side caching tools in the form of *fragment caching*. We also need to address a redirect issue related particularly to Openwave devices. This may be resolved in the final release version of the Mobile Internet Toolkit.

### Managing Device Cache

The following is the default cache setting at the client end with the Mobile Internet Toolkit

```
<meta http-equiv="Cache-Control" content="max-age=0">
```

This sets the client device cache to zero and encourages the device to always refer back to the server when making requests. This is the desired scenario when dealing with server-side events, programming, and dynamic data. However, given that a deck of several cards (or forms!) may have been downloaded to the device, in many circumstances it is better to take advantage of the cache and avoid unnecessary lag times. It also avoids the server spending time reprocessing information that we have already requested. We can do this at the device end by using local navigation (the Back softkey) to browse the cache. Many WML devices will use the cached copies of cards during backward navigation, even when the cache setting for content has been set to zero. However, cache sizes are fairly limited in most mobile devices and tend to get cleared regularly to make room for new content.

What happens when we return to the server and ask it to retrieve server-intensive information that has been previously generated (such as database requests)?

Mobile Web Forms allow us to perform fragment caching of a page (where we identify server intensive portions of the page, isolate them, and cache them separately for a specified time interval). The rest of the page can then be generated dynamically for each request.

### Managing Redirects

Though this is mentioned earlier, it is worth covering again: many mobile device/browser/ gateway configurations do not support relative addresses with redirects. Whenever possible use absolute or full addresses and make sure that the following tag is set up in your `Web.config` file:

```
<httpRuntime useFullyQualifiedRedirectUrl="true" />
```

## Working with Pagination

As we saw back in Chapter 5, "Designing for the Mobile Web," mobile devices are fairly limited when it comes to the file size of the information they are receiving. It is often a good idea to keep an eye on likely page sizes, particularly when you are constructing large decks or cards with lots of text and images. This applies equally to the Mobile Internet Toolkit as it does to any other development tool for the wireless Internet.

We can check the size of our compiled files using the trace tool, but this is of limited use when dealing with dynamic data when content length could vary widely. It's possible to program our way around this problem, but it can be tedious and it would be nice if there was an easier way.

Fortunately, Microsoft provides us with a pagination option with our Mobile Web Forms. We can opt for either custom pagination where we set the necessary parameters ourselves or automatic pagination where long-winded content is automatically split over multiple forms. To set this level of pagination, simply set the `Paginate` property to `true` on a form that is likely to contain large amounts of content.

To test this, open a new mobile project, drag a TextView control onto the Form control. Set the Form property `Paginate` to `true` and copy a large amount of text (i.e., a full page of text) into the TextView control text editor. Save and open the project in the mobile browser of your choice, and you should see the text split across two or more linked forms (see Figure 8.5).

We can alter the UI of the paginated form by changing the labels attached to the links between the forms. (By default, the links are simply labeled Next and Previous.)

FIGURE 8.5:

Document paginated
into two forms on the
Openwave browser

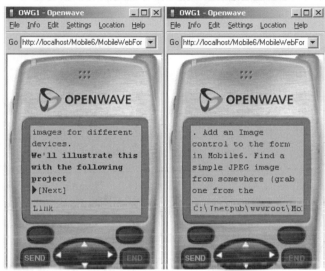

Image of UP.SDK courtesy Openwave Systems, Inc.

In the Properties box for the form you will find the PagerStyle property. Expand this by clicking the small + symbol and you will be presented with a range of properties for this object including NextPageText and PreviousPageText. In your project set the these two properties to the following:

| **Property** | **Setting** |
|---|---|
| NextPageText | Go to Page {0} |
| PreviousPageText | Return to Page {0} |

Save and test the project. The links should now be a little more meaningful (see Figure 8.6).

We can also control the styles under which the document is rendered using the PagerStyle properties.

Controls that inherit from the PagedControl base class (such as the List and ObjectList controls) offer extra capabilities for pagination. Using a process called *chunking*, we can limit any calculation or processing of data required to populate a list to just that portion of the list we are displaying on a paginated form. We will look at this in the next chapter.

Paginated document
showing customized
links

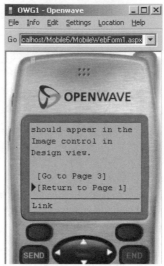

Image of UP.SDK courtesy Openwave Systems, Inc.

## Ensuring Security with the Mobile Internet Toolkit

There are three modes of authentication available to developers with ASP.NET. These are Windows, Passport, and Forms.

At the time of this writing, the Mobile Internet Toolkit doesn't support the wireless security protocol WTLS. Although developers can use Windows authentication, they are limited to basic mode (unencrypted) if they wish to service a wide range of devices. (Many mobile devices do not support SSL.) This means that using Windows authentication; authentication details are transmitted in plain text.

Alternatively, we can use Forms authentication to give us a more secure methodology but we need to configure it to cater for a cookieless environment. Forms authentication normally relies on cookies.

Passport authentication is currently available only to those devices that support HTML. This is expected to be extended to include WML devices at some point in the near future. However, until WML support is developed, it is not a practical solution for applications with an expected diverse user base.

Depending on which form of authentication we choose, we then return to our `Web.config` file to the `<authentication>` tag to set the appropriate type.

```
<authentication mode="Windows" />
```

The mode choices include: Windows, Forms, Passport, and None. (The default is Windows.) When using forms-based authentication, we also need to deny access to anonymous users in the `<authorization>` tag.

```
<authorization>
        <allow users="*" /> <!-- Allow all users -->
</authorization>
```

This needs to be set to the following:

```
<authorization>
        <deny users="?" /> <!-- Deny anonymous users -->
</authorization>
```

We then have to add the `System.Web.Security` namespace to our project by adding the following tag to the top of our ASPX form in HTML View:

```
<%@ Import Namespace="System.Web.Security" %>
```

If we choose Windows-based authentication, we need to configure IIS to the desired level of Windows authentication: Basic, Digest, or Integrated Windows.

Overall, in terms of the options we have, the forms-based authentication is part of the .NET Framework architecture and has definite advantages in terms of simplicity and reliability. Forms based authentication normally requires cookie support to work effectively but can be configured within the Mobile Internet Toolkit to work in cookieless mode. (We need to set our application's `cookieless="true"` attribute in the `<sessionState>` tag of the `Web.config` file.)

Forms authentication works as follows:

1. Server receives a request for a page.

2. Checks for an authentication cookie. If no cookie is found, it redirects the client to the login page.

3. The client completes and posts the login page.

4. The login is authenticated and the cookie is posted to the client, who is then redirected back to original page requested.

5. The cookie is checked and pages are delivered.

Essentially unauthorized clients are always directed back to a specific login page irrespective of which part of the application they manage to access. Once a client is authorized, they can move freely through the rest of the application. In cookieless mode, the authorization details are written into the query string of each request.

There are some other security features we can exploit in the `Web.config` file. The `<authorization>` tags can be used to allow or deny access to URL resources to individuals and/or groups. It can be configured to the HTTP method, making the request using the `verb` attribute (`Get` or `Post`).

Basic format of the `authorization` tag is shown in Listing 8.10.

---

**Listing 8.10**        **Use of *<authorization>* Tag to Set User Access**

```
<authorization>
    <allow VERB="POST" users="Jill,Fred,John,Jane" />
    <allow roles="SystemAdmin,Sales" />
    <allow VERB="GET" roles="GenStaff" />
    <deny users="?" />
</authorization>
```

---

In this example, we allow the users Jill, Fred, John, and Jane to POST to the resources. Members of SystemAdmin and Sales are granted access. Members of GenStaff are allowed to use GET to access the resources, and anonymous (unauthenticated) users (indicated by the ?) are denied access. If we wish to indicate all users, we use an *.

When URL authorization is used, the rules are read sequentially down and are checked until a match is found (or not as the case may be).

Chapter 19, "Morris's Wholesale Fruit & Vege: A Mobile Intranet," looks at the practical implementation of some security options using a Forms based system.

## Summary

In this chapter we have looked at some of the changes that have occurred in Visual Basic and how these will impact our applications. The reality is that for many applications, .NET (particularly when it comes to ASP.NET) is probably better suited for building new projects than trying to port existing ones.

However, the environment does offer clear advantages over what we have used before— even if there is a steepish learning curve involved. It finally gives VB, in particular, features that many developers, for some time, have been asking for.

We also took the opportunity to look a bit more under the hood at features delivered by the Mobile Internet Toolkit. In particular, we spent a lot of time with the `Web.config` file and the influence it can have over our applications. Some of the key bugbears for mobile developers (such as handling redirects, pagination, and state management) appear to have been handled very well by Microsoft in the toolkit. Some other areas, such as security, still seem to throw the developer back (to a certain extent) on his or her own resources, but with a bit of luck, by the time you read this, the final release of the Toolkit will be available and these issues will be largely resolved.

# PART IV

# Using the Mobile Internet Toolkit

# CHAPTER 9

# Data Access with the Mobile Internet Toolkit, Part 1 (List Controls)

- Data binding and the Mobile Internet Toolkit

- What's new in ADO.NET?

- Using the List control

- Using the ObjectList control

- Using the SelectionList control

- Paginating a list

**A**ccessing data is an essential ingredient of many applications, both online and offline. In this chapter, we will see how to exploit the capabilities of the Mobile Internet Toolkit to enable secure and reliable data access within our mobile applications.

## Data Binding and the Mobile Internet Toolkit

All the mobile controls directly inherit the Databind method from the System.Web.UI.Control class. In practice, one can often bind data to controls such as the list controls Labels, TextBox, and TextView.

Traditionally, Microsoft has provided developers with a range of tools to use for connecting to and exploiting data sources. In recent years, the company has invested its energies in developing ADO (ActiveX Data Objects), and .NET introduces the latest incarnation of ADO in the form of ADO.NET. As with all things .NET, this has resulted in some changes—although we are constantly reassured that our existing skills will be valuable grounding for the new technology! I will be using ADO.NET throughout this book, so be prepared for some shifts, both in the terminology and in the mind-set that you may be used to.

To access data, we first need to set up a data connection to the database or whatever data source we are using. We can use the Data tools from the toolbox in the Visual Studio .NET IDE. The Data Adapter Configuration Wizard can help take care of establishing the database connection. We can run this wizard by dragging either an OleDbDataAdapter object or a SqlDataAdapter object from the toolbox onto a form or component. Choose the object based on whether we are accessing an SQL database or another OLE-compliant database. (OLE stands for *object linking and embedding*.)

Once we have set up the adapter, we create a dataset, which represents the complete set of data (including tables and relationships) that we wish to access and then populate, using the data adapter. The dataset is like a virtual, in-memory holding pen for all the data that we wish to manage, and its methods and objects are consistent with the relational database model—it is a far more complex beast than the dear old recordset that we knew and loved. Within the dataset, we can further define DataTables and DataRelations. We can then bind a control (or controls) to the dataset.

A databound control may have the following properties:

*DataSource*    The source of the data to populate the list

*DataMember*    The table used in the selected DataSource

*DataTextField*    A field in the DataMember that can be associated with the Text property for each item in the control

*DataValueField*    A field in the DataMember that can be associated with the Value property for each item in the control

We can use either a simple binding (which binds a single data item) or a custom binding that can use expressions to create bindings between any properties on a page.

## What's New in ADO.NET?

ADO.NET essentially combines the simplicity and power of "classic" ADO with the flexibility of XML. We can still, if we wish, use ADO in .NET through the .NET COM operability services, but ADO.NET has been largely designed to work seamlessly with .NET and does some things very differently. In setting up and using data connections throughout this book, I will be employing ADO.NET.

As we saw in the preceding section, ADO.NET is very different in its approach from the plain-vanilla ADO that we are used to. To begin with, we no longer work with RecordSet objects or use cursors to manipulate our data. ADO.NET uses the DataSet object, which can contain multiple tables (DataTable objects). By comparison, the RecordSet object from ADO more closely resembled a single table. Additionally, ADO.NET is fully detached from the data source, so that cursors are not required.

Relationships can be set up between rows in various DataTable objects. Under ADO, we could use the Join query to create a single result table from multiple tables.

A dataset is transmitted as XML. This enables it to pass freely through firewalls, which has been a problem with taking a distributed approach to ADO in the past, with its use of COM marshalling. The use of COM marshalling has also required type conversions that can place an extra demand on system resources. The XML format doesn't have this requirement.

To finish off this brief overview of ADO.NET, it is worth noting that when we establish the initial connection object to the data source, we have the option of using a specific managed provider for SQL Server 7.0 or higher. This gives an optimized connection that directly accesses the internal API of the database server. ADO.NET provides a second managed provider for all other OLE DB (database) providers.

## Using the List Control

This is the simplest of the list controls, but there are many situations where it is all that we will require for our applications. In the following sections, we will see how to enter information directly into the control at design time and how to link it to other data sources to make it more flexible.

## Creating a Static List Using the *Items* Property

The List control is used to display a static list of items. The items can be entered via the Items property in the Properties window. Select the ellipsis in this property to generate a dialog box where we can add items (see Figure 9.1). Each item can also be given a value, which aids in programmatically manipulating the data in the list. In this example, we are creating a simple list of active Web links.

**FIGURE 9.1:**

The Properties dialog box for adding items to the List control

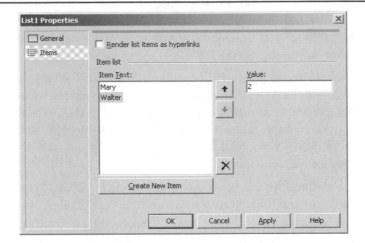

To set items as links, we can either select the Render List Items as HyperLinks check box in the List1 Properties dialog box or (if we exit the Properties dialog box) under the Behavior property section, set ItemsAsLinks to True to set the various items entered as links. If we then return to the Properties dialog box (selecting the ellipsis in the Items property), we can define the URLs so that they will attach to our links in the Value field (see Figure 9.2).

**FIGURE 9.2:**

Setting URLs for list items in the Properties dialog box

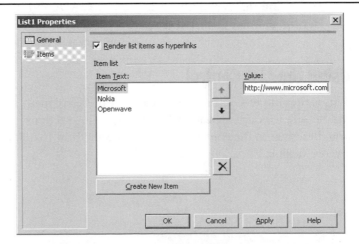

A simple list of links generated in this fashion appears as in Figure 9.3 in the Openwave browser.

FIGURE 9.3:

A simple list of links generated using the List control and illustrated in the Openwave emulator

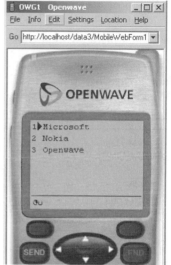

Image of UP.SDK courtesy Openwave Systems, Inc.

If we remember what we learned about WML, we can see in this example (Figure 9.3) that the list has been generated as Option On-Picks. If we view the list in the Nokia emulator, they are restricted to a list of HREFs.

We can do a lot more with this List control, however. We can databind it to a variety of sources including databases or programmatically generated arrays of information.

In the next example, we will step through the process of hooking up to a database and displaying some of its information in a list.

## Connecting the List Control to a Database

For the purpose of this exercise, we could use any OLE-compliant database that we have access to from our machine, and Microsoft's Northwind sample database is often a popular choice in various tutorials. However, in this example, we will create one from scratch, which will consist of a simple contact list of friends and their ages.

First, we need to build our database. Since most readers are likely to have access to Access (no pun intended!), I will use this for our data examples. However, any SQL/OLE-compliant database (such as SQL Server) will do the job.

## Creating the Database

Follow these steps to build your database:

1. Create a new, blank Access database.

2. Save it somewhere convenient (such as My Documents), and name it `mobiledb1.mdb`.

3. Select Create Table in Design View (this varies slightly between Access 97 and Access 2000 and higher).

4. In Design View, create the fields listed in Table 9.1.

**TABLE 9.1:** Field Descriptions for a Sample Database

| Field Name | Data Type |
| --- | --- |
| Id | AutoNumber (set to Primary key—right-click the gray box to the left of Field Name) |
| Name | Text |
| Age | Number |

5. Save the table as Table1 and enter DataSheet View.

6. Make up some dummy data by entering seven names and ages (see Figure 9.4 and Table 9.2); then close the database.

**FIGURE 9.4:**

The Table1 table with data entered

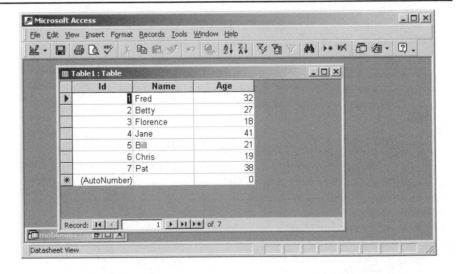

**TABLE 9.2:**  Sample Data Entered in Table1 Table in *mobiledb1.mdb* Database

| Id | Name | Age |
|----|------|-----|
| 1 | Fred | 32 |
| 2 | Betty | 27 |
| 3 | Florence | 18 |
| 4 | Jane | 41 |
| 5 | Bill | 21 |
| 6 | Chris | 19 |
| 7 | Pat | 38 |

### Building the Application

Now, create a new mobile Web application in Visual Studio .NET and name it Mobile-ListDemo1. Drag a List control onto the form in Design View and choose the Data toolset from the Toolbox on the left-hand side of the screen (see Figure 9.5).

**FIGURE 9.5:**

The Mobile Web Form with List control and Data tools visible

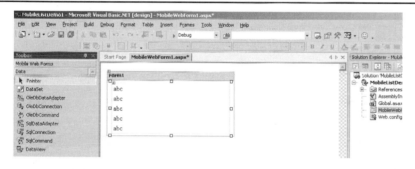

Since we are not using SQL Server, we will use the OleDbDataAdapter to make our connection (rather than the `SqlDataAdapter`). Drag a copy of the control onto Form1.

This should start the Data Adapter Configuration Wizard and place a reference to OleDbDataAdapter1 at the bottom of the ASPX page.

**1.** In the wizard, click Next.

**2.** Click the New Connection button; this should open the Data Link Properties dialog box (see Figure 9.6).

**3.** Click the Provider tab and choose Microsoft Jet 4.0 OLE DB Provider. (The default is Microsoft OLE DB Provider for SQL Server.) Click Next to shift from the Provider tab to the Connection tab. The dialog box should now appear as in Figure 9.7.

FIGURE 9.6:

The Data Link
Properties dialog box

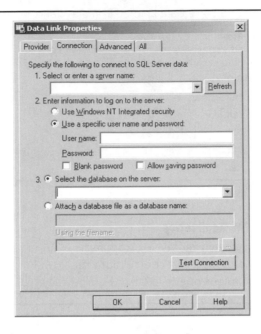

FIGURE 9.7:

The Connection tab
in the Data Link
Properties dialog box
after the Microsoft
Jet 4.0 OLE DB
Provider is selected

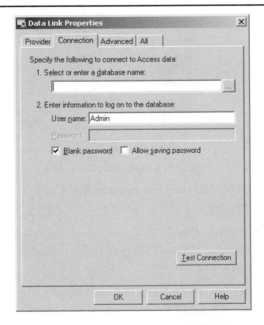

4. In the Select or Enter a Database Name text box, navigate to and select your copy of mobiledb1.mdb.

5. Click the Test Connection button to make sure all is well. Click OK. This should take you back to the first screen of the wizard; it should now have a connection string in the Which Data Connection Should the Data Adapter Use? box. Click the Next button.

6. In Choose a Query Type, select the Use SQL Statements option.

7. In the Generate the SQL Statements window, click the Query Builder button (see Figure 9.8).

**FIGURE 9.8:**

The Generate the SQL Statements window in the Data Adapter Configuration Wizard

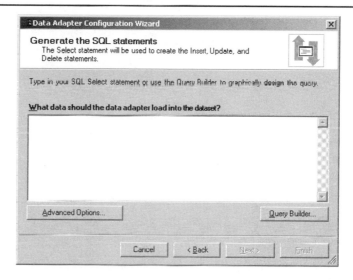

8. In the Add Table dialog box, choose the Table1 table, click the Add button, and then click Close (see Figure 9.9).

**FIGURE 9.9:**

The Add Table dialog box

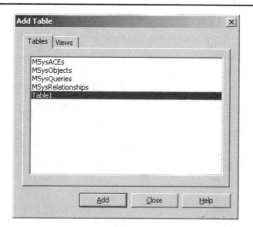

9. In the Table1 table in the top window of the Query Builder, select the All Columns check box. An appropriate SQL statement (SELECT Table1.* FROM Table1) should appear in the Query Builder (see Figure 9.10).

---

**FIGURE 9.10:**

The completed SQL statement in the Query Builder

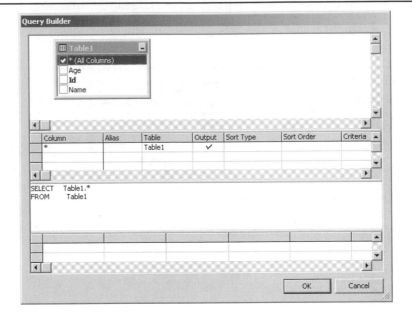

10. Click OK. The SQL statement should now appear in the Data Adapter Configuration Wizard. Click Next.

11. A final confirmation dialog box should now appear that lists the completed tasks, including Generated Select, Insert, Update, and Delete statements (see Figure 9.11). Click Finish to exit the wizard.

12. Right-click the OleDbDataAdapter1 object at the bottom of the screen and choose Generate Dataset from the menu (or choose Generate Dataset from the Data menu). Select the defaults in the Generate Dataset dialog box (see Figure 9.12) and click OK. Visual Studio .NET generates a typed dataset and a schema that defines the dataset. You can access this schema (DataSet1.xsd) from the Solution Explorer.

---

**NOTE**    The default view in Solution Explorer doesn't show all the files that constitute your application. A Show All Files button is included on the Solution Explorer toolbar.

**FIGURE 9.11:**

A successful Data
Adapter Configuration
confirmation box

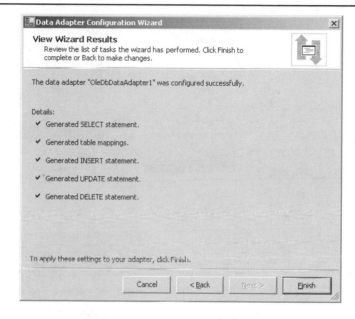

**FIGURE 9.12:**

The Generate Dataset
dialog box

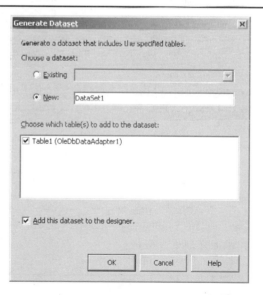

13. Right click the `OleDbDataAdapter1` object again and select Preview Data from the menu
(or choose Preview Data from the Data menu). Click the Fill Dataset button. This dialog box provides the opportunity to preview the data from our data source and to see
how it will look once we fill the dataset (see Figure 9.13). Click the Close button to exit
the dialog.

FIGURE 9.13:

The Data Adapter
Preview dialog box

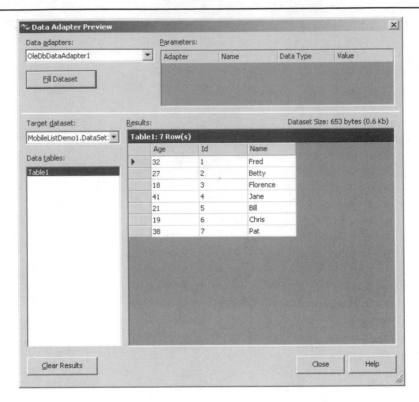

**14.** We have now set up all the objects needed to finish loading data from the database into the list. In Design View, select the List1 control on the form and set the properties listed in Table 9.3.

**TABLE 9.3:** Property Settings for the List1 Control

| Property | Setting |
| --- | --- |
| DataSource | DataSet1 |
| DataMember | Table1 |
| DataTextField | Name |
| DataValueField | Id |

**15.** In Code Behind View, add the code presented in Listing 9.1 to the Page_Load subroutine. This code actually loads data via the data adapter into the dataset and binds the List control to that dataset.

| Listing 9.1 | Code Behind to Fill a Dataset and to Databind to a List Control |
| --- | --- |

```
Private Sub Page_Load(ByVal sender As System.Object, ByVal e As
➡ System.EventArgs) Handles MyBase.Load
      'Put user code to initialize the page here
      OleDbDataAdapter1.Fill(DataSet11, "Table1")
      List1.DataBind()
   End Sub
```

**16.** Compile and view the project in your browser. In the Openwave browser, it should appear as in Figure 9.14.

**FIGURE 9.14:**

The databound list presented in the Openwave browser

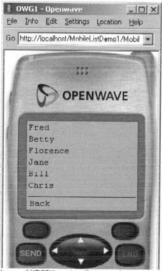

Image of UP.SDK courtesy Openwave Systems, Inc.

**NOTE**    If you double-clicked the List control to enter "code behind," you will find that the framework for an `ItemCommand` subroutine has been created. Leaving this in your code will result in the list items being displayed as links (that lead nowhere). Delete the `ItemCommand` sub, and the list items will appear normally.

We can also use the `Decoration` property to set list styles for devices capable of supporting something a little more fancy—if we can call a choice of "bulleted" or "numbered" fancy!

## Connecting the List Control to an Array

We can also bind controls to a variety of data sources other than databases, including arrays, text files, string variables, Microsoft Excel spreadsheets, XML data files, and so on.

In the next example, we will see how to connect a List control to data held in an array. Additionally, we will see how to code directly to the ASPX page rather than employing the code behind. We will build a Contacts application that is similar to the one in the preceding example, except that here we will have the data hard-coded into the array.

1. Create a new mobile application and name it `MobileListDemo2`.

2. Drag a List control onto the form and change to HTML View.

3. Complete the code on the ASPX page according to Listing 9.2.

**Listing 9.2**      **Example of a List Control Bound to Data Stored in an Array**

```vb
<%@ Page Language="vb" AutoEventWireup="true"
➥ Codebehind="MobileWebForm1.aspx.vb"
➥ Inherits="MobileListDemo2.MobileWebForm1" trace="False"%>
<%@ Register TagPrefix="mobile"
➥ Namespace="System.Web.UI.MobileControls"
➥ Assembly="System.Web.Mobile, Version=1.0.3300.0, Culture=neutral,
➥ PublicKeyToken=b03f5f7f11d50a3a" %>
<meta content="Microsoft Visual Studio.NET 7.0" name="GENERATOR">
<meta content="Visual Basic 7.0" name="CODE_LANGUAGE">
<meta content="http://schemas.microsoft.com/Mobile/Page"
➥ name="vs_targetSchema">
<script language="VB" runat="server">

Private Class Contacts

    Dim _name As String

    Public Sub New(name As String)
       _name = name
    End Sub

    Public ReadOnly Property name As String
       Get
           Return _name
       End Get
    End Property
End Class

Protected Sub Page_Load(sender As Object, e As EventArgs)

    If (Not IsPostBack)

        Dim myArray As New ArrayList()

        myArray.Add(New Contacts("Fred"))
        myArray.Add(New Contacts("Betty"))
        myArray.Add(New Contacts("Florence"))
```

```
        myArray.Add(New Contacts("Jane"))
        myArray.Add(New Contacts("Bill"))
        myArray.Add(New Contacts("Chris"))
        myArray.Add(New Contacts("Pat"))

        List1.DataSource = myArray
        List1.DataBind()

    End If

End Sub
</script>
<body Xmlns:mobile="http://schemas.microsoft.com/Mobile/WebForm">
    <mobile:Form runat="server" ID="Form1">
        <mobile:Label id="Label1" runat="server"
➡  StyleReference="title">
        Contacts</mobile:Label>
        <mobile:List id="List1" runat="server"
➡  DataTextField="name"></mobile:List>
    </mobile:Form>
</body>
```

**4.** Save and run the code in your browser. Figure 9.15 shows how it appears in the Openwave browser.

**FIGURE 9.15:**

Data generated from array, as displayed in the Openwave browser

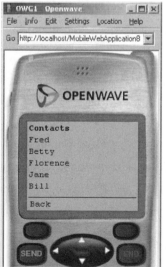

Image of UP.SDK courtesy Openwave Systems, Inc.

This is similar to (but much simpler than) the "Databinding to a List" example given in the Mobile Internet Toolkit QuickStart Tutorial. The example in QuickStart, which is worth looking at, demonstrates how to create a list of links that link in turn to a second form that dynamically renders data that is relevant to each link. (The data is also entered in the array.)

Essentially, in the preceding example, we created a new class (Contacts) that contains only one element (name); we could have given it more elements, such as age or address. We then loaded incidents of Contacts into an array, declared the array as the data source for the list, and databound it. At runtime, the DataTextField was bound to the name property of the data source object (myArray).

Note that we set the autoEventWireUp attribute of the @Page directive to True. This automatically enables page events and normally has a default of False in Mobile Web Pages.

---

**WARNING**     Note that one of the limitations in working in HTML View is that the intellisense and auto-complete facilities are fairly limited. We need to be very careful with typos when writing our code.

## Using the ObjectList Control

ObjectList is a strictly databound control that can be used to display a list of data objects. Each item in the list can then be linked to more data. The control can also be used to display data in a table with multiple columns, although the actual rendering of the table can vary according to device capabilities.

### Connecting the ObjectList Control to a Database

We will use the same database in this example as we used in the preceding section on the List control to create a very simple Contacts-style application.

1. Create a new mobile application and name it MobObjListDemo1.

2. Drag an ObjectList control onto the form.

3. Select the Data tools from the toolbox and set up an OleDbDataAdapter1 as described in the previous section on connecting the List control to a database (use mobiledb1 as your data source).

4. Select All Columns in the Query Builder to generate the following SQL statement:
   SELECT Age, Id, Name FROM Table1.

5. Generate a dataset (DataSet11) and check that everything is working properly by using the Preview Data option.

6. Select the ObjectList1 control on your form and set the properties listed in Table 9.4.

**TABLE 9.4:** Property Settings for the ObjectList Control Example

| Property | Setting |
|----------|---------|
| DataSource | DataSet11 |
| DataMember | Table1 |
| LabelField | Name |

7. In the TableFields property, click the ellipsis to open the ObjectList Properties dialog box (see Figure 9.16).

FIGURE 9.16:

The ObjectList
Properties dialog box

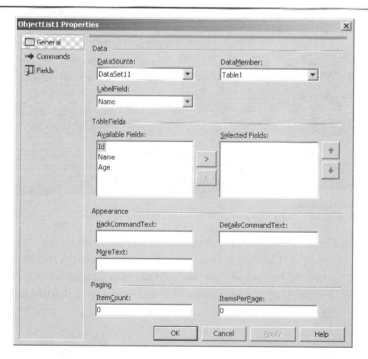

8. From the Available Fields window, move the Name, Age, and Id fields to the Selected Fields window. Use the Up and Down arrow keys to reorganize the fields into the order Id, Name, Age. Click OK. Your screen should now look something like Figure 9.17.

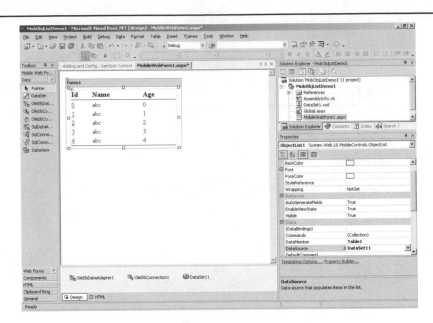

9. We now need to load the data into our dataset and bind the control. Select Code Behind
   View and add the lines shown in Listing 9.3 to the `Page_Load` subroutine.

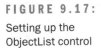

**Listing 9.3**          **Code Behind for *ObjectList* Example**

```
Private Sub Page_Load(ByVal sender As System.Object, ByVal e As
➥ System.EventArgs) Handles MyBase.Load
    OleDbDataAdapter1.Fill(DataSet11)
    ObjectList1.DataBind()
End Sub
```

10. Compile and run the project. In Internet Explorer, it should look something like Fig-
    ure 9.18. Using the Openwave browser, it should appear as in Figure 9.19. Notice that
    while IE can display the entire dataset as a table, in the Openwave browser the dataset is
    displayed as a list of names as links. Selecting a link then displays another card containing
    the full information for that name.

**FIGURE 9.18:**

ObjectList example running in Internet Explorer

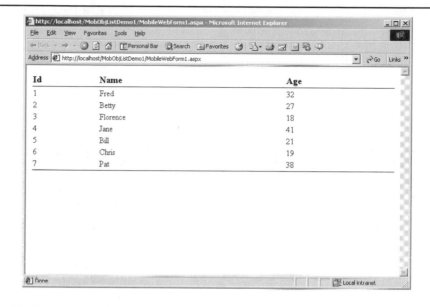

**FIGURE 9.19:**

ObjectList example running in the Openwave browser

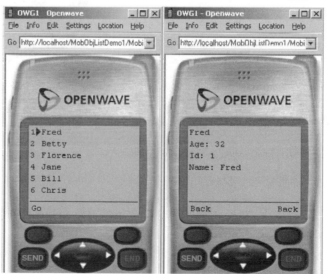

Image of UP.SDK courtesy Openwave Systems, Inc.

Note that by specifying the `LabelField` property as `Name` in the Properties dialog box, we can ensure that the Name field is displayed in the initial "links" window in the mobile browser. In this example, if we had not set the `LabelField` property, the Age field would have become the list of links that is initially displayed (see Figure 9.20). Although this would have affected the mobile browser, the use or non-use of the property would have had no impact on IE, since the entire table can be rendered in the browser window. In the next example, however, we will see where this may not be the case.

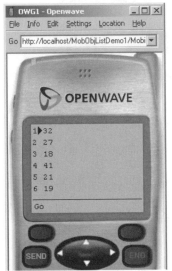

**FIGURE 9.20:**

The consequences of *not* setting the `LabelField` property in the ObjectList control

Image of UP.SDK courtesy Openwave Systems, Inc.

We can see from this example that it would be very easy to use this control to develop a Contacts-style application. We can also use the control to connect to a range of other data sources.

## Setting Up Custom Fields

We can also add custom fields to our control by using the `Fields` property:

1. Select the `Fields` property and click the ellipsis in the right corner. The ObjectList Properties box appears.

2. Click the Create New Field button and create a Field1.

3. From the DataField drop-down menu, choose the Age field.

4. We can use the DataFormatString box to apply custom string formatting to the field (type **{0} years**—without the parentheses for this example) and give it a custom title using the Title box (type **My Friend's Age**).

5. Select the Visible check box to make the field visible within the application. (See Figure 9.21.)

FIGURE 9.21:

Setting up a custom field in the ObjectList control

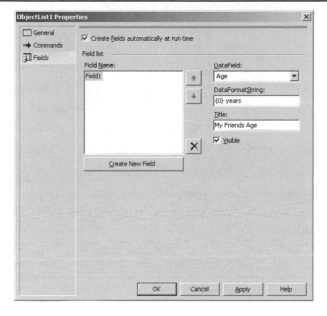

6. Delete the Age field from the TableFields property.

7. Run the project in Internet Explorer. The list should now appear as links with the first page showing only Name and Id. Selecting a link should now display the information for that link, including the My Friend's Age field. It should be formatted as "27 years," for example (see Figure 9.22).

FIGURE 9.22:

An ObjectList example with a custom field displayed in IE

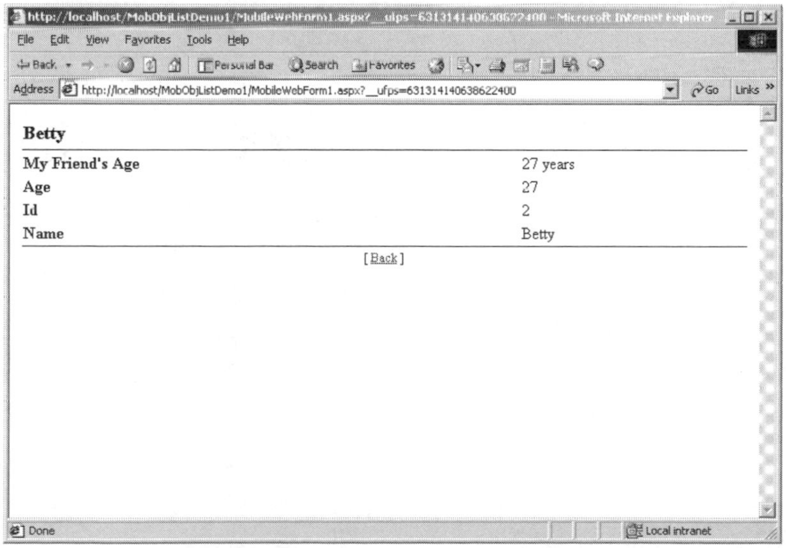

## Using the SelectionList Control

The SelectionList control is useful for showing short lists of items that users can select. It can be rendered (depending on the device) as a drop-down list, a selection list, or a list of check boxes or radio (option) buttons. The control supports data binding, and users can select more than one item. However, it does not support pagination.

As an example of using the SelectionList control, we will create a list of Websites. When a Website is selected, a second form will open, giving the site's URL.

1. Create a new mobile project and name it MobSelListDemo1.

2. Drag a SelectionList control onto the form.

3. As with the List control, we can add items to the control via a dialog box triggered from the ellipsis in the Items property. Add to the dialog the items and attached values that are listed in Table 9.5.

**TABLE 9.5:**  Item Text and Values for the SelectionList Control Example

| Item Text | Value |
| --- | --- |
| Microsoft | http://www.microsoft.com |
| Openwave | http://www.openwave.com |
| Nokia | http://www.forum.nokia.com |

4. The SelectionList Properties dialog box should appear as in Figure 9.23. Click OK.

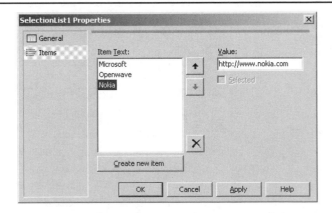

In the properties for the `SelectionList`, the `SelectType` property gives a choice of ways in which the control may be rendered, including these:

- Drop Down
- List Box
- Radio
- MultiSelect List Box
- Check Box

The default is Drop Down. It is worth noting, however, that many devices will support very few (if any) of these options.

As an example, Figure 9.24 shows how the Drop Down option appears in Internet Explorer and in the Openwave browser.

**FIGURE 9.24:**

The drop-down box from the SelectionList control rendered in IE and Openwave

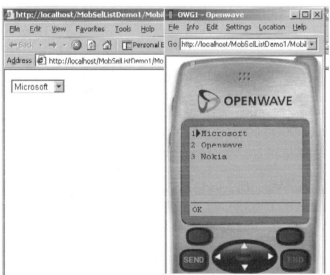

Image of UP.SDK courtesy Openwave Systems, Inc.

**5.** Select HTML View for the ASPX page and complete the code from Listing 9.4.

**Listing 9.4    Code Listing for the MobSelListDemo1 Example Using the SelectionList Control**

```
<%@ Page Language="vb" AutoEventWireup="true"
➡ Codebehind="MobileWebForm1.aspx.vb"
➡ Inherits="MobSelListDemo1.MobileWebForm1" trace="False"%>
<%@ Register TagPrefix="mobile"
➡ Namespace="System.Web.UI.MobileControls"
➡ Assembly="System.Web.Mobile, Version=1.0.3300.0, Culture=neutral,
```

```
➡ PublicKeyToken=b03f5f7f11d50a3a" %>
<meta content="Microsoft Visual Studio.NET 7.0" name="GENERATOR">
<meta content="Visual Basic 7.0" name="CODE_LANGUAGE">
<meta content="http://schemas.microsoft.com/Mobile/Page"
➡ name="vs_targetSchema">


<script language="vb" runat="server">
   Protected Sub Show_Address(sender As Object, e As EventArgs)
      Label2.Text = SelectionList1.Selection.Text
      Label3.Text = SelectionList1.Selection.Value
      ActiveForm = Form2
   End Sub
</script>

<body Xmlns:mobile="http://schemas.microsoft.com/Mobile/WebForm">
   <mobile:Form id="Form1" runat="server">
      <mobile:SelectionList id="SelectionList1" runat="server">
         <Item Value="http://www.microsoft.com"
➡ Text="Microsoft"></Item>
         <Item Value="http://www.openwave.com"
➡ Text="Openwave"></Item>
         <Item Value="http://www.nokia.com"
➡ Text="Nokia"></Item>
      </mobile:SelectionList>
      <mobile:Command id="Command1" runat="server"
➡ SoftkeyLabel="Details"
➡ OnClick="Show_Address">Details</mobile:Command>
   </mobile:Form>

<mobile:Form id="Form2" runat="server">
   <mobile:Label id="Label1" runat="server"
➡ StyleReference="title">Web Address</mobile:Label>
   <mobile:Label id="Label2" runat="server"></mobile:Label>
   <mobile:Label id="Label3" runat="server"></mobile:Label>
   </mobile:Form>

</body>
```

In the code from Listing 9.4, the Show_Address subroutine is triggered by the On_Click event of the Command1 control. This assigns the Text and Value values from the selection list for the currently selected Website to the text properties of Label2 and Label3 in Form2, and then calls Form2.

```
<script language="vb" runat="server">
   Protected Sub Show_Address(sender As Object, e As EventArgs)
      Label2.Text = SelectionList1.Selection.Text
      Label3.Text = SelectionList1.Selection.Value
      ActiveForm = Form2
   End Sub
</script>
```

**NOTE**     We did not need to graphically create the second form or the attached label controls in this part of the project, since these entities are all generated by the code from Listing 9.4. However, there is nothing to stop us from having used the graphical tools and property settings to save some typing of code. Take a look at the project in Design View—it looks as it would if we had graphically built it.

6. Compile and run the project in the Openwave browser. The completed project should appear as in Figure 9.25.

**FIGURE 9.25:**

The MobSelListDemo1 project, showing the use of the SelectionList control in the Openwave browser

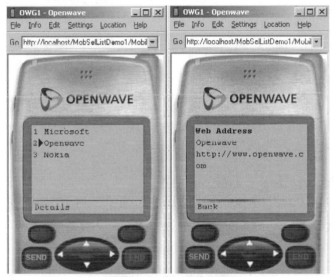

Image of UP.SDK courtesy Openwave Systems, Inc.

The Mobile Internet Toolkit QuickStart Tutorial includes a worked example demonstrating how to take advantage of the multiple selection functionality of the control. Note that this works for the control only when its `SelectType` property has been set to either `CheckBox` or `MultiSelectListBox`. Mobile browsers such as the Openwave browser support the multiple selection property by making use of the right softkey to "pick" the selections. A small *x* marks each selection. See Figure 9.26 for an illustrated example.

We can connect a SelectionList to a database in a similar fashion, as illustrated previously with the List and ObjectList controls.

A multiple selection
list displayed in the
Openwave browser

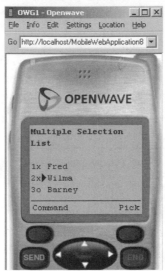

Image of UP.SDK courtesy Openwave Systems, Inc.

## Paginating a List

We can apply pagination to lists to control the amount of data that is presented on any one page. This can be handled in one of two ways:

- A large set of data can be broken up into smaller sets for display over a series of pages.
- Data that is calculated may be either processed in one hit and then broken up as above or calculated a page at a time (known as *chunking*).

We will look at both methods in this section.

Straightforward pagination is, as we have seen earlier, simply a case of setting the `pagination` property of the form to True. It is normally used with the List or ObjectList control. Microsoft advises that it is not a good idea to try and use it with the SelectionList control.

For a simple example, we will build an application that prints a list of consecutive numbers from 1 to 100.

1. Create a new mobile project and name it `MobileListDemo3`.

2. Drag a List and Label control to the form and set the form's pagination property to True. Set the label's text property to `Numbers` and its style property to `Title`.

3. In Code Behind View, copy the code from Listing 9.5 into the `Page_Load` subroutine.

---

**Listing 9.5    Paginating a List Control for the MobileListDemo3 Project**

```
Private Sub Page_Load(ByVal sender As System.Object, ByVal e As
➡ System.EventArgs) Handles MyBase.Load

    If (Not IsPostBack) then
        Dim n As Integer = 1
            Do While (n < 100)

            List1.Items.Add(n.ToString())
            n = n + 1
        Loop
        End If

    End Sub
```

---

4. Compile and test the code in IE and the Openwave browser. The list of numbers should be paginated.

---

**NOTE**    We use the `If (Not IsPostBack) then` code to prevent the sub from being re-executed every time we go back to the server for another page.

In the next example, we will see how to control the amount of data that is being processed and how to limit it for each page. This is an advantage in situations where potentially a very large amount of data might be processed by an application or where the calculations are very system intensive, but only a small section of the data needs to be viewed.

We can do this by handling our code through the `OnLoadItems` event of the List control rather than through the `Page_Load` event. We set the total amount of data available through the `ItemCount` property of the List control. This enables the control to paginate itself accordingly, even though it receives only one page of data at a time. Listing 9.6 demonstrates how this can be written in the HTML View of the ASPX page.

---

**Listing 9.6    Example of Chunking Pagination**

```
<%@ Page Language="vb" AutoEventWireup="true"
➡ Codebehind="MobileWebForm1.aspx.vb"
➡ Inherits="MobileListDemo3.MobileWebForm1" trace="False"%>
<%@ Register TagPrefix="mobile"
➡ Namespace="System.Web.UI.MobileControls"
➡ Assembly="System.Web.Mobile, Version=1.0.3300.0, Culture=neutral,
➡ PublicKeyToken=b03f5f7f11d50a3a" %>
<meta content="Microsoft Visual Studio.NET 7.0" name="GENERATOR">
<meta content="Visual Basic 7.0" name="CODE_LANGUAGE">
<meta content="http://schemas.microsoft.com/Mobile/Page"
➡ name="vs_targetSchema">
```

```
<script language="VB" runat="server">

Protected Sub Calculate(sender As Object, args As LoadItemsEventArgs)
     List1.Items.Clear
     Dim n As Integer

     For n = args.itemindex to args.ItemCount + args.itemindex
        Dim item As New MobileListItem(n.ToString())
        List1.Items.Add(item)
     Next

End Sub

</script>
<body Xmlns:mobile="http://schemas.microsoft.com/Mobile/WebForm">
   <mobile:Form id="Form1" runat="server" Paginate="True">
      <mobile:Label id="Label1" runat="server">Label</mobile:Label>
      <mobile:List id="List1" runat="server" ItemCount="50000"
➥ OnLoadItems="Calculate"></mobile:List>
   </mobile:Form>
</body>
```

Notice how, in the following code, I have set the `ItemCount` property for the List control to 50000. The number-generating code is now called `Calculate`. I have also set the loop in the `Calculate` sub to respond to the sum of the `ItemIndex` and `ItemCount` properties and for this sub to be raised by the `OnLoadItems` event.

```
<mobile:List id="List1" runat="server" ItemCount="50000"
➥ OnLoadItems="Calculate"></mobile:List>
```

Compile and run the code. The content of each page is now calculated only when it is called to display on the client. Note also that we haven't used the following statement, for obvious reasons!

```
If (Not IsPostBack) then
```

However, we can actually test whether our chunking is working as expected by inserting this argument. Repeated calls back to the server for the next set of numbers return only the original set, since the code isn't processed to produce the next lot of values.

## Summary

In this chapter, we have learned how to access data using the various list controls together with ADO.NET.

ADO.NET is probably going to take some getting used to for a number of people (it certainly is for me!), but it does promise greater flexibility than traditional methods, due to its disconnected approach and its support for XML.

The list controls in the Mobile Internet Toolkit offer us a range of tools that is possibly a bit limited in scope for those of us used to richer environments. However, we need to remember that the types of devices for which we are developing do not presently support the richer tools (in many cases, they only have limited support for the list controls currently supplied), and the existing list controls are very flexible and highly adaptable.

This chapter only touched the surface of data management, and it focused almost exclusively on accessing and reading data. In the next chapter, we will look at databinding controls other than the list controls and performing additional tasks with our data such as updating and deleting.

# CHAPTER 10

# Data Access with the Mobile Internet Toolkit, Part 2

- Reading data using non-List controls such as the Label control

- Customizing displayed text in a List control

- Modifying data

- Creating new records

- Deleting existing records

- Updating existing records in the database from the mobile device

- Full code listing for MyContacts

- Full code listing for MyContactsDR

I n this chapter we will further explore the use of lists and other controls in accessing and manipulating data with the Mobile Internet Toolkit. To illustrate this, we will set up two versions of a simple contact manager using the database originally created in Chapter 9, "Data Access with the Mobile Internet Toolkit, Part 1 (List Controls)".

Most of this stuff is basic fare for the experienced programmer, but it's worth remembering that we are going to be carrying out these tasks using ADO.NET—and things are not all as we may have been used to!

The purpose of this chapter is to give a brief overview of these tasks as related to using the Mobile Internet Toolkit and to introduce you to what's involved. Naturally I would assume that for serious data-intensive projects, you would refer to a text more specific to ADO.NET than this one.

We will create two versions of the simple contacts manager (MyContacts). One version (MyContacts) will use the DataSet approach new to ADO.NET and the other (MyContactsDR) will use the more traditional direct-from-the-datasource approach—except that we will be using ADO.NET to achieve this. Code listings for the projects' various elements are included as they are described throughout the chapter, and full code listings (including code-behind and ASPX pages) for the two projects are included at the end of the chapter.

## Setting Up MyContacts

In this section we will set up the basic forms for the application and illustrate several different methods that we can use to access and display data. These include the following:

- Accessing data from a DataSet
- Using a `DataView` object to access data from a DataSet
- Concatenating field contents for display in Label and List controls
- Using the `DataReader` object to access data from a database

### The Database

To build our simple Contacts Manager we will initially need to add more fields and dummy data to the `mobiledb1.mdb` database we created at the beginning of Chapter 9.

Open the database, then open Table1 in Design View. Add the following fields as listed in Table 10.1.

**TABLE 10.1:**  Field Additions to the Mobiledb1Database

| Field Name | Data Type |
|---|---|
| Surname | Text |
| Address | Text |
| Telephone | Text |
| Email | Text |
| Mobile | Text |
| City | Text |
| Zip | Text |
| Comments | Memo |

Save and switch to the Data Entry View. Enter the data as illustrated in Figure 10.1.

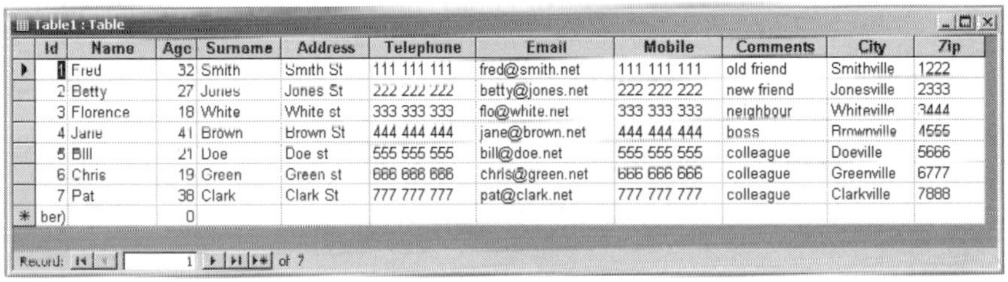

**FIGURE 10.1:**

Sample data entered into Mobiledb1

| Id | Name | Age | Surname | Address | Telephone | Email | Mobile | Comments | City | Zip |
|---|---|---|---|---|---|---|---|---|---|---|
| 1 | Fred | 32 | Smith | Smith St | 111 111 111 | fred@smith.net | 111 111 111 | old friend | Smithville | 1222 |
| 2 | Betty | 27 | Jones | Jones St | 222 222 222 | betty@jones.net | 222 222 222 | new friend | Jonesville | 2333 |
| 3 | Florence | 18 | White | White st | 333 333 333 | flo@white.net | 333 333 333 | neighbour | Whiteville | 3444 |
| 4 | Jane | 41 | Brown | Brown St | 444 444 444 | jane@brown.net | 444 444 444 | boss | Brownville | 4555 |
| 5 | Bill | 21 | Doe | Doe st | 555 555 555 | bill@doe.net | 555 555 555 | colleague | Doeville | 5666 |
| 6 | Chris | 19 | Green | Green st | 666 666 666 | chris@green.net | 666 666 666 | colleague | Greenville | 6777 |
| 7 | Pat | 38 | Clark | Clark St | 777 777 777 | pat@clark.net | 777 777 777 | colleague | Clarkville | 7888 |

## Building the Project

We are now ready to create the Mobile Web Project. Open a new mobile application project in Visual Studio .NET and name it MyContacts. Drag an OleDbDataAdapter (OleDbDataAdapter1) onto the form and set it to connect to the Mobiledb1 database. Select All from the SQL statement in the Query Builder. Generate DataSet11 and check that everything works by using Preview Data.

At this stage it is a good idea to get into the habit of creating projects that will properly accommodate the major mobile-phone browser types. As described in Chapter 8, "A Deeper Look at the Mobile Internet Toolkit and VB .NET," we need to open the Web.config file and set the cookieless attribute of the <sessionState> tag to TRUE to provide support for Nokia-based browsers. To cater to the redirect habits of Openwave-based browsers, ensure that the <httpRuntime> tag with the useFullyQualifiedRedirectUrl attribute set to TRUE is also present in the <system.web> section of Web.config:

```
<system.web>
 <httpRuntime useFullyQualifiedRedirectUrl="true" />
</system.web>
```

Drag a Label control and a List control to your Form1. Create a second form (Form2) and drag seven Label controls and a TextView control to the form. Type the text "**Phone:** " directly onto the form between Labels 5 and 6. Then type "**Mobile:** " between Labels 6 and 7, "**Email:** " between Labels 7 and 8, and "**Comments:** " between Label 8 and the TextView1 controls. Make sure to type a space after each of these headings. The eventual appearance of the two forms is illustrated later in Figure 10.4.

Set the properties of the various controls for Form1 as listed in Table 10.2.

**TABLE 10.2:** Property Settings for Form1 of the MyContacts Project

| Control | Property | Value |
| --- | --- | --- |
| Form1 | Title | My Contacts |
| | Pagination | True |
| | Pager Style – NextPageText | Go to Page {0} |
| | Pager Style – PreviousPageText | Return to Page {0} |
| Label1 | Style Reference | title |
| | Text | My Contacts |
| List1 | DataSource | DataSet11 |
| | DataMember | Table1 |
| | DataTextField | Name |
| | DataValueField | Id |

We will need to do a little more work before setting the properties on the controls for Form2.

## Accessing Data from DataSets

We will now look at how to access the data we have loaded into our DataSet. First we need to devise a way to populate the Label controls in Form2 with the relevant information for the particular contact we select from our list. We can do this several ways using ADO.NET. Later in the chapter, we will see how to use the `DataReader` object, but for the moment we will stick with extracting data from DataSets.

In this instance we can do one of the following:

- Create a DataSet from a new connection that uses a parameterized query to return the particular row of information that interests us.

- Loop through an instance of the existing DataSet until we find the particular row of information that concerns us.

We will look at both methods here. First, we will set up the rest of this part of the project using a parameterized query.

Drag an OleDbDataAdapter control to Form2 (OleDbDataAdapter2). Follow the Wizard through to the Query Builder. The object here is to create the following SQL statement:

```
SELECT Address, Age, City, Comments, Email, Id, Mobile, Name, Surname,
➡ Telephone, Zip FROM Table1 WHERE (Id = ?)
```

We can do this by either simply typing the statement into the SQL window or using the Query Builder by selecting all the fields and including a question mark in the Criteria column against Id.

Next, generate a new DataSet (DataSet21) and preview data. The preview dialog box will tell you that you must submit a value for the OleDbDataAdapter2 parameter. Click OK and exit the dialog box.

We can now set up the controls on Form2. In each case we are going to use the DataBindings property to bind the Text property of each control to the relevant field in the DataSet. For example, select Label3 and click the ellipsis in the DataBindings property under Data in the Properties box. The dialog box depicted in Figure 10.2 should appear.

FIGURE 10.2:

Label3 DataBindings
dialog box

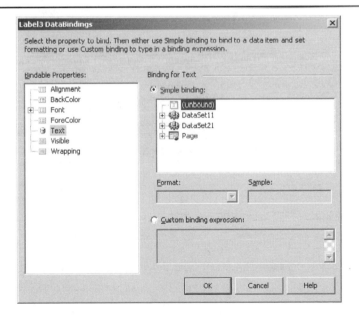

Expand the DataSet21 item and keep opening the sub-elements until you get to the individual fields. Choose the Address field; the Format box should now become active. Select General - {0} from the drop-down options. The final result should look something like Figure 10.3.

**FIGURE 10.3:**

Label3 DataBindings
completed

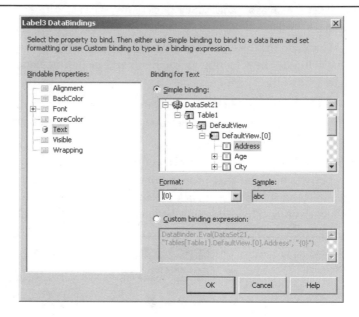

Click OK to return to the designer. Complete the property settings for Form2 as listed in Table 10.3.

**TABLE 10.3:** Property Settings for Form2 Controls in the MyContacts Project

| Control | Property | Value |
|---------|----------|-------|
| Form2 | Title | My Contacts - Details |
| Label2 | StyleReference | title |
| | Text | <empty> |
| Label3 | Font - Size | Small |
| | Text | <empty> |
| | DataBindings | DataBinder.Eval(DataSet21, "Tables[Table1].DefaultView.[0].Address","{0}") |

*Continued on next page*

**TABLE 10.3 CONTINUED:** Property Settings for Form2 Controls in the MyContacts Project

| Control | Property | Value |
|---------|----------|-------|
| Label4 | Font - Size | Small |
| | Text | <empty> |
| | DataBindings | DataBinder.Eval(DataSet21, "Tables[Table1].DefaultView.[0].City", "{0}") |
| Label5 | Font - Size | Small |
| | Text | <empty> |
| | DataBindings | DataBinder.Eval(DataSet21, "Tables[Table1].DefaultView.[0].Zip", "{0}") |
| Label6 | Font - Size | Small |
| | Text | <empty> |
| | DataBindings | DataBinder.Eval(DataSet21, "Tables[Table1].DefaultView.[0].Telephone", "{0}") |
| Label7 | Font - Size | Small |
| | Text | <empty> |
| | DataBindings | DataBinder.Eval(DataSet21, "Tables[Table1].DefaultView.[0].Mobile", "{0}") |
| Label3 | Font - Size | Small |
| | Text | <empty> |
| | DataBindings | DataBinder.Eval(DataSet21, "Tables[Table1].DefaultView.[0].Email", "{0}") |
| TextView1 | Font - Size | Small |
| | Text | <empty> |
| | DataBindings | DataBinder.Eval(DataSet21, "Tables[Table1].DefaultView.[0].Comments", "{0}") |

Figure 10.4 illustrates how the two forms should look after all the properties have been set.

We now need to write the code to first populate the two DataSets and then actually data-bind the relevant controls. Listing 10.1 contains the code behind for this project.

**NOTE**     I have made no attempt to manage this code; if something goes wrong it will simply fall over. This is only a demonstration project and I am trying to keep it as simple as possible to focus on the data manipulation aspects.

FIGURE 10.4:

MyContacts: layout for
Forms1 and 2

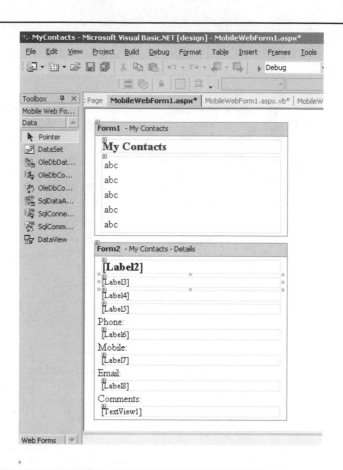

## Listing 10.1    Code Behind for the MyContacts Project

```
    Private Sub Page_Load(ByVal sender As System.Object, ByVal e As
➥ System.EventArgs) Handles MyBase.Load
        OleDbDataAdapter1.Fill(DataSet11, "Table1")
        List1.DataBind()
    End Sub

    Private Sub List1_ItemCommand(ByVal sender As System.Object, ByVal
➥ e As System.Web.UI.MobileControls.ListCommandEventArgs) Handles
➥ List1.ItemCommand

        Session("currID") = e.ListItem.Value
        ActiveForm = Form2
    End Sub
```

```
    Private Sub Form2_Activate(ByVal sender As System.Object, ByVal e
➡ As System.EventArgs) Handles Form2.Activate

        OleDbDataAdapter2.SelectCommand.Parameters("Id").Value =
➡ Session("currID")
        DataSet21.Clear()
        OleDbDataAdapter2.Fill(DataSet21, "Table1")
        Label2.Text = String.Format("{0} {1}",
➡ DataSet21.Table1.Rows(0).Item("Name"),
➡ DataSet21.Table1.Rows(0).Item("Surname"))
        Label3.DataBind()
        Label4.DataBind()
        Label5.DataBind()
        Label6.DataBind()
        Label7.DataBind()
        Label8.DataBind()
        TextView1.DataBind()

    End Sub
```

We declare a session variable Session ("currID") to pass a reference to the item that has been selected from Form1 to Form2.

The Page_Load sub contains the standard routine to load data into the DataSet and bind to a list control that we have seen previously:

```
Private Sub Page_Load(ByVal sender As System.Object, ByVal e As
➡ System.EventArgs) Handles MyBase.Load
        OleDbDataAdapter1.Fill(DataSet11, "Table1")
        List1.DataBind()
    End Sub
```

The List1_ItemCommand sub is raised in response to clicking one of the list items.

This routine assigns the current value of the DataValueField (ID number of the contact) to the session variable (currID) and opens Form2.

```
Private Sub List1_ItemCommand(ByVal sender As System.Object, ByVal e As
➡ System.Web.UI.MobileControls.ListCommandEventArgs) Handles
➡ List1.ItemCommand

        Session("currID") = e.ListItem.Value
        ActiveForm = Form2
End Sub
```

When Form2 activates, it calls the parameterized query that we set up using the value of currID as its argument. This returns the full row of information attached to that particular ID. We then empty any existing content out of DataSet21 and fill it with the new data.

```
OleDbDataAdapter2.SelectCommand.Parameters("Id").Value =
➥ Session("currID")
        DataSet21.Clear()
        OleDbDataAdapter2.Fill(DataSet21, "Table1")
```

The next line joins the contents of the Name and Surname fields into a single string and assigns it to Label2's Text property:

```
Label2.Text = String.Format("{0} {1}",
➥ DataSet21.Table1.Rows(0).Item("Name"),
➥ DataSet21.Table1.Rows(0).Item("Surname"))
```

Specifically, the DataSet21.Table1.Rows(0).Item("Name") statement reads the Name value from the DataSet at the specified row (which in this case is row(0) because we have only retrieved the one row).

We finish by databinding the set of Label and TextView controls:

```
Label3.DataBind()
        Label4.DataBind()
        Label5.DataBind()
        Label6.DataBind()
        Label7.DataBind()
        Label8.DataBind()
        TextView1.DataBind()
```

As mentioned earlier, we could also have accessed the information by looping through DataSet1 to find the appropriate record. The code for this approach is demonstrated in Listing 10.2. I have also taken the liberty here to illustrate a couple of other approaches to locating data within a DataSet. Replace the Form2_Activate sub in the code behind with the following listing.

---

**Listing 10.2**     **Alternative Ways to Read Data into the MyContacts Application**

```
Private Sub Form2_Activate(ByVal sender As System.Object, ByVal e As
➥ System.EventArgs) Handles Form2.Activate
        Dim n As Int32

        For n = 0 To (DataSet11.Table1.Rows.Count - 1)
            If DataSet11.Table1.Rows(n).Item("Id") =
➥ Session("currID")Then
                Label2.Text = String.Format("{0} {1}",
➥ DataSet11.Table1.Rows(n).Item("Name"),
➥ DataSet11.Table1.Rows(n).Item("Surname"))
                Label3.Text = DataSet11.Table1.Rows(n).Item("Address")
                Label6.Text =
➥ DataSet11.Table1.Rows(n).Item("Telephone")
                Label7.Text = DataSet11.Table1.Rows(n).Item("Mobile")
                Label8.Text = DataSet11.Table1.Rows(n).Item("Email")
```

```
            TextView1.Text =
➡ DataSet11.Table1.Rows(n).Item("Comments")
            Exit For
        End If
    Next

    Label4.Text =
➡ DataSet11.Table1.Rows.Find(Session("currID")).Item("City")

    Label5.Text =
➡ DataSet11.Table1.FindById(Session("currID")).Zip()


End Sub
```

The first part of the code is a straightforward For-Next loop that loops through the DataSet until it locates a record with an ID that matches the one specified in currID. We use `DataSet11.Table1Rows.Count` to determine the number of records present. We could set an exception handler here, if we wished, to pick up if the record count was zero.

You will notice that I haven't included Labels4 and 5 in the loop but used a different approach to assign their values from the DataSet. For Label4, I have used the Find function and for Label5, I have used FindBy(PrimaryKey), which in this case is FindById.

```
Label4.Text =
➡ DataSet11.Table1.Rows.Find(Session("currID")).Item("City")

Label5.Text = DataSet11.Table1.FindById(Session("currID")).Zip()
```

To make this code work, you don't need databinding properties set for the Form2 controls.

**TIP**   ADO.NET is feature rich, a euphemism for "if you need it, it's probably there; you just have to find it." It's a bit like the Microsoft Office of data access. If you use the code-behind area for your ADO.NET coding rather than the HTML View of your ASPX page, you gain the advantage of the Intellisense and Autocomplete functionalities.

Yet another way of accessing data from the DataSet is to use a `DataView` object. This is sort of a snapshot of the current state of the DataSet.

## Using a *DataView* Object to Access Data from a DataSet

To use a `DataView` object to access data, open the project in Design View, and drag a `DataView` object to your Form2 - DataView1. In the property box, set its `Table` property to `DataSet11` `.Table1`.

Databind all the controls on the form to their respective fields in DataView1 in the Data-Bindings dialog box. For example, Label3 should end up with the following expression in the dialog box (see Figure 10.5):

```
DataBinder.Eval(DataView1, "[0].Address", "{0}")
```

**FIGURE 10.5:**

Databinding settings for Label3 when using the DataView object

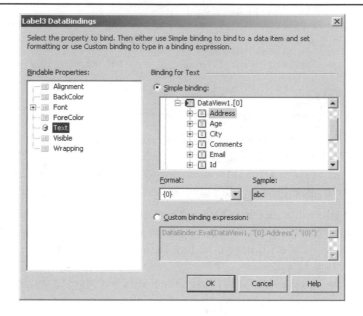

Switch to the Code Behind View and replace the Form2_Activate sub with the code as shown in Listing 10.3.

**Listing 10.3     Code Behind for the DataView Version of the MyContacts Project**

```
Private Sub Form2_Activate(ByVal sender As System.Object, ByVal e As
➡ System.EventArgs) Handles Form2.Activate
        DataView1.RowFilter = "id=" & Session("currID")

        Label2.DataBind()
        Label3.DataBind()
        Label4.DataBind()
        Label5.DataBind()
        Label6.DataBind()
        Label7.DataBind()
        Label8.DataBind()
        TextView1.DataBind()

    End Sub
```

The chief line to do all the work here is

```
DataView1.RowFilter = "id=" & Session("currID")
```

This filters our DataView to the desired row and then we just databind it to all our controls. Notice that in this example, I haven't used the string concatenation for the name and surname for Label2. We can illustrate a slightly different approach here, using the Data-Bindings dialog box back in Design View.

Open the dialog box for Label2 and select Custom Binding Expression. Add the following line to the window:

```
String.Format ("{0} {1}", DataBinder.Eval(DataView1, "[0].Name"),
➡ DataBinder.Eval(DataView1, "[0].Surname"))
```

The dialog box should now appear as in Figure 10.6.

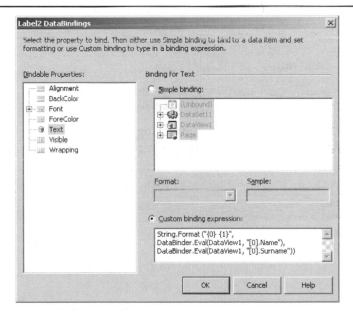

**FIGURE 10.6:**

DataBindings dialog box for Label2 with custom binding expression

If you look at this control in the HTML View of the ASPX page, you will see that this has overloaded the databinding event of the Text property of the control with our custom string.

We can use a similar approach to create customized entries for our list controls as demonstrated in the next section.

## Customizing the Displayed Text in a List Control

We can combine the contents of two or more fields from the database and present the results in a List control by overriding the `ItemDataBind` event of the control and setting its `Text` property to the desired outcome. We need to include the following code in our ASPX file (Listing 10.4):

---

**Listing 10.4**      **Code to Override the *ItemDataBind* Event of the List Control**

```vb
<script language="vb" runat="server">
protected sub List_bind(Sender as object, e as ListDataBindEventArgs)
    e.ListItem.Text = String.Format ("{0} {1}",
➥ DataBinder.Eval(e.DataItem, "Name"),  DataBinder.Eval(e.DataItem,
➥ "Surname"))
end sub
</script>
```

---

We also need to include `OnItemDataBind="List_bind"` in the `<mobile:List>` tag:

```
<mobile:List id="List1" runat="server"
➥ DataValueField="Id" DataTextField="Name" DataMember="Table1"
➥ DataSource="<%# DataSet11 %>"
➥ OnItemDataBind="List_bind"></mobile:List>
```

I have included the full code listing for the ASPX page in Listing 10.5. The desired output is demonstrated using the Openwave browser in Figure 10.7.

---

**FIGURE 10.7:**

MyContacts displayed in the Openwave browser using a customized `Text` property in the List control

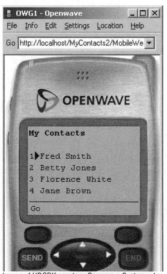

Image of UP.SDK courtesy Openwave Systems, Inc.

**Listing 10.5**      **Full ASPX Page Code for MyContacts with a Customized List Control**

```
<%@ Page Language="vb" AutoEventWireup="true"
➥ Codebehind="MobileWebForm1.aspx.vb"
➥ Inherits="MyContacts.MobileWebForm1" trace="False"%>
<%@ Register TagPrefix="mobile"
➥ Namespace="System.Web.UI.MobileControls"
➥ Assembly="System.Web.Mobile, Version=1.0.3300.0, Culture=neutral,
➥ PublicKeyToken=b03f5f7f11d50a3a" %>
<meta content="Microsoft Visual Studio.NET 7.0" name="GENERATOR">
<meta content="Visual Basic 7.0" name="CODE_LANGUAGE">
<meta content="http://schemas.microsoft.com/Mobile/Page"
➥ name="vs_targetSchema">

<script language="vb" runat="server">
protected sub List_bind(Sender as object, e as ListDataBindEventArgs)
   e.ListItem.Text = String.Format ("{0} {1}",
➥ DataBinder.Eval(e.DataItem, "Name"), DataBinder.Eval(e.DataItem,
➥ "Surname"))
end sub
</script>
<body Xmlns:mobile="http://schemas.microsoft.com/Mobile/WebForm">
   <mobile:form id="Form1" title="My Contacts" runat="server"
➥ PagerStyle-PreviousPageText="Return to Page {0}"
➥ PagerStyle-NextPageText="Go to Page {0}" Paginate="True">
      <mobile:Label id="Label1" runat="server"
➥ StyleReference="title">My Contacts</mobile:Label>
         <mobile:List id="List1" runat="server"
➥ DataValueField="Id"
➥ DataTextField="Name" DataMember="Table1" DataSource="<%# DataSet11
➥ %>" OnItemDataBind="List_bind"></mobile:List>
   </mobile:form>
   <mobile:form id="Form2" title="My Contacts - Details"
➥ runat="server">
      <P>
<mobile:Label id="Label2" runat="server" StyleReference="title"
➥ Text='<%# String.Format ("{0} {1}", DataBinder.Eval(DataView1,
➥ "[0].Name"), DataBinder.Eval(DataView1, "[0].Surname"))
➥ %>'></mobile:Label>
<mobile:Label id="Label3" runat="server"
➥ Text='<%# DataBinder.Eval(DataView1, "[0].Address", "{0}") %>'
➥ Font-Size="Small"></mobile:Label>
<mobile:Label id="Label4" runat="server"
➥ Text='<%# DataBinder.Eval(DataView1, "[0].City", "{0}") %>'
➥ Font-Size="Small"></mobile:Label>
<mobile:Label id="Label5" runat="server"
➥ Text='<%# DataBinder.Eval(DataView1, "[0].Zip", "{0}") %>'
➥ Font-Size="Small"></mobile:Label>Phone:
<mobile:Label id="Label6" runat="server"
➥ Text='<%# DataBinder.Eval(DataView1, "[0].Telephone", "{0}") %>'
```

```
➥ Font-Size="Small"></mobile:Label>Mobile:
<mobile:Label id="Label7" runat="server"
➥ Text='<%# DataBinder.Eval(DataView1, "[0].Mobile", "{0}") %>'
➥ Font-Size="Small"></mobile:Label>Email:
<mobile:Label id="Label8" runat="server"
➥ Text='<%# DataBinder.Eval(DataView1, "[0].Email", "{0}") %>'
➥ Font-Size="Small"></mobile:Label>Comments:
<mobile:TextView id="TextView1" runat="server"
➥ Text='<%# DataBinder.Eval(DataView1, "[0].Comments", "{0}") %>'
➥ Font-Size="Small"></mobile:TextView></P>
   </mobile:form>
</body>
```

## Using the DataReader to Access Data

The DataSet object is a powerful tool to access information in our databases, and we have
only scratched the surface of its capabilities so far. It is useful when we want to carry out
complex operations such as work with multiple tables and their various relationships. However, in a lot of cases all we wish to do is access a simple list of data (as we basically have in
these examples). For simple, direct database access, Microsoft has provided another tool, the
DataReader. The DataReader acts as a fast, read-only cursor and is ideal for reading the contents of either a single record or a series of records.

To set up a simple example of the DataReader, create a new Mobile application and name it
MyContactsDR.

Drag a List and OleDbDataAdapter control to Form1. Use the Wizard to set the
OleDbDataAdapter1 to connect to the Mobiledb1 database and the SQL statement to
retrieve the content of all fields. *Do not create a DataSet.*

Whenever we create these adapters, you will probably notice that several additional SQL
statements are also generated. These include SELECT, INSERT, UPDATE, and DELETE. They can
be previewed in the Code Behind View if you expand the Web Forms Designer Generated
Code tab. These statements are autogenerated for the purpose of updating the original datasource from a modified DataSet. However, more on this later. In this case, we will borrow
the SELECT statement for use with our DataReader.

Switch to the Code Behind View and enter the contents of Listing 10.6 into the Page_
Load sub.

---

**Listing 10.6      Using a DataReader to Access and Display Data in MyContactsDR**

```
Private Sub Page_Load(ByVal sender As System.Object, ByVal e As
➥ System.EventArgs) Handles MyBase.Load

    OleDbConnection1.Open()
```

```
        Dim dbRead As OleDb.OleDbDataReader
        dbRead = OleDbSelectCommand1.ExecuteReader
        While dbRead.Read()
            List1.Items.Add(dbRead.Item("Name"))
        End While
        OleDbConnection1.Close()
    End Sub
```

OleConnection1 is one of the objects created when we generated OleDbDataAdapter1 and contains the connection string to our database. OleDbConnection1.Open() establishes the connection to our database. We use Dim dbRead As OleDb.OleDbDataReader to create our instance of the DataReader and we use the SELECT statement generated when we created the OleDbDataAdapter1 (OleDbSelectCommand1) to access the records in our database. The While loop loads the contents of the Name field into the List. We close the connection to finish.

We could also have created a specific SELECT statement for this operation by either using the graphical OleDbCommand object from the Data Tools menu or writing the code ourselves in either Code Behind or HTML View.

To use the OleDbCommand object, drag a copy to Form1; an instance should now be listed with the other data objects as OleDbCommand1. In the Properties box, set the Connection property to OleDbConnection1 and select the ellipsis in the CommandText property. This opens the Query Builder, which you can use to generate the following query:

```
SELECT Name FROM Table1
```

Alter the dbRead expression in Listing 10.6 to read as follows:

```
dbRead = OleDbCommand1.ExecuteReader
```

Compile and run the program.

To write your own SQL statement in the code, refer to Listing 10.7.

---

**Listing 10.7**    **DataReader Example with the Custom *Command* Object Declared Programatically**

```
Private Sub Page_Load(ByVal sender As System.Object, ByVal e As
➥ System.EventArgs) Handles MyBase.Load

        Dim MyOleDbCommand As OleDb.OleDbCommand
        MyOleDbCommand = New OleDb.OleDbCommand()
        MyOleDbCommand.Commandtext = "SELECT Name FROM
➥ Table1"
        MyOleDbCommand.Connection = OleDbConnection1

    OleDbConnection1.Open()
        Dim dbRead As OleDb.OleDbDataReader
        dbRead = MyOleDbCommand.ExecuteReader
```

```
        While dbRead.Read()
            List1.Items.Add(dbRead.Item("Name"))
        End While
        OleDbConnection1.Close()
    End Sub
```

In this example we use `Dim MyOleDbCommand As OleDb.OleDbCommand` to declare `MyOle-DbCommand` and then initialize it with `MyOleDbCommand = New OleDb.OleDbCommand()`. We set the `SELECT` statement with `MyOleDbCommand.Commandtext = "SELECT Name FROM Table1"`. We attach it to a data connection with `MyOleDbCommand.Connection = OleDb-Connection1`. It is then used in our dbRead expression with `dbRead = MyOleDbCommand.ExecuteReader`.

## Summary of Data Access

As we can see, Microsoft has provided a regular smorgasbord of possibilities when it comes to accessing our data. (And we haven't even touched on the SQL Server database tools!) Choosing which way to go will in many cases come down to what you, the developer, are most comfortable with. However, issues such as performance do matter when you are deciding. Ultimately it depends on the nature of the project and the answer to the question, "If I go this way, what are the advantages and tradeoffs?"

# Modifying Data

The automatically generated `SELECT`, `UPDATE`, `INSERT`, and `DELETE` commands are created specifically for use when updating the database based on changes in the DataSet. However, their application scope is limited; they can be used only where the DataTable is generated from, or maps to, a single database table. The commands are generated when the `SELECT` statement is created when configuring the `DataAdapter` object. In addition, the table must contain a primary key for the commands to be created.

We normally access these commands via the DataAdapter's `Update` method. When we call the `Update` method, it checks the DataSet for any modifications such as inserts, deletes, or updates (edits). It then calls the appropriate `INSERT`, `DELETE`, and/or `UPDATE` commands to push the changes onto the datasource. If several changes have been implemented on the DataSet, they are carried out in the same sequential order of rows as returned by the initial `UPDATE` statement (which is not the same as the order in which they have been implemented). This can sometimes cause data conflicts and it is worth considering how users are likely to use your application, where the conflicts may occur, and what can be done to avoid them.

Depending on how we have set up our data access and how we choose to carry it out, there are several possibilities for how we might modify our data at the source. In our original MyContacts application, we used a DataSet that essentially provides us with a memory resident copy of our database that has been disconnected from the original.

In this situation we can either

- Modify data in the DataSet and then use the changes in the DataSet to update the datasource.

- Modify data directly at the datasource and then update the DataSet.

Because one advantage of using a DataSet is that we can carry out a range of data manipulations and then update them in the datasource all at once (providing performance advantages especially in distributed applications), the first option is the one we are more likely to use. However, in some situations it may be desirable to use a DataSet for certain of its features but not for updating the datasource. In these instances, we would use the second option.

Our database may also perform some direct data manipulation, such as autoenter on ID numbers or setting default values, so whichever approach we use, we should still refresh our DataSet after the datasource has been updated.

Where we do not use a DataSet (such as in MyContactsDR), we are still able to update and manipulate data directly at the datasource.

In the following sections we will work both with the MyContacts application to add, modify, and delete records via the DataSet and with the MyContactsDR project to directly manipulate the datasource. I have used SQL commands in these examples but you can also set up and use stored procedures.

## Adding a Record via a DataSet

There are two steps to adding a record. First, we add a record (row) to the DataSet and then we use the Update method of the DataAdapter to update the datasource (database). Adding a record to a DataSet consists of creating a new DataTable row, adding content to each of the columns (fields) in the row, and then adding the row to the DataTable.

### Setting Up MyContacts

We will require a third Form control in MyContacts to provide us with a data entry screen for creating new contacts. Open the MyContacts project and add a new Form to the Mobile Web Page. Drag a Label control, nine TextBox controls, and a Command control to Form3. By typing directly on the form, give a title to each TextBox matching one of the fields in the database. Delete the contents of the Text property for the Label control. Set the Text property on the Command control to "Create New Contact". See Figure 10.8 for the suggested layout.

Layout for Form3 of the MyContacts project

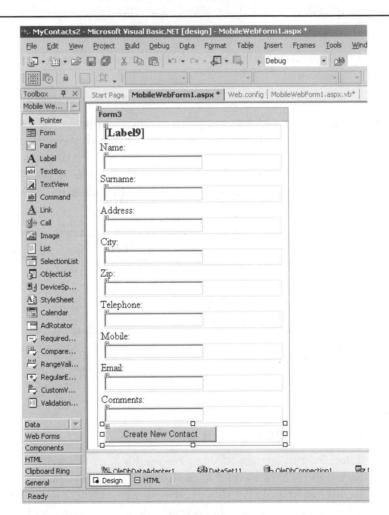

Add a Command control to Form1 and set its Text property to New Contact.

Double-click the Command control on Form1 (Command2) to open the Code Behind View and enter the following code from Listing 10.8.

Listing 10.8 **Code for the Command2 Control on Form1 in the MyContacts Project**

```
Private Sub Command2_Click(ByVal sender As System.Object, ByVal e As
➡ System.EventArgs) Handles Command2.Click
        ActiveForm = Form3
        Label9.Text = "Enter Details:"
End Sub
```

## Code for Inserting a New Record

We will attach the code for adding the new record to the Command1 control. Copy the code from Listing 10.9 to your code behind.

Listing 10.9 **Insert Record Code for the Command1 Control in the MyContacts Project**

```
Private Sub Command1_Click(ByVal sender As System.Object, ByVal e As
➡ System.EventArgs) Handles Command1.Click

    Dim myContact As DataRow
        myContact = DataSet11.Tables("Table1").NewRow

        myContact("Name") = TextBox1.Text
        myContact("Surname") = TextBox2.Text
        myContact("Address") = TextBox3.Text
        myContact("City") = TextBox4.Text
        myContact("Zip") = TextBox5.Text
        myContact("Telephone") = TextBox6.Text
        myContact("Mobile") = TextBox7.Text
        myContact("Email") = TextBox8.Text
        myContact("Comments") = TextBox9.Text

        DataSet11.Tables("Table1").Rows.Add(myContact)

        OleDbDataAdapter1.Update(DataSet11, "Table1")

        ActiveForm = Form1

    End Sub
```

Although we still have a bit to do before this will actually work properly in our project, this segment of code will create a new record in DataSet11's Table1, based on whatever information we have entered in our TextBoxes, and it will return us to Form1.

Essentially, the lines

```
Dim myContact As DataRow
    myContact = DataSet11.Tables("Table1").NewRow
```

declare and initialize our new datarow. The following lines

```
myContact("Name") = TextBox1.Text
        myContact("Surname") = TextBox2.Text
```

drop our data entry from the TextBoxes into the respective field in the row, and

```
DataSet11.Tables("Table1").Rows.Add(myContact)
```

adds the completed row to Table1.

---

**NOTE**    We can either use the syntax DataSet11.Tables("Table1").etc or DataSet11.Table1 .etc to access Table1 in our DataSet.

However, returning to Form1 will not yet display our new entry in the List. We can fix this by moving the List1.DataBind() instruction from the Page_Load event to the Form1_Activate event. For example,

```
Private Sub Form1_Activate(ByVal sender As System.Object, ByVal e As
➡ System.EventArgs) Handles Form1.Activate

        List1.DataBind()

End Sub
```

This should create a new link in List1 to the new contact. We still need to give the record an ID number and update the original database. We give the record an ID number by writing some code to increment the Id field, and we update the original database by using the Update method of the DataAdapter. There are a couple ways to increment the Id field, but first we'll look at calling the Update method.

Calling the Update method is performed by the line

```
OleDbDataAdapter1.Update(DataSet1, "Table1")
```

from Listing 10.9. This statement calls the Update method of the OleDbDataAdapter1, which in turn will invoke the UPDATE command created when we first set up the DataAdapter.

To increment the Id field, we can place the following line of code into an appropriate part of our Command1_Click sub, somewhere before we call the Add method for the new row:

```
MyContact("Id") = DataSet11.Tables("Table1").Rows.Count + 1
```

Our other alternative is to use the table columns' AutoIncrement property. Normally we would need to decide carefully how to handle all of this because multiple users, all generating new records in detached DataSets, could easily end up with conflicting primary keys. In this example, which is essentially for a single user, this is not likely to be an issue.

To use the AutoIncrement property, we need to add the following code to the Page_Load event (see Listing 10.10).

---

**Listing 10.10**    **Using the *AutoIncrement* Property to Generate ID Values**

```
Private Sub Page_Load(ByVal sender As System.Object, ByVal e As
➡ System.EventArgs) Handles MyBase.Load
        OleDbDataAdapter1.Fill(DataSet11, "Table1")

        Dim numRows As Integer
        NumRows = DataSet11.Tables("Table1").Rows.Count - 1
        DataSet11.Tables("Table1").Columns("Id").AutoIncrement = True
        DataSet11.Tables("Table1").Columns("Id").AutoIncrementSeed =
➡ (DataSet11.Tables("Table1").Rows(numRows).Item("Id")) + 1
        DataSet11.Tables("Table1").Columns("Id").AutoIncrementStep = 1

End Sub
```

---

Initially, we find out how many rows we have and assign the value to the numRows variable. Then we set the AutoIncrement property of the Id column to True. We then give it a starting value equivalent to the ID value of the last row incremented by 1. Next, we set the ID value to increase by 1 at each increment.

Finally, we need to add some Home navigation links to Forms2 and 3 and tidy up the consequences of not having added an entry into one of the TextBox fields. Add Command controls to the bottom of both Form2 and Form3. Set their Text and SoftKeyLabel properties to Home. Enter code behind and add the following line of code to the click events of both controls:

```
ActiveForm = Form1
```

The default for Access databases is not to accept zero-length data entries. We can get around this by opening the database table in Design View and setting the Allow Zero Length property of each field to Yes. (The property box is underneath the table of fields in Design View.) Or we can programmatically set a default of white space in each field from VS .NET. To do this, set the following code in the Form3_Activate sub (see Listing 10.11).

---

**Listing 10.11**    **Setting Field Defaults for the MyContacts Project**

```
Private Sub Form3_Activate(ByVal sender As System.Object, ByVal e As
➡ System.EventArgs) Handles Form3.Activate

        TextBox1.Text = " "
        TextBox2.Text = " "
        TextBox3.Text = " "
        TextBox4.Text = " "
        TextBox5.Text = " "
        TextBox6.Text = " "
        TextBox7.Text = " "
```

```
        TextBox8.Text = " "
        TextBox9.Text = " "

    End Sub
```

## Adding a Record Directly

We can also add a record directly to a database when it is not appropriate to use a DataSet. For our example, we will use the MyContactsDR project.

At this stage we will also make a few cosmetic and functional changes to MyContactsDR to take some of the rough edges off the project. Start by adding a second form to the Mobile Web Page. Next, add a label and Command control to Form1. Then add a Label, two TextBoxes, and two Command controls to Form2. Type the following directly onto the form, above the two TextBoxes: **Enter Name** and **Enter Surname**. (Refer to Figure 10.9.)

**FIGURE 10.9:**

Layout for revised
MyContactsDR

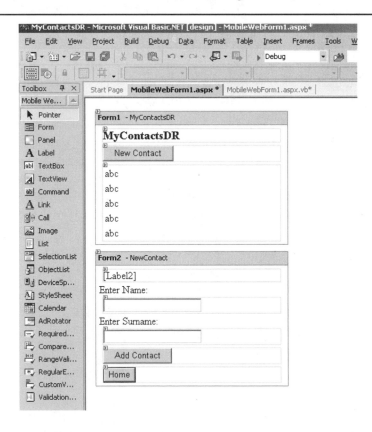

Set the control properties as listed in Table 10.4.

**TABLE 10.4:** Property Settings for MyContactsDR

| Control | Property | Value |
| --- | --- | --- |
| Form1 | Paginate | True |
| | PagerStyle | |
| | NextPageText | Next Page |
| | PreviousPageText | Previous |
| | Title | MyContactsDR |
| Label1 | StyleReference | Title |
| | Text | MyContactsDR |
| Command1 | Text | NewContact |
| | SoftKeyLabel | NewContact |
| List1 | | |
| Form2 | Title | NewContact |
| Label2 | Text | <empty> |
| TextBox1 | | |
| TextBox2 | | |
| Command2 | Text | Add Contact |
| | SoftKeyLabel | Add Contact |
| Command3 | Text | Home |
| | SoftKeyLabel | Home |

To finish setting up the project, enter the code behind and cut and paste the code from Page_Load into Form1_Activate. This will enable the List to be updated with any new entries that we generate. We also need to add the following line:

    List1.Items.Clear()

to the beginning of the Form1_Activate code. Listing 10.12 provides the code we will need for this part of the project.

**Listing 10.12** **Code for MyContactsDR with New Record Capability**

```
Private Sub Command1_Click(ByVal sender As System.Object, ByVal e
 As System.EventArgs) Handles Command1.Click
    ActiveForm = Form2
    Label2.Text = "New Contact"
    Label2.StyleReference = "title"
End Sub
```

```
    Private Sub Command2_Click(ByVal sender As System.Object, ByVal e
➥ As System.EventArgs) Handles Command2.Click
        Dim MyOleDbInsertCommand As OleDb.OleDbCommand
        MyOleDbInsertCommand = New OleDb.OleDbCommand()
        MyOleDbInsertCommand.CommandText = "INSERT INTO Table1
➥(Name, Surname) VALUES (?, ?)"
        MyOleDbInsertCommand.Connection = OleDbConnection1
        MyOleDbInsertCommand.Parameters.Add
➥(New OleDb.OleDbParameter("Name", OleDb.OleDbType.Char, 50))
        MyOleDbInsertCommand.Parameters.Add
➥(New OleDb.OleDbParameter("Surname", OleDb.OleDbType.Char, 50))
        MyOleDbInsertCommand.Parameters.Item("Name").Value =
➥ TextBox1.Text
        MyOleDbInsertCommand.Parameters.Item("Surname").Value =
➥ TextBox2.Text
        OleDbConnection1.Open()
        MyOleDbInsertCommand.ExecuteNonQuery()
        OleDbConnection1.Close()
        ActiveForm = Form1
    End Sub

    Private Sub Form1_Activate(ByVal sender As System.Object, ByVal e
➥ As System.EventArgs) Handles Form1.Activate
        List1.Items.Clear()
        Dim MyOleDbCommand As OleDb.OleDbCommand
        MyOleDbCommand = New OleDb.OleDbCommand()
        MyOleDbCommand.CommandText = "SELECT Name FROM Table1"
        MyOleDbCommand.Connection = OleDbConnection1
        OleDbConnection1.Open()
        Dim dbRead As OleDb.OleDbDataReader
        dbRead = MyOleDbCommand.ExecuteReader
        While dbRead.Read()
            List1.Items.Add(dbRead.Item("Name"))
        End While
        OleDbConnection1.Close()
    End Sub

    Private Sub Command3_Click(ByVal sender As System.Object, ByVal e
➥ As System.EventArgs) Handles Command3.Click
        ActiveForm = Form1
    End Sub
```

Form1_Activate now holds the code formerly in Page_Load, and Command3_Click navigates the user back to Form1. Command1_Click navigates the user to Form2 and sets the Text property of the heading label in Form2 to something appropriate. Command2_Click handles the real work of creating the new record.

Initially, we set up our MyOleDbInsertCommand for creating a new database record:

```
Dim MyOleDbInsertCommand As OleDb.OleDbCommand
MyOleDbInsertCommand = New OleDb.OleDbCommand()
```

The next line sets up the SQL statement to carry out the task of creating the new record. We then link the command to a connection:

```
MyOleDbInsertCommand.CommandText = "INSERT INTO Table1(Name, Surname) VALUES
➥(?, ?)"
MyOleDbInsertCommand.Connection = OleDbConnection1
```

Here, we have declared the parameters that we will use in our INSERT statement. At this point, developers experienced with SQL and unfamiliar with ADO.NET are probably starting to have slight heart palpitations and are demanding to know "What is this 'parameter' hogwash!?" We could have used a simple, traditional INSERT-style SQL statement if we had wished, and we will later as an example.

```
        MyOleDbInsertCommand.Parameters.Add
➥(New OleDb.OleDbParameter("Name", OleDb.OleDbType.Char, 50))
        MyOleDbInsertCommand.Parameters.Add
➥(New OleDb.OleDbParameter("Surname", OleDb.OleDbType.Char, 50))
```

The answer to this question is, "This is how we do it in ADO.NET." By setting our parameters externally to the SQL statement, we can use the assembled features of the technology to do things such as update our datasource via a DataSet, or choose from a whole range of other management options. In the next two lines we assign the relevant values (content of the two TextBoxes) to the parameters:

```
        MyOleDbInsertCommand.Parameters.Item("Name").Value =
➥ TextBox1.Text
        MyOleDbInsertCommand.Parameters.Item("Surname").Value =
➥ TextBox2.Text
```

Next we open our connection, execute the query, close the connection, and return to Form1:

```
        OleDbConnection1.Open()
        MyOleDbInsertCommand.ExecuteNonQuery()
        OleDbConnection1.Close()
        ActiveForm = Form1
```

When we execute the query, we have a couple of choices. While ExecuteNonQuery does the deed and returns the number of rows affected, we could also have chosen to use ExecuteScalar, which returns the first column of the first row in the result set of the query.

We might also have used a traditional SQL INSERT-style statement as follows:

```
MyOleDbInsertCommand.CommandText = "INSERT INTO Table1(Name, Surname)
➥ VALUES ( '" & TextBox1.Text & "', '" & TextBox2.Text & "' )"
```

The Command2_Click code amended for this type of statement is demonstrated in Listing 10.13.

---

**Listing 10.13**      *Command2_Click* **Code with a Traditional SQL Statement**

```
Private Sub Command2_Click(ByVal sender As System.Object, ByVal e As
➥ System.EventArgs) Handles Command2.Click
        Dim MyOleDbInsertCommand As OleDb.OleDbCommand
        MyOleDbInsertCommand = New OleDb.OleDbCommand()
        MyOleDbInsertCommand.CommandText = "INSERT INTO Table1
➥(Name, Surname) VALUES ( '" & TextBox1.Text & "', '" & TextBox2.Text
➥ & "' )"
        MyOleDbInsertCommand.Connection = OleDbConnection1
        OleDbConnection1.Open()
        MyOleDbInsertCommand.ExecuteNonQuery()
        OleDbConnection1.Close()
        ActiveForm = Form1
    End Sub
```

---

Note that this record insertion code will only work if we have set the ID field in Access to AutoNumber (which automatically increments for each new record).

## Deleting a Record via a DataSet

The process of both deleting and updating records when using DataSets is very similar to that of adding a record. Because we have already covered the basics, we can move through fairly quickly.

### Setting Up MyContacts for Record Deletion

Open the MyContacts project in Design View. Add a Command control to the bottom of Form2 (the Details form), and set its Text property to Delete Contact and its SoftKeyLabel property to Delete. Refer to Figure 10.10.

**FIGURE 10.10:**

Layout for Form2 with
the `Delete` command

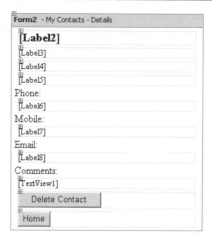

Create a fourth form on the ASPX page; this will become our delete confirmation form.
Place three Label and two Command controls on the form as shown in Figure 10.11.

**FIGURE 10.11:**

Layout for Form4 in
MyContacts

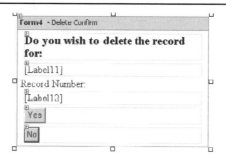

Note that I have typed Record Number: directly onto the form between Labels11 and 12.
Set the properties on the new form as shown in Table 10.5.

**TABLE 10.5:** Property Settings for Delete Confirmation in MyContacts

| Control | Property | Value |
| --- | --- | --- |
| Form2 | | |
| Command5 | Text | Delete Contact |
| | SoftKeyLabel | Delete |
| Form4 | Title | Delete Confirm |
| Label10 | StyleReference | Title |
| | Text | Do you wish to delete the record for: |
| Label11 | Text | <empty> |

*Continued on next page*

**TABLE 10.5 CONTINUED:** Property Settings for Delete Confirmation in MyContacts

| Control | Property | Value |
| --- | --- | --- |
| Label12 | Text | <empty> |
| Command6 | Text | Yes |
| | SoftKeyLabel | Yes |
| Command7 | Text | No |
| | SoftKeyLabel | No |

Command7 returns the user to Form1 if they decide not to delete the record. Set Command7_Click as follows:

```
ActiveForm = Form1
```

Command5 takes the user to the delete confirmation form and copies the name/surname of the record into Label11. Write the following code for the Command5_Click sub:

```
ActiveForm = Form4
Label11.Text = Label2.Text
Label12.Text = Session("currID")
```

## Setting Up the *Delete* Command

Switch to Code Behind View for MyContacts. Listing 10.14 gives the code to actually delete the record. It is attached to the Command6 control (the Yes link/button).

**Listing 10.14    Delete Code for MyContacts**

```
Private Sub Command6_Click(ByVal sender As System.Object, ByVal e As
➥ System.EventArgs) Handles Command6.Click

    DataSet11.Tables("Table1").Rows.Find(Label12.Text).Delete()
    OleDbDataAdapter1.Update(DataSet11, "Table1")

    ActiveForm = Form1

End Sub
```

The line

```
DataSet11.Tables("Table1").Rows.Find(Label12.Text).Delete()
```

performs a find on Table1 in the DataSet based on the primary key of the record to be deleted, as obtained from the Label12.Text property. It then deletes this row. The next line, OleDbDataAdapter1.Update(DataSet11, "Table1"), calls the DataAdapter Update method and updates the original datasource with the changes from the DataSet (as we did in the Create New Record example).

## Deleting a Record Directly

To delete a record directly, we set up our SQL DELETE statement in MyContactsDR as shown in the upcoming sections. In the interest of brevity, I have kept this example as simple as possible. As with the rest of this project, we will target and delete our contact on first-name basis only and not bother with any confirmation messages.

### Setting Up MyContactsDR for Deleting a Record

Open MyContactsDR in Design View. Add a Command control to Form1 and set its Text property to Delete Record and its SoftKeyLabel to Delete.

Create a third form; place a Label, Command, and List control on it. Set their properties as follows in Table 10.6.

**TABLE 10.6:**  Property Settings for Form3 in MyContactsDR

| Control | Property | Value |
| --- | --- | --- |
| Form3 | Title | Delete Contact |
| Label3 | StyleReference | title |
|  | Text | Click Contact to Delete: |
| Command5 | Text | Home |
|  | SoftKeyLabel | Home |
| List2 | No property changes | |

The form should appear as shown in Figure 10.12.

**FIGURE 10.12:**
Layout for Form3 in
MyContactsDR

The user selects Command4 (Delete Record) to navigate to Form4. The Command4_Click event invokes code we have previously discussed to populate List2 with the set of names. (See Listing 10.15.)

**Listing 10.15        Code for *Command4_Click* in the MyContactsDR Project**

```
Private Sub Command4_Click(ByVal sender As System.Object, ByVal e
➥ As System.EventArgs) Handles Command4.Click
        ActiveForm = Form3
        List2.Items.Clear()
        Dim MyOleDbCommand2 As OleDb.OleDbCommand
        MyOleDbCommand2 = New OleDb.OleDbCommand()
        MyOleDbCommand2.CommandText = "SELECT Name FROM Table1"
        MyOleDbCommand2.Connection = OleDbConnection1
        OleDbConnection1.Open()
        Dim dbRead As OleDb.OleDbDataReader
        dbRead = MyOleDbCommand2.ExecuteReader
        While dbRead.Read()
            List2.Items.Add(dbRead.Item("Name"))
        End While
        OleDbConnection1.Close()
    End Sub
```

Selecting an item in List2 identifies and deletes the record we have clicked in the List. This is handled by List2_ItemCommand.

The code for List2_ItemCommand is given in Listing 10.16.

**Listing 10.16        Code for Record Deletion in MyContactsDR**

```
Private Sub List2_ItemCommand(ByVal sender As System.Object, ByVal e
➥ As System.Web.UI.MobileControls.ListCommandEventArgs) Handles
➥ List2.ItemCommand

        Dim MyOleDbDeleteCommand As OleDb.OleDbCommand
        MyOleDbDeleteCommand = New OleDb.OleDbCommand()
        MyOleDbDeleteCommand.CommandText = "DELETE FROM Table1 WHERE
➥ (Name = ?)"
        MyOleDbDeleteCommand.Parameters.Add
➥(New OleDb.OleDbParameter("Name", OleDb.OleDbType.Char, 50))
        MyOleDbDeleteCommand.Parameters.Item("Name").Value =
➥ e.ListItem.Value
        MyOleDbDeleteCommand.Connection = OleDbConnection1
        OleDbConnection1.Open()
        MyOleDbDeleteCommand.ExecuteNonQuery()
        OleDbConnection1.Close()
        ActiveForm = Form1

    End Sub

    Private Sub Command5_Click(ByVal sender As System.Object, ByVal e
➥ As System.EventArgs) Handles Command5.Click
        ActiveForm = Form1
    End Sub
```

The main item of interest here is the DELETE statement:

```
MyOleDbDeleteCommand.CommandText = "DELETE FROM Table1 WHERE
➡ (Name = ?)"
```

Again it uses parameters:

```
MyOleDbDeleteCommand.Parameters.Add(New OleDb.OleDbParameter
➡("Name", OleDb.OleDbType.Char, 50))
MyOleDbDeleteCommand.Parameters.Item("Name").Value = e.ListItem.Value
```

And again, we could have replaced it entirely with a straightforward SQL DELETE statement such as

```
MyOleDbDeleteCommand.CommandText = "DELETE FROM Table1 WHERE
➡ (Name = '" & e.ListItem.Value & "')"
```

We complete the code for this section with some navigation functionality on the Command5 (Home) link.

## Updating a Record via a DataSet

To update a record via a DataSet, we again make changes to the DataSet and then call the Update method, which in turn identifies the changes and invokes the UPDATE statement that was automatically generated. For situations more complex than a single table, we need to create our own UPDATE statements (and all the associated parameter settings) to handle the task.

The process is similar to what we have already experienced using INSERT and DELETE. To update the DataSet, we identify the fields (columns) of the particular row (record) in the relevant table.

For example, to make some changes to the contents of the first record in our DataSet we could use the following line of code:

```
DataSet11.Tables("Table1").Rows(0)("Name")="Franky"
```

where Rows(0) is the first record. This will change the contents of the Name field for the first record from Fred to Franky.

Again, to update our datasource, we would then call the Update method of the DataAdapter as follows:

```
OleDbDataAdapter1.Update(DataSet11, "Table1")
```

The full code listing for MyContacts at the end of this chapter illustrates how an update routine might be implemented for this project.

## Updating a Record Directly

To update a record directly, we again take a similar approach to what we have used previously. We can use a traditional SQL statement. This is illustrated in Listing 10.17.

**Listing 10.17    Directly Updating a Record**

```
Dim MyOleDbUpdateCommand As OleDb.OleDbCommand
        MyOleDbUpdateCommand = New OleDb.OleDbCommand()
        MyOleDbUpdateCommand.CommandText = "UPDATE Table1 SET
➡ Surname = '" & TextBox2.Text & "' WHERE
➡ (Name = '" & TextBox1.Text & "')"
        MyOleDbUpdateCommand.Connection = OleDbConnection1
        OleDbConnection1.Open()
        MyOleDbUpdateCommand.ExecuteNonQuery()
        OleDbConnection1.Close()
```

In this example, we are updating a surname field from the contents of TextBox2 based on the name field from TextBox1. A simple implementation of this is included in the full code listing for MyContactsDR.

## Full Code Listing for MyContacts

Listing 10.18 includes all the code completed in the previous sections as well as an Update module. In this module, we use the TextBoxes originally created as a new record function in Form2 to now serve as data entry fields for the Update role. The form also retains its new record functionality. To enable the update facility to work, you will need to also change the type of the Id field in the Mobiledb1 database from autonumber to number.

Listing 10.18 contains the code from the code behind, and Listing 10.19 contains the ASPX code. Together, they should give you some idea of how everything fits together. Because I have explained most things at length earlier in the chapter, I have only lightly commented this code.

**Listing 10.18    The Full Code from the Code Behind of MyContacts**

```
        'On page load, the DataSet is populated from
        'the DataAdapter and the ID column of the DataSet
        'is set to autoincrement when a new entry is made

Private Sub Page_Load(ByVal sender As System.Object, ByVal e As
➡ System.EventArgs) Handles MyBase.Load
        OleDbDataAdapter1.Fill(DataSet11, "Table1")
```

```
        Dim numRows As Integer
        numRows = DataSet11.Tables("Table1").Rows.Count - 1
        DataSet11.Tables("Table1").Columns("Id").AutoIncrement = True
        DataSet11.Tables("Table1").Columns("Id").AutoIncrementSeed =
➥ (DataSet11.Tables("Table1").Rows(numRows).Item("Id")) + 1
        DataSet11.Tables("Table1").Columns("Id").AutoIncrementStep = 1

    End Sub

    'Selecting a contact in List1 sets the session
➥ variable
    '(currID) to current list item value (ID) and
➥ navigates user
    'to Form2

    Private Sub List1_ItemCommand(ByVal sender As System.Object, ByVal
➥ e As System.Web.UI.MobileControls.ListCommandEventArgs) Handles
➥ List1.ItemCommand

        Session("currID") = e.ListItem.Value
        ActiveForm = Form2
    End Sub

    'Form2 displays details on chosen contact. The
    'chosen record is filtered from the DataView1 and
    'each of the labels are databound to display
    'relevant data

    Private Sub Form2_Activate(ByVal sender As System.Object, ByVal e
➥ As System.EventArgs) Handles Form2.Activate
        DataView1.RowFilter = "id=" & Session("currID")
        Label13.DataBind()
        Label2.DataBind()
        Label3.DataBind()
        Label4.DataBind()
        Label5.DataBind()
        Label6.DataBind()
        Label7.DataBind()
        Label8.DataBind()
        TextView1.DataBind()

    End Sub

    'Command2 navigates to Form3 and sets Label9 text
➥ property

    Private Sub Command2_Click(ByVal sender As System.Object, ByVal e
➥ As System.EventArgs) Handles Command2.Click
        ActiveForm = Form3
        Label9.Text = "Enter Details:"
    End Sub
```

```
'Code in the Form1_Activate event databinds List1 and sets
'Commands1 and 9 to defaults

    Private Sub Form1_Activate(ByVal sender As System.Object, ByVal e
➥ As System.EventArgs) Handles Form1.Activate
        List1.DataBind()
        Command1.Visible = True
        Command9.Visible = False
End Sub

        'On Form3_Activate, whitespace is set in all
➥ TextBoxes

Private Sub Form3_Activate(ByVal sender As System.Object, ByVal e
➥ As System.EventArgs) Handles Form3.Activate
        TextBox1.Text = " "
        TextBox2.Text = " "
        TextBox3.Text = " "
        TextBox4.Text = " "
        TextBox5.Text = " "
        TextBox6.Text = " "
        TextBox7.Text = " "
        TextBox8.Text = " "
        TextBox9.Text = " "

    End Sub

    'Command1 creates a new DataRow in the DataSet table
    'and loads the contents of the textboxes into each of
    'the relevant columns in the row. It then updates
    'the database from the modified DataSet.

    Private Sub Command1_Click(ByVal sender As System.Object, ByVal e
➥ As System.EventArgs) Handles Command1.Click
        Dim myContact As DataRow
        myContact = DataSet11.Tables("Table1").NewRow

        myContact("Name") = TextBox1.Text
        myContact("Surname") = TextBox2.Text
        myContact("Address") = TextBox3.Text
        myContact("City") = TextBox4.Text
        myContact("Zip") = TextBox5.Text
        myContact("Telephone") = TextBox6.Text
        myContact("Mobile") = TextBox7.Text
        myContact("Email") = TextBox8.Text
        myContact("Comments") = TextBox9.Text

        DataSet11.Tables("Table1").Rows.Add(myContact)

        OleDbDataAdapter1.Update(DataSet11, "Table1")
```

```
        ActiveForm = Form1

    End Sub

    'Command3 navigates user back to Form1

    Private Sub Command3_Click(ByVal sender As System.Object, ByVal e
➥ As System.EventArgs) Handles Command3.Click
        ActiveForm = Form1
    End Sub

    'Command4 navigates user back to Form1 and sets
    'Command1 and 9 visible properties back to default

    Private Sub Command4_Click(ByVal sender As System.Object, ByVal e
➥ As System.EventArgs) Handles Command4.Click
        ActiveForm - Form1
        Command1.Visible = True
        Command9.Visible = False
    End Sub

    'Command7 navigates user back to Form1

    Private Sub Command7_Click(ByVal sender As System.Object, ByVal e
➥ As System.EventArgs) Handles Command7.Click
        ActiveForm = Form1
    End Sub

    'Command5 navigates user to Form4 and sets the
    'Label11 and 12 text properties to selected
    'contact name and ID.

    Private Sub Command5_Click(ByVal sender As System.Object, ByVal e
➥ As System.EventArgs) Handles Command5.Click
        ActiveForm = Form4
        Label11.Text = Label2.Text
        Label12.Text = Session("currID")
    End Sub

    'Command6 deletes the selected record from the
➥ DataSet
    'and updates the database

    Private Sub Command6_Click(ByVal sender As System.Object, ByVal e
➥ As System.EventArgs) Handles Command6.Click
        DataSet11.Tables("Table1").Rows.Find(Label12.Text).Delete()
        OleDbDataAdapter1.Update(DataSet11, "Table1")
        ActiveForm = Form1
    End Sub

    'Command8_Click sets up the textbox fields with
    'existing details ready for updating. Disables the
```

```vb
'NewRecord command
'and enables the UpdateRecord command

Private Sub Command8_Click(ByVal sender As System.Object, ByVal e
➥ As System.EventArgs) Handles Command8.Click
        Dim intCurrId
        intCurrId = Session("currID")
        ActiveForm = Form3
        Command1.Visible = False
        Command9.Visible = True
        Label9.Text = "Enter Changes:"
        TextBox1.Text =
➥ DataSet11.Tables("Table1").Rows.Find(intCurrId).Item("Name")
        TextBox2.Text =
➥ DataSet11.Tables("Table1").Rows.Find(intCurrId).Item("Surname")
        TextBox3.Text =
➥ DataSet11.Tables("Table1").Rows.Find(intCurrId).Item("Address")
        TextBox4.Text =
➥ DataSet11.Tables("Table1").Rows.Find(intCurrId).Item("City")
        TextBox5.Text =
➥ DataSet11.Tables("Table1").Rows.Find(intCurrId).Item("Zip")
        TextBox6.Text =
➥ DataSet11.Tables("Table1").Rows.Find(intCurrId).Item("Telephone")
        TextBox7.Text =
➥ DataSet11.Tables("Table1").Rows.Find(intCurrId).Item("Mobile")
        TextBox8.Text =
➥ DataSet11.Tables("Table1").Rows.Find(intCurrId).Item("Email")
        TextBox9.Text =
➥ DataSet11.Tables("Table1").Rows.Find(intCurrId).Item("Comments")

    End Sub

    'Command9_Click updates the DataSet with any changes
    'listed in the textboxes and then calls the update
    'method to write back to the database.

Private Sub Command9_Click(ByVal sender As System.Object, ByVal e
➥ As System.EventArgs) Handles Command9.Click
        Dim intCurrId As Integer = Session("currID")
        Command1.Visible = True
        Command9.Visible = False
        DataSet11.Tables("Table1").Rows.Find(intCurrId).Item("Name") =
➥ TextBox1.Text
        DataSet11.Tables("Table1").Rows.Find(intCurrId).Item("Surname")
➥ = TextBox2.Text
        DataSet11.Tables("Table1").Rows.Find(intCurrId).Item("Address")
➥ = TextBox3.Text
        DataSet11.Tables("Table1").Rows.Find(intCurrId).Item("City") =
➥ TextBox4.Text
        DataSet11.Tables("Table1").Rows.Find(intCurrId).Item("Zip") =
➥ TextBox5.Text
```

```
        DataSet11.Tables("Table1").Rows.Find(intCurrId).Item("Telephone") =
➥ TextBox6.Text
        DataSet11.Tables("Table1").Rows.Find(intCurrId).Item("Mobile")
➥ = TextBox7.Text
        DataSet11.Tables("Table1").Rows.Find(intCurrId).Item("Email") =
➥ TextBox8.Text
        DataSet11.Tables("Table1").Rows.Find(intCurrId).Item("Comments") =
➥ TextBox9.Text
        OleDbDataAdapter1.Update(DataSet11, "Table1")
        ActiveForm = Form1

    End Sub
End Class
```

**Listing 10.19**    **Code for the ASPX Page for MyContacts**

```
<%@ Page Language="vb" AutoEventWireup="true"
➥ Codebehind="MobileWebForm1.aspx.vb"
➥ Inherits="MyContacts.MobileWebForm1" trace="False"%>
<%@ Register TagPrefix="mobile"
➥ Namespace="System.Web.UI.MobileControls"
➥ Assembly="System.Web.Mobile, Version=1.0.3300.0, Culture=neutral,
➥ PublicKeyToken=b03f5f7f11d50a3a" %>
<meta content="Microsoft Visual Studio.NET 7.0" name="GENERATOR">
<meta content="Visual Basic 7.0" name="CODE_LANGUAGE">
<meta content="http://schemas.microsoft.com/Mobile/Page"
➥ name="vs_targetSchema">

<script language="vb" runat="server">
protected sub List_bind(Sender as object, e as ListDataBindEventArgs)
    e.ListItem.Text = String.Format ("{0} {1}",
➥ DataBinder.Eval(e.DataItem, "Name"),  DataBinder.Eval(e.DataItem,
➥ "Surname"))
end sub
</script>
<body Xmlns:mobile="http://schemas.microsoft.com/Mobile/WebForm">
    <mobile:form id="Form1" title="My Contacts" runat="server"
➥ PagerStyle-PreviousPageText="Return to Page {0}"
➥ PagerStyle-NextPageText="Go to Page {0}" Paginate="True">
        <mobile:Label id="Label1" runat="server"
➥ StyleReference="title">My Contacts</mobile:Label>
        <mobile:List id="List1" runat="server"
➥ OnItemDataBind="List_bind" DataSource="<%# DataSet11 %>"
➥ DataMember="Table1" DataTextField="Name" DataValueField="Id">
 </mobile:List>
        <mobile:Command id="Command2" runat="server">New
➥ Contact</mobile:Command>
    </mobile:form>
    <mobile:form id="Form3" runat="server">
        <P>
```

```
<mobile:Label id="Label9" runat="server"
➥ StyleReference="title"></mobile:Label>Name:
<mobile:TextBox id="TextBox1" runat="server"></mobile:TextBox>Surname:
<mobile:TextBox id="TextBox2" runat="server"></mobile:TextBox>Address:
<mobile:TextBox id="TextBox3" runat="server"></mobile:TextBox>City:
<mobile:TextBox id="TextBox4" runat="server"></mobile:TextBox>Zip:
<mobile:TextBox id="TextBox5"
➥ runat="server"></mobile:TextBox>Telephone:
<mobile:TextBox id="TextBox6" runat="server"></mobile:TextBox>Mobile:
<mobile:TextBox id="TextBox7" runat="server"></mobile:TextBox>Email:
<mobile:TextBox id="TextBox8" runat="server"></mobile:TextBox>Comments:
<mobile:TextBox id="TextBox9" runat="server"></mobile:TextBox>
<mobile:Command id="Command1" runat="server">Create New
➥ Contact</mobile:Command>
<mobile:Command id="Command9" runat="server" SoftkeyLabel="Change"
➥ Visible="False">Change Details</mobile:Command>
<mobile:Command id="Command4" runat="server"
➥ SoftkeyLabel="Home">Home</mobile:Command></P>
   </mobile:form>
   <mobile:form id="Form2" title="My Contacts - Details"
➥ runat="server">
      <P>
<mobile:Label id="Label2" runat="server" StyleReference="title"
➥ Text='<%# String.Format ("{0} {1}", DataBinder.Eval(DataView1,
➥ "[0].Name"), DataBinder.Eval(DataView1, "[0].Surname"))
➥ %>'></mobile:Label>ID
Number:
<mobile:Label id="Label13" runat="server"
➥ Text='<%# DataBinder.Eval(DataView1, "[0].Id", "{0}") %>'
➥ Font-Size="Small"></mobile:Label>Address:
<mobile:Label id="Label3" runat="server"
➥ Text='<%# DataBinder.Eval(DataView1, "[0].Address", "{0}") %>'
➥ Font-Size="Small"></mobile:Label>
<mobile:Label id="Label4" runat="server"
➥ Text='<%# DataBinder.Eval(DataView1, "[0].City", "{0}") %>'
➥ Font-Size="Small"></mobile:Label>
<mobile:Label id="Label5" runat="server"
➥ Text='<%# DataBinder.Eval(DataView1, "[0].Zip", "{0}") %>'
➥ Font-Size="Small"></mobile:Label>Phone:
<mobile:Label id="Label6" runat="server"
➥ Text='<%# DataBinder.Eval(DataView1, "[0].Telephone", "{0}") %>'
➥ Font-Size="Small"></mobile:Label>Mobile:
<mobile:Label id="Label7" runat="server"
➥ Text='<%# DataBinder.Eval(DataView1, "[0].Mobile", "{0}") %>'
➥ Font-Size="Small"></mobile:Label>Email:
<mobile:Label id="Label8" runat="server"
➥ Text='<%# DataBinder.Eval(DataView1, "[0].Email", "{0}") %>'
➥ Font-Size="Small"></mobile:Label>Comments:
<mobile:TextView id="TextView1" runat="server"
➥ Text='<%# DataBinder.Eval(DataView1, "[0].Comments", "{0}") %>'
➥ Font-Size="Small"></mobile:TextView>
```

```
<mobile:Command id="Command5" runat="server"
➥ SoftkeyLabel="Delete">Delete Contact</mobile:Command>
<mobile:Command id="Command8" runat="server">Change
➥ Details</mobile:Command>
<mobile:Command id="Command3" runat="server"
➥ SoftkeyLabel="Home">Home</mobile:Command></P>
    </mobile:form>
    <mobile:form id="Form4" title="Delete Confirm" runat="server">
      <P>
<mobile:Label id="Label10" runat="server" StyleReference="title">Do you
➥ wish to delete the record for:</mobile:Label>
<mobile:Label id="Label11" runat="server"></mobile:Label>Record
Number:
<mobile:Label id="Label12" runat="server"></mobile:Label>
<mobile:Command id="Command6" runat="server"
➥ SoftkeyLabel="Yes">Yes</mobile:Command>
<mobile:Command id="Command7" runat="server"
➥ SoftkeyLabel="No">No</mobile:Command></P>
    </mobile:form>
</body>
```

## Full Code Listing for MyContactsDR

Code Listings 10.20 and 10.21 contain the code behind and ASPX for MyContactsDR,
including Update functionality, although you may have to reinstate autonumber on the Id
field in your Mobiledb1 database to make this work properly.

**Listing 10.20**    **Code Behind for MyContactsDR**

```
Private Sub Page_Load(ByVal sender As System.Object, ByVal e As
➥ System.EventArgs) Handles MyBase.Load
    End Sub

    Private Sub Command1_Click(ByVal sender As System.Object, ByVal e
➥ As System.EventArgs) Handles Command1.Click
        ActiveForm = Form2
        Label2.Text = "New Contact"
        Label2.StyleReference = "title"
    End Sub

    'Command2 creates a new record in the database based
➥ on the
        'contents of the two text boxes in Form2

    Private Sub Command2_Click(ByVal sender As System.Object, ByVal e
➥ As System.EventArgs) Handles Command2.Click
        Dim MyOleDbInsertCommand As OleDb.OleDbCommand
```

```
        MyOleDbInsertCommand = New OleDb.OleDbCommand()
        MyOleDbInsertCommand.CommandText = "INSERT INTO
➥ Table1(Name, Surname) VALUES (?, ?)"
        MyOleDbInsertCommand.Connection = OleDbConnection1
        MyOleDbInsertCommand.Parameters.Add
➥(New OleDb.OleDbParameter("Name", OleDb.OleDbType.Char, 50))
        MyOleDbInsertCommand.Parameters.Add
➥(New OleDb.OleDbParameter("Surname", OleDb.OleDbType.Char, 50))
        MyOleDbInsertCommand.Parameters.Item("Name").Value =
➥ TextBox1.Text
        MyOleDbInsertCommand.Parameters.Item("Surname").Value =
➥ TextBox2.Text
        OleDbConnection1.Open()
        MyOleDbInsertCommand.ExecuteNonQuery()
        OleDbConnection1.Close()
        ActiveForm = Form1
    End Sub

    'Form1_Activate loads up List1 with values from
    'the database using a SELECT statement

    Private Sub Form1_Activate(ByVal sender As System.Object, ByVal e
➥ As System.EventArgs) Handles Form1.Activate
        Command2.Visible = True
        Command8.Visible = False
        List1.Items.Clear()
        Dim MyOleDbCommand As OleDb.OleDbCommand
        MyOleDbCommand = New OleDb.OleDbCommand()
        MyOleDbCommand.CommandText = "SELECT Name FROM Table1"
        MyOleDbCommand.Connection = OleDbConnection1
        OleDbConnection1.Open()
        Dim dbRead As OleDb.OleDbDataReader
        dbRead = MyOleDbCommand.ExecuteReader
        While dbRead.Read()
            List1.Items.Add(dbRead.Item("Name"))
        End While
        OleDbConnection1.Close()
    End Sub

    Private Sub Command3_Click(ByVal sender As System.Object, ByVal e
➥ As System.EventArgs) Handles Command3.Click
        ActiveForm = Form1
        Command2.Visible = True
        Command8.Visible = False
    End Sub

    'List2_select takes the item selected from list2
    'and deletes it from the database using a DELETE
➥ statement

    Private Sub List2_ItemCommand(ByVal sender As System.Object, ByVal
```

```
➥ e As System.Web.UI.MobileControls.ListCommandEventArgs) Handles
➥ List2.ItemCommand

        Dim MyOleDbDeleteCommand As OleDb.OleDbCommand
        MyOleDbDeleteCommand = New OleDb.OleDbCommand()
        MyOleDbDeleteCommand.CommandText = "DELETE FROM Table1 WHERE
➥ (Name = ?)"
        MyOleDbDeleteCommand.Parameters.Add
➥(New OleDb.OleDbParameter("Name", OleDb.OleDbType.Char, 50))
        MyOleDbDeleteCommand.Parameters.Item("Name").Value =
➥ e.ListItem.Value
        MyOleDbDeleteCommand.Connection = OleDbConnection1
        OleDbConnection1.Open()
        MyOleDbDeleteCommand.ExecuteNonQuery()
        OleDbConnection1.Close()
        ActiveForm = Form1

    End Sub

    'List3_select sets up Form2 in data update mode
    'and loads current values into the textboxes in
➥ Form2.

    Private Sub List3_ItemCommand(ByVal sender As System.Object, ByVal
➥ e As System.Web.UI.MobileControls.ListCommandEventArgs) Handles
➥ List3.ItemCommand

        Session("name") = e.ListItem.Text
        ActiveForm = Form2
        Command2.Visible = False
        Command8.Visible = True
        Dim MyOleDbCommand As OleDb.OleDbCommand
        MyOleDbCommand = New OleDb.OleDbCommand()
        MyOleDbCommand.CommandText = "SELECT Surname FROM Table1 WHERE
➥ (Name = '" & Session("name") & "')"
        MyOleDbCommand.Connection = OleDbConnection1
        OleDbConnection1.Open()
        Dim dbRead As OleDb.OleDbDataReader
        dbRead = MyOleDbCommand.ExecuteReader
        While dbRead.Read()
            TextBox2.Text = dbRead.Item("Surname")
        End While
        OleDbConnection1.Close()
        TextBox1.Text = Session("name")
        Label2.Text = "Enter Changes to the Surname:"
    End Sub

    Private Sub Command5_Click(ByVal sender As System.Object, ByVal e
➥ As System.EventArgs) Handles Command5.Click
        ActiveForm = Form1
    End Sub
```

```
      'Command4 Navigates user to form3 (delete selection
➥ form)
      'and loads contact names into list2

    Private Sub Command4_Click(ByVal sender As System.Object, ByVal e
➥ As System.EventArgs) Handles Command4.Click
        ActiveForm = Form3
        List2.Items.Clear()
        Dim MyOleDbCommand2 As OleDb.OleDbCommand
        MyOleDbCommand2 = New OleDb.OleDbCommand()
        MyOleDbCommand2.CommandText = "SELECT Name FROM Table1"
        MyOleDbCommand2.Connection = OleDbConnection1
        OleDbConnection1.Open()
        Dim dbRead As OleDb.OleDbDataReader
        dbRead = MyOleDbCommand2.ExecuteReader
        While dbRead.Read()
            List2.Items.Add(dbRead.Item("Name"))
        End While
        OleDbConnection1.Close()
    End Sub

    Private Sub Command6_Click(ByVal sender As System.Object, ByVal e
➥ As System.EventArgs) Handles Command6.Click
        ActiveForm = Form1
    End Sub

      'Command7 navigates user to Form4 (Update)
      'and loads values into List3.

    Private Sub Command7_Click(ByVal sender As System.Object, ByVal e
➥ As System.EventArgs) Handles Command7.Click
        ActiveForm = Form4
        List3.Items.Clear()
        Dim MyOleDbCommand3 As OleDb.OleDbCommand
        MyOleDbCommand3 = New OleDb.OleDbCommand()
        MyOleDbCommand3.CommandText = "SELECT Name FROM Table1"
        MyOleDbCommand3.Connection = OleDbConnection1
        OleDbConnection1.Open()
        Dim dbRead As OleDb.OleDbDataReader
        dbRead = MyOleDbCommand3.ExecuteReader
        While dbRead.Read()
            List3.Items.Add(dbRead.Item("Name"))
        End While
        OleDbConnection1.Close()
    End Sub

      'Command8 invokes the SQL statement to update
      'the database with any changes entered in the
      'surname textbox.

    Private Sub Command8_Click(ByVal sender As System.Object, ByVal e
```

```
➥ As System.EventArgs) Handles Command8.Click
        Command2.Visible = True
        Command8.Visible = False
        Dim MyOleDbUpdateCommand As OleDb.OleDbCommand
        MyOleDbUpdateCommand = New OleDb.OleDbCommand()
        MyOleDbUpdateCommand.CommandText = "UPDATE Table1 SET
➥ Surname = '" & TextBox2.Text & "' WHERE (Name = '" & TextBox1.Text
➥ & "')"
        MyOleDbUpdateCommand.Connection = OleDbConnection1
        OleDbConnection1.Open()
        MyOleDbUpdateCommand.ExecuteNonQuery()
        OleDbConnection1.Close()
        ActiveForm = Form1

    End Sub
End Class
```

**Listing 10.21    ASPX Code for MyContactsDR**

```
<%@ Page Language="vb" AutoEventWireup="true"
➥ Codebehind="MobileWebForm1.aspx.vb"
➥ Inherits="MyContactsDR.MobileWebForm1" trace="False"%>
<%@ Register TagPrefix="mobile"
➥ Namespace="System.Web.UI.MobileControls"
➥ Assembly="System.Web.Mobile, Version=1.0.3300.0, Culture=neutral,
➥ PublicKeyToken=b03f5f7f11d50a3a" %>
<meta content="Microsoft Visual Studio.NET 7.0" name="GENERATOR">
<meta content="Visual Basic 7.0" name="CODE_LANGUAGE">
<meta content="http://schemas.microsoft.com/Mobile/Page"
➥ name="vs_targetSchema">

<body Xmlns:mobile="http://schemas.microsoft.com/Mobile/WebForm">
    <mobile:form id="Form1" title="MyContactsDR" runat="server"
➥ Paginate="True" PagerStyle-NextPageText="Next Page"
➥ PagerStyle-PreviousPageText="Previous">
        <mobile:Label id="Label1" runat="server"
➥ StyleReference="title">MyContactsDR</mobile:Label>
        <mobile:Command id="Command1" runat="server"
➥ SoftkeyLabel="New Contact">New Contact</mobile:Command>
        <mobile:Command id="Command4" runat="server"
➥ SoftkeyLabel="Delete">Delete Contact</mobile:Command>
        <mobile:Command id="Command7" runat="server"
➥ SoftkeyLabel="Update">Update Contact</mobile:Command>
        <mobile:List id="List1" runat="server"></mobile:List>
    </mobile:form>
    <mobile:form id="Form2" title="NewContact" runat="server">
        <P>
<mobile:Label id="Label2" runat="server"></mobile:Label>Enter Name:
<mobile:TextBox id="TextBox1" runat="server"></mobile:TextBox>Enter
```

```
➡ Surname:
<mobile:TextBox id="TextBox2" runat="server"></mobile:TextBox>
<mobile:Command id="Command2" runat="server" SoftkeyLabel="Add
➡ Contact">Add Contact</mobile:Command>
<mobile:Command id="Command8" runat="server" SoftkeyLabel="Change"
➡ Visible="False">Change Details</mobile:Command>
<mobile:Command id="Command3" runat="server"
➡ SoftkeyLabel="Home">Home</mobile:Command></P>
   </mobile:form>
   <mobile:form id="Form4" title="Update Contact" runat="server">
      <mobile:Label id="Label4" runat="server"
➡ StyleReference="title">Click Contact to Update:</mobile:Label>
      <mobile:Command id="Command6" runat="server"
➡ SoftkeyLabel="Home">Home</mobile:Command>
      <mobile:List id="List3" runat="server">
</mobile:List>
   </mobile:form>
   <mobile:form id="Form3" title="Delete Contact" runat="server">
      <mobile:Label id="Label3" runat="server"
➡ StyleReference="title">Click Contact to Delete:</mobile:Label>
      <mobile:Command id="Command5" runat="server"
➡ SoftkeyLabel="Home">Home</mobile:Command>
      <mobile:List id="List2" runat="server">
</mobile:List>
   </mobile:form>
</body>
```

## Summary

In this chapter we have built a simple contacts manager that has enabled us to see how the process of viewing, updating, and deleting data from a database works with the Mobile Internet Toolkit and ADO.NET. The examples presented in this chapter are, by necessity, fairly simple. MyContactsDR, in particular, is only meant to highlight various techniques using the technology. The examples are solely intended to illustrate various data management techniques with ADO.NET and the Mobile Internet Toolkit. At the very least, for a full-scale application, we would need to include appropriate error handling and validation (a good opportunity to road test our validation controls!). It is also a good idea to split the application across at least a couple individual ASPX pages to eliminate any device-caching problems that may arise. In addition, it is desirable to give the user some form of opening menu to select the various functions of the application, and to use a selection list control to enable multiple deletes. I have revised this application with a more complete and rounded version in Chapter 20, "*MyNewContacts*: MyContacts Revisited," later in this book. In Chapter 20 we also use the SQL Server connection objects to connect to a SQL Server version of the mobiledb1 database. We will also briefly cover the use of stored procedures with the Mobile Internet Toolkit and ADO.NET.

We have only scratched the surface of ADO.NET with these examples, and it should be fairly clear that there are many differences between this and the way we used to do things with ASP and old-fashioned ADO. The information should, however, be enough to get you started. If you are getting into serious data manipulation with your applications, it is worth reading some specialized references on the topic, such as *ADO and ADO.NET Programming* by Mike Gunderloy (Sybex, February 2002).

In the next chapter, we will take a look at using styles and templates with the Mobile Internet Toolkit.

# CHAPTER 11

# Using Styles and Templates in the Mobile Internet Toolkit

- Using Styles with the MIT revisited

- Creating an external style sheet

- Using template scts in style sheets

- Using `MobileCapabilities`

W e have previously taken a brief look at the use of the StyleSheet control back in Chapter 7, "The Runtime Controls." In this chapter we will see how we can extend the capabilities of the StyleSheet control by defining it in an external style sheet. By creating this separate file, we can access the style properties from multiple mobile pages on a site. It is possible when using an external style sheet to achieve and maintain a consistent look and feel for a whole suite of applications with a minimum of fuss.

We can also establish templates to define device-specific rendering for various mobile controls. If a target device for the template is used, the control is rendered specifically for that device. Otherwise, the standard adaptive rendering is used. We can set up template sets of multiple templates and link them to a style sheet to be shared amongst multiple forms.

Finally, in this chapter, we will look at the MobileCapabilities object and how we can use it to identify the capabilities of a particular device. We can use this information to optimize our applications for specific devices. We will also see how we can extend the MobileCapabilities object by adding our own device filters.

## Using Styles with the MIT Revisited

There are a number of possible methods that we can use to access or change styles with the Mobile Internet Toolkit. The most obvious ones include the following:

- Using style-related properties. On a per-control basis we can access style properties such as BackColor or FontSize. Setting these properties on container objects (such as Forms or Panels) determines the style properties of objects such as Labels placed within those container controls.

- Using the preset StyleReference property with built-in values (such as title, subcommand, and error).

- Use a StyleSheet control and the <Style> element to set common styles for a single mobile page.

We have used all these approaches previously in projects in this book. As we advanced a little, we saw how we could use the DeviceSpecific control to identify the specific device and set some of the style options that we want to use specifically for that device or range of devices.

We then looked at how to take advantage of the templating options of the DeviceSpecific control to further determine the rendering of individual controls on particular devices. For example, we saw how to customize the Header/Footer template of a Form control.

## Creating an External Style Sheet

In this section, we will create a sample project that draws its style settings from an external style sheet. We will see how we can create the style sheet and access its properties.

NOTE One thing to watch when working with external style sheets is that the applied styles only appear at runtime. This is unlike what happens when you set the styles internally—the applied styles appear at design time and we can see what they look like without having to compile and run the project. The other difficulty with working with external styles is that the list of available styles will not appear in the drop-down list of the `StyleReference` property of any given control.

Be aware also that, for your average mobile phone, the ability to display much in the way of styles is very limited. This will change as the technology and bandwidth improves, but for the moment any style implementations are mainly for the benefit of any PDA's that may access your site. However, don't let this limit your implementation, as the Mobile Internet Toolkit will adaptively render your site back down to something acceptable to the accessing device, even if it cannot handle the styles that you have applied.

Follow these steps to create the sample project:

1. Create a new mobile project, mobilestyle1, and drop two Label controls and a Link control onto Form1.

2. Create a second form and place a Panel, a Label, and a Link control on this form. Keep the Label inside the Panel control and the Link control below the Panel.

3. Drag a StyleSheet control onto the Mobile Web Page.

   Figure 11.1 shows the suggested layout for this project.

Before we assign any properties to our controls, we need to create our external style sheet. We can do this simply by opening up Notepad, typing in the appropriate code, and saving the thing as an ASCX file in the root directory of our application.

We can then access this style sheet by setting the `ReferencePath` property of the Stylesheet1 control to the location of our style sheet. The main disadvantages I have found to creating the style sheet this way in Visual Studio is that if you try to locate the file using the dialog box from the `ReferencePath` property, it can have some unpredictable consequences and the file isn't referenced in the Solution Explorer. We can fix the latter by right-clicking the mobilestyle1 reference in the Solution Explorer and choosing the Add Existing Item option from the Add submenu (or choose Add Existing Item from the main Project menu in the Visual Studio IDE). Navigate to the location of the style sheet, choose it, and click Yes when asked if you wish to create a new class file (although this is not strictly necessary).

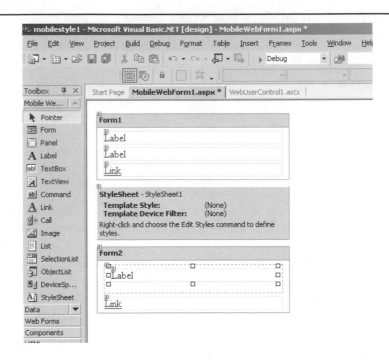

If you do use the Notepad application, remember to use Save As and save your file with the
.ascx file extension. In the Save As Type field, select the All Files option.

An alternative is to choose Add Web User Control from the Project menu. This creates
a new Web user control, which is an ASCX file. Name it something appropriate (such as
MyStyleSheet.ascx) and click the Open button. You can then switch to HTML View,
delete any existing code, and add all the relevant code. You will still have to set the path
to MyStyleSheet from the StyleSheet control using its ReferencePath property.

Add the code to your stylesheet (by whichever method that you have used to produce it!) as
presented in Listing 11.1.

**Listing 11.1      Code for External Style Sheet for mobilestyle1 Project**

```
<%@ Register TagPrefix="mobile"
➥ Namespace="System.Web.UI.MobileControls"
➥ Assembly="System.Web.Mobile" %>
<%@ Control  Language="vb" AutoEventWireup="false"
➥ Inherits="System.Web.UI.MobileControls.MobileUserControl" %>

<mobile:Stylesheet runat="server" id="Stylesheet1">

    <Style name="Font" Font-Name="Comic Sans MS" />
```

```
    <Style name="Form" StyleReference="Font" BackColor="#C0C000"
➥ ForeColor="#C00000" />
    <Style name="Head" Font-Bold="True" Font-Size="Large"
➥ Font-Name="Impact" />
    <Style name="Panel" Font-Name="Arial" ForeColor="Black" />
    <Style name="Link" Font-Italic="True" Font-Size="Small" />

</mobile:Stylesheet>
```

This style sheet creates a number of different styles that we can call:

**Font**   Sets the font to Comic Sans. It is also used internally within the style sheet by the Form style.

**Form**   Sets the background color to some ugly shade of green and the foreground color to red. (This is unlikely to be a problem, even if you do suffer from some form of red/green color blindness, because most cell phones simply won't display it!)

**Head**   A heading style with bigger, bolder, Impact font text.

**Panel**   Sets the font to plain, black Arial.

**Link**   Makes links small and italic (although for demonstration purposes, I don't use this property for the link on the second form).

Switch back to Design View of the MobileWebForm1 and set the Control properties to those listed in Table 11.1.

**TABLE 11.1:**  Property Settings for Controls in mobilestyle1

| Control | Property | Value |
| --- | --- | --- |
| Form1 | StyleReference | Form |
| Label1 | Text | MobileStyle1 |
|  | StyleReference | Head |
| Label2 | Text | Some text goes in here |
| Link1 | StyleReference | Link |
|  | Text | Next Form |
|  | NavigateURL | #Form2 |
| StyleSheet1 | ReferencePath | MyStyleSheet.ascx |
| Form2 | StyleReference | Form |
| Panel1 | StyleReference | Panel |
| Label3 | Text | Hi there! |
| Link2 | Text | Previous Form |
|  | NavigateURL | #Form1 |

Compile and run the project.

This project will only fully reflect these styles in a browser capable of rendering them. The simplest option is Internet Explorer. You should be able to see the range of styles and the contexts in which they have been applied.

Open the project in the Openwave browser, and you will see very few of these style settings reflected (see Figure 11.2).

FIGURE 11.2:

The mobilestyle1 project demonstrated in the Openwave browser and Internet Explorer

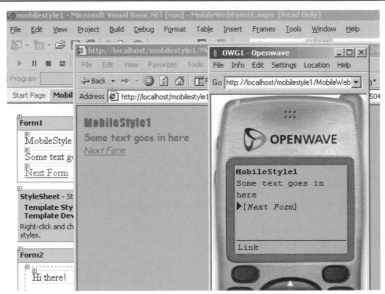

Image of UP.SDK courtesy Openwave Systems, Inc.

## Using Template Sets in Style Sheets

In Chapter 7, we created the Mobile8 project that demonstrated the use of a template to identify Openwave browsers and apply a custom header. Of interest here is the ASPX code, which we did not really examine at the time. Take a look at the code for this project in Listing 11.2.

**Listing 11.2**    **ASPX Code for Mobile8 Project Demonstrating the Use of Templates**

```
<%@ Page Language="vb" AutoEventWireup="false"
➥ Codebehind="MobileWebForm1.aspx.vb" Inherits="Mobile8too.MobileWebForm1"
➥ %>
<%@ Register TagPrefix="mobile"
➥ Namespace="System.Web.UI.MobileControls"
```

```
➥ Assembly="System.Web.Mobile, Version=1.0.3300.0, Culture=neutral,
➥ PublicKeyToken=b03f5f7f11d50a3a" %>
<meta name="GENERATOR" content="Microsoft Visual Studio.NET 7.0">
<meta name="CODE_LANGUAGE" content="Visual Basic 7.0">
<meta name="vs_targetSchema"
➥ content="http://schemas.microsoft.com/Mobile/Page">
<body Xmlns:mobile="http://schemas.microsoft.com/Mobile/WebForm">
    <mobile:Form id="Form1" runat="server" StyleReference="Style2"
➥ Paginate="True">Hello There
<mobile:SelectionList id="SelectionList1"
➥ runat="server"></mobile:SelectionList>
<mobile:DeviceSpecific id="DeviceSpecific1" runat="server">
    <Choice
➥ Xmlns="http://schemas.microsoft.com/mobile/html32template"
➥ StyleReference="title"
➥ Filter="isUP4x">
        <HeaderTemplate>
            <mobile:Label id="Label1" runat="server">Hello
➥ Openwave User</mobile:Label>
        </HeaderTemplate>
    </Choice>
    <Choice
➥ Xmlns="http://schemas.microsoft.com/mobile/html32template"
➥  StyleReference="subcommand"
➥ Filter="isMME"></Choice>
</mobile:DeviceSpecific>
<mobile:TextView id="TextView1" runat="server">The Image
➥ control......<br /></mobile:TextView></mobile:Form>
    <mobile:StyleSheet id="StyleSheet1" runat="server">
        <Style Name="Style1"></Style>
        <Style Font-Size="Large" Font-Bold="True"
➥ Name="Style2"></Style>
    </mobile:StyleSheet>
</body>
```

The main area of our focus is the DeviceSpecific code:

```
<mobile:DeviceSpecific id="DeviceSpecific1" runat="server">
    <Choice
➥ Xmlns="http://schemas.microsoft.com/mobile/html32template"
➥ StyleReference="title"
➥ Filter="isUP4x">
        <HeaderTemplate>
            <mobile:Label id="Label1" runat="server">Hello
➥ Openwave User</mobile:Label>
        </HeaderTemplate>
    </Choice>
    <Choice
➥ Xmlns="http://schemas.microsoft.com/mobile/html32template"
➥  StyleReference="subcommand"
➥ Filter="isMME"></Choice>
</mobile:DeviceSpecific>
```

In this section we use the Choice tags to choose the relevant filters for the devices we wish to customize for. We can include a range of filters, and .NET evaluates each one, in order, against the target device. In this example, we then made use of a header template to apply a custom header to Openwave (UP) browsers. Back in Chapter 7, we actually set this up graphically using the GUI tools, but we could also have simply coded it as we did here.

We can include the template sets inside a `<style>` element in a style sheet. We can then access these templates by setting the StyleReference property of a control to the relevant style (that contains the templates). We will recreate Mobile8, using an external style sheet containing the template set that we set up.

Create a new project named Mobile8too and drag a Label and TextArea control to the form. Drag a StyleSheet control to the page.

Using one of the approaches described in the previous section, create an external style sheet (ASCX page) containing the code described in Listing 11.3. Name it MyStyleSheet.

---

**Listing 11.3**       **Code for the External Style Sheet for Mobile8too (MyStyleSheet)**

```
<%@ Register TagPrefix="mobile"
➥ Namespace="System.Web.UI.MobileControls"
➥ Assembly="System.Web.Mobile" %>
<%@ Control Language="vb"
➥ AutoEventWireup="false"
➥ Inherits="System.Web.UI.MobileControls.MobileUserControl"
➥ %>
<mobile:Stylesheet runat="server" id="Stylesheet1">
    <Style name="Font" Font-Name="Comic Sans MS" />
    <Style name="Form" StyleReference="Font" BackColor="#C0C000"
➥ ForeColor="#C00000">
        <DeviceSpecific>
            <Choice Filter="isUP4x">
                <HeaderTemplate>
                    <mobile:Label id="Label1"
➥ runat="server">
                        Hello Openwave
➥ User</mobile:Label>
                </HeaderTemplate>
            </Choice>
            <Choice Filter="isMME">
            </Choice>
        </DeviceSpecific>
    </Style>
    <Style name="Head" Font-Bold="True" Font-Size="Large"
➥ Font-Name="Impact" />
    <Style name="Panel" Font-Name="Arial" ForeColor="Black" />
    <Style name="Link" Font-Italic="True" Font-Size="Small" />
</mobile:Stylesheet>
```

---

Essentially, we have duplicated exactly the same style sheet that we created with Listing 11.1, except we have included the DeviceSpecific and Template reference from the Mobile8 project, Listing 11.2. We have placed this reference inside the Form style. If we wished, we could place a sequence of choice filters in here, targeting individual devices and utilizing specific templates. For example, there is an additional reference to the isMME filter, although we have not used it to actually do anything in this example (other than to illustrate where it goes!).

Return to Design View of the MobileWebForm1 and set the properties of the controls as shown in Table 11.2.

**TABLE 11.2:** Property Settings for Controls in Mobile8too

| Control | Property | Value |
|---------|----------|-------|
| Form1 | StyleReference | Form |
| Label1 | StyleReference | Head |
| | Text | Mobile8too |
| TextView1 | Text | Could contain lots of text |
| StyleSheet1 | ReferencePath | MyStyleSheet.ascx |

Listing 11.4 gives the ASPX code for the project (HTML View).

**Listing 11.4　　ASPX Code for Mobile8too**

```
<%@ Page Language="vb" AutoEventWireup="false"
➥ Codebehind="MobileWebForm1.aspx.vb" Inherits="Mobile8too.MobileWebForm1"
➥ %>
<%@ Register TagPrefix="mobile"
➥ Namespace="System.Web.UI.MobileControls"
➥ Assembly="System.Web.Mobile, Version=1.0.3300.0, Culture=neutral,
➥ PublicKeyToken=b03f5f7f11d50a3a" %>
<meta name="GENERATOR" content="Microsoft Visual Studio.NET 7.0">
<meta name="CODE_LANGUAGE" content="Visual Basic 7.0">
<meta name="vs_targetSchema"
➥ content="http://schemas.microsoft.com/Mobile/Page">
<body Xmlns:mobile="http://schemas.microsoft.com/Mobile/WebForm">

    <mobile:Form id="Form1" runat="server" StyleReference="Form">
        <mobile:Label id="Label1" runat="server"
➥ StyleReference="Head">Mobile8too</mobile:Label>
        <mobile:TextView id="TextView1" runat="server">Could
➥ contain lots of text....</mobile:TextView>
    </mobile:Form>
    <mobile:StyleSheet id="StyleSheet1" runat="server"
➥ ReferencePath="MyStyleSheet.ascx"></mobile:StyleSheet>
</body>
```

Run the project in both Internet Explorer and the Openwave browser. They should look something like Figure 11.3. You will observe that the device-specific features for Openwave are present and the rest of the styles are represented in the IE rendition.

FIGURE 11.3:

Mobile8too in
both Openwave and
Internet Explorer

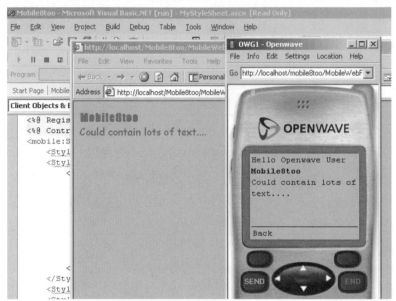

Image of UP.SDK courtesy Openwave Systems, Inc.

## Using *MobileCapabilities*

The MobileCapabilities object enables us to identify individual and collective capabilities of particular devices. It extracts the information from a number of sources, principally the HTTP headers returned by the device.

To demonstrate our ability to collect this information, we can simply display it in our application. The QuickStart Tutorials supplied with the Mobile Internet Toolkit include code for displaying all the publicly available properties of a device (that can be extracted by the MobileCapabilities object) in a list. Clicking a property will open a second form, which gives the value of that property for that particular device.

The following example is a simpler project that demonstrates how we can display the value of a couple of properties in two Label controls.

Drag two Label controls to the form in the Mobile8too project. Switch to Code Behind View and copy the code from Listing 11.5 into the Form_Load sub.

**Listing 11.5**     **Using the *MobileCapabilities* Object in Mobile8too**

```
Private Sub Page_Load(ByVal sender As System.Object, ByVal e As
➡ System.EventArgs) Handles MyBase.Load
        Dim myProperties As Mobile.MobileCapabilities = Request.Browser
        Label2.Text = myProperties.Browser
        Label3.text = myProperties.Version
    End Sub
```

The `Request.Browser` property contains the `MobileCapabilities` object and is used to get information about the client.

In this example, we have loaded the values of two client properties (browser type and version number) into our two Label controls. Figure 11.4 shows how this information is presented in both the Openwave browser and Internet Explorer.

**FIGURE 11.4:**

Extracting browser type and version number using `MobileCapabilities`

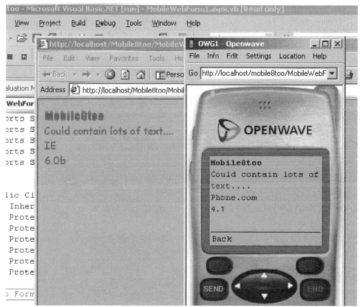

Image of UP.SDK courtesy Openwave Systems, Inc.

There are many more properties we could have chosen from for accessing client device characteristics from the `MobileCapabilities` class that are packaged with the Mobile Internet Toolkit. They are listed in Table 11.3. They also give us an idea of the range of factors involved when designing for the large number of different mobile devices and browsers that exist.

**TABLE 11.3:** Properties Belonging to the *MobileCapabilities* Class and Their Associated Client Device Characteristic

| Property | Brief Description | Return Value | Default Value |
|---|---|---|---|
| Browser | Type of browser | Browser type as string | Unknown |
| CanCombineFormsInDeck | Determines if device can handle multiple forms as separate cards | True if device has capability | True |
| CanInitiateVoiceCall | Checks if device can initiate voice call | True if device can initiate a voice call | False |
| CanRenderEmptySelects | Indicates if device can render empty select statements | True/False | True |
| CanRenderInputAnd ➥SelectElements ➥Together | Indicates if <input> and <select> elements can be rendered together | True/False | |
| CanRenderMixedSelects | Indicates device can handle <select> tags that include <option> elements with both onpick and value attributes | True/False | True |
| CanRenderOneventAnd ➥PrevElementsTogether | If device can handle <onevent> and <do type> tags together | True/False | True |
| CanRenderPostbackCards | Determines if device can use postback cards | True/False | True |
| CanRenderSetvarZero ➥WithMultiSelectionList | Determines if device can accept <setvar> with value = 0 | True/False | True |
| CanSendMail | Checks if device can send mail | True if device can send mail | True |
| GatewayMajorversion | Major version number of wireless gateway used to access the server | Version number | 0 |
| GatewayMinorVersion | Minor version number of wireless gateway used to access the server | Version number | 0 |
| GatewayVersion | Version of gateway used to access server | Version | None |

*Continued on next page*

**TABLE 11.3 CONTINUED:** Properties Belonging to the *MobileCapabilities* Class and Their Associated Client Device Characteristic

| Property | Brief Description | Return Value | Default Value |
|---|---|---|---|
| HasBackButton | Checks for Back button | True if device has dedicated back button | True |
| HidesRightAligned ➥MultiSelectScrollbars | Determines if right aligned scrollbars can be hidden | True/False | False |
| InputType | Type of input supported on device | Type of input | Empty string |
| IsColor | Checks if device can handle color | True if device has color display | True |
| IsMobileDevice | Determines if device is recognized mobile device | True/False | True |
| Item | Enables lookup of arbitrary capability values by name | String | Null |
| MaximumRenderedPageSize | Max length of page in bytes that device can display | Number of bytes | 2000 |
| MaximumSoftKeyLabelLength | Maximum length of text that softkey can support | Number | 8 |
| MobileDeviceManufacturer | Name of manufacturer | As text | Unknown |
| MobileDeviceModel | Model name | As text | Unknown |
| NumberOfSoftkeys | Detects number of Softkeys | Number | 0 |
| PreferredImageMIME | Preferred MIME type of image | Image type | image/gif |
| PreferredRenderingMIME | Preferred MIME type of content | MIME type | text/html |
| PreferredRenderingType | Type of content the device prefers | Returns type | html32 |
| RendersBreaksBefore ➥WmlSelectAndInput | Returns True if device inserts additional break after WML <select> or <input> | True/False | False |
| RendersBreaksAfter ➥HtmlLists | If device already renders breaks after HTML list tags | True/False | True |

*Continued on next page*

**TABLE 11.3 CONTINUED:** Properties Belonging to the *MobileCapabilities* Class and Their Associated Client Device Characteristic

| Property | Brief Description | Return Value | Default Value |
|---|---|---|---|
| RendersBreaksAfter ➥WmlAnchor | If device produces break after standalone anchor | True/False | False |
| RendersBreaksAfter ➥WmlInput | If device produces break after input elements received | True/False | False |
| RendersWmlDoAccepts ➥Inline | If device renders <do>-based form, accepts construct as inline button | True/False | True |
| RendersWmlSelects ➥AsMenuCards | True if <select> state-ments rendered as cards rather than combo box | True/False | False |
| RequiredMetaTagNameValue | Returns meta tag required by some devices | Meta tag | Null |
| RequiresContentType ➥MetaTag | Returns True if user is browsing with Pocket IE | True/False | False |
| RequiresAttribute ➥ColonSubstitution | Determines if browser requires colons to be replaced in tag names | True/False | False |
| RequiresHtmlAdaptive ➥ErrorReporting | Determines if HTML device must get default ASP.NET error message | True/False | False |
| RequiresLeadingPageBreak | Determines if page ignores a <br> if first element on page | True/False | False |
| RequiresNoBreak ➥InFormatting | Determines if format-ting tags not allowed to contain <br> tag | True/False | False |
| RequiresOutput ➥Optimization | If set to True, adapters aim for minimal output size | True/False | False |
| RequiresPhoneNumbers ➥AsPlainText | If device, supports dialing based only on plain text | True/False | False |
| RequiresSpecialView ➥StateEncoding | Determines if device requires special encoding | True/False | False |

*Continued on next page*

**TABLE 11.3 CONTINUED:** Properties Belonging to the *MobileCapabilities* Class and Their Associated Client Device Characteristic

| Property | Brief Description | Return Value | Default Value |
|---|---|---|---|
| RequiresUniqueFile ➥PathSuffix | Helps resolve caching issues on some devices and gateways | True/False | False |
| RequiresUniqueHtml ➥CheckboxNames | If it is HTML, <input> tag requires unique name attribute values | True/False | False |
| RequiresUrlEncoded ➥PostfieldValues | If during postback, text is encoded in value attribute of postfield | True/False | False |
| ScreenBitDepth | Depth of display | Bits per pixel | 1 |
| ScreenCharactersHeight | Height of display | Number of character lines | 6 |
| ScreenCharactersWidth | Width of display | Number of characters | 12 |
| ScreenPixelsHeight | Height of display | Number of pixels | 72 |
| ScreenPixelsWidth | Width of display | Number of pixels | 96 |
| SupportsAccesskey ➥Attribute | Determines if device can handle Accesskey attribute for <a> and <input> tags | True/False | False |
| SupportsBodyColor | If bgcolor of <body> tag supported | True/False | True |
| SupportsBold | If <b> tag supported | True/False | False |
| SupportsCacheControl ➥MetaTag | If Cache-Control: max-age-0 tag is supported | True/False | True |
| SupportCSS | For font properties if device supports cascading style sheets | True/False | False |
| SupportsDivAlign | If align attribute within <DIV> tag | True/False | True |
| SupportsDivNoWrap | If nowrap attribute within <DIV> tag | True/False | False |
| SupportsFontColor | If color attribute of <font> tag | True/False | True |
| SupportsFontName | If name attribute of <font> tag | True/False | False |
| SupportsFontSize | If size attribute of <font> tag | True/False | False |

*Continued on next page*

**TABLE 11.3 CONTINUED:** Properties Belonging to the *MobileCapabilities* Class and Their Associated Client Device Characteristic

| Property | Brief Description | Return Value | Default Value |
|---|---|---|---|
| SupportsImageSubmit | If device can handle images that submit the form | True/False | False |
| SupportsIModeSymbols | If device supports i-mode symbols | True/False | False |
| SupportsInputIStyle | If istyle attribute of <input> tag | True/False | False |
| SupportsInputMode | If supports mode attribute for <input> tag | True/False | False |
| SupportsItalic | If supports <i> tag | True/False | False |
| SupportsJPhoneMulti ➡MediaAttributes | If supports J-Phone multimedia attributes | True/False | False |
| SupportsJPhoneSymbols | If supports J-Phone picture symbols | True/False | False |
| SupportsQueryString ➡InFormAction Property | If the device supports a query string in the action attribute of a <form> tag | True/False | True |
| SupportsUncheck | Determines if the changed state of a deselected HTML check box is reflected in the post fields | True/False | True |

Once we have extracted the information we need, we can then use it to programmatically respond to the particular device capabilities. For example, we might use the IsColor property to determine whether or not we use particular styles from our style sheet when rendering an application.

A particularly useful tool here is the HasCapability method. It can be used to determine if a particular device satisfies a particular device filter, meets a MobileCapabilities property, or matches an item in the MobileCapabilities dictionary.

As an example of applying this method, we can add some color-only styles to MyStyleSheet from the Mobile8too project and then utilize them only when the IsColor property returns True when queried by the HasCapability method.

The "new" version of MyStyleSheet is contained in Listing 11.6.

**Listing 11.6    MyStyleSheet Updated to Distinguish between Color and Non-Color-Related Styles**

```
<%@ Register TagPrefix="mobile"
➥ Namespace="System.Web.UI.MobileControls"
➥ Assembly="System.Web.Mobile" %>
<%@ Control Language="vb"
➥ AutoEventWireup="false"
➥ Inherits="System.Web.UI.MobileControls.MobileUserControl"
➥ %>
<mobile:Stylesheet runat="server" id="Stylesheet1">
    <Style name="Font" Font-Name="Comic Sans MS" />
    <Style name="Form" StyleReference="Font" BackColor="#C0C000"
➥ ForeColor="#C00000">
        <DeviceSpecific>
            <Choice Filter="isUP4x">
                <HeaderTemplate>
                    <mobile:Label id="Label1"
➥ runat="server">
                        Hello Openwave
➥ User</mobile:Label>
                </HeaderTemplate>
            </Choice>
            <Choice Filter="isMME">
            </Choice>
        </DeviceSpecific>
    </Style>

    <Style name="Head" Font-Bold="True" Font-Size="Large" />
    <Style name="Panel" Font-Italic="True" />
    <Style name="Link" Font-Bold="True" Font-Size="Small" />
    <Style name="Fonttype" Font-Name="Comic Sans MS" />
    <Style name="cForm" StyleReference="Fonttype" BackColor="#C0C000"
➥ ForeColor="#C00000" />
    <Style name="cHead" Font-Bold="True" Font-Size="Large"
➥ Font-Name="Impact" />
    <Style name="cPanel" Font-Name="Arial" ForeColor="Black" />
    <Style name="cLink" Font-Italic="True" Font-Size="Small" />

</mobile:Stylesheet>
```

In this example, the styles prefixed with c are specifically for use in a color environment and, presumably, one that supports a few fonts (i.e., cForm, cHead, cPanel, and cLink).

The revised Page_Load procedure that takes advantage of these styles is described in Listing 11.7. I have added a Link control to the form to illustrate the use of the cLink style.

**Listing 11.7**      **Revised Page_Load Sub for Mobile8too Utilizing the *HasCapability* Method**

```
Private Sub Page_Load(ByVal sender As System.Object, ByVal e As
➥ System.EventArgs) Handles MyBase.Load

    Dim myProperties As Mobile.MobileCapabilities = Request.Browser

    If myProperties.HasCapability("IsColor", True) Then
        Form1.StyleReference = "cForm"
        Label1.StyleReference = "cHead"
        Link1.StyleReference = "cLink"
    End If

    Label2.Text = myProperties.Browser
    Label3.Text = myProperties.Version

End Sub
```

The piece of code that is doing the work here is the following snippet:

```
If myProperties.HasCapability("IsColor", True) Then
        Form1.StyleReference = "cForm"
        Label1.StyleReference = "cHead"
    Link1.StyleReference = "cLink"
End If
```

It tests the device to see if it returns True for the IsColor property. If it does, then it reassigns the StyleReference properties of the Form1, Label1, and Link1 controls.

Listing 11.8 has the full ASPX code for the revised Mobile8too including the additional Link control.

**Listing 11.8**      **Revised Code for ASPX Page of Mobile8too with Additional Link Control**

```
<%@ Page Language="vb" AutoEventWireup="false"
➥ Codebehind="MobileWebForm1.aspx.vb" Inherits="Mobile8too.MobileWebForm1"
➥ %>
<%@ Register TagPrefix="mobile"
➥ Namespace="System.Web.UI.MobileControls"
➥ Assembly="System.Web.Mobile, Version=1.0.3300.0, Culture=neutral,
➥ PublicKeyToken=b03f5f7f11d50a3a" %>
<meta name="GENERATOR" content="Microsoft Visual Studio.NET 7.0">
<meta name="CODE_LANGUAGE" content="Visual Basic 7.0">
<meta name="vs_targetSchema"
➥ content="http://schemas.microsoft.com/Mobile/Page">
<body Xmlns:mobile="http://schemas.microsoft.com/Mobile/WebForm">

    <mobile:form id="Form1" runat="server" StyleReference="Form">
```

```
        <mobile:Label id="Label1" runat="server"
➥ StyleReference="Head">Mobile8too</mobile:Label>
        <mobile:TextView id="TextView1" runat="server">Could
➥ contain lots of text....</mobile:TextView>
        <mobile:Label id="Label2"
➥ runat="server">Label</mobile:Label>
        <mobile:Label id="Label3"
➥ runat="server">Label</mobile:Label>
        <mobile:Link id="Link1" runat="server"
➥ StyleReference="Link">Link</mobile:Link>
    </mobile:form>
    <mobile:stylesheet id="StyleSheet1" runat="server"
➥ ReferencePath="MyStyleSheet.ascx"></mobile:stylesheet>
</body>
```

## Adding Device Filters

We can extend the MobileCapabilities object by adding our own device filters to the application. Device filters are specified in the Web.config file (see Chapter 8, "A Deeper Look at the Mobile Internet Toolkit and VB .NET"). There are two types of filter that we can specify:

**Comparison-based filter**    For a simple evaluation.

**Evaluator delegate-based filter**    For a complex evaluation.

A comparison-based filter has the following syntax:

```
<filter name="capability" compare="capabilityName" argument="argument" />
```

An example of this is as follows:

```
<filter name="IsBW" compare="IsColor" argument="false" />
```

This is a little simple, but to illustrate its use, modify the If...then statement from Listing 11.7 to read as follows:

```
If Not myProperties.HasCapability("IsBW", True) Then
        Form1.StyleReference = "cForm"
        Label1.StyleReference = "cHead"
        Link1.StyleReference = "cLink"
    End If
```

Copy the IsBW filter into the <deviceFilters> section of your Web.config file. Run it and I'm sure that you will get the idea. It should give exactly the same result as the previous setup.

We can either use these filters directly in the HasCapability method or indirectly in the <Choice> element. If you drop a DeviceSpecific control onto your form, right-click it to take a look at the available device filters; you will see our little IsBW filter happily awaiting use.

We can also write more complex filters using the following syntax:

```
<filter name="capability" type="className" method = "methodName" />
```

This is an evaluator delegate-based filter for which we will need to write and compile our own method. For example, if we wanted to do something a little more fancy (such as determining the exact color capability of a device), we would need to write some code to extract the information and could then link it to a filter using the approach discussed here.

We can also configure our existing Device Filters from the `AppliedDeviceFilters` property on each of the mobile controls. The Device Filter Editor is accessed via the ellipsis in the `AppliedDeviceFilters` property. Choose the filter to edit from the Available Device Filters drop-down list. Click the Edit button and make the desired changes. The order of device filters as they appear in the `Web.config` file can also be changed from the Device Filter Editor.

## Summary

To a certain extent we have almost come full circle with our styles. We use tools such as the Mobile Internet Toolkit to avoid having to code for individual devices, and then once we start using the Toolkit, we get excited because we find that we can use it to code for individual devices!

The reality is that in the rapidly changing world of mobile computing, we need all the flexibility that we can get and the differences between some devices that may be accessing our sites are just too great for a truly successful "one size fits all" approach.

We can also use styles to create a consistent set of "look and feel" criteria for our applications that is simple to apply, maintain, and update. This is extremely important with large, complex applications and, particularly, if they have a distributed architecture.

In the next chapter, we will look at how to create and customize our own mobile controls.

# CHAPTER 12

# Creating Custom Controls

- Customizing controls

- Creating user controls

- Using inheritance to create a custom control

- Creating a composite control that is made up of several other controls

- Using device-specific controls that behave differently for different devices

- Building your own original control

**A** powerful mechanism for extending the capabilities of the Mobile Internet Toolkit is the ability to create and customize our own controls, and Microsoft provides a number of mechanisms for achieving this with the Mobile Internet Toolkit.

## Customizing Controls

The key advantage of customizing a control is that we can encapsulate some functionality that we have built for our user (i.e., some chunk of code that does something useful) and reuse it across any number of pages.

There are two ways in which we can create controls for our Mobile applications. The first is to create user controls using similar techniques to those we have previously employed to create our applications. The second is to create and compile Custom Controls separately in the language of our choice (i.e., Visual Basic .NET!).

### Creating User Controls

We will begin by looking at how to create what Microsoft terms as user controls. As with the external style sheets, we use the .ascx file extension for pages that contain our reusable control code.

In Chapter 10, "Data Access with the Mobile Internet Toolkit, Part 2," we saw how we can customize the displayed text in a List control to contain the contents of multiple fields by overriding the ItemDataBind event. In this example, we will see how we can take this approach to build a custom List control that we can reuse across pages:

1. Create a new project and name it CustomMobileControl1.

2. From the Project menu, select Add Web User Control, name it MyControl.ascx in the Add New Item dialog box, and click Open.

3. Switch to HTML View and add the code from Listing 12.1. (You should delete any existing code.)

4. Switch back to Design View. You may see a warning that the control is not supported in Design View when placed inside a Web User Control. (This is OK!)

5. Drag an OleDbDataAdapter to the page and use the wizard to configure a connection to mobiledb1.mdb. Set the SQL statement to All Columns (see Figure 12.1).

6. Switch to Code Behind View, and copy the code from Listing 12.2 into the Page_Load sub.

---

**Listing 12.1**          **Code to Add to HTML View of *MyControl.ascx* Page**

```vb
<%@ Register TagPrefix="mobile"
➥ Namespace="System.Web.UI.MobileControls"
➥ Assembly="System.Web.Mobile" %>
<%@ Control Language="vb" AutoEventWireup="false"
➥ Codebehind="MyControl.ascx.vb"
➥ Inherits="CustomMobileControl1.MyControl" %>
<script language="vb" runat="server">
   Protected sub List_bind(sender As Object, e As
➥ ListDataBindEventArgs)
      e.ListItem.text = String.Format ("{0} {1}",
➥ DataBinder.Eval(e.DataItem, "Name"), DataBinder.Eval(e.DataItem,
➥ "Surname"))
   End sub
</script>
<mobile:List id="ContactList" runat="server" DataValueField="id"
➥ DataMember="Table1" DataSource="<%# DataSet11 %>"
➥ OnItemDataBind="List_bind" />
```

---

**FIGURE 12.1:**

Page layout for
MyContol.ascx

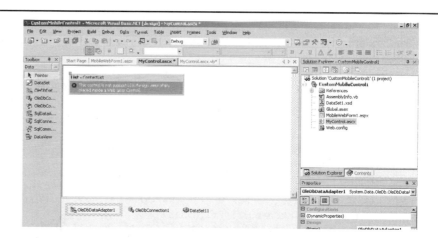

---

**Listing 12.2**          **Code Behind for *MyControl.ascx***

```vb
Private Sub Page_Load(ByVal sender As System.Object, ByVal e As
➥ System.EventArgs) Handles MyBase.Load
      OleDbDataAdapter1.Fill(DataSet11, "Table1")
      ContactList.DataBind()
End Sub
```

---

The code in Listing 12.1 should be familiar as a declaration for a mobile List control with an override attached to the ItemDataBind event. The code in Code Behind View fills the DataSet and databinds the List.

There are two ways that we can implement this control. We can use the @ Register directive or programmatically load the control using the (surprise!) LoadControl method. We will look at using both these methods, but first we need to set up our form to run the custom control.

Switch back to MobileWebForm1.aspx and open it in Design View. Drag a Label control to the form and set its StyleReference property to title and its Text property to My Custom Control.

### Using the @ *Register* Directive to Deploy a User Control

To use the @ Register directive, choose HTML View for MobileWebForm1.aspx. Add the following Register to the top of the page (underneath the other two directives):

```
<%@ Register TagPrefix="uc1" TagName="MyControl"
➥ Src="MyControl.ascx" %>
```

Add the following tag to <mobile:Form>:

```
<uc1:MyControl id="MyControl1" runat="server"></uc1:MyControl>
```

The final code should appear as it does in Listing 12.3.

---

**TIP**    Rather than type in the code as we have done to add our user control, it is simpler to drag a copy of the user control from the Solution Explorer to the Mobile Web Form in Design View.

---

**Listing 12.3      The Full ASPX Code for the CustomMobileControl1 Project**

```
<%@ Page Language="vb" AutoEventWireup="false"
➥ Codebehind="MobileWebForm1.aspx.vb"
➥ Inherits="CustomMobileControl1.MobileWebForm1" %>
<%@ Register TagPrefix="uc1" TagName="MyControl"
➥ Src="MyControl.ascx" %>
<%@ Register TagPrefix="mobile"
➥ Namespace="System.Web.UI.MobileControls"
➥ Assembly="System.Web.Mobile, Version=1.0.3300.0, Culture=neutral,
➥ PublicKeyToken=b03f5f7f11d50a3a" %>
<meta name="GENERATOR" content="Microsoft Visual Studio.NET 7.0">
<meta name="CODE_LANGUAGE" content="Visual Basic 7.0">
<meta name="vs_targetSchema"
➥ content="http://schemas.microsoft.com/Mobile/Page">
<body Xmlns:mobile="http://schemas.microsoft.com/Mobile/WebForm">
    <mobile:Form id="Form1" runat="server">
        <mobile:Label id="Label1" runat="server"
➥ StyleReference="title">My Custom Control</mobile:Label>
        <uc1:MyControl id="MyControl1" runat="server"></uc1:MyControl>
    </mobile:Form>
</body>
```

Run the project and view it in a browser. The list of names and surnames from the database should be displayed (see Figure 12.2).

FIGURE 12.2:

Browser display for
CustomMobileControl1
project

**TIP** You can also use the control on a form by simply dragging it from the Solution Explorer directly onto the form. (It saves typing out the code in HTML View!)

## Using the *LoadControl* Method to Deploy a User Control

The second way to utilize the control is to use the LoadControl method.

From the Project menu, select the Add Web Form option. Choose a Mobile Web Form and click Open. The Solution Explorer should now contain a reference to MobileWebForm2 .aspx. Right-click this and select Set As Start Page from the drop-down menu.

**TIP** You can easily alter which page the application opens by right-clicking the page in Solution Explorer and choosing Set As Start Page from the drop-down menu.

Switch to Code Behind View and add the code from Listing 12.4 to the Form_Load event.

**Listing 12.4    Using *LoadControl* to Deploy a User Control in an Application**

```
Private Sub Page_Load(ByVal sender As System.Object, ByVal e As
➡System.EventArgs) Handles MyBase.Load
       Dim custcontrol As MyControl
       custcontrol = LoadControl("MyControl.ascx")
       Form1.Controls.Add(custcontrol)
End Sub
```

Compile and run the application. The list should be displayed in the browser (similar to Figure 12.2 without the heading).

## Using Inheritance to Create a Custom Control

The second main group of controls that we can create is the custom controls. We create the controls by writing separate classes in a language such as VB .NET and compiling them into an assembly. The advantage offered by this approach is greater flexibility when writing the controls. We can use this approach to create complex controls that combine existing controls or exhibit device-specific composition at runtime.

When using inheritance, we use an existing mobile control and inherit from its base class for core functionality (such as rendering), but we can also extend it with custom properties and behavior.

In our example, we will create a simple custom control that consists of a List control containing a sequence of numbers (very useful for those occasions when you forget how to count!). The QuickStart Tutorials that ship with the Mobile Internet Toolkit contain a more practical (and more complicated) example featuring a List control that acts as a summary container for the contents of multiple forms, which is also worth taking a look at. However, in the following example I have given greater emphasis to the steps required to actually set up the control and get it working.

To create the control, open a new project in Visual Basic using the Class Library template. Name it something imaginative, like ClassLibrary1 (the default). It should open to an almost blank page, Class1.vb. Delete anything on it and copy the code from Listing 12.5 into it.

**Listing 12.5**    **Code for *Class1.vb* in Classlibrary1 (the Custom Control)**

```
Imports System
Imports System.Web.UI
Imports System.Web.UI.MobileControls
Namespace MyCompany.CustomControl
    Public Class MyList : Inherits System.Web.UI.MobileControls.List
        Protected Overrides Sub OnLoad(ByVal e As EventArgs)
            Dim n As Integer

            For n = 1 To 10
                Dim item As MobileListItem = New MobileListItem()
                item.Text = n
                item.Value = n
                Items.Add(item)
            Next

        End Sub
    End Class
End Namespace
```

You will also need to add references to the Web and mobile control class libraries. From the Project menu, select Add Reference. Then from within the .NET list, choose `System .Web.dll` and `System.Web.Mobile.dll`. Click OK. (All the squiggly blue lines should now disappear.) Complete the control by compiling the project using the `Build` command from the Build menu.

This example contains one class (`MyList`) that inherits from the List Mobile Web control. We then use a simple For/Next loop to populate the list with the numbers one through to ten by overriding the `OnLoad` event.

The control is now ready to be deployed within an application. (Make a note of where the project has been saved—this will come in handy for the next step.)

Create a new Mobile Web application in Visual Basic (CustomMobileControl2). In Design View, drag a Label control to the form, set its text property to `Custom Control` and its style property to `title`.

Add a reference to your custom control by selecting Add Reference from the Project menu. Use the Browse button to locate your custom control. You are looking for a file called `ClassLibrary1.dll` (or if you named the control *somethingelse*, it would be `somethingelse .dll`). You can expect to find it in the Bin directory, inside the ClassLibrary1 directory. Click OK and make sure that it has been referenced correctly by expanding the References node in the Solution Explorer and seeing if it is now listed there.

Switch back to HTML View on the MobileWebForm and add the code from Listing 12.6. (Note that most of this will already be there.)

**Listing 12.6       ASPX Code for CustomMobileControl2**

```
<%@ Register TagPrefix="mobile"
➥ Namespace="System.Web.UI.MobileControls"
➥ Assembly="System.Web.Mobile, Version=1.0.3300.0, Culture=neutral,
➥ PublicKeyToken=b03f5f7f11d50a3a" %>
<%@ Page Language="vb" AutoEventWireup="false"
➥ Codebehind="MobileWebForm1.aspx.vb"
➥ Inherits="CustomMobileControl2.MobileWebForm1" %>
<%@ Register TagPrefix="MyCompanyName"
➥ Namespace="ClassLibrary1.MyCompany.CustomControl"
➥ Assembly="ClassLibrary1" %>
<meta name="GENERATOR" content="Microsoft Visual Studio.NET 7.0">
<meta name="CODE_LANGUAGE" content="Visual Basic 7.0">
<meta name="vs_targetSchema"
➥ content="http://schemas.microsoft.com/Mobile/Page">
<body Xmlns:mobile="http://schemas.microsoft.com/Mobile/WebForm">
    <mobile:Label id="Label1" runat="server" StyleReference="Title">
```

```
          Custom Control</mobile:Label>
       <MyCompanyName:MyList id="MyList1" runat="server">
       </MyCompanyName:MyList>
    </mobile:Form>
```

Of principle interest here is the @ Register directive added for our custom control:

```
<%@ Register TagPrefix="MyCompanyName"
➥ Namespace="ClassLibrary1.MyCompany.CustomControl"
➥ Assembly="ClassLibrary1" %>
```

We set a TagPrefix (MyCompanyName) that is used further along the code when we call the control. The NameSpace is built from the Assembly name (ClassLibrary1) and the NameSpace declared within the control itself (see Listing 12.5)—MyCompany.CustomControl. The Assembly is the assembly name as listed in the References in the Solution Explorer (ClassLibrary1).

If you switch back to Design View, the List should now appear as a List control in Form1 as depicted in Figure 12.3. You may also notice that the control has a full property suite in the Properties window. We can set all the usual List properties (such as StyleReference, Alignment, etc.).

---

**FIGURE 12.3:**

CustomMobileControl2 in Design View

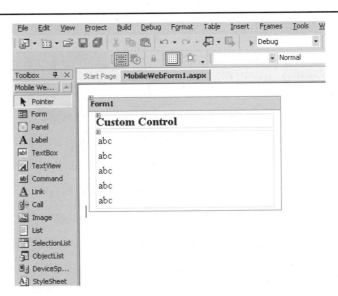

Compile and view the project in a browser. Figure 12.4 shows how the project should appear in the Openwave browser.

FIGURE 12.4:

CustomMobileControl2
running in the
Openwave browser

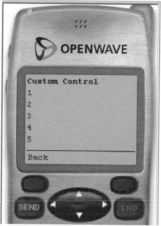

Image of UP.SDK courtesy Openwave Systems, Inc.

## Creating a Composite Control

One of the advantages of using custom controls is that we can create sophisticated controls made up of a number of standard mobile controls. In this section we shall see how to create one of these composite controls.

When I first considered writing this section, I thought that what would make a very good example of a composite control would be a login form. I then went over to the QuickStart Tutorials to see what Microsoft had done there—and guess what—a login form! So, for a very good example of a login form built as a custom control, please have a look at the QuickStart Tutorials. Here, we will do something else....

The following example builds a composite control that consists of two labels and a PhoneCall control. The labels are designed to hold a name and surname and the PhoneCall control provides a phone number that can be dialed with a single click on appropriate devices. This could be used as a standard signature control across multiple forms or even to display expanded details from a contacts list such as those we have built in earlier projects.

The example also demonstrates how you can create and expose your own public properties for the control.

Open a new Class Library project and name it ClassLibrary2. Delete any existing code and copy the code from Listing 12.7 into it.

**Listing 12.7**     **Code for ClassLibrary2: A Composite Custom Control**

```vb
Imports System
Imports System.Web.UI
Imports System.Web.UI.MobileControls
Namespace MyCompany.CustomCompControl

    Public Class MyComposite : Inherits MobileControl
        Implements INamingContainer

        Dim _MyName As String
        Dim _MySurname As String
        Dim _MyPhoneNumber As String


        Public Property MyName() As String
            Get
                Return _MyName
            End Get
            Set(ByVal Value As String)
                _MyName = Value
            End Set
        End Property
        Public Property MySurname() As String
            Get
                Return _MySurname
            End Get
            Set(ByVal Value As String)
                _MySurname = Value
            End Set
        End Property

        Public Property MyPhoneNumber() As String
            Get
                Return _MyPhoneNumber
            End Get
            Set(ByVal Value As String)
                _MyPhoneNumber = Value
            End Set
        End Property

        Protected Overrides Sub CreateChildControls()
            Dim Surname As Label
            Dim Name As Label
            Dim dialler As [PhoneCall]

            Name = New Label()
            Name.Text = "Name: " & MyName
            Controls.Add(Name)
```

```
            Surname = New Label()
            Surname.Text = "Surname: " & MySurname
            Controls.Add(Surname)

            dialler = New [PhoneCall]()
            dialler.PhoneNumber = MyPhoneNumber
            Controls.Add(dialler)
        End Sub

    End Class
End Namespace
```

Again, remember to add references to `System.Web.dll` and `System.Web.Mobile.dll` using Add Reference from the Project menu.

The first part of the code is the familiar `Imports` and `Namespace` statements from the previous project. We also have the following:

```
Implements INamingContainer
```

We need to ensure that we implement `INamingContainer` if we wish to do any databinding at all. It gives each of the child controls (that make up the composite control) a unique ID.

We then set up our public properties with the following code:

```
        Dim _MyName As String
        Dim _MySurname As String
        Dim _MyPhoneNumber As String


        Public Property MyName() As String
            Get
                Return _MyName
            End Get
            Set(ByVal Value As String)
                _MyName = Value
            End Set
        End Property
        Public Property MySurname() As String
            Get
                Return _MySurname
            End Get
            Set(ByVal Value As String)
                _MySurname = Value
            End Set
        End Property
```

```
Public Property MyPhoneNumber() As String
    Get
        Return _MyPhoneNumber
    End Get
    Set(ByVal Value As String)
        _MyPhoneNumber = Value
    End Set
End Property
```

In this code we are establishing three properties: MyName, MySurname, and MyPhoneNumber, which we can attach to our child controls and expose for use. You will notice that as soon as you start typing **Public Property**, the IDE autogenerates a code template of the following:

```
Public Property MyProperty() As SomeType
    Get

    End Get
    Set(ByVal Value As SomeType)

    End Set
End Property
```

This is property template is basically empty, and we just have to fill in the gaps. The third main part of the code declares the three child controls and assigns the values of our public properties to them.

```
Protected Overrides Sub CreateChildControls()
    Dim Surname As Label
    Dim Name As Label
    Dim dialler As [PhoneCall]

    Name = New Label()
    Name.Text = "Name: " & MyName
    Controls.Add(Name)

    Surname = New Label()
    Surname.Text = "Surname: " & MySurname
    Controls.Add(Surname)

    dialler = New [PhoneCall]()
    dialler.PhoneNumber = MyPhoneNumber
    dialer.Text = "Call"
    Controls.Add(dialler)
End Sub
```

Once we have declared each child control, we need to add it to the configuration by calling Controls.Add(). Finish off by saving and compiling the control. (Select Build from the Build menu.)

Open a new Mobile Web application and name it CustomMobileControl3. Add a reference to ClassLibrary2 using Add Reference from the Project menu. Switch to Design View and complete the ASPX code to look like Listing 12.8.

**Listing 12.8**     **ASPX Code for CustomMobileControl3 Project**

```
<%@ Register TagPrefix="MyCompany"
➡ NameSpace="ClassLibrary2.MyCompany.CustomCompControl"
➡ Assembly="ClassLibrary2" %>
<%@ Page Language="vb" AutoEventWireup="false"
➡ Codebehind="MobileWebForm1.aspx.vb"
➡ Inherits="CustomMobileControl3.MobileWebForm1" %>
<%@ Register TagPrefix="mobile"
➡ Namespace="System.Web.UI.MobileControls"
➡ Assembly="System.Web.Mobile, Version=1.0.3300.0, Culture=neutral,
➡ PublicKeyToken=b03f5f7f11d50a3a" %>
<meta name="GENERATOR" content="Microsoft Visual Studio.NET 7.0">
<meta name="CODE_LANGUAGE" content="Visual Basic 7.0">
<meta name="vs_targetSchema"
➡ content="http://schemas.microsoft.com/Mobile/Page">
    <mobile:Label id="Label1"
➡ runat="server">Label</mobile:Label>
    <MyCompany:MyComposite id="MyComposite1"
➡ runat="server">
    </MyCompany:MyComposite>
  </mobile:Form>
</body>
```

I have highlighted those sections of the code that you will need to add. Switch back to Design View. The public properties that we established for the control should now be available in the Properties box under the Misc section. Type a sample name, surname, and phone number into the properties. Your application should now look something like Figure 12.5. Notice that the properties common to all three child controls are now exposed in the Properties box; we can change StyleReference and others for the composite control. As well as using the GUI interface, we could also have worked programmatically with the MyName, MySurname, and MyPhoneNumber properties.

FIGURE 12.5:

FIGURE 12.5:

Screen layout and
Properties box for the
CustomMobileControl3
project

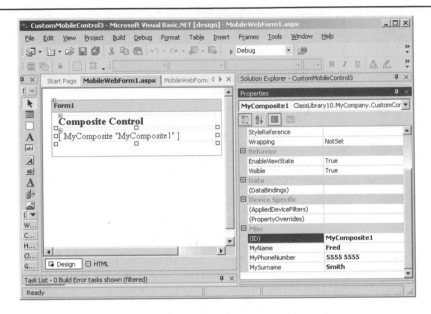

Compile and run the project. In the Openwave browser, it should appear similar to
Figure 12.6.

FIGURE 12.6:

CustomMobileControl3
project displayed in the
Openwave browser

Image of UP.SDK courtesy Openwave Systems, Inc.

## Using Device-Specific Controls That Behave Differently for Different Devices

There are a couple of ways that we can specify device-specific behavior for our controls. One approach is to insert device-specific behavior into the CreateChildControls method of the control. However, Microsoft doesn't recommend this approach, because the idea of mobile controls is to keep them as device independent as possible. This allows for modifications and updates to devices to occur without having to rewrite the code used in an application (or in its controls).

The other approach is to write device-specific control adapters. We will look at how to do this in the next chapter, "Customizing the Device Adapters."

## Building Your Own Original Control

It is possible to build a complete control from scratch. For instance, at the time of the Beta2 release, the Mobile Internet Toolkit contained no timer control. However, I am aware of a couple of people who have built their own custom timer control for the MIT.

Microsoft supplies some basic guidelines for building your own control. They include the following:

- Inherit from the MobileControl base class rather than a Web Forms Control class. To exploit logic from a Web Forms control, use containment to include the control in a mobile control.

- The code of your control should be device independent.

- Create device-specific adapters where you need different rendering of the control for specific devices.

- Design your code so that other developers can inherit properties and methods from the control.

## Summary

The Mobile Internet Toolkit is extensible in a number of areas. One of the most useful is the ability to create and customize your own controls. This chapter has given us a brief overview of how to create both user controls and custom controls.

While it is arguably easier to write user controls, custom controls are the more flexible of the two and ultimately provide us with controls that can benefit from inheritance, can expose properties, and can be easily applied across projects.

In the next chapter we will look briefly at the process of customizing the device adapters for the Mobile Internet Toolkit.

# CHAPTER 13

# Customizing the Device Adapters

- Locating the adapter source files

- Compiling the adapters

- Deploying the modified adapters in a project

- Modifying `Web.config`

This chapter will briefly examine the process of creating and modifying device adapters. There is a lot more to this process than I have covered here, and I recommend referring to the Microsoft documentation if you are planning on making some major changes to the device adapters. Additionally, the adapters that ship with the Mobile Internet Toolkit are written in C#, which is a language I don't cover in this book.

We may wish to modify device adapters for a number of reasons, but typically the need may arise when we have created a custom control that we wish to exhibit some device-specific behavior. Or you may be a device manufacturer and wish to develop and ship an adapter that supports your device. Note that we are looking at modifying the behavior of controls for specific devices in this instance rather than modifying control behavior for different browser types, which we can do by editing the `Web.config` (application level) or `machine.config` (server level) files. The set of devices supported by the Mobile Internet toolkit is listed in Chapter 6, "Getting Started with the Mobile Internet Toolkit."

There are two main steps to the process. First we have to make the desired modifications, and then we have to compile and deploy the customized adaptors into our projects. I will focus in this chapter on the second of these steps—compiling and deploying the customized adapters in our projects.

## Locating the Adapters

The source code for the adapters is normally found in `c:\Program Files\Microsoft .NET\ Mobile Internet Toolkit\Adapter Source`, assuming that you followed the defaults on the original install.

---

**TIP**    It is always a good idea to make a backup of the adapter source files *before* you begin any modifications to them.

---

The adapters come in three categories (at least in Beta2): WML, cHTML, and HTML. Within each category you will find a selection of files that each correspond to a particular mobile control. For example, you can find adapters for the Calendar control across all three categories: `ChtmlCalendarAdapter.cs`, `HtmlCalendarAdapter.cs`, and `WmlCalendarAdapter .cs`. In some cases it may be necessary to modify all three files.

Once you have located the particular adapters of concern to you, open them in a suitable editor and make the modifications that you require. Save the file, and exit the editor.

## Compiling the Adapters

Once we are satisfied with the changes we have made to the adapter code, our next step is to compile the adapters. Back at the start of this book, I promised to steer clear of command line compilers. However, there are some tasks in .NET where their use is fairly unavoidable, and this is one of them. (Another occurs if you wish to create a multifile assembly—not something that is required for everyday projects!)

Visual Studio .NET ships with its own command prompt optimized for its environment (see Figure 13.1). This can be found by selecting Start ➢ Programs ➢ Microsoft Visual Studio .NET 7.0 ➢ Visual Studio .NET Tools ➢ Visual Studio .NET Command Prompt.

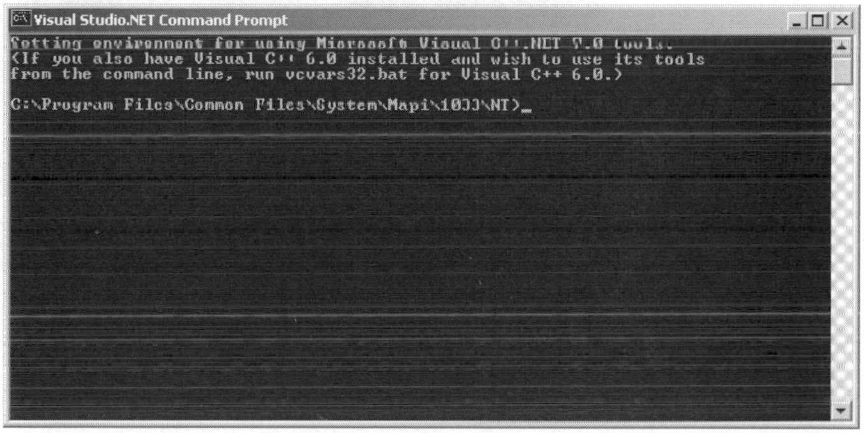

FIGURE 13.1:

Visual Studio .NET Command Prompt window

Once you have opened the command prompt, navigate to the directory containing the adapters by typing the following and then pressing Enter. This assumes that you have used the default locations for your installation.

```
cd c:\Program Files\Microsoft.NET\Mobile Internet Toolkit\Adapter
➥ Source
```

The command prompt should now give the full path to the Adapter Source directory as its current location.

The next step is to run the compiler. At the command prompt, type the following and then press Enter.

```
csc /debug+ /target:library
➥ /out:System.Web.UI.MobileControls.ShippedAdapterSource.dll
➥ /r:System.Web.Mobile.dll /D:COMPILING_FOR_SHIPPED_SOURCE *.cs
```

If you get no messages saying that things have come unstuck, then chances are it has all worked without drama.

Take a look in the Adapter Source directory. (You may need to press F5 to refresh.) The directory should now contain two additional files: `System.Web.UI.MobileControls.Shipped` `.AdapterSource.pdb` and `System.Web.UI.MobileControls.Shipped.AdapterSource.dll`.

Refer to Figure 13.2 for how the command prompt window should appear after a successful compile.

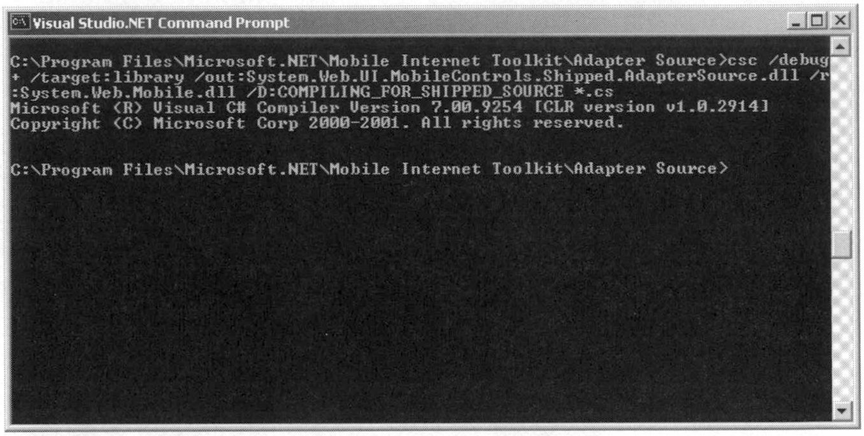

**FIGURE 13.2:**

Visual Studio .NET Command Prompt window after successful compile of adapter code

## Deploying the Modified Adapters in a Project

Once we have created and compiled our adapters, we need to deploy them in our projects. We can do this within individual projects with the following process:

1. Back in Visual Studio .NET, in the project that is to use the modified adapters, click the Show All Files button at the top of the Solution Explorer.

2. Right-click the Bin folder, and select Include in Project from the context menu. It should now appear as an open folder rather than as an outline.

3. Right-click the Bin folder again, and choose Add ➢ Add Existing Item.

4. Navigate to the Adapter Source directory and choose the `System.Web.UI.MobileControls` `.Shipped.AdapterSource.dll` that you created earlier (see Figure 13.3). You may need to change the Files of Type option to All Files.

**FIGURE 13.3:**

Solution Explorer with included adapter file

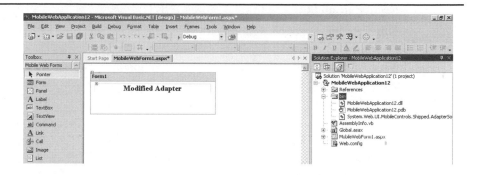

## Modifying *Web.config*

The last step is to modify the Web.config file so that the application knows to use the modified adapters. In the Adapter Source directory, you will find a file named web .config-shippedAdapters. If you have created extra adapters, you will need to modify this file accordingly. Otherwise, if you have just modified existing adapters, then use the file as it is.

Open the file in an appropriate editor such as Notepad. Copy all the contents between the <system.web> tags. Paste the code into the Web.config file of your project (somewhere between the <system.web> tags) in Visual Studio .NET.

---

**TIP**    If you plan to edit the web.config-shippedAdapters using a plain text editor, use WordPad rather than Notepad—the formatting will make more sense!

---

If you are using custom attributes, you may also need to set the allowCustomAttributes property of the <mobileControls> tag to True.

Take a quick look at the code in the web.config-shippedAdapters file. It is grouped into the three main categories of WML, HTML, and cHTML inside specific <device> tags. Within each category, each control is listed along with its associated adapter. If you have created a new control and associated adapters, it is a fairly straightforward process to add them to this file. Refer to Listing 13.1 for an example of the syntax where the control is called MyControl and the adapter is named HtmlMyControlAdapter:

**Listing 13.1**    **Example Syntax for a Control Adapter Reference in *web.config-shippedAdapters***

```
<control name="System.Web.UI.MobileControls.MyControl"
➥ adapter="System.Web.UI.MobileControls.ShippedAdapterSource
➥.HtmlMyControlAdapter,System.Web.UI.MobileControls
➥.ShippedAdapterSource"/>
```

Recompile and test your Visual Studio .NET project.

Note that the sort of configuration information contained in the `web.config-shippedAdapters` file is normally accessed from the `machine.config` file. So far in this book we have not looked at this file, but it provides much of the overall configuration settings common across applications. The file can normally be found (on a Windows 2000 machine) in the `C:\WINNT\Microsoft.NET\ Framework\v.[current build]\CONFIG` directory.

If a new device comes out on the market that uses a browser already supported by the Mobile Internet Toolkit, adding support for that device is simply a case of adding an appropriate entry into the `machine.config` file. The file is far too large to reproduce here, but it is well laid out and easy to navigate (particularly if you open it with WordPad rather than Notepad).

## Summary

Although making the necessary changes to the device adapter code can be quite fiddly, involving numerous small changes across multiple files, the process of implementing the modified code is quite straightforward. It potentially offers a powerful way to extend the Mobile Internet Toolkit and enables us to expand the device support of our applications as new devices become available.

In the next chapter we will revisit building distributed applications using XML Web Services.

# CHAPTER 14

# Using XML Web Services to Build Distributed Applications

- Creating a simple XML Web Service

- Building the database

- Building the XML Web Service

- Consuming the XML Web Service

- XML Web Service directories

- Using the Add Web Reference dialog box

- The Discovery files

- The SOAP Toolkit

We introduced XML Web Services back in Chapter 1, "What Is .NET?" Essentially, an XML Web Service is a software component or data library that can be accessed either locally or over the Internet. We can use XML Web Services to include additional functionality in our applications without having to write all the code ourselves. In theory, an entire application could be built whose functionality relies on a number of XML Web Services sourced from different locations, and the local code could simply consist of a user interface and some simple "plumbing" to access and exploit the XML Web Services.

What makes XML Web Services different from the traditional COM approach is that they rely on XML to package the data and commands that are exchanged between clients and XML Web Services. The XML approach in turn makes use of the Simple Object Access Protocol (SOAP) to give it a consistent representation that can be readily interpreted by otherwise unrelated clients and providers. Thus, the key advantage is that XML Web Services can operate relatively unimpeded on the Internet, whereas other technologies such as COM can often run afoul of firewalls and other security constraints. Microsoft also produces a SOAP Toolkit that can apply a SOAP "wrapper" to existing COM objects, which enables them to behave as XML Web Services. (See "The SOAP Toolkit" later in this chapter.)

## Creating a Simple XML Web Service

Creating an XML Web Service is a reasonably straightforward proposition in Visual Studio .NET, depending of course on the complexity of the service itself! Because a detailed study of XML Web Services is beyond the scope of this book, this sample will be quite simple.

For the sample service, we will create an object that returns a thought for the day. Many site's authors use some form of daily homily to add a bit of interest or a discussion point to their normal presentation. Additionally, a thought for the day gives the impression that a site is regularly updated. The thought-for-the-day service here will provide a randomly selected quotation that can be changed each time the site is accessed. The quotes are stored in a database, allowing them to be easily changed or added to.

---

**NOTE**    Note that we could achieve the same type of effect by using the AdRotator mobile control.

---

We need to first set up the database of quotes. Because this is an example, we are not going to store huge numbers of quotes or build an industrial-strength database. A simple database in Microsoft Access or, if you prefer, SQL Server will suffice. The following instructions apply to Access.

## Building the Database

To build the database, follow these steps:

1. Open a new blank Access database.

2. Name it `quotedb.mdb` and save it somewhere convenient, such as in My Documents.

3. From the database window, select Create Table in Design View.

4. Name the first field `id` and give it the datatype `autonumber`. Make it the primary key by right-clicking the small arrow to the left of the field name and selecting Primary Key.

5. Name the second field `quote` and set the datatype as `memo`.

6. Close the Design View for the table and save as `Table1`.

7. Double-click Table1 and create 10 entries of suitable quotes that you might like your service to provide. See Figure 14.1.

Table1 of the database with some stored quotes

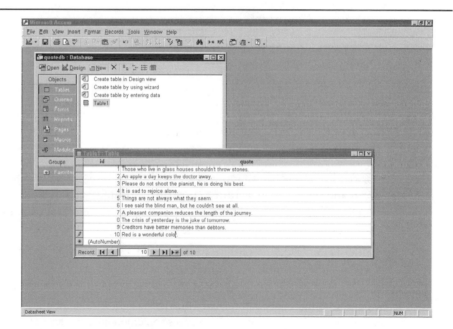

## Building the XML Web Service

Fire up Visual Studio .NET and select New Project. From the dialog window, choose Visual Basic Projects (we could also choose C# or C++, but we're using Visual Basic because that's what this book is about) from the left-hand pane and ASP.NET Web Service from the right-hand pane. You will be prompted to give the project a name. Because the exercise is meant to be a demonstration application, we will choose something distinctive such as the default `WebService1`. Then follow these steps:

1. Select the Code Behind window by right-clicking the form and selecting View Code.

2. This window offers the opportunity to create a simple "Hello World" example XML Web Service by removing comments from a few lines of code and then compiling the code. Feel free to give this a spin, as it will give you a feel for how an XML Web Service is put together and how it looks when functioning. See Figure 14.2.

**FIGURE 14.2:**

The example code included in Visual Studio .NET, illustrating a "Hello World" XML Web Service

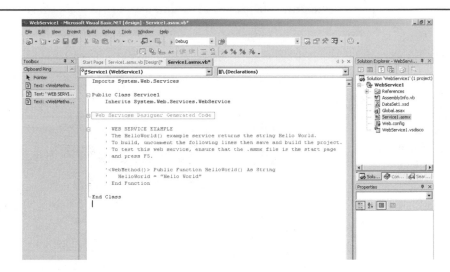

3. Switch back to Design View and select the data tools. Drag an OleDataAdapter onto the form and set up a connection to the `quotedb` database. (Click New Connection, choose Microsoft Jet 4.0 OLE DB Provider from the Provider tab, click Next, locate the database, test the connection, and click OK.)

4. In the Data Adapter Configuration Wizard, choose Use SQL Statements and in the Query Builder choose All Columns.

**TIP**    We can test the query in the Query Builder by right-clicking somewhere in the query table and selecting the Run option. Doing so should populate the lower table with the results of the query.

5. Click OK and in Advanced Options deselect everything, as we won't be using any of the options.

6. Click Next and Finish.

7. Right-click the OleDbDataAdapter1 that is in Design View and select Generate DataSet. (Check the Add This Dataset to the Designer box.) Click OK and use the Preview Data option by right-clicking the OleDbDataAdapter1 to check that everything worked as expected.

8. Switch to code behind. At the end of the "Hello World" example in the Service1 class, add the code in Listing 14.1 (and then delete the "Hello World" example!).

**Listing 14.1    The Thought for the Day Web Service**

```
<WebMethod()> Public Function DailyThought() As String

    Dim intRanValue As Integer
          OleDbDataAdapter1.Fill(DataSet11, "Table1")

          intRanValue = Int((10 * Rnd()) + 1)
          DailyThought =
➥ DataSet11.Tables("Table1").Rows.Find(intRanValue).Item
➥("quote")

End Function
```

The code is straightforward. First, we fill our DataSet. The following line generates a random value between 1 and 10, which we can match against the primary key values in our database:

```
rValue = Int((10 * Rnd()) + 1)
```

The next line retrieves the appropriate quote matching the randomly generated primary-key value:

```
DailyThought =
    DataSet11.Tables("Table1").Rows.Find(intRanValue).Item("quote")
```

This line assigns the returned string containing the thought for the day to the return value of the DailyThought function.

Click the Play (Start) button or press F5 to compile and view the project. (This process is now far more reminiscent of Visual C++ than good old Visual Basic. We now have to sit through build windows and whatever while it all happens. And at the end of the day, there will now no longer be a File ➢ Make *MyReallyCoolProgram.exe*. The compile process is all handled in Build!)

If the project compiles successfully, it should generate an instance of Internet Explorer (assuming that IE is your default browser) containing a link to the service and a warning about using the default namespace when the service is made public. Details are provided on how to change the namespace, but, as this is only a sample running locally, we won't bother with it yet. Refer to Figure 14.3.

**FIGURE 14.3:**

Internet Explorer
showing a link to the
newly created XML
Web Service, and the
recommendation
concerning
namespaces

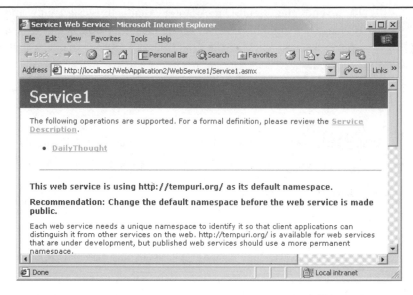

**FIGURE 14.3:**

Internet Explorer
showing a link to the
newly created XML
Web Service, and the
recommendation
concerning
namespaces

Clicking the link to DailyThought will open another page containing an Invoke button
and a sample SOAP request and response showing the Post and Get calls to and from our
XML Web Service. They are written in XML but are reasonably self-explanatory even if
you are unfamiliar with the language. See Figure 14.4.

**FIGURE 14.4:**

Internet Explorer
showing the Invoke
button (for the
`DailyThought`
function) and part of
the sample SOAP
request/response

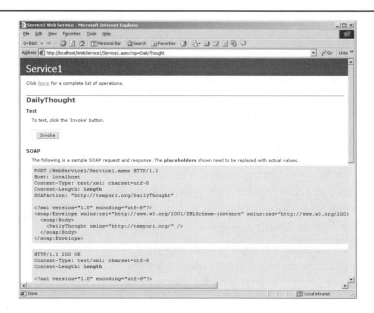

Click the Invoke button. IE should come up with a bit of XML containing one of the quotes that was entered in the database. See Figure 14.5.

**FIGURE 14.5:**

The XML response containing the thought for the day

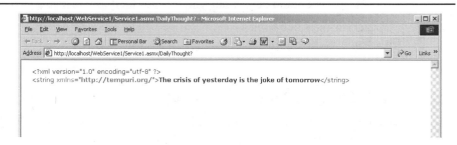

Finally, we will see how to change the namespace reference within the XML Web Service. Stop running the project and return to Code View. You'll see the following class declaration:

```
Public Class Service1
```

Immediately before it, add the following line:

```
<WebService(namespace:="http://www.MyFantasticWebServiceSite.com")>
```

*MyFantasticWebServiceSite.com* represents the URL over which you have some control and where the XML Web Service will probably reside.

The full code appears in Listing 14.2.

**Listing 14.2     The Entire Code for the Thought for the Day Web Service**

```
Imports System.Web.Services

<WebService(namespace:="http://www.MyFantasticWebServiceSite.com")>
➡ Public Class Service1
    Inherits System.Web.Services.WebService

Web Services Designer Generated Code

    <WebMethod()> Public Function DailyThought() As String
        Dim intRanValue As Integer
        OleDbDataAdapter1.Fill(DataSet11, "Table1")
        intRanValue = Int((10 * Rnd()) + 1)
        DailyThought =
➡ DataSet11.Tables("Table1").Rows.Find(intRanValue).Item("quote")
    End Function

End Class
```

Note that I haven't included all the code collapsed in the Web Services Designer Generated Code node. If you run the project again, you will also notice that the warning concerning namespaces should have disappeared from the initial instance of Internet Explorer.

If everything is behaving as it should, we will be ready to call up our XML Web Service from some of the mobile applications that we will be creating.

## Consuming an XML Web Service

Making use of an XML Web Service is termed as *consuming* that XML Web Service. An XML Web Service is normally available somewhere online and is located and included in your projects as a *Web Reference*. You can consume an XML Web Service whether the XML Web Service is located on the local Web server or somewhere else. However, if the XML Web Service is located on the local computer, you can also include it via a standard reference. In a mobile application, to consume the XML Web Service that we have just created, follow these steps:

1. Create a new mobile project in Visual Basic (MobileWebService1).

2. Right-click References in the Solution Explorer and use either Add Reference (for the local machine) or Add Web Reference (if the XML Web Service is elsewhere and online) to locate and add your XML Web Service. (In this case, you will use Add Reference. You are looking for the `WebService1.dll` file, which, if you have followed the defaults, should be found at `c:\Inetpub\wwwroot\WebService1\bin`.)

3. From the Project menu, use Add Reference to add a reference to the `System.Web`
`.Services.dll`.

4. In Design View, add a TextView control and a Command control to Form1. (See TextView1 and Command1 in Figure 14.6.)

---

**FIGURE 14.6:**

Form1 layout for
MobileWebService1

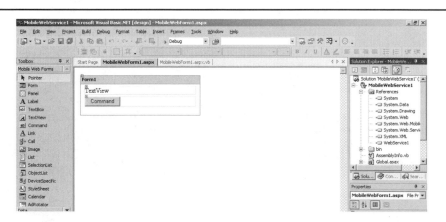

**5.** Double-click the Command control to enter code behind and add the code shown in Listing 14.3.

**6.** Compile and run the project. Figure 14.7 illustrates how it should appear in the Openwave browser after clicking the Command1 link.

---

**Listing 14.3**    **The Code Behind for MobileWebService1**

```
Private Sub Command1_Click(ByVal sender As System.Object, ByVal e
➡ As System.EventArgs) Handles Command1.Click

  Dim myService As WebService1.Service1 = New
➡ WebService1.Service1()

      TextView1.Text = myService.DailyThought

  End Sub
```

---

**FIGURE 14.7:**

MobileWebService1 running in the Openwave browser

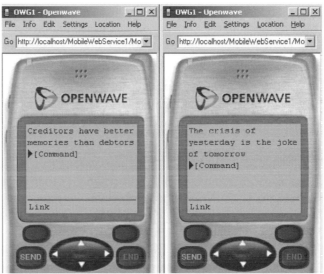

Image of UP.SDK courtesy Openwave Systems, Inc.

What we've just created is a very bare-bones XML Web Service. We can very easily make the code a little more robust by using the new exception-handling capabilities of Visual Basic .NET and one of the features from ADO.NET. Listing 14.4 contains the amended code for WebService1.

---

**Listing 14.4** **Amended Code, WebService1**

```
<WebMethod()> Public Function DailyThought() As String
        Dim intRanValue As Integer
        Dim intNumRows As Integer

        Try
            OleDbDataAdapter1.Fill(DataSet11, "Table1")
            intNumRows = DataSet11.Tables("Table1").Rows.Count()
            intRanValue = Int((intNumRows * Rnd()) + 1)
            DailyThought =
➡ DataSet11.Tables("Table1").Rows.Find(intRanValue).Item("quote")
        Catch
            DailyThought = "Tomorrow is another day!"

        End Try

End Function
```

---

The random-number generator has been modified so that it bases its output on the number of records found in the DataSet. So we can add additional quotes without having to continuously update the code. The exception handler is set up to return a standard quote ("Tomorrow is another day!") if for any reason the database (or the record we are after) is unavailable.

In practice, we would put the code into the Form_Load event so that the thought is displayed when the form is called rather than in response to the Command button.

## Web-Service Directories

As long as we are connected to the Internet, we can make use of XML Web Services that have been made available by other providers for public consumption. Some of these services may be on a fee-paying basis, whereas others are free. One starting point for locating online XML Web Services is the Microsoft UDDI Directory, and a possible option for test services to use during development is the Test Microsoft UDDI Directory. The UDDI (Universal Description, Discovery, and Integration) directories provide online business directories that can be searched using a range of techniques, including visual mapping mechanisms. Note that there is much more to UDDI than just XML Web Services and that Microsoft provides extensive documentation and links from its UDDI site (http://uddi.microsoft.com) that are worth spending considerable quality time with if you are at all interested in this aspect of information technology.

**WARNING**    You need to be aware that many available XML Web Services might be totally inappropriate for mobile Websites. You need to take into account factors such as likely processing times, data sizes, type of security used, and data formats. The current limitations on mobile devices apply equally to XML Web Services as they do to anything you may use to construct and deliver your mobile sites.

We can access both of these directories directly from the Add Web Reference dialog box from the Project ➢ Add Web Reference menu (or by right-clicking References in the Solution Explorer). Refer to Figure 14.8.

**FIGURE 14.8:**

The Add Web Reference dialog box

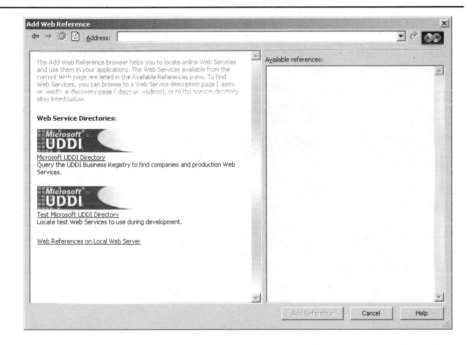

Alternatively, we can enter URLs directly into the Address bar. There are a number of good starting points for XML Web Services, such as www.salcentral.com or www.xmltoday .com. It is a good idea to use our Web browser to locate a desired XML Web Service from such a site and then copy its URL into the Add Web Reference dialog box.

## Using the Add Web Reference Dialog

To see how to add an XML Web Service as a Web Reference, we will need to create a new mobile project: MobileWebService2. Drag a TextView control to Form1 and select Add Web Reference from the Project menu.

To add the XML Web Service that we created earlier using this dialog (rather than using Add Reference, as we did previously), type **http://localhost/WebService1/Service1.asmx** into the navigation bar of the Add Web Reference dialog box. We could also try using the dynamic discovery option provided by the link Web References on Local Web Server that appears in the left-hand pane of the dialog box. Or, as you will see later in this chapter, we can make use of any static discovery files we may have created.

The details for Service1 should now appear in the left-hand pane of the dialog box, and links to View Contract and View Documentation should appear in the right-hand pane. Refer to Figure 14.9.

**FIGURE 14.9:**

The Add Web Reference dialog box containing the details for WebService1

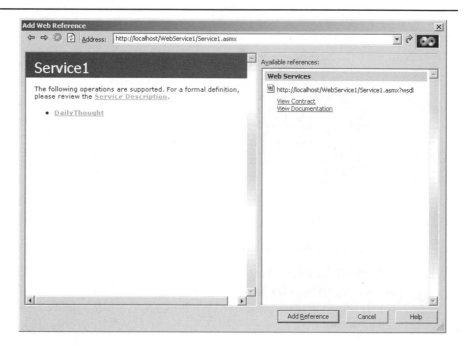

Click the Add Reference button (which should now be active) to add the XML Web Service to our project. In Solution Explorer, a Web Reference folder should now be visible. Expanding this node should reveal our Service1 references, as in Figure 14.10.

**FIGURE 14.10:**

Solution Explorer for
MobileWebService2,
displaying Web
Reference details
for Service1
(WebService1)

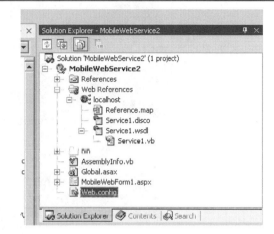

Switch to code behind and add the code from Listing 14.5 to the Page_Load subroutine.

**Listing 14.5        Code Behind for the MobileWebService2 Project**

```
Private Sub Page_Load(ByVal sender As System.Object, ByVal e As
➡ System.EventArgs) Handles MyBase.Load
       Dim myService As localhost.Service1 = New localhost.Service1()

       TextView1.Text = myService.DailyThought

End Sub
```

**NOTE**     Note that because we have added WebService1 as a *Web Reference,* we can now access Service1 directly rather than via WebService1 (as we did when adding the Web Service as a straight reference). Using the Add Web Reference option automatically includes a project reference to the System.Web.Services.dll.

Compile and run the project. Figure 14.11 illustrates the project running in the Openwave browser.

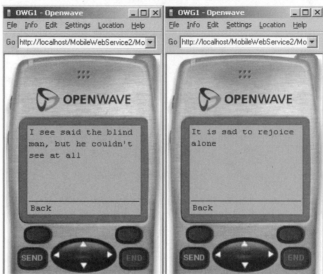

Image of UP.SDK courtesy Openwave Systems, Inc.

## The Discovery Files

Discovery files are XML documents that enable the programmatic location and interrogation of XML Web Service descriptions. They contain the links to resources that describe the XML Web Service.

Dynamic discovery files (ending in the extension .vsdisco) and static discovery files (with the extension .disco) are the two main types of discovery files. The dynamic discovery approach enables discovery of XML Web Services through the directory tree. The file is automatically generated when an XML Web Service is created, and a default.vdisco file is located in the root of the Web server. The file can be edited to exclude specific subdirectories from the search.

To create a static discovery file for our XML Web Service, we can create the document with a simple text editor such as Notepad and save it with the .disco file extension, use the Add New Item dialog box from the Project menu, or right-click the project name in Solution Explorer and select Add New Item from the New submenu. Choose Static Discovery File from the dialog box. A file named Disco1.disco will be created and listed in the Solution Explorer.

We can add relevant code to the basic framework to reference service contract(s) and/or other discovery document(s). References to service contracts are added with a <contractRef> tag, whereas references to other discovery documents employ a <discoveryRef> tag.

Listing 14.6 illustrates a simple discovery file for Service1.

---

**Listing 14.6**       **A Simple Discovery File for Service1 (WebService1)**

```
<?xml version="1.0" encoding="utf-8" ?>
<discovery xmlns="http://schemas.xmlsoap.org/disco/">
   <discoveryRef ref="http://localhost/Webservice1/Service1.asmx" />
</discovery>
```

---

Save the file as `Disco1.disco` (the default). The discovery file can be accessed from Add Web Reference in the Project menu by typing its URL directly into the address bar (i.e., `http://localhost/WebService1/Disco1.disco`). The right-hand pane of the Add Web Reference dialog should then display a link to `http://localhost/Webservice1/Service1.asmx`. (See Figure 14.12.) Clicking that link should expose the descriptions for Service1. (Refer to Figure 14.9.)

---

**FIGURE 14.12:**

Using the discovery file to access Service1 in the Add Web Reference dialog

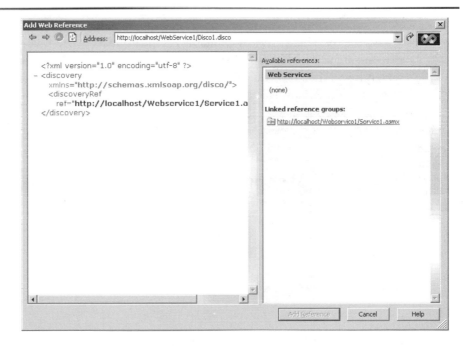

If we wish to make our XML Web Services available for public consumption without expecting our potential clients to poke blindly around in our directory structures looking for them, we can provide direct links to our disco files from a Web page.

For example, the code contained in Listing 14.7 establishes a very simple Web page to provide a link to our `Disco1.disco` file. This code could be very easily incorporated as a separate page or link into an existing Website that we might control and use to advertise our XML Web Services.

**Listing 14.7    A Simple Web Page with a Link to the XML Web Service Discovery File**

```
<HTML>
<HEAD>
<TITLE>Web Service Discovery Links</TITLE>
</HEAD>
<BODY>
<H1>Web Service Discovery Links for MySite
<BR>
<A HREF="http://localhost/WebService1/Disco1.disco">Service1</A>
</H1>
</BODY>
</HTML>
```

Save the file as `ws1.html` by using the All Files option in the Save as Type dialog (assuming that you are using Notepad). Drop the `ws1.html` file into the root directory of your Web server. It will then be accessed by using the Add Web Reference dialog in a Visual Studio .NET project and provides a direct link to the relevant discovery files. See Figure 14.13.

**FIGURE 14.13:**

The Add Web Reference dialog displaying the `ws1.html` Web page

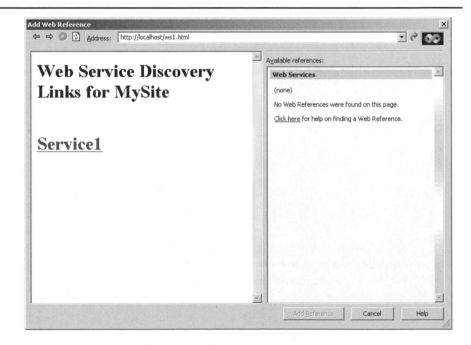

Another approach is to add the link to the <HEAD> tag of the preferred Web page. For example, the code in Listing 14.8 might be placed in the default page for our site so that if a client calls our site from the Add Web Reference dialog, the relevant links will be displayed. This approach has the advantage of using the right-hand pane of the dialog box to display the links to the XML Web Services, and our users are automatically presented with the XML Web Service links.

**Listing 14.8** **A Default Web Page with Discovery-Link Details Placed in the Header**

```
<HTML>
<HEAD>
<TITLE>Web Service Discovery Links</TITLE>
<LINK TYPE="text/xml" REL="alternate"
➥ HREF="WebService1/Disco1.disco" />
</HEAD>
<BODY>
<H1>Web Service Discovery Links for MySite</H1>
</BODY>
</HTML>
```

Save the code from Listing 14.8 as `Default.htm` and place it in the root of your Web server.

**WARNING** Please don't replace any existing `Default.htm` that you might already be using in root of your Web server. (You will then wonder why your Website has gone pear-shaped!) You can insert the <LINK> tag into an existing page and then delete it later if necessary.

Figure 14.14 illustrates how this approach should look in the Add Web Reference dialog.

**NOTE** We have used the `.htm` file extension rather than `.html`. The default in IIS is the `.htm` extension. If you are like me—normally fussy about using the `.html` extension—you will need to sort it out in Default Web Site Properties in IIS Manager.

Finally, a command-line tool (`disco.exe`) is also available that can help locate XML Web Services at a given URL. To take advantage of it, follow these steps:

1. Create a suitable directory into which to download the XML Web Service information—such as `c:\wsdump`.

2. Open the Visual Studio .NET Command Prompt (Start Menu ➤ Programs ➤ Microsoft Visual Studio .NET 7.0 ➤ Visual Studio .NET Tools ➤ Visual Studio. NET Command Prompt). At the command prompt, type the following and press Enter:

```
Disco /out:wsdump http://localhost/WebService1/Disco1.disco
```

The `Default.htm`
document displayed
in the Add Web
Reference dialog

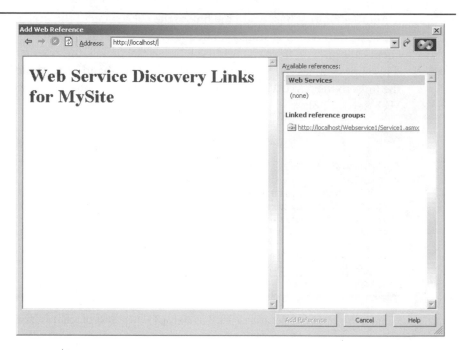

If everything works correctly (see Figure 14.15), the contents of the wsdump directory
should include copies of the following files: `Disco1.disco`, `results.discomap`, `Service1`
`.disco`, and `Service1.wsdl`.

**FIGURE 14.15:**

Running `disco.exe`
at the command
prompt

Assuming that we have obtained these files from a remote server somewhere, they can now be perused at leisure for information regarding the available XML Web Services. (They can also be accessed from the Add Web Reference dialog using a local path such as `c:\wsdump\Disco1.disco`.)

A range of switches and options are available with the `disco.exe` tool. Type: **`disco /?`** at the command prompt for more details.

---

**TIP**    Documentation is another important aspect of XML Web Services. Presumably, if we wish others to access our XML Web Services, we need to provide relevant instructions. There are some quite simple yet impressive techniques for extracting key information from the XML descriptions to help build appropriate documentation. Refer to the relevant Microsoft support documentation for further information.

## The SOAP Toolkit

You may quite likely have a range of existing and suitable COM objects that you may wish to give XML Web Service functionality to without having to rebuild them extensively. You can do so through the SOAP Toolkit, which is available for download from the (Microsoft) MSDN downloads site at `http://msdn.microsoft.com/downloads`.

The toolkit includes the following:

- A high-level API (including the SOAP Toolkit Wizard) for applying a SOAP wrapper to COM objects
- The SOAP Messaging Objects Framework
- A low-level API for direct control over the process
- A range of sample clients and services
- The Microsoft SOAP Trace Tool

For many simple objects, the SOAP process can be handled easily by the SOAP Toolkit Wizard, which pretty much takes care of everything. However, if the object has some complexities, such as custom data types, or if you prefer to keep control of the process, the low-level API allows the developer to manage all aspects of the process, such as customizing the SOAP headers.

A detailed exploration of the SOAP Toolkit is really a topic for another book. Microsoft provides extensive documentation on the topic in the Visual Studio .NET help files.

---

**NOTE**    One concern expressed by developers about the use of XML Web Services is security. Currently, XML Web Services offer the same set of security options available to any other Web application and can make use of the standard set of Microsoft security options, such as SSL, Basic authentication, Integrated Windows authentication, and client certificate authentication. At the time of this writing, there are long-term plans for introducing encryption standards into the SOAP specification.

## Summary

XML Web Services provide us with a powerful tool for extending the functionality of our applications. They could also provide another source of income for developers, as individuals and organizations develop and provide online services in commercial settings.

We have only scratched the surface of building XML Web Services. Many other options are available for extending and improving the performance of XML Web Services. These include the ability to build asynchronous functionality into XML Web Services so that the client is able to perform other tasks while waiting for a response from an XML Web Service and the use of tools such as the XML Web Services Description Language Tool (`wsdle.exe`).

In the next chapter, we will touch on using output caching to improve performance of our Mobile Web applications. Output caching can also be applied to XML Web Services.

# CHAPTER 15

# Building Performance Applications

- Caching output

- Caching portions of a Mobile Web Page

- Session management

- Additional performance hints

**M**aximizing performance is always desirable and, given the limitations of the mobile Internet, is particularly desirable when building our projects for this environment.

Many performance tweaks are application-specific, but we can apply a range of techniques to most (if not all) of our mobile projects to help them along. The techniques cover areas such as sensible management of state, taking advantage of some of the caching opportunities in ASP.NET, and making use of properties such as Page.IsPostBack. In this chapter, we will look at some of these techniques.

## Caching Output

ASP.NET offers two approaches to caching page output. The first is output caching and the second takes the more traditional approach to application caching.

The advantage of caching is that we can cut down on the amount of work being processed by the server. This is particularly relevant with dynamic Web applications that may have processing-intensive components. Caching requests that are likely to be repeated can have a significant overall positive impact on application performance. The page is dynamically generated for the first request, but subsequent requests for the same information can be delivered directly from cache without the performance overhead of reprocessing the request.

If we take the traditional approach to cache management, we can use the Page.Response property to programmatically manipulate the HttpCachePolicy class in code behind. This is illustrated in the following code:

```
Dim ts As New TimeSpan(0, 0, 30)
Response.Cache.SetMaxAge(ts)
```

Alternatively, cache can be controlled using the @ OutputCache directive. We simply add this directive to the top of the ASPX page and control it via its attributes. For example, consider this code:

```
<%@ OutputCache Duration="10" VaryByParam="None" %>
```

Added to the top of an ASPX page (in HTML View), this directive will ensure that the page will be cached on the server for 10 seconds after a client originally requests it and that any pages matching the original request will receive the cached version.

The Duration attribute sets the life of the cache in seconds. The VaryByParam attribute is required and enables multiple versions of the page to be generated and cached if need be.

For example, if we have a page that provides a response in return for user input as either GET or POST HTTP methods, then we can specify the parameter type that we wish to cache any responses to. If one of our responses was based on a request for gender, we could specify that with VaryByParam="gender". Presumably, the code would result in two sets of responses being cached. We can specify multiple parameters by separating the parameters with a semi-colon. For example, VaryByParam="gender;age" would separately cache any pages that returned with different age and gender combinations.

Using the none value, as in the OutputCache directive example, ensures that a single version of the page is cached.

We can use a range of other attributes to manage our output caching. These are discussed in the Microsoft documentation, but it is worth mentioning the VaryByHeader and VaryByCustom attributes. The former can be used to cache pages based on header content, such as the Accept-Language headers, and can be used to handle multiple headers. The latter can be used to cache pages based on browser type or other custom strings written by the developer. It can also be used to extend the functionality of the output cache by overriding the HttpApplication .GetVaryByCustomString method.

## Caching Portions of a Mobile Web Page

Also known as fragment caching, caching portions of a Mobile Web Page enables us to cache those elements that are either static or are processor intensive but likely to be subject to multiple requests. Thus, caching can improve performance and continue to dynamically generate the remaining sections of the page that require dynamic production or constant updating.

Essentially, after identifying those areas of the page that we wish to cache, we write them into user controls (the ASCX file—see Chapter 12, "Creating Custom Controls"). We then specify appropriate output caching for each user control by using the approach outlined in the previous section.

When using this approach to cache portions of a page, be aware that we cannot programmatically manipulate our user control from our page when the user control contains an @ OutputCache directive. Anything we need to do with the control must be programmed directly into the control using its own Page_Load event.

## Session Management

Session state is the continuity that a client is able to create with a server while the client is making use of a particular application from that server. Although from the client's point of view the server is maintaining ongoing communication, as far as the server is concerned it is simply receiving a series of independent requests. The ability to respond to the client's sequence of requests as if the requests were an ongoing communication is called *session management* and it is used to maintain a *state* with the client. It can be maintained in Mobile Forms using session- and application-level variables. These are declared and assigned values in a very similar fashion to the way we used to do it in good old ASP pages.

## Session Variables

We used an example of declaring a session variable back in Listing 10.1, which was the My-Contacts example. Session variables can be essentially used as global variables to hold relevant information between requests from a client. We can declare and use a session variable very simply in our code behind. For example, we used the following in the MyContacts application:

```
Session("currID") = e.ListItem.Value
```

That line created the currID session variable and assigned its value to e.ListItem.Value. To use the session variable, we simply reference Session("currID").

## Application Variables

We can use an application variable as a sort of "super" global variable. It can be used to share information between different sessions or to keep track of information relevant (and often administrative) to the application as a whole—such as the number of consecutive users. We declare application variables in a similar fashion to session variables. Here's an example:

```
Application ("Number_of_Users")  =  0
```

Another way of looking at the difference between application and session variables is to consider that if we have 20 simultaneous users of our application, we may have 20 separate sessions running and therefore 20 copies of a particular session variable (such as currID). There will, however, be only one copy of the application variable (such as Number_of_Users).

## Disabling Session State

Despite the usefulness of session state, it does introduce some overhead in terms of application performance, and there are plenty of situations where our applications have no need of it. For example, we might be just providing a static page with standard information. In such situations, we can disable session state to gain some performance boost. We can do so on a page-by-page basis or at the application level.

To disable session state for a page, switch to Design View and click somewhere in the general page area to set the Properties box (in the right-hand corner of the IDE) to Document. Within the Properties box, set the enableSessionState and enableViewState attributes to false. Alternatively, we can write these directly into the @ Page directive in HTML View. The following code is an example:

```
<%@ Page Language="vb" AutoEventWireup="false"
    Codebehind="MobileWebForm1.aspx.vb"
    Inherits="MobileWebApplication1.MobileWebForm1"
    enableSessionState="false" enableViewState="false"%>
```

To disable session state at the application level, we will need to also set the mode attribute to Off in the sessionState section of the Web.config file.

| TIP | An alternative situation is where we may need to read session variables but not create or modify them. For these circumstances, we can set the enableSessionState attribute to ReadOnly. |
| --- | --- |

## Using ViewState

In the section on "Handling Cookies and State Management" in Chapter 8, "A Deeper Look at the Mobile Internet Toolkit and VB. NET," we briefly looked at ViewState management. That process provides a powerful degree of page-level state management. In terms of application performance, we can make quite a difference by activating or deactivating ViewState for individual pages and controls.

It is worth spending some time with ViewState, particularly when maximizing performance for mobile applications, as the ViewState operates slightly differently with Mobile Web Forms than it does with ordinary Web Forms. In the case of Web Forms, ViewState is sent back to the client, but in the case of Mobile Web Forms, to save bandwidth, ViewState is saved on the server in the user's session. This can add overhead to the server, which can, in turn, degrade performance. Judicious use of ViewState (and setting the enableViewState to false in the Document or individual control properties box) can make quite a difference for heavily used applications where performance is vital.

An example is where a particular document contains a considerable amount of text. With ViewState enabled, multiple users accessing the document will result in multiple copies of it being cached on the server. By disabling ViewState, we can limit the number of server copies to one.

# Additional Performance Hints

The following includes a number of additional hints for optimizing your code. Microsoft also includes documentation on the issue, and undoubtedly you will create your own bag of tricks the more you use these tools.

## Page.IsPostback

We can use the Page.IsPostback property to determine if a particular request has been processed by the server for the first time or if it is a subsequent request. In many cases (such as when populating a list), we may only need to process a request once for any given session, so we can use this property to conditionally execute code. Listing 15.1 is an example, in pseudocode.

| Listing 15.1 | An Example Use of *Page.IsPostback* to Conditionally Execute Code |
| --- | --- |

```
Sub Page_Load(sender As Object, e As EventArgs)
    If Not (Page.IsPostBack)
        Connect to database
        Grab some data
        Populate a list
    End If

    Display the List
End Sub
```

The contents of the If statement direct the computer to connect to the database, download data, and populate the list on the first request, but on subsequent requests, the computer ignores these steps.

## Exception Handling

Although Visual Basic .NET's new exception-handling ability is wonderfully simple and versatile, it does carry overhead. It is more efficient to programmatically avoid known common problems rather than rely on the exception handler to trap the lot. For example, in the Simple Calculator example in Listing 8.3 (Chapter 8), we deliberately set up a divide-by-zero exception as an example to trap. However, it would have been more efficient in terms of application performance to use an If…Then statement to avoid the problem.

## Data Connections

Wherever possible, use the managed provider for SQL Server (in conjunction with SQL Server) to handle your data. The combination of the two is optimized for maximum performance. Where possible, make use of the SqlDataReader, as it allows for extremely fast data reads directly from a database connection.

When using the SqlDataAdapter, make use of stored procedures in SQL Server as much as possible to access data, as they are more efficient than ad-hoc queries.

## Disable Debug Mode

Remember to disable Debug mode (along with any tracing!) when your application is complete and ready for deployment. Debug is disabled in the Web.config file. (Refer to "Debugging Our Projects" in Chapter 8.)

### Code Behind vs. HTML View

Because it is possible to write virtually all of our code in HTML View, and most of the Microsoft examples seem to be in HTML View, there is a strong temptation to stick with this when creating our projects.

However, making use of code behind (as I have tended to do throughout this book) enables us to separate our business logic from the presentation logic. This helps the code's understandability and also enables it to be more easily adaptable and updateable. I have also found that (at least with the beta products) data access tends to be more stable when utilized from code behind.

## Summary

Optimizing performance is particularly desirable with online mobile applications, which present restrictions over which we have little control (such as limited bandwidth).

We can take a number of issues into account when boosting the performance of our applications. These include caching, session management, and the sensible use of techniques such as employing the Page.IsPostback property. Microsoft has also included a number of significant performance-boosting tools, such as the dedicated managed-data providers.

However, each application will be different, and we shouldn't take something for granted simply because it has worked before. Maximizing performance requires careful testing and performance measurement, not only on the test bench but also in the anticipated deployment environment.

# PART V

# Building Applications with the Mobile Internet Toolkit

# CHAPTER 16

# Sample Mobile Website: My Computer Shop

- Using a naming convention

- Rationale

- Planning the application

- The database

- The User control

- Finishing touches

- Running the application

- Some considerations

- Full ASPX code

I n this chapter, we will build an application that provides an online (mobile) presence for a small computer store. Within the application, users can specify the type of system they are interested in and obtain an immediate price quote.

The project highlights the use of a User control to create a header and logo that can be used consistently on each form (card) of the application, the generation of a dynamic list (using a SelectionList control) from a database source, the use of session variables, and some basic exception handling.

## Using a Naming Convention

Before we begin, I have a confession to make. I have never been terribly good at sticking to a consistent naming convention for variables and controls. Now, I know that there have been accepted conventions in Visual Basic for years, but I have continued to stray!

You may have already noticed with the examples we have completed that my naming conventions have been a little less than consistent. However, for the purposes of the applications illustrated in the next few chapters, I have adopted a convention that uniquely identifies controls and, where appropriate, indicates which form and page they belong to.

I'll describe my convention as follows:

- For specific-purpose controls such as a Command control to retrieve processor details and display them in a list, I have used the familiar `cmdProcessor` approach.

- I have identified generic header and text labels with their page and form location, like so: `lblPg2Fm1`.

- With Link controls, I have identified their location and destination; for example, `lnkPg2Fm1Pg1Fm1` where the Mobile Web Page changes or `lnkPg2Fm1Fm4` where navigation occurs between forms on a single page.

This convention will enable us to refer to various controls in this section of the book without having to constantly specify which form or page they belong to.

## Rationale

In this example, we will build an online mobile presence for the mythical My Computer Shop. This is a small store that builds "beige boxes" for domestic and small-scale commercial use. The store requires an online presence that enables it to easily update the computer components it uses as well as component prices. As the store builds computers to customer specifications, it needs an online solution that enables customers to specify their needs and obtain an individual quote. Once users have obtained their quote, the store requires some way of enabling customers to order their computer.

## Planning the Application

We will use a database to store component prices, as it provides an easily updateable and flexible solution. Because this is only a demonstration application, we will keep the database very simple and continue to use Microsoft Access. We will not build an administrative front end for the database. The mobile application links to the database and provides the user with a simple interface for setting the preferred design specifications. The application then returns the price of the proposed system. We will make use of the PhoneCall control to provide quick phone ordering facilities for the customer. Customers should also have the opportunity to test different component configurations and obtain a range of prices. The application will also provide contact information for the store.

### Proposed Deck and Card Layout

I have designed the application with three decks and have used, during the building of the application, a separate Mobile Web Form to represent each deck, although this is not strictly necessary. Figure 16.1 illustrates the proposed layout.

**FIGURE 16.1:**

The deck and card layout for the My Computer Store application

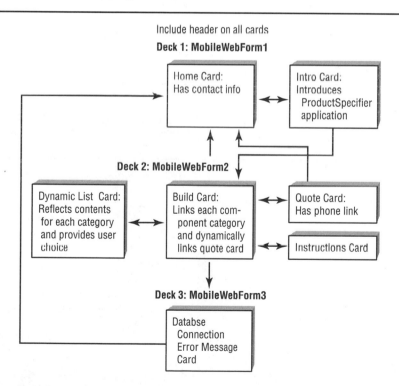

This proposed structure is a bit of a compromise between a desirable card-deck structure and the practicalities of working with Mobile Web Forms. If we were using a traditional

ASP/WML approach, we would probably split the cards in Deck 2 into separate decks. (Cards 1 and 4 would form a single deck and Cards 2 and 3 would be separate.) With Mobile Web Forms, we can place everything on a single page if we wish, as the page is only dished up one form at a time.

However, using the structure proposed offers a certain logical architecture to the application in that the brochure-type information is on one Mobile Web Page, all the business logic is contained in a second page, and any error messages are delivered from a third.

## The Database

Using Microsoft Access, create a new database and name it products.mdb. Create a single table in the database and set the fields as outlined in Table 16.1.

**TABLE 16.1:** Field Definitions for the *products.mdb* Database

| Field | Data Type |
| --- | --- |
| id | AutoNumber |
| product | Text |
| type | Text |
| price | Number |

Save the table as Table1, switch to Data View, and enter a range of data as depicted in Figure 16.2.

**FIGURE 16.2:**

Data values for the products.mdb database

| id | product | type | price |
| --- | --- | --- | --- |
| 1 | 2.0 GHz | Processor | 250 |
| 2 | 2.3 GHz | Processor | 400 |
| 3 | 2.5 GHz | Processor | 500 |
| 4 | 128 MB | Ram | 60 |
| 5 | 256 MB | Ram | 80 |
| 6 | 512 MB | Ram | 110 |
| 7 | 40 GB | Harddrive | 300 |
| 8 | 60 GB | Harddrive | 420 |
| 9 | CD ROM | Multimedia | 65 |
| 10 | CD Burner | Multimedia | 200 |
| 11 | DVD | Multimedia | 160 |
| 12 | 17 inch | Monitor | 250 |
| 13 | 19 inch | Monitor | 350 |
| 14 | 21 inch | Monitor | 550 |
| (AutoNumber) | | | 0 |

Record: I◀ ◀ | 1 | ▶ ▶I ▶✳ of 14

## The User Control

For a consistent look, we can use a consistent header across each form or card. In this example, I have used a combination of a WBMP image in an Image control and the shop title in a Label control. Rather than recreate this combination for each and every form, it is simpler to create a custom user control containing the header elements and apply it to each form.

We'll begin by creating a new Mobile Web project using Visual Basic .NET in Visual Studio .NET. Name the project ProductSpecifier, save the project, and minimize it for the moment.

### Creating a WBMP Image

We need to create an image that we can use for our shop logo. We will create a simple WBMP image using the Nokia tool from the Nokia SDK. Note that if you do not have the SDK, any other WBMP creation tool will do, or you can use any other available image as long as it is compatible with your mobile browser(s). We will use the WBMP format because this application is aimed squarely at mobile phones with WAP browsers. However, we could extend the application using alternative image formats in conjunction with the device-specific capabilities of the Mobile Internet Toolkit. For example, we could also create a color JPEG image for use with HTML browsers on appropriate devices. Note that I have used version 2 of the Nokia SDK in creating the images for this application. At the time of writing, version 3 of the Nokia SDK was available.

Open the Nokia WAP Toolkit and, from the File menu, select New and WBMP Image. This opens a simple drawing tool for creating WBMP images. Enter dimensions into the New Dimensions dialog box. (I used 39 width and 33 height for my image.) The drawing tools are fairly basic and offer Draw, Line, Rectangle, and Circle. The color range consists of black and white! Build your image and save it back to the `ProductSpecifier` directory as `comp.wbmp` (in your Visual Studio Projects directory if you have followed the defaults). Refer to Figure 16.3 for the simple image that I created for this application. Note that this view of the image is at twice the actual size.

FIGURE 16.3:

The computer image
for the application logo

| TIP | We can also use the Nokia SDK to import JPEG and GIF files to the WBMP format by choosing Open from the File menu and then Images for Import to WBMP from the Files of Type: option in the Open dialog box. |
|-----|---|

## Building the User Control

Return to the ProductSpecifier project in Visual Studio .NET. From the Project menu, select Add Web User Control and name the control `Title.ascx` in the dialog box that appears. Click the Open button to confirm the choice. Refer to Figure 16.4.

**FIGURE 16.4:**

The dialog box to create User control `Title.ascx`

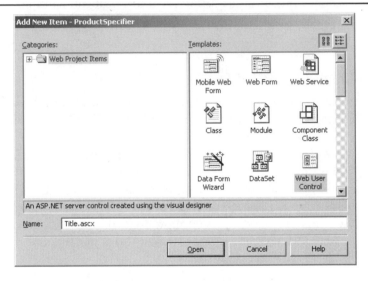

Switch to HTML View from the `Title.ascx` page. Delete any existing code and enter the code from Listing 16.1.

**Listing 16.1    Code for *Title.ascx***

```
<%@ Register TagPrefix="mobile"
➥ Namespace="System.Web.UI.MobileControls"
➥ Assembly="System.Web.Mobile" %>
<%@ Control Language="vb" AutoEventWireup="false"
➥ Codebehind="Title.ascx.vb"
➥ Inherits="ProductSpecifier.Title" %>
<mobile:Image id="Image1" runat="server" Alignment="Left"
➥ ImageURL="http://localhost/ProductSpecifier/comp.wbmp"
➥ AlternateText="The very best in computers!">
</mobile:Image>
<mobile:Label id="Label1" runat="server"
➥ Font-Italic="True" StyleReference="title">
   The Local Computer Shop!</mobile:Label>
```

The `Title.ascx` User control should be visible in the Solution Explorer and can now be available for use on any forms we create. Note that we have used a full address for the image

URL rather than a relative one, as a bit of insurance against choosy browsers. To use the control, simply drag it from the Solution Explorer to the Form control.

## Mobile Web Page 1

The first Mobile Web Page (MobileWebForm1) will require two Form controls. Drag a second Form control to the page and add the controls with the property settings as specified in Table 16.2. Set the ID property of Form1 to Pg1Form1 and the ID property of Form2 to Pg1Form2.

**TABLE 16.2:** Controls and Properties for MobileWebForm1

| Form | Control | Property | Value |
|------|---------|----------|-------|
| Pg1Form1 | UserControl-Title | | |
| | PhoneCall | Text | Tel. 555 555 555 |
| | | Alternative Format | {0} |
| | | SoftkeyLabel | Call |
| | | ID | cllPhoneNo |
| | | PhoneNumber | 555555555 |
| | Label | Text | 25 Swanton Way |
| | | ID | lblStreetAddress |
| | Label | Text | MyTown, MyState |
| | | ID | lblCityAddress |
| | Link | Text | Specify Your New Computer |
| | | SoftkeyLabel | Build |
| | | ID | lnkPg1Fm1Fm2 |
| | | NavigateURL | #Pg1Form2 |
| Pg1Form2 | UserControl - Title | | |
| | TextView | Text | In this part of our site, you can specify the computer system that you would like us to build for you and find out how much it will cost. In the following screens, select your preferred components to build your dream computer. Once you are happy with your selections, click the "Our Quote" link that will appear on the "Build" screen to get the price. |

*Continued on next page*

**TABLE 16.2 CONTINUED:** Controls and Properties for MobileWebForm1

| Form | Control | Property | Value |
|---|---|---|---|
| | | ID | txtvwPg1Fm2 |
| | Link | Text | Let's Start Building! |
| | | SoftkeyLabel | Build |
| | | ID | lnkPg1Fm2Pg2Fm1 |
| | | NavigateURL | MobileWebForm2.aspx (document relative) |
| | Link | Text | Home |
| | | SoftkeyLabel | Home |
| | | ID | lnkPg1Fm2Fm1 |
| | | NavigateURL | #Pg1Form1 |

The two forms should appear as in Figure 16.5.

**FIGURE 16.5:**

MobileWebForm1 of the ProductSpecifier application

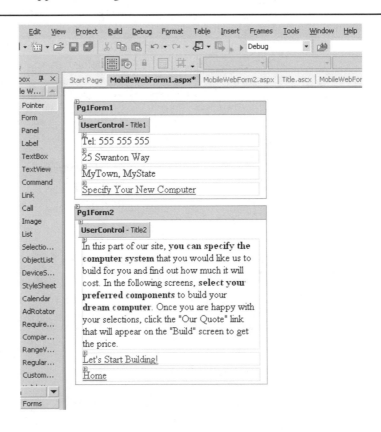

TIP    It may be easier to complete the NavigateURL properties for the Links after all the forms and pages have been created.

## Mobile Web Page 2

Mobile Web Page 2 (MobileWebForm2) is where the actual ProductSpecifier application is handled. The first page provides an entry point to the site and contact details but has no dynamic content.

From the Project menu, select Add Web Form. From the Add New Item dialog box, choose Mobile Web Form from the right-hand Templates window (as in Figure 16.6). Name the Mobile Web Form MobileWebForm2.aspx and click the Open button.

FIGURE 16.6:

Using the Add New Item dialog box to create a new Mobile Web Form

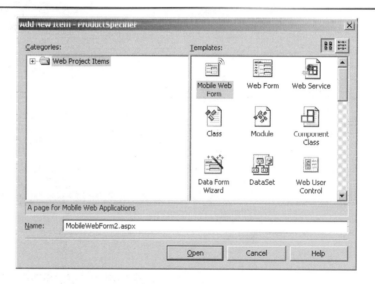

Drag an OleDbDataAdapter (OleDbDataAdapter1) from the data tools to MobileWebForm2. Within the Data Adapter Wizard, click the New Connection button to open the Data Link Properties dialog box and connect to the products.mdb database. Click the Provider tab and choose Microsoft Jet 4.0 OLE DB Provider. See Figure 16.7.

Click the Next button and click the ellipsis button next to Select or Enter a Database Name: to locate the products database. See Figure 16.8.

**FIGURE 16.7:**

Choosing the correct
provider from the
Data Link Properties
dialog box

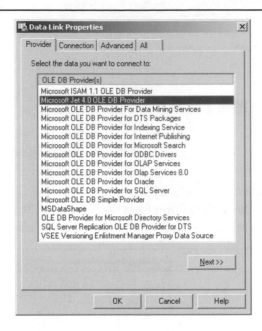

**FIGURE 16.8:**

Locating the database
in the Connection set-
tings of the Data Link
Properties dialog box

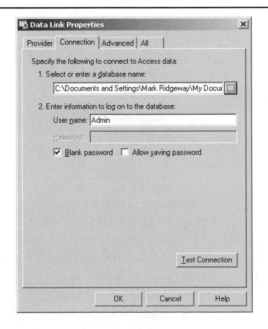

Click the Test Connection button to test the connection and if everything checks out, click OK. Complete the Data Adapter Wizard, selecting everything from Table1 in the Query Builder. See Figure 16.9.

FIGURE 16.9:

Using the Query Builder dialog box to select the entire contents of Table1

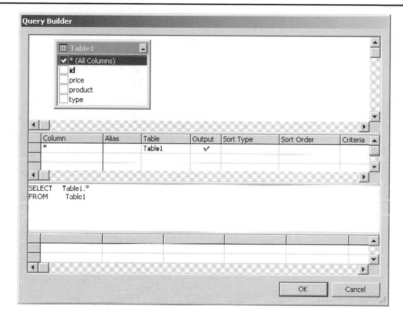

When you return to the Generate the SQL Statements screen in the Data Adapter Configuration Wizard, click the Advanced Options button and deselect the three options available in it, as we will not be using any of them. Click through the wizard and select Finish.

Back at the MobileWebForm2 in Design View, right-click the reference to OleDbDataAdapter1 and select the Generate DataSet option. Create a DataSet (DataSet11).

Drag a DataView control (DataView1) to the form and set its Table property to DataSet11.Table1.

Create four forms on MobileWebForm2 and name them Pg2Form1, Pg2Form2, Pg2Form3, and Pg2Form4. Table 16.3 contains the properties and settings of the various controls to place on these forms.

**TABLE 16.3:** Controls and Properties for MobileWebForm2

| Form | Control | Property | Value |
|------|---------|----------|-------|
| Pg2Form1 | UserControl - Title Label | Text | Build Your New Computer: |

*Continued on next page*

**TABLE 16.3 CONTINUED:** Controls and Properties for MobileWebForm2

| Form | Control | Property | Value |
|---|---|---|---|
| | | ID | lblPg2Fm1 |
| | Link | Text | Instructions |
| | | SoftkeyLabel | Instr |
| | | ID | lnkPg2Fm1Fm4 |
| | | NavigateURL | #Pg2Form4 |
| | Command | Text | Processor |
| | | SoftkeyLabel | Procr |
| | | ID | cmdProcessor |
| | Command | Text | RAM |
| | | SoftkeyLabel | RAM |
| | | ID | cmdRAM |
| | Command | Text | Hard Drive |
| | | SoftkeyLabel | Hdriv |
| | | ID | harddrive |
| | Command | Text | MultiMedia |
| | | SoftkeyLabel | MMed |
| | | ID | cmdMultimedia |
| | Command | Text | Monitor |
| | | SoftkeyLabel | Mon |
| | | ID | cmdMonitor |
| | Command | Text | Start Again |
| | | SoftkeyLabel | Start |
| | | ID | cmdClear |
| | Command | Text | Our Quote |
| | | SoftkeyLabel | Quote |
| | | Visible | False |
| | | ID | cmdOurquote |
| | Link | Text | Home |
| | | SoftkeyLabel | Home |
| | | ID | lnkPg2Fm1Pg1Fm1 |
| | | NavigateURL | MobileWebForm1.aspx (document relative) |
| Pg2Form2 | UserControl - Title | | |
| | Label | Text | Make your selection from the following list: |

*Continued on next page*

**TABLE 16.3 CONTINUED:** Controls and Properties for MobileWebForm2

| Form | Control | Property | Value |
|------|---------|----------|-------|
| | Label | ID | lblPg2Fm2 |
| | | Text | \<empty> |
| | SelectionList | ID | lblPg2Fm21 |
| | | SelectType | Radio |
| | | DataSource | DataView1 |
| | | DataTextField | product |
| | | DataValueField | price |
| | | ID | slstCategories |
| | Command | Text | Return to Build Your Computer |
| | | SoftkeyLabel | Build |
| | | ID | cmdBuild |
| Pg2Form3 | UserControl - Title | | |
| | Label | Text | You have chosen the following system: |
| | | ID | lblPg2Fm3 |
| | Label | Text | \<empty> |
| | | ID | lblProcessor |
| | Label | Text | \<empty> |
| | | ID | lblRAM |
| | Label | Text | \<empty> |
| | | ID | lblHarddrive |
| | Label | Text | \<empty> |
| | | ID | lblMultimedia |
| | Label | Text | \<empty> |
| | | ID | lblMonitor |
| | Label | Text | Our quote for the system is: |
| | | ID | lblPg2Fm31 |
| | Label | Text | \<empty> |
| | | ID | lblPrice |
| | PhoneCall | Text | Call: 555-555-555 |
| | | AlternateFormat | {0} |
| | | ID | cllPhone2 |
| | | SoftKeyLabel | Call |
| | | PhoneNumber | 555555555 |

*Continued on next page*

**TABLE 16.3 CONTINUED:** Controls and Properties for MobileWebForm2

| Form | Control | Property | Value |
|------|---------|----------|-------|
| | Label | Text | if you wish to purchase. |
| | | ID | lblPg2Fm33 |
| | Link | Text | Return to Build Your Computer |
| | | SoftkeyLabel | Build |
| | | ID | lnkPg2Fm3Fm1 |
| | | NavigateURL | #Pg2Form1 |
| | Link | Text | Home |
| | | SoftkeyLabel | Home |
| | | ID | lnkPg2Fm3Pg1Fm1 |
| | | NavigateURL | MobileWebForm1.aspx (document relative) |
| Pg2Form4 | UserControl - Title | | |
| | Label | Text | Instructions: |
| | | ID | lblPg2Fm4 |
| | TextView | Text | Make a selection from each of the following categories. Once you have completed all categories an "Our Quote" link will appear to give you the quote on your dream computer! If you need to change an entry, just choose from that category again. |
| | | ID | txtvwPg2Fm4 |
| | Link | Text | Build Your Computer |
| | | SoftkeyLabel | Build |
| | | ID | lnkPg2Fm4Fm1 |
| | | NavigateURL | #Pg2Form1 |

Figure 16.10 illustrates how the completed forms look in Design View.

**FIGURE 16.10:**

MobileWebForm2 in
Design View—note
that I have
superimposed
Forms 3 and 4
next to Forms 1 and 2

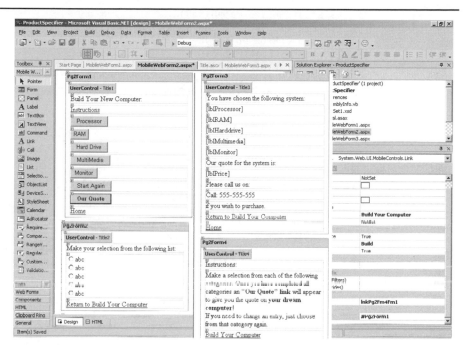

The next step is to code MobileWebForm2. Switch to code behind and add the code from
Listing 16.2.

**Listing 16.2    Code Behind for MobileWebForm2**

```
Private Sub Page_Load(ByVal sender As System.Object,
➥ ByVal e As System.EventArgs) Handles MyBase.Load
      Try
          DataSet11.Clear()
          OleDbDataAdapter1.Fill(DataSet11, "Table1")
      Catch

  RedirectToMobilePage("http://localhost/
➥ProductSpecifier/MobileWebForm3.aspx")
      End Try

   End Sub


   Private Sub cmdProcessor_Click(ByVal sender As
➥ System.Object, ByVal e As System.EventArgs)
➥ Handles cmdProcessor.Click

      ActiveForm = Pg2Form2()
      Session("category") = "Processor"
      slstCategories.Items.Clear()
      DataView1.RowFilter = "type='Processor'"
```

```
        slstCategories.DataBind()
        lblPg2Fm21.Text = "Choose a Processor:"
        Session("Proc_price") =
➡ slstCategories.Items(0).Value
        Session("Processor") =
➡ slstCategories.Items(0).Text
        cmdProcessor.Text = slstCategories.Items(0).Text
➡ & " Processor"

    End Sub

    Private Sub cmdRAM_Click(ByVal sender As
➡ System.Object,
➡ ByVal e As System.EventArgs) Handles cmdRAM.Click
        Session("category") = "Ram"
        ActiveForm = Pg2Form2()
        slstCategories.Items.Clear()
        DataView1.RowFilter = "type='Ram'"
        slstCategories.DataBind()
        lblPg2Fm21.Text = "Choose your RAM:"
        Session("Ram_price") =
➡ slstCategories.Items(0).Value
        Session("Ram") = slstCategories.Items(0).Text
        cmdRAM.Text = slstCategories.Items(0).Text &
➡ " RAM"

    End Sub

    Private Sub cmdHarddrive_Click(ByVal sender As
➡ System.Object, ByVal e As System.EventArgs)
➡ Handles cmdHarddrive.Click

        Session("category") = "Harddrive"
        ActiveForm = Pg2Form2()
        slstCategories.Items.Clear()
        DataView1.RowFilter = "type='Harddrive'"
        slstCategories.DataBind()
        lblPg2Fm21.Text = "Choose your HardDrive:"
        Session("Hdrive_price") =
➡ slstCategories.Items(0).Value
        Session("Harddrive") =
➡ slstCategories.Items(0).Text
        cmdHarddrive.Text = slstCategories.Items(0).Text
➡ & " HardDrive"

    End Sub

    Private Sub cmdMultimedia_Click(ByVal sender As
➡ System.Object,
➡ ByVal e As System.EventArgs) Handles
➡ cmdMultimedia.Click
```

```
        Session("category") = "Multimedia"
        ActiveForm = Pg2Form2()
        slstCategories.Items.Clear()
        DataView1.RowFilter = "type='Multimedia'"
        slstCategories.DataBind()
        lblPg2Fm21.Text = "Choose your MultiMedia:"
        Session("MM_price") =
➡ slstCategories.Items(0).Value
        Session("Multimedia") =
➡ slstCategories.Items(0).Text
        cmdMultimedia.Text = slstCategories.Items(0).Text
➡ & " Multimedia"

    End Sub

    Private Sub cmdMonitor_Click(ByVal sender As
➡ System.Object, ByVal e As System.EventArgs) Handles
➡ cmdMonitor.Click
        Session("category") = "Monitor"
        ActiveForm = Pg2Form2()
        slstCategories.Items.Clear()
        DataView1.RowFilter = "type='Monitor'"
        slstCategories.DataBind()
        lblPg2Fm21.Text = "Choose your Monitor:"
        Session("Mon_price") =
➡ slstCategories.Items(0).Value
        Session("Monitor") = slstCategories.Items(0).Text
        cmdMonitor.Text = slstCategories.Items(0).Text &
➡ " Monitor"

    End Sub

    Private Sub slstCategories_SelectedIndexChanged(ByVal
➡ sender As System.Object, ByVal e As System.EventArgs)
➡ Handles slstCategories.SelectedIndexChanged
        Select Case Session("category")
            Case "Processor"
                cmdProcessor.Text =
➡ slstCategories.Selection.Text & " Processor"
                Session("Proc_price") =
➡ slstCategories.Selection.Value
                Session("Processor") =
➡ slstCategories.Selection.Text

            Case "Ram"
                cmdRAM.Text =
➡ slstCategories.Selection.Text & " RAM"
                Session("Ram_price") =
➡ slstCategories.Selection.Value
                Session("Ram") =
➡ slstCategories.Selection.Text
```

```
                    Case "Harddrive"
                         cmdHarddrive.Text =
➡ slstCategories.Selection.Text & " Hard Drive"
                         Session("Hdrive_price") =
➡ slstCategories.Selection.Value
                         Session("Harddrive") =
➡ slstCategories.Selection.Text
                    Case "Multimedia"
                         cmdMultimedia.Text =
➡ slstCategories.Selection.Text
                         Session("MM_price") =
➡ slstCategories.Selection.Value
                         Session("Multimedia") =
➡ slstCategories.Selection.Text
                    Case "Monitor"
                         cmdMonitor.Text =
➡ slstCategories.Selection.Text & " Monitor"
                         Session("Mon_price") =
➡ slstCategories.Selection.Value
                         Session("Monitor") =
➡ slstCategories.Selection.Text
            End Select

    End Sub


    Private Sub cmdOurquote_Click(ByVal sender As
➡ System.Object, ByVal e As System.EventArgs) Handles
➡ cmdOurquote.Click
        Dim total As Integer
        Dim Proc_price As Integer = Session("Proc_price")
        Dim Ram_price As Integer = Session("Ram_price")
        Dim Hdrive_price As Integer =
➡ Session("Hdrive_price")
        Dim MM_price As Integer = Session("MM_price")
        Dim Mon_price As Integer = Session("Mon_price")

        ActiveForm = Pg2Form3
        lblProcessor.Text = Session("Processor") &
➡ " Processor"
        lblRAM.Text = Session("Ram") & " RAM"
        lblHarddrive.Text = Session("Harddrive") &
➡ " Hard Drive"
        lblMultimedia.Text = Session("Multimedia")
        lblMonitor.Text = Session("Monitor") & " Monitor"

        total = Proc_price + Ram_price + Hdrive_price +
➡ MM_price + Mon_price + 300
        lblPrice.Text = "$" & total & ".00"

    End Sub
```

```
    Private Sub cmdClear_Click(ByVal sender As
➥ System.Object, ByVal e As System.EventArgs) Handles
➥ cmdClear.Click
        cmdProcessor.Text = "Processor"
        cmdRAM.Text = "RAM"
        cmdHarddrive.Text = "Hard Drive"
        cmdMultimedia.Text = "MultiMedia"
        cmdMonitor.Text = "Monitor"
        Session("Proc_price") = 0
        Session("Processor") = ""
        Session("Ram_price") = 0
        Session("Ram") = ""
        Session("Hdrive_price") = 0
        Session("Harddrive") = ""
        Session("MM_price") = 0
        Session("Multimedia") = ""
        Session("Mon_price") = 0
        Session("Monitor") = ""
        cmdOurquote.Visible = False
        lblPg2Fm21.Text = ""
    End Sub

    Private Sub cmdBuild_Click(ByVal sender As
➥ System.Object, ByVal e As System.EventArgs) Handles
➥ cmdBuild.Click
        ActiveForm = Pg2Form1
        Dim Proc_price As Integer = Session("Proc_price")
        Dim Ram_price As Integer = Session("Ram_price")
        Dim Hdrive_price As Integer =
➥ Session("Hdrive_price")
        Dim MM_price As Integer = Session("MM_price")
        Dim Mon_price As Integer = Session("Mon_price")

        If (Proc_price > 0 And Ram_price > 0 And
➥ Hdrive_price > 0 And MM_price > 0 And Mon_price > 0)
➥ Then
            cmdOurquote.Visible = True
        Else : cmdOurquote.Visible = False
        End If
    End Sub
End Class
```

In the Page_Load sub (as illustrated in the following code), we fill the DataSet and add an exception handler in case there are any problems. If the database connection fails, the application redirects to the error message on MobileWebPage3 (which we have yet to create!):

```
Private Sub Page_Load(ByVal sender As System.Object,
➥ ByVal e As System.EventArgs) Handles MyBase.Load
        Try
            DataSet11.Clear()
```

```
            OleDbDataAdapter1.Fill(DataSet11, "Table1")
        Catch
            RedirectToMobilePage("http://localhost/
➥ProductSpecifier/MobileWebForm3.aspx")
        End Try

    End Sub
```

Note that we use the `RedirectToMobilePage` rather than a `Response.Redirect` object to navigate between Mobile Web Pages. The `RedirectToMobilePage`, coupled with a full URL, tends to guarantee a less accident-prone link between Mobile Web Pages.

Then follows a succession of code for each of the Command controls on Pg2Form1. For example, consider the `cmdProcessor` Command control:

```
Private Sub cmdProcessor_Click(ByVal sender As System.Object,
➥ ByVal e As System.EventArgs) Handles cmdProcessor.Click
        ActiveForm = Pg2Form2()
        Session("category") = "Processor"
        slstCategories.Items.Clear()
        DataView1.RowFilter = "type='Processor'"
        slstCategories.DataBind()
        lblPg2Fm21.Text = "Choose a Processor:"
        Session("Proc_price") =
➥ slstCategories.Items(0).Value
        Session("Processor") =
➥ slstCategories.Items(0).Text
        cmdProcessor.Text = slstCategories.Items(0).Text
➥ & " Processor"

    End Sub
```

For each of these controls, we set the `Category` session variable to reflect whichever Command control (or link) has been selected. We then make Pg2Form2 (which contains the Selection List—`slstCategories`) the active form, filter the appropriate items from the DataSet11 into `DataView1`, and load the list from the `DataView1` object. Thus clicking on the `cmdProcessor` Command control opens up the Selection List with the various processor types contained in the database. Previously, we set the text content of this list to reflect the types of components retrieved and the value content to contain their individual prices. The last four lines of code set a default value for the Processor option in the List.

In the next section of code, choosing an item in the Selection List sets the `Text` property of the relevant Command control in Pg2Form1 to the text value of that item selected in the list. A session variable is also set to hold the text value of the item chosen, and another session variable is set to hold the price. These session variables are maintained for the purpose of assembling the final quote. This part of the process is handled within the `Select Case` statement of the code.

Clicking the cmdOurquote Command control directs the user to Pg2Form3 (as illustrated in the next code). It also loads the contents of the various session variables that hold the items chosen into the relevant Label controls on Pg2Form3. Additionally, the code adds up the various prices of the items selected (and adds $300 for unspecified costs!) and presents the quote in the lblPrice Label control. Here's the code:

```
Private Sub cmdOurquote_Click(ByVal sender As
➡ System.Object, ByVal e As System.EventArgs) Handles
➡ cmdOurquote.Click
        Dim total As Integer
        Dim Proc_price As Integer = Session("Proc_price")
        Dim Ram_price As Integer = Session("Ram_price")
        Dim Hdrive_price As Integer = Session("Hdrive_price")
        Dim MM_price As Integer = Session("MM_price")
        Dim Mon_price As Integer = Session("Mon_price")

        ActiveForm = Pg2Form3

        lblProcessor.Text = Session("Processor") &
➡ " Processor"
        lblRAM.Text = Session("Ram") & " RAM"
        lblHarddrive.Text = Session("Harddrive") &
➡ " Hard Drive"
        lblMultimedia.Text = Session("Multimedia")
        lblMonitor.Text = Session("Monitor") & " Monitor"

        total = Proc_price + Ram_price + Hdrive_price +
➡ MM_price + Mon_price + 300
        lblPrice.Text = "$" & total & ".00"

    End Sub
```

Selecting the cmdClear Command control (as illustrated in the following code) resets all the session variables (text) back to empty strings and the session variables (price) to zero. It resets the text properties of the Command controls on Pg2Form1 back to their default values and hides cmdOurquote again. Here's the code:

```
Private Sub cmdClear_Click(ByVal sender As System.Object,
➡ ByVal e As System.EventArgs) Handles cmdClear.Click
        cmdProcessor.Text = "Processor"
        cmdRAM.Text = "RAM"
        cmdHarddrive.Text = "Hard Drive"
        cmdMultimedia.Text = "MultiMedia"
        cmdMonitor.Text = "Monitor"
        Session("Proc_price") = 0
        Session("Processor") = ""
        Session("Ram_price") = 0
```

```
        Session("Ram") = ""
        Session("Hdrive_price") = 0
        Session("Harddrive") = ""
        Session("MM_price") = 0
        Session("Multimedia") = ""
        Session("Mon_price") = 0
        Session("Monitor") = ""
        cmdOurquote.Visible = False
    End Sub
```

In the code handling the cmdBuild_Click event, local values are taken from the session variables (so that they can be handled as integers), and all the component prices are checked (for a greater-than-zero value) to see if the full range of components has been selected. Once all the categories have been filled, the Visible property of the cmdOurquote Command control is set to True, which enables the user to navigate to the next form (Pg2Form3).

## Mobile Web Page 3

This final Mobile Web Page (MobileWebForm3) contains a single form to present an error message if for any reason the database is inaccessible.

Create a new Mobile Web Page by selecting Add Web Form from the Project menu. Name it MobileWebForm3.aspx. Set the ID property of the Form control on the page to Pg3Form1.

Add the controls and set their properties as outlined in Table 16.4.

**TABLE 16.4:** Controls and Properties for MobileWebForm3

| Form | Control | Property | Value |
|------|---------|----------|-------|
| Pg3Form1 | UserControl - Title | | |
| | TextView | Text | Our database appears to be temporarily unavailable at the moment. Please try again. |
| | | ID | txtvwP3Fm1 |
| | Link | Text | Home |
| | | SoftkeyLabel | Home |
| | | ID | lnkPg3Fm1Pg1Fm1 |
| | | NavigateURL | MobileWebForm1.aspx (document relative) |

MobileWebForm3 should now appear as in Figure 16.11.

FIGURE 16.11:

MobileWebForm3 in
the ProductSpecifier
application

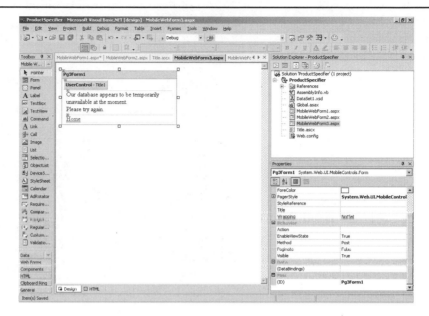

Save the project. (You have been saving as you have been going along, haven't you?)

## Finishing Touches

Finally, we need to edit our Web.config file to ensure that everything will work as it should across the various mobile device/browser/gateway combinations.

Open up Web.config from the Solution Explorer window and ensure that the <httpRuntime useFullyQualifiedRedirectUrl="true" /> tag is set, as explained in Chapter 8.

Scroll down to the <sessionState> tag and set cookieless="true".

Once you have tested and debugged the application, to improve runtime performance, set debug="false" in the <compilation> tag. Save the changes.

## Running the Application

Compile and view the application in a suitable browser such as Openwave. (Internet Explorer will be adequate, but the result won't be as pretty!) The user is initially presented with contact information with an automatic-dial option from their cell phone to the shop, as depicted in Figure 16.12.

**FIGURE 16.12:**

Opening screen for the ProductSpecifier application

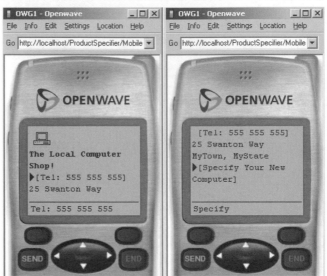

Image of UP.SDK courtesy Openwave Systems, Inc.

Selecting the Specify Your New Computer link opens the form Pg1Form2 on the emulator. See Figure 16.13. Note that I have made a bit of use of the formatting options in the TextView control to style some parts of the text in bold.

**FIGURE 16.13:**

Pg1Form2 of the ProductSpecifier application depicted in the Openwave browser

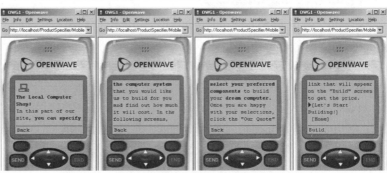

Image of UP.SDK courtesy Openwave Systems, Inc.

If we then select the Let's Start Building link, we should be directed to the screen depicted in Figure 16.14. If the database were not available, however, we would see the screen from Figure 16.15.

FIGURE 16.14:

The Build screen in
the ProductSpecifier
application

FIGURE 16.14:

The Build screen in
the ProductSpecifier
application

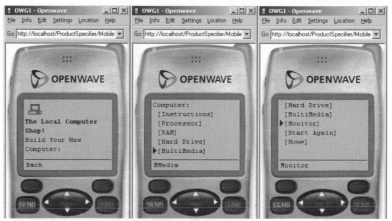

Image of UP.SDK courtesy Openwave Systems, Inc.

FIGURE 16.15:

The database-
connection error
screen in the
ProductSpecifier
application

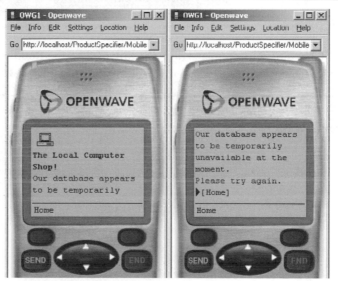

Image of UP.SDK courtesy Openwave Systems, Inc.

From the Build screen, selecting one of the component types takes you to a list of the available components in that type. For example, clicking the Processor link takes us to a list of the available processors. See Figure 16.16.

FIGURE 16.16:

The List screen
displaying available
processor types

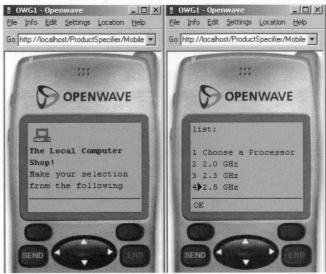

Image of UP.SDK courtesy Openwave Systems, Inc.

Choosing a list item and then the link back to the Build screen should result in the chosen item now being displayed in the Build screen. See Figure 16.17.

FIGURE 16.17:

The Build screen after
a 2.5Ghz processor
has been chosen

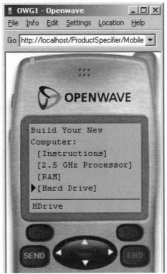

Image of UP.SDK courtesy Openwave Systems, Inc.

Once all the categories have been chosen, the Our Quote link will appear in the Build screen. See Figure 16.18. Note that selecting the Start Again link will set all the Build links back to their defaults.

FIGURE 16.18:

The Our Quote link in
the Build screen

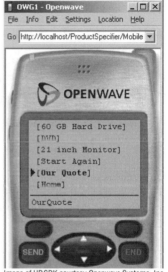

Image of UP.SDK courtesy Openwave Systems, Inc.

Finally, selecting Our Quote will take the user to a screen that lists the identified components and gives a quote for the proposed system. It also provides for cell phones an auto-dial service back to the store. Refer to Figure 16.19.

FIGURE 16.19:

The quote screen in
the ProductSpecifier
application

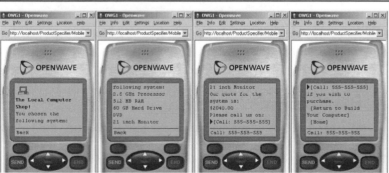

Image of UP.SDK courtesy Openwave Systems, Inc.

## Some Considerations

Not surprisingly, with the Mobile Internet Toolkit, file sizes can start to rapidly increase (in mobile terms) as programmers add controls to a form. We can easily check the compiled size of our forms by using the Phone Information window of the Openwave SDK. Refer to Figure 16.20.

Reading the size of the compiled binary in the Phone Information window of the Openwave SDK

```
               --------- DATA SIZE ---------
Uncompiled data from HTTP is 1238 bytes.
...found Content-Type: text/vnd.wap.wml.
Compiled WAP binary is 811 bytes.

cache hit: <
                    <http://localhost/ProductSpecifier/comp.wbmp>
              }
```

Most of the forms created in the ProductSpecifier application exceed the recommended 500-byte limit. Because this recommendation applies to maximizing performance over limited bandwidth, it is not a critical problem. However, Pg2Form1 can run perilously close to the 1MB maximum that applies to some phones. This is less of a problem for the newer phones on the market, but it may mean reducing the file size by either deleting the image, modifying the form, or creating some device-specific alternatives if maximum device availability is required.

If the ProductSpecifier lists had become particularly large, we could have introduced some pagination to control them.

If we were after flat-out performance, we would need to cut out all unnecessary text and formatting and shave the forms back to the absolute bare minimum to maximize delivery speeds to the device. Placing all of the forms on the one Mobile Web Page would help speed things at the server end. Ultimately, however, we need to strike a balance between the usability and functionality of our application. We need to measure the speed of its delivery and weigh it against the design and scalability of its architecture.

## Full ASPX Code

Listings 16.3, 16.4, and 16.5 show the full ASPX code for MobileWebForm1, MobileWebForm2, and MobileWebForm3, respectively.

**Listing 16.3    Full ASPX Code for MobileWebForm1**

```
<%@ Register TagPrefix="mobile"
➥ Namespace="System.Web.UI.MobileControls"
➥ Assembly="System.Web.Mobile, Version=1.0.3300.0,
➥ Culture=neutral, PublicKeyToken=b03f5f7f11d50a3a" %>
```

```
<%@ Page Language="vb" AutoEventWireup="false"
➥ Codebehind="MobileWebForm1.aspx.vb"
➥ Inherits="ProductSpecifier.MobileWebForm1" %>
<%@ Register TagPrefix="uc1" TagName="Title"
➥ Src="Title.ascx" %>
<meta name="GENERATOR" content="Microsoft Visual
➥ Studio.NET 7.0">
<meta name="CODE_LANGUAGE" content="Visual Basic 7.0">
<meta name="vs_targetSchema"
➥ content="http://schemas.microsoft.com/Mobile/Page">
<body Xmlns:mobile="http://schemas.microsoft.com/Mobile/
➥WebForm">
   <mobile:form id="Pg1Form1" runat="server">
      <uc1:Title id="Title1" runat="server"></uc1:Title>
      <mobile:Label id="lblStreetAddress"
➥ runat="server">25 Swanton Way</mobile:Label>
      <mobile:Label id="lblCityAddress"
➥ runat="server">MyTown, MyState</mobile:Label>
      <mobile:Link id="lnkPg1Fm1Fm2" runat="server"
➥ SoftkeyLabel="Build" NavigateURL="#Pg1Form2">Specify
➥ Your New Computer</mobile:Link>
      <mobile:PhoneCall id="cllPhoneNo" runat="server"
➥ SoftkeyLabel="Call" PhoneNumber="555555555"
➥ AlternateFormat="{0}">Tel: 555 555
➥ 555</mobile:PhoneCall>
   </mobile:form>
   <mobile:form id="Pg1Form2" runat="server">
      <uc1:Title id="Title2" runat="server"></uc1:Title>
      <mobile:TextView id="txtvwPg1Fm2" runat="server">In
➥ this part of our site, <b>you can
➥ specify the computer system </b>that you would like
➥ us to build for you and find out how much it will
➥ cost. In the following screens, <b>
➥ select your preferred components </b>to build your
➥ <b>dream computer</b>. Once you are happy with your
➥ selections, click the "Our Quote" link that will
➥ appear on the "Build" screen to get the
➥ price.</mobile:TextView>
      <mobile:Link id="lnkPg1Fm2Pg2Fm1" runat="server"
➥ SoftkeyLabel="Build"
➥ NavigateURL="MobileWebForm2.aspx">Let's Start
➥ Building!</mobile:Link>
      <mobile:Link id="lnkPg1Fm2Fm1" runat="server"
➥ SoftkeyLabel="Home"
➥ NavigateURL="#Pg1Form1">Home</mobile:Link>
   </mobile:form>
</body>
```

**Listing 16.4     Full ASPX Code for MobileWebForm2**

```
<%@ Register TagPrefix="mobile"
➥ Namespace="System.Web.UI.MobileControls"
```

```
➥ Assembly="System.Web.Mobile, Version=1.0.3300.0,
➥ Culture=neutral, PublicKeyToken=b03f5f7f11d50a3a" %>
<%@ Register TagPrefix="uc1" TagName="Title"
➥ Src="Title.ascx" %>
<%@ Page Language="vb" AutoEventWireup="false"
➥ Codebehind="MobileWebForm2.aspx.vb"
➥ Inherits="ProductSpecifier.MobileWebForm2" %>
<meta name="GENERATOR" content="Microsoft Visual
➥ Studio.NET 7.0">
<meta name="CODE_LANGUAGE" content="Visual Basic 7.0">
<meta name="vs_targetSchema"
➥ content="http://schemas.microsoft.com/Mobile/Page">
<body Xmlns:mobile="http://schemas.microsoft.com/Mobile/
➥WebForm">
<mobile:form id="Pg2Form1" runat="server">
      <uc1:Title id="Title1" runat="server"></uc1:Title>
      <mobile:Label id="lblPg2Fm1" runat="server">Build
➥ Your New Computer:</mobile:Label>
      <mobile:Link id="lnkPg2Fm1Fm4" runat="server"
➥ SoftkeyLabel="Instr"
➥ NavigateURL="#Pg2Form4">Instructions</mobile:Link>
      <mobile:Command id="cmdProcessor" runat="server"
➥ SoftkeyLabel="Proc">Processor</mobile:Command>
      <mobile:Command id="cmdRAM" runat="server"
➥ SoftkeyLabel="RAM">RAM</mobile:Command>
      <mobile:Command id="cmdHarddrive" runat="server"
➥ SoftkeyLabel="HDriv">Hard Drive</mobile:Command>
      <mobile:Command id="cmdMultimedia" runat="server"
➥ SoftkeyLabel="MMed">MultiMedia</mobile:Command>
      <mobile:Command id="cmdMonitor" runat="server"
➥ SoftkeyLabel="Mon">Monitor</mobile:Command>
      <mobile:Command id="cmdClear" runat="server"
➥ SoftkeyLabel="Start">Start Again</mobile:Command>
      <mobile:Command id="cmdOurquote" runat="server"
➥ SoftkeyLabel="Quote" Visible="False"
➥ Font-Bold="True">Our Quote</mobile:Command>
      <mobile:Link id="lnkPg2Fm1Pg1Fm1" runat="server"
➥ SoftkeyLabel="Home"
➥ NavigateURL="MobileWebForm1.aspx">Home</mobile:Link>
  </mobile:form>
<mobile:form id="Pg2Form2" runat="server">
      <uc1:Title id="Title2" runat="server"></uc1:Title>
      <mobile:Label id="lblPg2Fm2" runat="server">Make
➥ your selection from the following
➥ list:</mobile:Label>
      <mobile:Label id="lblPg2Fm21"
➥ runat="server"></mobile:Label>
      <mobile:SelectionList id=slstCategories
➥ runat="server" DataValueField="price"
➥ SelectType="Radio" DataTextField="product"
➥ DataSource="<%# DataView1 %>">
```

```
        </mobile:SelectionList>
        <mobile:Command id="cmdBuild" runat="server"
➡ SoftkeyLabel="Build">Return to Build Your
➡ Computer</mobile:Command>
    </mobile:form>
<mobile:form id="Pg2Form3" runat="server">
        <uc1:Title id="Title3" runat="server"></uc1:Title>
        <mobile:Label id="lblPg2Fm3" runat="server">You
➡ have chosen the following system:</mobile:Label>
        <mobile:Label id="lblProcessor"
➡ runat="server"></mobile:Label>
        <mobile:Label id="lblRAM"
➡ runat="server"></mobile:Label>
        <mobile:Label id="lblHarddrive"
➡ runat="server"></mobile:Label>
        <mobile:Label id="lblMultimedia"
➡ runat="server"></mobile:Label>
        <mobile:Label id="lblMonitor"
➡ runat="server"></mobile:Label>
        <mobile:Label id="lblPg2Fm31" runat="server">Our
➡ quote for the system is:</mobile:Label>
        <mobile:Label id="lblPrice"
➡ runat="server"></mobile:Label>
        <mobile:Label id="lblPg2Fm32" runat="server">Please
➡ call us on:</mobile:Label>
        <mobile:PhoneCall id="cllPhone2" runat="server"
➡ SoftkeyLabel="Call" PhoneNumber="555555555"
➡ AlternateFormat="{0}">Call: 555 555
➡ 555</mobile:PhoneCall>
        <mobile:Label id="lblPg2Fm33" runat="server">if you
➡ wish to purchase.</mobile:Label>
        <mobile:Link id="lnkPg2Fm3Fm1" runat="server"
➡ SoftkeyLabel="Build" NavigateURL="#Pg2Form1">Return
➡ to Build Your Computer</mobile:Link>
        <mobile:Link id="lnkPg2Fm3Pg1Fm1" runat="server"
➡ SoftkeyLabel="Home"
➡ NavigateURL="MobileWebForm1.aspx">Home</mobile:Link>
    </mobile:form>
<mobile:form id="Pg2Form4" runat="server">
        <uc1:Title id="Title4" runat="server"></uc1:Title>
        <mobile:Label id="lblPg2Fm4"
➡ runat="server">Instructions:</mobile:Label>
        <mobile:TextView id="txtvwPg2Fm4"
➡ runat="server">Make a selection from each of the
➡ following categories. Once you have completed all
➡ categories an <b>
➡ "Our Quote" link</b> will appear to give you the
➡ quote on <b>your dream
➡ computer</b>!<br />If you need to change an entry,
➡ just choose from that category
➡ again.</mobile:TextView>
```

```
          <mobile:Link id="lnkPg2Fm4Fm1" runat="server"
➥ SoftkeyLabel="Build" NavigateURL="#Pg2Form1">Build
➥ Your Computer</mobile:Link>
       </mobile:form>
    </body>
```

**Listing 16.5**      **Full ASPX Code for MobileWebForm3**

```
<%@ Register TagPrefix="mobile"
➥ Namespace="System.Web.UI.MobileControls"
➥ Assembly="System.Web.Mobile, Version=1.0.3300.0,
➥ Culture=neutral, PublicKeyToken=b03f5f7f11d50a3a" %>
<%@ Register TagPrefix="uc1" TagName="Title"
➥ Src="Title.ascx" %>
<%@ Page Language="vb" AutoEventWireup="false"
➥ Codebehind="MobileWebForm3.aspx.vb"
➥ Inherits="ProductSpecifier.MobileWebForm3" %>
<meta name="GENERATOR" content="Microsoft Visual
➥ Studio.NET 7.0">
<meta name="CODE_LANGUAGE" content="Visual Basic 7.0">
<meta name="vs_targetSchema"
➥ content="http://schemas.microsoft.com/Mobile/Page">
<body Xmlns:mobile="http://schemas.microsoft.com/Mobile/
➥WebForm">
   <mobile:form id="Pg3Form1" runat="server">
      <uc1:Title id="Title1" runat="server"></uc1:Title>
      <mobile:TextView id="txtvwP3Fm1" runat="server">Our
➥ database appears to be temporarily unavailable at the
➥ moment.<br />Please try again.</mobile:TextView>
      <mobile:Link id="lnkPg3Fm1Pg1Fm1" runat="server"
➥ SoftkeyLabel="Home"
➥ NavigateURL="MobileWebForm1.aspx">Home</mobile:Link>
   </mobile:form>
</body>
```

## Summary

This particular application is a simple example of how we could set up a site for facilitating a commercial transaction, and it also provides an engine that could easily be scaled up to a more sophisticated "big-screen" site. We have also canvassed design considerations such as navigation between separate Mobile Web Pages and exception handling.

In the next chapter, we will look at creating an online application that makes use of an XML Web Service.

# CHAPTER 17

# The HomeLoanCalculator

- Rationale

- Planning the application

- The XML Web Service: WebServiceHomeLoanCalc

- The Mobile Web Page

- The code behind

- Finishing touches

- Running the application

- Full ASPX code listing

H ome-loan calculators are a fairly ubiquitous item on the Internet. (They seem to be offered by just about every online real-estate agent!) In this application, we see how we can set up a calculator as an XML Web Service that could be accessed by either a mobile or a "big-screen" site. This XML Web Service will be a little more interactive than our example in the previous chapter, as we will have to post data to it and anticipate a response.

We will then create a Mobile Website to consume the XML Web Service. The example gives us the opportunity to exercise some of the Validation controls provided in the Toolkit and to make practical use of a Style Sheet control.

## Rationale

We want to have a site that enables a user to choose from a range of possible calculations, including:

- The ability to calculate the maximum amount that the user could afford to borrow as a loan

- The ability to calculate the size of the repayments for a given loan

- The ability to calculate how much is owed on a loan at any given time

Once the user has chosen their calculation type, we need to have a data-entry screen with some form of validation on the data fields and a Calculate option. The Calculate command should take the user to a form that not only presents the results of the calculation but also the parameters that they entered.

An important feature of the application should be the ability to rapidly test different values in the calculation so that users can quickly get a picture of what they are able to afford or how much something is going to cost them.

## Planning the Application

The application is in two separate parts:

- The XML Web Service: WebServiceHomeLoanCalc

- The Mobile Website: HomeLoanCalculator

### WebServiceHomeLoanCalc

The XML Web Service offers three separate calculation services:

**Amount**    The amount that can be borrowed

**Repayment**    The size of the repayment

**Outstanding**    The amount owed on a loan

The XML Web Service should be able to request the necessary input data and return the result of the calculation rounded to two decimal places (to make the value meaningful in currency terms).

## HomeLoanCalculator

We will set HomeLoanCalculator up as five forms on a single Mobile Web Page. Figure 17.1 illustrates the role of each form (or card).

**FIGURE 17.1:**

The card layout for the HomeLoanCalculator application

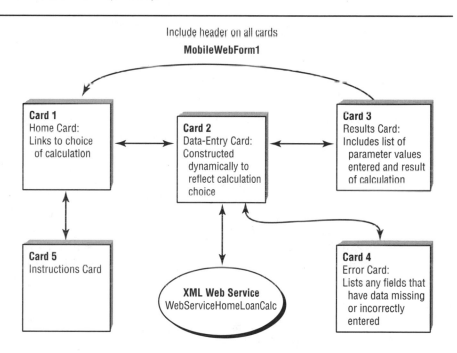

If we were building the application using a more traditional ASP/WML approach, we would probably group cards 1 and 5 into a single deck and have cards 2, 3, and 4 on separate ASP pages, each essentially comprising single-card decks. When using the Mobile Internet Toolkit, there are no real logical or design advantages in splitting this application across separate Mobile Web Pages as there were with the previous ProductSpecifier application. Therefore, we can happily place all five forms on the single page. These forms all stay under the 1,000-byte mark when compiled, so the application should perform well in the wireless mobile space.

## The XML Web Service: WebServiceHomeLoanCalc

To calculate the home loan, we need a formula that we can manipulate programmatically. There are a number of methods to calculate a reducing-balance loan, which is what we are doing here. The process of paying out a liability (consisting of principal and interest) by a series of equal payments over a period of time is known as *amortization*, and once the debt is cleared, it is said to have been *amortized*.

The formula we will use is $A = PR^n - (Q(R^n - 1)/(R - 1))$, where $R = 1 + r/100$ and $A$ is the amount owed after $n$ periods or payments, $n$ is the total number of periods or payments, $r$ is the interest rate per period, $Q$ is the size of repayment, and $P$ is the principal or amount borrowed.

This is a fairly easy formula to manipulate programmatically. Its one drawback is that it can only be used to calculate loans where the repayment is made at the same time as the interest calculation. So if repayments are made monthly, then the calculation can only work if the interest is calculated monthly as well.

Within the code (see Listing 17.1), we have grouped some elements of the formula to help visually with putting it all together. For example, if we take a look at the second WebMethod used to calculate the amount of loan still outstanding, we'll see that we can begin by requesting a yearly interest rate from the user, as that is the value that most people will have. We also request the number of payments the user makes each year and combine these two figures to come up with the interest rate ($i$) for each repayment period that we need to use in the formula.

So $i = Rate/Periods$ and $R = 1 + i/100$. We then determine the total number of repayments that are to be made over the life of the loan ($n$) by evaluating $n = Years * Periods$. *Years* equals the total number of years that the user expects to be repaying the loan for, and *Periods* represents the number of repayments that the user makes each year.

Another aspect of the original formula that we have simplified and assigned to a value ($x$) is $x = R^n$. This equation is written in Visual Basic .NET using the functions from the Maths library and is written like so:

```
x = Math.Pow(R, n)
```

The Pow function allows us to raise the value $R$ to the power of $n$.

We then make use of our $x$ value and the *Repayment* value as entered by the user to calculate $y$ where $y = (Repayment * (x - 1)) / (R - 1)$.

This picks up the following part of the original formula: $Q(R^n - 1)/(R - 1)$. We then finish it off with: $A = (Principal * x) - y$.

$A$ is our amount outstanding. We can then use the Round function from the Maths library to round our calculated value ($A$) off to two decimal places:

```
Outstanding = Math.Round(A, 2)
```

The value Outstanding is the figure returned by the WebMethod.

We can also set up additional WebMethods based on the amortization formula to calculate other aspects of housing loans. For example, we can rearrange the formula to calculate the amount that can be borrowed for a given repayment, interest rate, and repayment period.

Consider the original formula, $A = PR^n - Q(R^n - 1)/(R - 1)$. When the loan is amortized, the amount outstanding equals zero, hence $0 = PR^n - Q(R^n - 1)/(R - 1)$. Thus, $PR^n = Q(R^n - 1)/(R - 1)$ or $P = Q(R^n - 1)/((R - 1) * R^n)$. We have built this version of the formula into the third WebMethod (Amount).

We can also calculate the repayment for a given loan by algebraically rearranging the formula as follows (again using a final amount owed of 0): $0 = PR^n - Q(R^n - 1)/(R - 1)$ or $PR^n = Q(R^n - 1)/(R - 1)$ or $Q = (R - 1) * PR^n/(R^n - 1)$.

This version of the formula has been built into the first WebMethod (Repayment).

Open Visual Studio .NET and create a new XML Web Service using Visual Basic. Name the XML Web Service WebServiceHomeLoanCalc.

Switch to code behind (or Code View, as it is described in the Web Service interface) and add the code from Listing 17.1.

---

**Listing 17.1        Code Behind for the WebServiceHomeLoanCalc XML Web Service**

```
Imports System.Web.Services

<WebService(namespace:="http://www.MyFantasticWebService
➡Site.com")> Public Class Loan_Calculator
    Inherits System.Web.Services.WebService

+ Web Services Designer Generated Code

    <WebMethod()> Public Function Repayment(ByVal
➡ Principal As Double, ByVal Rate As Double, ByVal
➡ Years As Double, ByVal Periods As Integer) As Double
        Dim i As Double
        Dim R As Double
        Dim n As Double
        Dim x As Double
        Dim Q As Double
        i = Rate / Periods
        R = 1 + (i / 100)
        n = Years * Periods
        x = Math.Pow(R, n)
```

```
        Q = (R - 1) * Principal * x / (x - 1)
        Repayment = Math.Round(Q, 2)
    End Function

    <WebMethod()> Public Function Outstanding(ByVal
➥ Principal As Double, ByVal Repayment As Double, ByVal
➥ Rate As Double, ByVal Years As Double, ByVal Periods
➥ As Integer) As Double
        Dim i As Double
        Dim R As Double
        Dim n As Double
        Dim x As Double
        Dim y As Double
        Dim A As Double
        i = Rate / Periods
        R = 1 + (i / 100)
        n = Years * Periods
        x = Math.Pow(R, n)
        y = (Repayment * (x - 1)) / (R - 1)
        A = (Principal * x) - y
        Outstanding = Math.Round(A, 2)
    End Function

    <WebMethod()> Public Function Amount(ByVal Repayment
➥ As Double, ByVal Rate As Double, ByVal Years As
➥ Double, ByVal Periods As Integer) As Double
        Dim i As Double
        Dim R As Double
        Dim n As Double
        Dim x As Double
        Dim P As Double
        i = Rate / Periods
        n = Years * Periods
        R = 1 + (i / 100)
        x = Math.Pow(R, n)
        P = (Repayment * (x - 1)) / (x * (R - 1))
        Amount = Math.Round(P, 2)
    End Function

End Class
```

Although the project is called WebServiceHomeLoanCalc, we have named the actual class
Loan_Calculator and given it three methods, Repayment, Outstanding, and Amount. Notice,
too, that we have set up a dummy Web address within the namespace to avoid the warning
messages when testing the XML Web Service in Internet Explorer:

```
<WebService(namespace:="http://www.MyFantasticWebService
➥Site.com")>
```

In practice, we would either add a real Web URL from where we could host the XML Web Service or leave it out.

Compile the project and open it in Internet Explorer. Figure 17.2 illustrates how the XML Web Service should appear.

**FIGURE 17.2:**

The Loan_Calculator (WebServiceHome-LoanCalc) in Internet Explorer

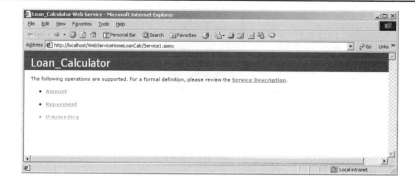

Click the link for Amount. Figure 17.3 illustrates how the Amount service appears when running in Internet Explorer.

**FIGURE 17.3:**

The Amount service when running in Internet Explorer

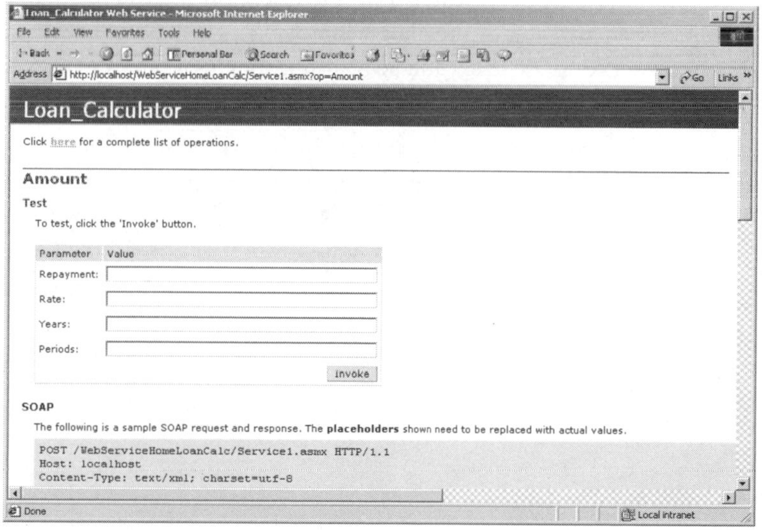

We can enter values to test the service. For example, we could enter 500 for the Repayment, 10 for the Rate, 25 for Years, and 12 for Periods.

Selecting the Invoke button should produce the result illustrated in Figure 17.4.

The value returned
by the Amount
service from the
Loan_Calculator

Once you are satisfied that everything is behaving as it should, close the project, as our next step is to create the Mobile Website.

## The Mobile Web Page

Open a new Mobile Web Application in Visual Studio .NET using Visual Basic. Name the project HomeLoanCalculator.

Set the Mobile Web Page up with five forms (Form1, Form2, Form3, Form4, and Form5). Drag a Style Sheet control to the page. Right-click the Style Sheet control (StyleSheet1) and select Edit Styles from the menu. This will open the Styles Editor dialog box, where you will choose Style from the Style Types window (in the top left-hand corner of the dialog box). In the Properties box of the dialog (bottom right-hand corner) expand the Font properties by clicking the small +. Set the `Bold` subproperty of `Font` to True and the `Size` subproperty to Large. Right-click Style1 and select Rename from the context menu. Set the name to Title1. Refer to Figure 17.5.

The Styles Editor
dialog box displaying
settings for
StyleSheet1

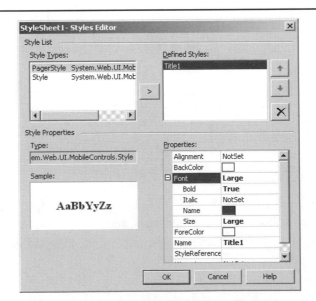

The style that we have created should now be available in the `StyleReference` property of the individual mobile controls as Title1.

Use Table 17.1 as a guide to set up the five forms with the controls and properties listed.

**TABLE 17.1:** Controls and Properties for MobilewebForm1

| Form | Control | Property | Value |
| --- | --- | --- | --- |
| Form1 | Label | StyleReference | Title1 |
| | | Text | Home Loan Calculator |
| | | ID | lblFm1 |
| | Link | Text | Instructions |
| | | SoftKeyLabel | Instr |
| | | ID | lnkFm1Fm5 |
| | | NavigateURL | #Form5 |
| | Label | Text | Choose your calculation: |
| | | ID | lblFm11 |
| | Command | Text | Amount You Can Borrow |
| | | SoftKeyLabel | Brrw |
| | | ID | cmdBorrow |
| | Command | Text | Repayment Size |
| | | SoftKeyLabel | Repay |
| | | ID | cmdRepayment |
| | Command | Text | Amount Outstanding |
| | | SoftKeyLabel | Owe |
| | | ID | cmdOutstanding |
| Form2 | Label | StyleReference | Title1 |
| | | Text | Home Loan Calculator |
| | | ID | lblFm2 |
| | Command | Text | Home |
| | | SoftKeyLabel | Home |
| | | ID | cmdHome |
| | Label | Font | |
| | | Bold | True |
| | | Text | Input Screen |
| | | ID | lblFm21 |
| | Label | Text | <Empty> |
| | | ID | lblFm22 |

*Continued on next page*

**TABLE 17.1 CONTINUED:**  Controls and Properties for MobilewebForm1

| Form | Control | Property | Value |
|------|---------|----------|-------|
| | TextBox | Text | <Empty> |
| | | ID | txtInput1 |
| | Label | Text | <Empty> |
| | | ID | lblFm23 |
| | TextBox | Text | <Empty> |
| | | ID | txtInput2 |
| | Label | Text | <Empty> |
| | | ID | lblFm24 |
| | TextBox | Text | <Empty> |
| | | ID | txtInput3 |
| | Label | Text | <Empty> |
| | | ID | lblFm25 |
| | TextBox | Text | <Empty> |
| | | ID | txtInput4 |
| | Label | Text | <Empty> |
| | | ID | lblFm26 |
| | TextBox | Text | <Empty> |
| | | ID | txtInput5 |
| | Command | Text | Calculate |
| | | SoftKeyLabel | Calc |
| | | ID | cmdCalculate |
| | Command | Text | Home |
| | | SoftKeyLabel | Home |
| | | ID | cmdHome1 |
| | RequiredField ➡Validator | ErrorMessage | <Empty> |
| | | ControlToValidate | txtInput1 |
| | | ID | rfvInput1 |
| | RequiredField ➡Validator | ErrorMessage | <Empty> |
| | | ControlToValidate | txtInput2 |
| | | ID | rfvInput2 |
| | RequiredField ➡Validator | ErrorMessage | <Empty> |
| | | ControlToValidate | txtInput3 |
| | | ID | tfvInput3 |

*Continued on next page*

**TABLE 17.1 CONTINUED:** Controls and Properties for MobilewebForm1

| Form | Control | Property | Value |
|------|---------|----------|-------|
| | RequiredField ➡Validator | ErrorMessage | <Empty> |
| | | ControlToValidate | txtInput4 |
| | | ID | rfvInput4 |
| | RequiredField ➡Validator | ErrorMessage | <Empty> |
| | | ControlToValidate | txtInput5 |
| | | ID | rfvInput5 |
| Form3 | Label | StyleReference | Title1 |
| | | Text | Home Loan Calculator |
| | | ID | lblFm3 |
| | ValidationSummary | BackLabel | Return to Input Screen |
| | | HeaderText | Return to the Input Screen and complete the following: |
| | | FormToValidate | Form2 |
| | | ID | vsFm3 |
| | Label | Text | <Empty> |
| | | ID | lblFm31 |
| | Link | Text | Return to Input Screen |
| | | SoftKeyLabel | Input |
| | | ID | lnkFm3Fm2 |
| | | NavigateURL | #Form2 |
| Form4 | Label | StyleReference | Title1 |
| | | Text | Home Loan Calculator |
| | | ID | lblFm4 |
| | Label | Text | <Empty> |
| | | ID | lblFm41 |
| | Label | Text | <Empty> |
| | | ID | lblResult |
| | Label | Text | Based on the following values: |
| | | ID | lblFm42 |
| | Label | Text | <Empty> |
| | | ID | lblFm43 |
| | Label | Text | <Empty> |
| | | ID | lblFm44 |

*Continued on next page*

**TABLE 17.1 CONTINUED:** Controls and Properties for MobilewebForm1

| Form | Control | Property | Value |
|---|---|---|---|
| | Label | Text | <Empty> |
| | | ID | lblFm45 |
| | Label | Text | <Empty> |
| | | ID | lblFm46 |
| | Label | Text | <Empty> |
| | | ID | lblFm47 |
| | Link | Text | Return to Input Screen |
| | | SoftKeyLabel | Input |
| | | ID | lnkFm4Fm2 |
| | | NavigateURL | #Form2 |
| | Link | Text | Home |
| | | SoftKeyLabel | Home |
| | | ID | lnkFrm4Frm1 |
| | | NavigateURL | #Form1 |
| Form5 | Label | StyleReference | Title1 |
| | | Text | Home Loan Calculator |
| | | ID | lblFm5 |
| | TextView | Text | Instructions: |
| | | | This calculator can be used to determine |
| | | | * how much you can afford to borrow |
| | | | * how large your repayments might be |
| | | | * how much is left on your loan to pay |
| | | | Select the relevant link to calculate the information you need. Please note that this calculator only works for loans where the interest calculation period (eg: monthly) matches the repayment periods (eg: monthly). |
| | | ID | txtvwFm5 |
| | Link | Text | Home |
| | | SoftKeyLabel | Home |
| | | ID | lnkFm5Fm1 |
| | | NavigateURL | #Form1 |

The completed forms should appear as illustrated in Figures 17.6, 17.7, and 17.8. Note that I have reorganized the order of the forms on the Mobile Web Page to assist with fitting them into the screen shots.

FIGURE 17.6:

MobileWebForm1 for
HomeLoanCalculator
in design view,
displaying Forms 1
and 5

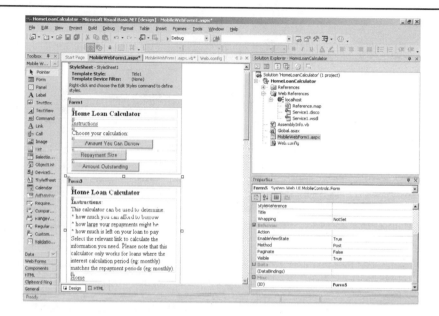

FIGURE 17.7:

MobileWebForm1 for
HomeLoanCalculator
in design view,
displaying Form 2

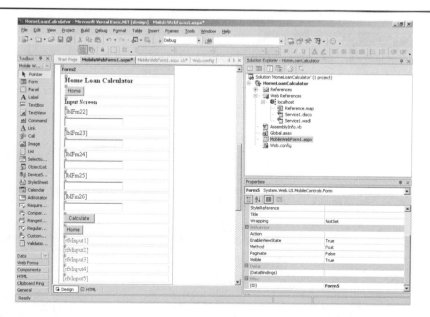

**FIGURE 17.8:**

MobileWebForm1 for HomeLoanCalculator in design view, displaying Forms 2 and 3

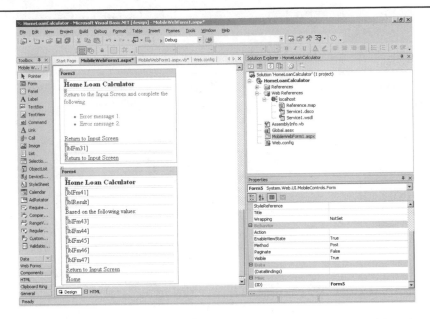

We need to add a reference to the XML Web Service that we created. Select Add Web Reference from the Project menu and use the Add Web Reference dialog box to locate and create a reference to the WebServiceHomeLoanCalc XML Web Service.

## The Code Behind

Switch to Code Behind View and add the code from Listing 17.2 to the MobileWebForm class.

**Listing 17.2    Code Behind for HomeLoanCalculator**

```
Private Sub cmdCalculate_Click(ByVal sender As
➥ System.Object, ByVal e As System.EventArgs) Handles
➥ cmdCalculate.Click

      Dim myService As localhost.Loan_Calculator = New
➥ localhost.Loan_Calculator()

      If Page.IsValid Then
          ActiveForm = Form4
      Else : ActiveForm = Form3
          lblFm31.Text = lblFm31.Text.Empty
          lnkFm3Fm2.Visible = False
      End If
      Try
```

```
                    Dim Y As Double = txtInput4.Text
                    Dim P As Double = txtInput3.Text
                    Dim R As Double = txtInput2.Text
                    Dim Q As Double = txtInput1.Text


            Select Case Session("Calc")
                    Case 1
                            lblFm41.Text = "The amount you would
➥ be able to borrow is:"
                            lblResult.Text = "$" &
➥ myService.Amount(Q, R, Y, P)
                            lblFm43.Text = "Your repayments are
➥ $" & Q
                            lblFm44.Text = "Your Interest rate =
➥ " & R & "%"
                            lblFm45.Text = "Life of the Loan = "
➥ & Y & " years"
                            lblFm46.Text = "Number of payments
➥ per year = " & P
                            lblFm47.Visible = False
                    Case 2
                            lblFm41.Text = "The size of your
➥ regular repayment would be:"
                            lblResult.Text = "$" &
➥ myService.Repayment(Q, R, Y, P)
                            lblFm43.Text = "Your Loan = $" & Q
                            lblFm44.Text = "Your Interest rate =
➥ " & R & "%"
                            lblFm45.Text = "Life of the Loan = "
➥ & Y & " years"
                            lblFm46.Text = "Number of payments
➥ per year = " & P
                            lblFm47.Visible = False
                    Case 3
                            Dim Pr As Double = txtInput5.Text
                            lblFm47.Visible = True
                            lblFm41.Text = "The amount
➥ outstanding on your loan is:"
                            lblResult.Text = "$" &
➥ myService.Outstanding(Pr, Q, R, Y, P)
                            lblFm43.Text = "Your Loan = $" & Pr
                            lblFm44.Text = "Your repayments are
➥ $" & Q
                            lblFm45.Text = "Your Interest rate =
➥ " & R & "%"
                            lblFm46.Text = "After making
➥ repayments for: " & Y & " years"
                            lblFm47.Text = "Number of payments
➥ per year = " & P

            End Select
        Catch
```

```
            ActiveForm = Form3
            lblFm31.Text = "Please check that you have
➟ only entered numbers in the fields and that there are
➟ no spaces or other characters. Otherwise, if your
➟ figures are OK, the Calculator may be temporarily
➟ unavialable."
            lnkFm3Fm2.Visible = True
        End Try
    End Sub

    Private Sub cmdBorrow_Click(ByVal sender As
➟ System.Object, ByVal e As System.EventArgs) Handles
➟ cmdBorrow.Click
        Session("Calc") = 1
        ActiveForm = Form2

        txtInput5.Visible = False
        rfvInput5.Visible = False
        lblFm26.Visible = False
        txtInput1.Text = txtInput1.Text.Empty
        txtInput2.Text = txtInput2.Text.Empty
        txtInput3.Text = txtInput3.Text.Empty
        txtInput4.Text = txtInput4.Text.Empty

        lblFm22.Text = "Enter your preferred repayment in
➟ dollars:"
        lblFm23.Text = "Enter your expected yearly
➟ Interest rate:"
        lblFm24.Text = "Enter how many times a year that
➟ you make your repayment:"
        lblFm25.Text = "Enter the number of years that
➟ you wish to borrow the money for:"

        rfvInput1.ErrorMessage = "Please enter your
➟ preferred repayment in dollars."
        rfvInput2.ErrorMessage = "Please enter your
➟ expected yearly Interest rate."
        rfvInput3.ErrorMessage = "Please enter how many
➟ times a year that you make your repayment."
        rfvInput4.ErrorMessage = "Please enter the number
➟ of years that you wish to borrow the money for."
    End Sub

    Private Sub cmdRepayment_Click(ByVal sender As
➟ System.Object, ByVal e As System.EventArgs) Handles
➟ cmdRepayment.Click
        Session("Calc") = 2
        ActiveForm = Form2

        txtInput5.Visible = False
        rfvInput5.Visible = False
        lblFm26.Visible = False
```

```
        txtInput1.Text = txtInput1.Text.Empty
        txtInput2.Text = txtInput2.Text.Empty
        txtInput3.Text = txtInput3.Text.Empty
        txtInput4.Text = txtInput4.Text.Empty

        lblFm22.Text = "Enter the amount you wish to
➥ borrow in dollars:"
        lblFm23.Text = "Enter your expected yearly
➥ Interest rate:"
        lblFm24.Text = "Enter how many times a year that
➥ you make your repayment:"
        lblFm25.Text = "Enter the number of years that
➥ you wish to borrow the money for:"

        rfvInput1.ErrorMessage = "Please enter the amount
➥ you wish to borrow in dollars."
        rfvInput2.ErrorMessage = "Please enter your
➥ expected yearly Interest rate."
        rfvInput3.ErrorMessage = "Please enter how many
➥ times a year that you make your repayment."
        rfvInput4.ErrorMessage = "Please enter the number
➥ of years that you wish to borrow the money for."
    End Sub

    Private Sub cmdOutstanding_Click(ByVal sender As
➥ System.Object, ByVal e As System.EventArgs) Handles
➥ cmdOutstanding.Click
        Session("Calc") = 3
        ActiveForm = Form2

        txtInput5.Visible = True
        rfvInput5.Visible = True
        lblFm26.Visible = True
        txtInput1.Text = txtInput1.Text.Empty
        txtInput2.Text = txtInput2.Text.Empty
        txtInput3.Text = txtInput3.Text.Empty
        txtInput4.Text = txtInput4.Text.Empty
        txtInput5.Text = txtInput5.Text.Empty

        lblFm22.Text = "Enter your preferred repayment in
➥ dollars:"
        lblFm23.Text = "Enter your expected yearly
➥ Interest rate:"
        lblFm24.Text = "Enter how many times a year that
➥ you make your repayment:"
        lblFm25.Text = "Enter the number of years that
➥ you wish to calculate the amount outstanding at:"
        lblFm26.Text = "Enter the amount you wish to
➥ borrow in dollars:"

        rfvInput1.ErrorMessage = "Please enter the amount
➥ you wish to borrow in dollars."
```

```
        rfvInput2.ErrorMessage = "Please enter your
➥ expected yearly Interest rate."
        rfvInput3.ErrorMessage = "Please enter how many
➥ times a year that you make your repayment."
        rfvInput4.ErrorMessage = "Please enter the number
➥ of years that you wish to calculate the amount
➥ outstanding at."
        rfvInput5.ErrorMessage = "Please enter the amount
➥ you wish to borrow in dollars."
    End Sub


    Private Sub cmdHome_Click(ByVal sender As
➥ System.Object, ByVal e As System.EventArgs) Handles
➥ cmdHome.Click
        ActiveForm = Form1
    End Sub

    Private Sub cmdHome1_Click(ByVal sender As
➥ System.Object, ByVal e As System.EventArgs) Handles
➥ cmdHome1.Click
        ActiveForm = Form1
    End Sub

End Class
```

We haven't made any use of the Page_Load event, so its default code template isn't included in this listing. However, the code from Listing 17.2 would be entered immediately after the Page_Load code template.

As can be seen in the following code, when we trigger the cmdCalculate_Click event, we create our link to the XML Web Service and check the validation controls. If any of the validation controls have tripped up, Page.IsValid will return false, and the user will be directed to Form 3, which contains the validation summary information. Otherwise, Form 4 (the results form) becomes the active form:

```
Dim myService As localhost.Loan_Calculator = New
➥ localhost.Loan_Calculator()

        If Page.IsValid Then
            ActiveForm = Form4
        Else : ActiveForm = Form3
            lblFm31.Text = lblFm31.Text.Empty
            lnkFm3Fm2.Visible = False
        End If
```

We have placed an exception handler around the remaining code in this subroutine to pick up any problems with the way that the user has entered data or in connecting to the XML

Web Service. We could have taken much more care with finding and correcting likely data-entry errors rather than handling them with a generic exception handler, and this is something we may wish to do if we were to extend the application. If the exception handler is tripped, Form3 is again made active with an appropriate error message.

---

**WARNING**    There may be some temptation to provide a validation layer at the control level by setting the TextBox numeric property to true. However, doing so prohibits the use of nonnumeric characters such as the decimal point, which automatically invalidates much of the data that our users may wish to enter.

Essentially, the remaining code of cmdCalculate_Click checks the status of the session variable Calc to identify which method of calculation has been chosen and then sets up the Results form (Form4) to reflect the selection. It reads data from the input TextBoxes from Form2 and calls the appropriate WebMethod from the XML Web Service to carry out the calculation.

The next three subroutines respond to the user's choice of calculation. Each subroutine sets up both the Data Entry form (Form2) and the Validation Summary form (Form3) to reflect the choice. We can see this in the following code, which is the cmdBorrow_Click subroutine:

```
Private Sub cmdBorrow_Click(ByVal sender As
➥ System.Object, ByVal e As System.EventArgs) Handles
➥ cmdBorrow.Click
        Session("Calc") = 1
        ActiveForm = Form2

        txtInput5.Visible = False
        rfvInput5.Visible = False
        lblFm26.Visible = False
        txtInput1.Text = txtInput1.Text.Empty
        txtInput2.Text = txtInput2.Text.Empty
        txtInput3.Text = txtInput3.Text.Empty
        txtInput4.Text = txtInput4.Text.Empty

        lblFm22.Text = "Enter your preferred repayment in
➥ dollars:"
        lblFm23.Text = "Enter your expected yearly
➥ Interest rate:"
        lblFm24.Text = "Enter how many times a year that
➥ you make your repayment:"
        lblFm25.Text = "Enter the number of years that
➥ you wish to borrow the money for:"

        rfvInput1.ErrorMessage = "Please enter your
➥ preferred repayment in dollars."
```

```
        rfvInput2.ErrorMessage = "Please enter your
➡ expected yearly Interest rate."
        rfvInput3.ErrorMessage = "Please enter how many
➡ times a year that you make your repayment."
        rfvInput4.ErrorMessage = "Please enter the number
➡ of years that you wish to borrow the money for."
    End Sub
```

Putting the Validation Summary set-up code into a separate subroutine may be slightly better in terms of performance and logical design (which is something else to consider when extending the project).

Note that the following subroutine only needs four inputs from the user and that it hides the fifth TextBox control and associated labels. It also ensures that the TextBoxes are empty when accessed from Form1 (although the local cache on a mobile device may have its own ideas on this!):

```
txtInput5.Visible = False
rfvInput5.Visible = False
lblFm26.Visible = False
txtInput1.Text = txtInput1.Text.Empty
txtInput2.Text = txtInput2.Text.Empty
txtInput3.Text = txtInput3.Text.Empty
txtInput4.Text = txtInput4.Text.Empty
```

The last two subroutines in Listing 17.2 provide some navigation links for the user from Form2 to return to Form1.

---

**TIP**     We have used Command controls rather than Link controls because some mobile devices can be a little creative in the way that a combination of Command and Link controls is rendered at the end of a data-entry sequence. (Try replacing the cmdHome1 control with a Link control and then view it using the Openwave browser. The Calculate command becomes a little tricky to access.)

---

**TIP**     We have placed a Home link (in the form of a Command control) near the top of Form2, again to accommodate the way in which data input is rendered by the Openwave browser. Each input field is given a separate screen, which could prove a little tedious if you wish to quickly return to the first form.

---

Save and compile the project.

## Finishing Touches

As with the ProductSpecifier application (Chapter 16, "Sample Mobile Website: My Computer Shop"), we need to finalize a couple of operational aspects of our project before we can realistically deploy it.

We need to edit our `Web.config` file to ensure that everything will work as it should across the various mobile device/browser/gateway combinations.

Open up `Web.config` from the Solution Explorer window and check that the `<httpRuntime useFullyQualifiedRedirectUrl="true" />` tag is set in the `<system.web>` section, as explained in Chapter 8, "A Deeper Look at the Mobile Internet Toolkit and VB .NET." Scroll down to the `<sessionState>` tag and set `cookieless="true"`.

Once we have tested and debugged the application, set `debug="false"` in the `<compilation>` tag, to improve performance. Save the changes.

## Running the Application

Compile and view the application in a suitable browser. The user is initially presented with the choice of which calculation they wish to make. See Figure 17.9.

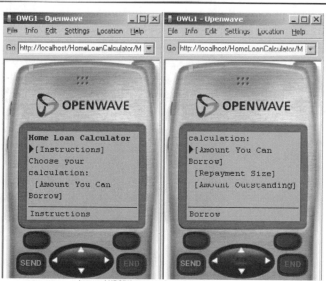

Image of UP.SDK courtesy Openwave Systems, Inc.

The user then chooses one of the calculations, in this case Amount You Can Borrow, and is presented with Form2, which has been rendered to reflect the choice. See Figure 17.10. The second view of the browser in Figure 17.10 illustrates a repayment entry of $500.

**FIGURE 17.10:**

The data-entry screen for Amount You Can Borrow, rendered in the Openwave browser

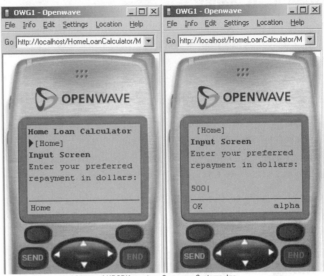

Image of UP.SDK courtesy Openwave Systems, Inc.

Notice that the Openwave browser presents each input option as a separate screen. Clicking OK presents the next and subsequent inputs as depicted in Figure 17.11. In these examples, we have entered values of 5% for the interest rate, 12 for the number of repayments each year, and 25 for the life of the loan in years.

**FIGURE 17.11:**

The sequence of data-entry screens, as depicted by the Openwave browser, for the HomeLoanCalculator application

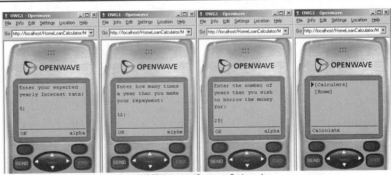

Image of UP.SDK courtesy Openwave Systems, Inc.

Selecting the Calculate link returns the Results form, as depicted in Figure 17.12.

**FIGURE 17.12:**

The results of the calculation

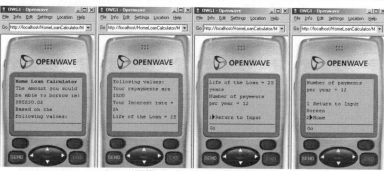

Image of UP.SDK courtesy Openwave Systems, Inc.

If we had left one or more of the fields blank or had incorrectly entered data, we would have had the validation summary or error message from Form3 returned, as illustrated in Figures 17.13 and 17.14.

**FIGURE 17.13:**

The validation messages returned by the HomeLoanCalculator application when a data item is omitted

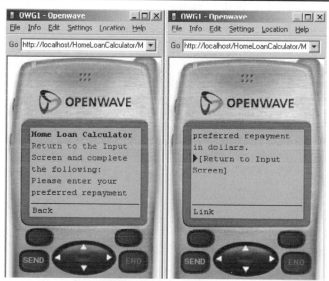

Image of UP.SDK courtesy Openwave Systems, Inc.

**FIGURE 17.14:**

The error message
returned by the
HomeLoanCalculator
when a percent sign is
entered into one of
the fields

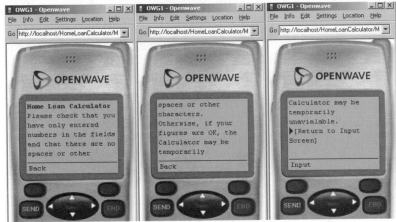

Image of UP.SDK courtesy Openwave Systems, Inc.

## Full ASPX Code Listing

Listing 17.3 contains the full ASPX code for the HomeLoanCalculator.

**Listing 17.3    Full ASPX Code for the HomeLoanCalculator Application**

```
<%@ Register TagPrefix="mobile"
➥ Namespace="System.Web.UI.MobileControls"
➥ Assembly="System.Web.Mobile, Version=1.0.3300.0,
➥ Culture=neutral, PublicKeyToken=b03f5f7f11d50a3a" %>
<%@ Page Language="vb" AutoEventWireup="false"
➥ Codebehind="MobileWebForm1.aspx.vb"
➥ Inherits="HomeLoanCalculator.MobileWebForm1" %>
<meta name="GENERATOR" content="Microsoft Visual
➥ Studio.NET 7.0">
<meta name="CODE_LANGUAGE" content="Visual Basic 7.0">
<meta name="vs_targetSchema"
➥ content="http://schemas.microsoft.com/Mobile/Page">
<body Xmlns:mobile="http://schemas.microsoft.com/Mobile/
➥WebForm">
    <mobile:stylesheet id="StyleSheet1" runat="server">
        <Style Font-Size="Large"
➥ Font-Bold="True" Name="Title1"></Style>
    </mobile:stylesheet>
    <mobile:form id="Form1" runat="server">
        <mobile:Label id="lblFm1" runat="server"
➥ StyleReference="Title1">Home Loan
➥ Calculator</mobile:Label>
```

```
        <mobile:Link id="lnkFm1Fm5" runat="server"
  SoftkeyLabel="Instr"
  NavigateURL="#Form5">Instructions</mobile:Link>
        <mobile:Label id="lblFm11" runat="server">Choose
  your calculation:</mobile:Label>
        <mobile:Command id="cmdBorrow" runat="server"
  SoftkeyLabel="Brrw">Amount You Can
  Borrow</mobile:Command>
        <mobile:Command id="cmdRepayment" runat="server"
  SoftkeyLabel="Repay">Repayment
  Size</mobile:Command>
        <mobile:Command id="cmdOutstanding" runat="server"
  SoftkeyLabel="Owe">Amount
  Outstanding</mobile:Command>
    </mobile:form>
    <mobile:form id="Form5" runat="server">
        <mobile:Label id="lblFm5" runat="server"
  StyleReference="Title1">Home Loan
  Calculator</mobile:Label>
        <mobile:TextView id="txtvwFm5"
  runat="server"><b>Instructions:</b> <br />This
  calculator can be used to determine:<br /><b>*</b>
  how much you can afford to borrow<br /><b>*</b> how
  large your repayments might be<br /><b>*</b> how much
  is left on your loan to pay<br />Select the relevant
  link to calculate the information you need. Please
  note that this calculator only works for loans where
  the interest calculation period (eg: monthly) matches
  the repayment periods (eg:
  monthly).</mobile:TextView>
        <mobile:Link id="lnkFm5Fm1" runat="server"
  SoftkeyLabel="Home"
  NavigateURL="#Form1">Home</mobile:Link>
    </mobile:form>
    <mobile:form id="Form2" runat="server">
        <mobile:Label id="lblFm2" runat="server"
  StyleReference="Title1">Home Loan
  Calculator</mobile:Label>
        <mobile:Command id="cmdHome" runat="server"
  SoftkeyLabel="Home">Home</mobile:Command>
        <mobile:Label id="lblFm21" runat="server" Font-
  Bold="True">Input Screen</mobile:Label>
        <mobile:Label id="lblFm22"
  runat="server"></mobile:Label>
        <mobile:TextBox id="txtInput1"
  runat="server"></mobile:TextBox>
        <mobile:Label id="lblFm23"
  runat="server"></mobile:Label>
        <mobile:TextBox id="txtInput2"
  runat="server"></mobile:TextBox>
        <mobile:Label id="lblFm24"
  runat="server"></mobile:Label>
```

```
    <mobile:TextBox id="txtInput3"
➡ runat="server"></mobile:TextBox>
    <mobile:Label id="lblFm25"
➡ runat="server"></mobile:Label>
    <mobile:TextBox id="txtInput4"
➡ runat="server"></mobile:TextBox>
    <mobile:Label id="lblFm26"
➡ runat="server"></mobile:Label>
    <mobile:TextBox id="txtInput5"
➡ runat="server"></mobile:TextBox>
    <mobile:Command id="cmdCalculate" runat="server"
➡ SoftkeyLabel="Calc">Calculate</mobile:Command>
    <mobile:Command id="cmdHome1" runat="server"
➡ SoftkeyLabel="Home">Home</mobile:Command>
    <mobile:RequiredFieldValidator id="rfvInput1"
➡ runat="server" ControlToValidate="txtInput1"></mobile:RequiredFieldVa
➡lidator>
    <mobile:RequiredFieldValidator id="rfvInput2"
➡ runat="server" ControlToValidate="txtInput2"></mobile:RequiredFieldVa
➡lidator>
    <mobile:RequiredFieldValidator id="rfvInput3"
➡ runat="server" ControlToValidate="txtInput3"></mobile:RequiredFieldVa
➡lidator>
    <mobile:RequiredFieldValidator id="rfvInput4"
➡ runat="server" ControlToValidate="txtInput4"></mobile:RequiredFieldVa
➡lidator>
    <mobile:RequiredFieldValidator id="rfvInput5"
➡ runat="server" ControlToValidate="txtInput5"></mobile:RequiredFieldVa
➡lidator>
  </mobile:form>
  <mobile:form id="Form3" runat="server">
    <mobile:Label id="lblFm3" runat="server"
➡ StyleReference="Title1">Home Loan
➡ Calculator</mobile:Label>
    <mobile:ValidationSummary id="vsFm3" runat="server"
➡ FormToValidate="Form2" HeaderText="Return to the
➡ Input Screen and complete the following:"
➡ BackLabel="Return to Input
➡ Screen"></mobile:ValidationSummary>
    <mobile:Label id="lblFm31"
➡ runat="server"></mobile:Label>
    <mobile:Link id="lnkFm3Fm2" runat="server"
➡ SoftkeyLabel="Input" NavigateURL="#Form2">Return to
➡ Input Screen</mobile:Link>
  </mobile:form>
  <mobile:form id="Form4" runat="server">
    <mobile:Label id="lblFm4" runat="server"
➡ StyleReference="Title1">Home Loan
➡ Calculator</mobile:Label>
    <mobile:Label id="lblFm41"
➡ runat="server"></mobile:Label>
```

```
        <mobile:Label id="lblResult"
➥ runat="server"></mobile:Label>
        <mobile:Label id="lblFm42" runat="server">Based on
➥ the following values:</mobile:Label>
        <mobile:Label id="lblFm43"
➥ runat="server"></mobile:Label>
        <mobile:Label id="lblFm44"
➥ runat="server"></mobile:Label>
        <mobile:Label id="lblFm45"
➥ runat="server"></mobile:Label>
        <mobile:Label id="lblFm46"
➥ runat="server"></mobile:Label>
        <mobile:Label id="lblFm47"
➥ runat="server"></mobile:Label>
        <mobile:Link id="lnkFm4Fm2" runat="server"
➥ SoftkeyLabel="Input" NavigateURL="#Form2">Return to
➥ Input Screen</mobile:Link>
        <mobile:Link id="lnkFrm4Frm1" runat="server"
➥ SoftkeyLabel="Home"
➥ NavigateURL="#Form1">Home</mobile:Link>
    </mobile:form>
</BODY>
```

## Summary

This chapter demonstrated an interactive mobile application linked to an XML Web Service. We could easily expand this site to encompass a full Internet solution using a "big-screen" HTML presence, as well as the mobile solution.

Within the mobile solution, we have demonstrated the practical application of Validation controls and a Style Sheet and explored some of the additional functionality of Visual Basic .NET with the Maths library.

The application itself could easily be extended with additional calculation options and various performance enhancements such as detecting and compensating for common input errors (such as placing percentage signs at the end of interest values or misplacing a decimal point).

# CHAPTER 18

# MyTipple: A Wine Lover's Portal

- Planning the application

- Setting up the images

- Writing the User control

- Setting up the AdRotator

- Setting up the Mobile Web Page

- Writing the code behind

- Finishing touches

- Running the application

- Further enhancements

- Full ASPX listing

Y ou know the drill. That important client is due in a couple of hours, and they've just rung to ask if you could have something knocked up for them to take a look at!

This project is about creating a "quick-and-dirty," database-driven Mobile Website. The code isn't elegant, optimized, or particularly clever, but it works and doesn't take too long to cobble together. We can use it to demonstrate just how quickly we can put together a functional and reasonably sophisticated online mobile presence using the Mobile Internet Toolkit.

The project also illustrates some of the principles of creating a dynamic site that can be totally controlled from a database, gives us the chance to play with the AdRotator control, and lets us further explore the various permutations of using the List Style mobile controls. Later in the chapter, in the section "Finishing Touches," we will explore some of the enhancements and extensions we could make to this project.

## Rationale

MyTipple is a mythical wine enthusiast's club looking to provide an online mobile presence that can be used as a promotional tool, a service to members, and a portal site to wine-related news and links on the Mobile Web.

The services to be provided include:

- Latest club news
- Calendar of events
- Links to and details of club sponsors
- Advertising
- Categorized links to sponsors, organizations, relevant news, and information, etc.

We could do a lot more with a portal site, but we need to keep this project down to the size of one chapter!

The site needs to be easily updated, which suggests that we use a database with its own interface.

Our aim is to build this site in less than three hours, so we will focus on using those tools that will produce the quickest results rather than those that may be regarded as the best tools for the task.

# Planning the Application

The term *portal* means many things to many people, and we could absolutely go to town in building an all-singing, all-dancing site that illustrates every conceivable aspect of cutting-edge mobile computing—but we won't.

The emphasis here is on speed and simplicity. We'll use Microsoft Access to build a flat-file database with a separate table for each set of data that we need. We'll use the Access form wizards to quickly whip up an interface to the database. If we were to build this for real, we would probably create a Web-based front end and a relational structure (and not use Access!), but this is quick and serves our purpose of creating something with which we can illustrate functionality. (The clock is ticking!)

Table 18.1 illustrates the proposed table and field structure for the database.

**TABLE 18.1:**  Table and Field Structure for MyTipple Database

| Table: | Field Name: | Field Type: |
| --- | --- | --- |
| Table 1 | news_id | AutoNumber |
| | news_item | Text |
| | news_text | Memo |
| | news_date | Date/Time |
| | news_current | Text |
| Table 2 | sponsor_id | AutoNumber |
| | sponsor_name | Text |
| | sponsor_address | Text |
| | sponsor_tel | Text |
| Table 3 | link_id | AutoNumber |
| | link_category | Text |
| | link_URL | Text |
| | link_name | Text |
| Table 4 | calendar_id | AutoNumber |
| | calendar_date | Text |
| | calendar_event | Text |
| | calendar_details | Memo |
| | calendar_current | Text |

The next step is to set up our site structure. Again, for simplicity, we will use a single Mobile Web Page. Figure 18.1 illustrates the form (card) structure for our site.

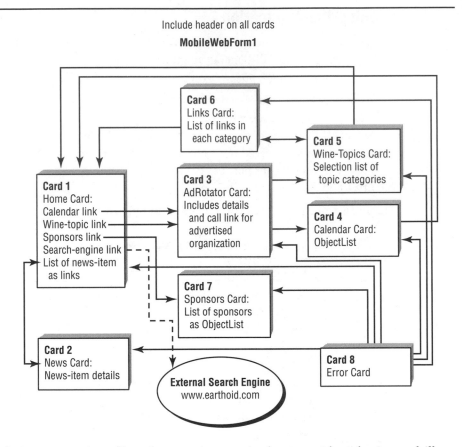

**FIGURE 18.1:**

The site structure for MyTipple

Include header on all cards

**MobileWebForm1**

The main design concept is to allow the user to access site features without having to drill too deep but at the same time to be exposed to some of our sponsor's advertising while they browse the site. This happens with Card3, through which the user is directed when they access the calendar or wine-topic link areas of the site. Whether the user should also go through the advertising card when accessing the news links might be something that we need to think about, and we won't bother with advertising when the user accesses the sponsor lists.

A common feature of this sort of site is to have some type of user authentication that enables the user to customize their site experience and for the site to provide some form of individualized services. We haven't included user authentication in this example, but it might be something we could look at when extending the application.

## Creating the Database

The emphasis on this application is speed of development. We are not interested in any level of sophistication in our database. This is going to be a plain-old flat-file job. Create a new database in Access and name it MyTipple.mdb.

Set up the tables and fields as outlined in Table 18.1. Once the basic structure is set up, we will use the Form Wizard to create some data-entry and management facilities for the database. (We could simply add the data straight into the tables, but this is not really practical in a deployed application, and we are looking to impress our prospective client.)

We also need to specialize a couple of the fields we have created. Open up Table 1 in Design View. Select the news_current field and in the Data Type column choose Lookup Wizard. Once in the wizard, choose the I Will Type in the Values That I Want radio button and click the Next button. In the second window, set the Number of Columns to 1 and in the Col 1 data field, type in **Yes** in the first row and **No** in the second row. Click the Next button and then Finish to exit the wizard. In the Properties box at the bottom of the Table 1 Design View, set the Default Value for the news_current field to True. While we are in this table, set the Default Value of news_date to Date().

Follow a similar process for the calendar_current field of Table 4. Set the Default Value of calendar_current to True. In Table 3, select the link_category field and, using a similar process with the Lookup Wizard, enter the values Reds, Whites, Fortifieds, and Spirits into the Col 1 data field.

To use the Form Wizard, from the Database Window select the Form tab and double-click the Create Form by Using Wizard option. See Figure 18.2.

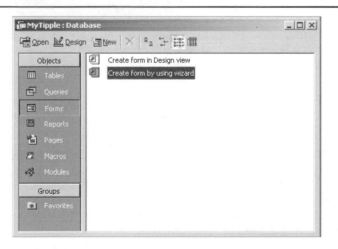

From the first of the Form Wizard windows, choose Table 1 from the Tables/Queries combo and click the arrow buttons to move all the fields from the Available Fields pane into the Selected Fields pane. See Figure 18.3. Click the Next button.

**FIGURE 18.3:**

The first of the Form Wizard windows

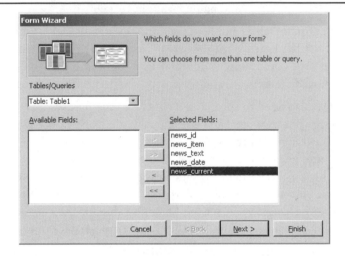

In the second window of the Form Wizard, choose the Justified option. Refer to Figure 18.4. Click Next.

**FIGURE 18.4:**

The second of the Form Wizard windows

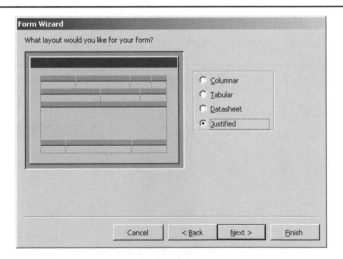

At the next window, choose one of the stunning styles available (being "adventurous," I went with Standard) and click Next. In the final window, set the form title to News and select the Modify the Form's Design option. See Figures 18.5 and 18.6. The form in Design View should look something like Figure 18.6.

**FIGURE 18.5:**

Final window in the
Form Wizard

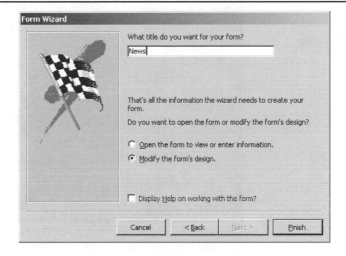

**FIGURE 18.6:**

The form in
Design View

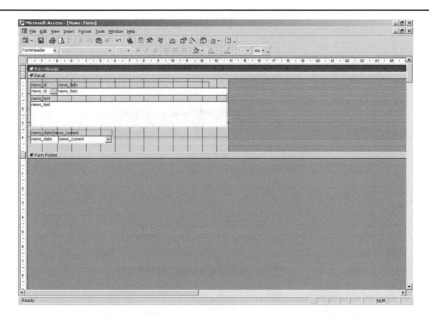

Make any adjustments that you wish to improve the appearance of the form. Carry out a similar process for the other three tables, naming them Sponsors, Links, and Calendar. Figure 18.7 illustrates the four data-management forms. Notice that I have already entered data into the database, which is reflected in these forms.

FIGURE 18.7:

The News,
Sponsors, Links,
and Calendar forms

FIGURE 18.7:

The News,
Sponsors, Links,
and Calendar forms

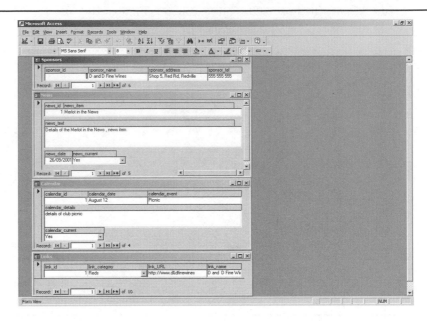

Finally, we need to add some dummy data into the database. It is simplest to enter it from the forms, but I have illustrated the data here directly from the tables, as it is a little easier to display it on a single page in this format. Enter the data illustrated in Figures 18.8, 18.9, 18.10, and 18.11.

FIGURE 18.8:

Data entered in
Table 1

| news_id | news_item | news_text | news_date | news_current |
|---|---|---|---|---|
| 1 | Merlot in the News | Details of the Merlot in the News , news item | 26/09/2001 | Yes |
| 2 | Chardonnay Specials for Club m | Details of the Chardonnay Specials for Club members news item | 26/09/2001 | Yes |
| 3 | Club Picnic! | Details of the Club Picnic news item | 26/09/2001 | Yes |
| 4 | Not a news item | rhubarb, rhubarb | 26/09/2001 | No |
| 5 | Lots of text news item | Open a new Mobile Web Application in Visual Studio .NET using Visu | 26/09/2001 | Yes |
| (AutoNumber) | | | 27/09/2001 | Yes |

Note that in Table 1, the Lots of Text news item actually has a couple of pages of text entered to test the pagination we will eventually introduce into the application. The Not a News Item item is designed to test the result of setting the news_current flag to No.

FIGURE 18.9:

Data entered in
Table 2

| sponsor_id | sponsor_name | sponsor_address | sponsor_tel |
|---|---|---|---|
| 1 | D and D Fine Wines | Shop 5, Red Rd, Redville | 555 555 555 |
| 2 | Discount Plonk | 7 Savignon Plce, GrapeTown | 444 444 444 |
| 3 | C and C Very Fine Wines | Shop 3, White St, WhiteCity | 222 222 222 |
| 4 | H and H Wines | 12 Merlot Crt, GrapeTown | 333 333 333 |
| 5 | G and G Wine and Spirits | Shop 8, Red Rd, Redville | 111 111 111 |
| 6 | B and S Beverages | Shop 9, White St, WhiteCity | 000 000 000 |
| (AutoNumber) | | | |

**FIGURE 18.10:**

Data entered in
Table 3

| | link_id | link_category | link_URL | link_name |
|---|---|---|---|---|
| Table3 : Table | | | | |
| | 1 | Reds | http://www.d&dfinewines | D and D Fine Wines |
| | 2 | Reds | http://www.discountplonk | Discount Plonk |
| | 3 | Whites | http://www.d&dfinewines | D and D Fine Wines |
| | 4 | Whites | http://www.c&cveryfinewines | C and C Very Fine Wines |
| | 5 | Whites | http://www.h&hwines | H and H Wines |
| | 6 | Fortifieds | http://www.discountplonk | Discount Plonk |
| | 7 | Fortifieds | http://www.c&cveryfinewines | C and C Very Fine Wines |
| | 8 | Spirits | http://www.discountplonk | Discount Plonk |
| | 9 | Spirits | http://www.g&gwine&spirits | G and G Wine and Spirits |
| | 10 | Spirits | http://www.b&sbeverages | B and S Beverages |
| ▶ | (AutoNumber) | | | |

**FIGURE 18.11:**

Data entered in
Table 4

| | calendar_id | calendar_date | calendar_event | calendar_details | calendar_current |
|---|---|---|---|---|---|
| Table4 : Table | | | | | |
| ▶ | 1 | August 12 | Picnic | details of club picnic | Yes |
| | 2 | August 18 | AGM | details of AGM | Yes |
| | 3 | August 31 | Winery tour | details of Winery tour | Yes |
| | 4 | September 3 | Club meeting | details of Club meeting | Yes |
| * | (AutoNumber) | | | | Yes |

We can now use the data-management forms to easily demonstrate the site management to our prospective client.

## Setting Up the Images

We are going to require four separate WBMP images for this project. The first will form part of our site header, and the other three will act as advertising images for use with the AdRotator. We need to fire up our favorite WBMP editor—in this instance I used the Nokia SDK (version 2) WBMP editor, as described in Chapter 16, "Sample Mobile Website: My Computer Shop."

I find with the Nokia editor that adjusting the view scale to 1,000 times makes it a little easier to build images, as we are normally working a pixel at a time. It took me about 20 minutes to create the four images depicted in Figure 18.12. I could have saved this time by using some stock images from a WBMP library.

**TIP**     Appendix C "Internet Resources," has a list of sites where various SDKs can be obtained.

**FIGURE 18.12:**

Images for the
MyTipple application

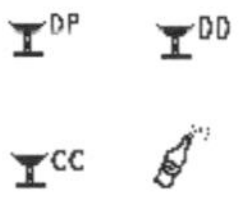

For the MyTipple site, I have used the bottle image as the generic site image (saved as logo.wbmp). The remaining images are used as the advertising logos, saved as dd.wbmp, dp.wbmp, and cc.wbmp, respectively.

## Writing the User Control

Open Visual studio .NET and create a new Mobile Web Application called MyTipple. Once the application is set up, minimize the Visual Studio IDE and move the image that you are planning to use as the generic site image to the root Web directory of the application (the default is c:\Inetpub\wwwroot\MyTipple\).

Expand Visual Studio and from the Projects menu choose Add Web User Control. In the Add New Item dialog box, name the control as logo.ascx and click Open.

Switch to HTML View, delete any existing code, and add the code from Listing 18.1.

**Listing 18.1**    **Code for the *logo.ascx* User Control**

```
<%@ Control Language="vb" AutoEventWireup="false"
➡ Codebehind="logo.ascx.vb" Inherits="MyTipple.logo" %>
<%@ Register TagPrefix="mobile"
➡ Namespace="System.Web.UI.MobileControls"
➡ Assembly="System.Web.Mobile" %>
<mobile:Image id="Image1" runat="server"
➡ ImageURL="http://localhost/MyTipple/logo.wbmp"
➡ AlternateText="A Wine Lover's Portal">
</mobile:Image>
<mobile:Label id="Label1" runat="server"
➡ Font-Italic="true" StyleReference="title">
   MyTipple!</mobile:Label>
```

You may find it a little quicker to copy and paste the code from the User control in Chapter 16 (ProductSpecifier) and make appropriate adjustments. This step should only cost us five minutes.

## Setting Up the AdRotator

We need to do a little background work before we can make use of the AdRotator control in the project. Initially, take the three images we created earlier for advertising purposes and place them in a folder named Ads in the root Web directory of the application (the default is c:\Inetpub\wwwroot\MyTipple\). An example of the image URLs can be seen in the fourth line of Listing 18.2.

Next, we need to create the XML document that the AdRotator control references. Listing 18.2 illustrates the code for this document.

---

**Listing 18.2**        *Ad1.xml* **for the AdRotator Control in MyTipple**

```xml
<?xml version="1.0"?>
<Advertisements>
    <Ad>
    <ImageUrl>http://localhost/MyTipple/ads/dd.wbmp</Image
➡Url>
        <MonoImageUrl>http://localhost/MyTipple/ads/dd.wbmp
➡</MonoImageUrl>
        <NavigateUrl></NavigateUrl>
        <AlternateText>D and D Fine Wines</AlternateText>
        <KeywordFilter>reds</KeywordFilter>
        <Impressions>80</Impressions>
    </Ad>
<Ad>
        <ImageUrl>http://localhost/MyTipple/ads/dp.wbmp
➡</ImageUrl>
        <MonoImageUrl>http://localhost/MyTipple/ads/dp.wbmp
➡</MonoImageUrl>
        <NavigateUrl></NavigateUrl>
        <AlternateText>Discount Plonk</AlternateText>
        <KeywordFilter>whites</KeywordFilter>
        <Impressions>80</Impressions>
    </Ad>
<Ad>
        <ImageUrl>http://localhost/MyTipple/ads/cc.wbmp
➡</ImageUrl>
        <MonoImageUrl>http://localhost/MyTipple/ads/cc.wbmp
➡</MonoImageUrl>
        <NavigateUrl></NavigateUrl>
        <AlternateText>C and C Very Fine
➡ Wines</AlternateText>
        <KeywordFilter>whites</KeywordFilter>
        <Impressions>80</Impressions>
    </Ad>
</Advertisements>
```

---

The simplest way to create this document is to select Add New Item from the Project menu. Select XML File from the Templates pane in the Add New Item dialog box, name the document Ads.xml, and click the Open button. See Figure 18.13.

Visual Studio .NET should now open to the code window for Ads.xml, and we can add the code from Listing 18.2. Note that it may be quicker to copy and paste the code used for this purpose back in Chapter 7, "The Runtime Controls," for the Mobile6 project (Listing 7.1) and make appropriate adjustments.

**FIGURE 18.13:**

Creating an XML file
using the Add New
Item dialog in the
MyTipple application

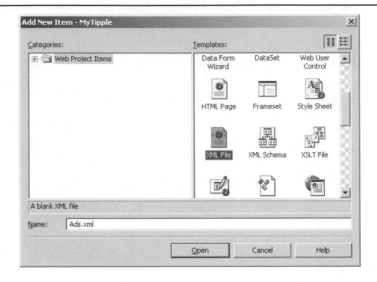

When copying and pasting code from a word processor such as Microsoft Word into Visual Studio, a large amount of unwanted formatting text seems to travel with it. Use the Paste As HTML option in the Edit menu to avoid this problem.

The only note to make about this code is that the contents of the AlternateText tags must match the name of the sponsor as entered in the database exactly, as we will be using this for search criteria in one of our SQL SELECT statements in the MyTipple application. We have also included the `link_category` values from the database as our `KeyWordFilter` values. This gives us the opportunity if we wish to display relevant sponsors if, for example, we ran a special week promoting only red wines.

`Ads.xml` should now be available in the Solution Explorer. It took me a little over an hour to bring the project to this stage.

## Setting Up the Mobile Web Page

Click back to `MobileWebForm1.aspx` in Design View. Set the page up with eight Form controls. We are also going to need seven `OleDbDataAdapters` hooked to the MyTipple database. Use the same process to create a connection that we have followed previously (Chapter 9).

Table 18.2 lists the SQL statements that we wish to create for each DataAdapter. In each case, deselect the Advanced Options in the Generate SQL Statements section of the Data Adapter Configuration Wizard.

**TABLE 18.2:** SQL Statements Generated for DataAdapters in the MyTipple Application

| OleDbDataAdapter | SQL statement |
|---|---|
| OleDbDataAdapter1 | SELECT news_current, news_date, news_id, news_item, news_text FROM Table1 WHERE (news_current = 'Yes') |
| OleDbDataAdapter2 | SELECT sponsor_name, sponsor_address, sponsor_tel, sponsor_id FROM Table2 |
| OleDbDataAdapter3 | SELECT DISTINCT link_category FROM Table3 |
| OleDbDataAdapter4 | SELECT calendar_date, calendar_details, calendar_event, calendar_id FROM Table4 WHERE (calendar_current = 'Yes') |
| OleDbDataAdapter5 | SELECT news_current, news_date, news_id, news_item, news_text FROM Table1 WHERE (news_id = ?) |
| OleDbDataAdapter6 | SELECT link_id, link_name, link_URL, link_category FROM Table3 WHERE (link_category = ?) |
| OleDbDataAdapter7 | SELECT sponsor_name, sponsor_tel, sponsor_id, sponsor_address FROM Table2 WHERE (sponsor_name = ?) |

For each DataAdapter (except for OleDbDataAdapter6), generate a table in DataSet1 by following the defaults. This should create the following:

- OleDbDataAdapter1 (Table1)

- OleDbDataAdapter2 (Table2)

- OleDbDataAdapter3 (Table3)

- OleDbDataAdapter4 (Table4)

- OleDbDataAdapter5 (Table1)

- OleDbDataAdapter7 (Table2)

In the case of OleDbDataAdapter6, create a new DataSet—DataSet2 (Table3).

Switch back to Design View and set up the Mobile Web Page with the controls, properties, and settings listed in Table 18.3. If you need a refresher on data-binding mobile controls such as Labels, refer to Chapter 10. Note also that in Table 18.3 we will need to set the DataSource property on individual controls before setting the DataMember property. To add the User control (logo.ascx), drag a copy from the Solution Explorer to each of the Form controls.

**TABLE 18.3:** Controls and Properties for MobileWebForm1

| Form | Control | Property | Value |
|---|---|---|---|
| Form1 | | Paginate | True |
| | User (logo.ascx) | ID | Logo1 |
| | Label | Font | |

*Continued on next page*

**TABLE 18.3 CONTINUED:** Controls and Properties for MobileWebForm1

| Form | Control | Property | Value |
|------|---------|----------|-------|
| | | Size | Small |
| | | Text | A Portal for Wine Lovers |
| | | ID | LblFm1 |
| | Command | Text | Club Calendar |
| | | ID | cmdCalendar |
| | Command | Text | Wine Related Links |
| | | ID | cmdWineLinks |
| | Link | Text | Our Sponsors |
| | | SoftKeyLabel | Sponsors |
| | | ID | lnkFm1Fm7 |
| | | NavigateURL | #Form7 |
| | Link | Text | Search the Mobile Web |
| | | SoftKeyLabel | Search |
| | | ID | lnkWebsrch |
| | | NavigateURL | http://www.earthoid.com |
| | Form1 | | Type **Latest Club News -** directly on the form between lnkWebrch and lstFm1[*] |
| | List | Decoration | Numbered |
| | | DataMember | Table1 |
| | | DataSource | DataSet11 |
| | | DataTextField | news_item |
| | | DataValueField | news_id |
| | | ID | lstFm1 |
| Form2 | User (logo.ascx) | ID | Logo2 |
| | Command | Text | Home |
| | | ID | cmdHome |
| | Label | ID | lblFm2 |
| | | DataBindings | Bind Text to DataBinder .Eval(DataSet11, "Tables[Table1]. DefaultView.[0].news_ date", "{0:D}") using the lblFm2 DataBindings dialog box[*] |
| | Label | Font | |
| | | Bold | True |
| | | ID | lblFm21 |

*Continued on next page*

**TABLE 18.3 CONTINUED:** Controls and Properties for MobileWebForm1

| Form | Control | Property | Value |
|------|---------|----------|-------|
| | | DataBindings | Bind Text to DataBinder .Eval(DataSet11, "Tables[Table1]. DefaultView.[0]. news_item", "{0}")[*] |
| | TextView | ID | txtvFm2 |
| | | DataBindings | Bind Text to DataBinder.Eval (DataSet11, "Tables[Table1]. DefaultView.[0]. news_text", "{0}")[*] |
| Form3 | User (logo.ascx) | ID | Logo3 |
| | Label | Text | Proudly supported by |
| | | ID | lblFm3 |
| | AdRotator | AdvertisementFile | Ads.xml |
| | | ID | adrFm3 |
| | Label | Text | <empty> |
| | | ID | lblFm31 |
| | Label | ID | lblFm32 |
| | | DataBindings | Bind Text to DataBinder .Eval(DataSet11, "Tables[Table2]. DefaultView.[0].sponsor_ address", "{0}")[*] |
| | PhoneCall | Text | Please Call Us: |
| | | ID | cllFm3 |
| | | PhoneNumber | 0 |
| | Link | Text | Next |
| | | SoftKeyLabel | Next |
| | | ID | lnkFm3dynamic |
| | | NavigateURL | <empty> |
| Form4 | User (logo.ascx) | ID | Logo4 |
| | Link | Text | Home |
| | | SoftKeyLabel | Home |
| | | ID | lnkFm4Fm1 |
| | | NavigateURL | #Form1 |
| | ObjectList | DataMember | Table4 |
| | | DataSource | DataSet11 |
| | | ID | oblFm4 |

*Continued on next page*

**TABLE 18.3 CONTINUED:** Controls and Properties for MobileWebForm1

| Form | Control | Property | Value |
| --- | --- | --- | --- |
| Form5 | User (logo.ascx) | ID | Logo5 |
| | Link | Text | Home |
| | | SoftKeyLabel | Home |
| | | ID | lnkFm5Fm1 |
| | | NavigateURL | #Form1 |
| | SelectionList | SelectType | Radio |
| | | DataMember | Table3 |
| | | DataSource | DataSet11 |
| | | DataTextField | link_category |
| | | ID | selFm5 |
| | Command | Text | Listing |
| | | ID | cmdListing |
| Form6 | User (logo.ascx) | ID | Logo6 |
| | | Paginate | True |
| | Link | Text | Home |
| | | SoftKeyLabel | Home |
| | | ID | lnkFm6Fm1 |
| | | NavigateURL | #Form1 |
| | Link | Text | Return to Categories |
| | | SoftKeyLabel | Categories |
| | | ID | lnkFm6Fm5 |
| | | NavigateURL | #Form5 |
| | TextView | Text | <empty> |
| | | ID | txtvFm6 |
| | List | ItemsAsLinks | True |
| | | DataMember | Table3 |
| | | DataSource | DataSet21 |
| | | DataTextField | link_name |
| | | DataValueField | link_URL |
| | | ID | lstFm6 |
| Form7 | User (logo.ascx) | ID | Logo7 |
| | Link | Text | Home |
| | | SoftKeyLabel | Home |
| | | ID | lnkFm7Fm1 |

*Continued on next page*

**TABLE 18.3 CONTINUED:** Controls and Properties for MobileWebForm1

| Form | Control | Property | Value |
|------|---------|----------|-------|
| | | NavigateURL | #Form1 |
| | ObjectList | DataMember | Table2 |
| | | DataSource | DataSet11 |
| | | ID | oblFm7 |
| Form8 | User (logo.ascx) | ID | Logo8 |
| | Label | Text | <empty> |
| | | ID | lblFm8 |
| | Link | Text | Return |
| | | SoftKeyLabel | Return |
| | | ID | lnkFm8 |
| | | NavigateURL | <empty> |

*The information here is an instruction, not a value.

Figures 18.14, 18.15, 18.16, and 18.17 illustrate the completed forms.

**FIGURE 18.14:**

Forms 1 and 2 in the
MyTipple application

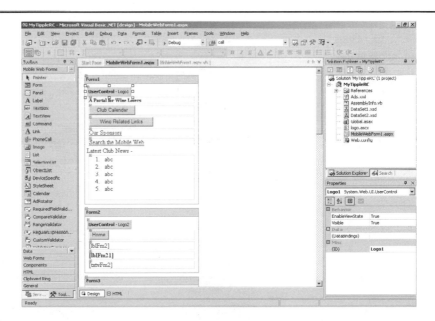

**FIGURE 18.15:**

Forms 3 and 4 in the MyTipple application

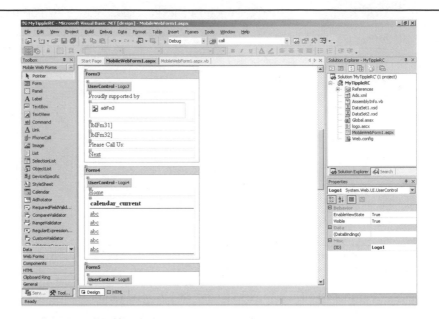

**FIGURE 18.16:**

Forms 5 and 6 in the MyTipple application

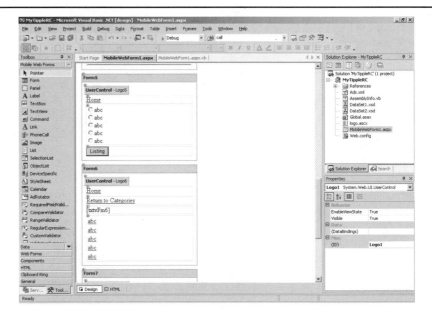

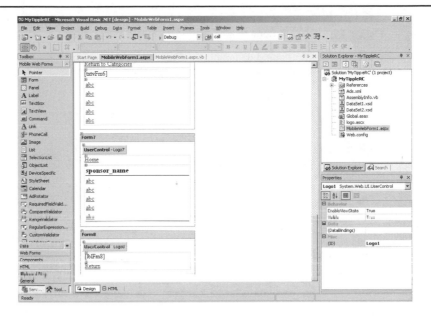

There are a few things to consider when setting up these forms. The first is the placement of Links and Command controls on the forms containing lists. If we place the Link and Command controls after the List controls, they are not always rendered "cleanly" by some mobile browsers, such as the Openwave browser. Openwave doesn't display the link until after the user has selected a list item, when it is then displayed as an option. This can prove a little confusing and make for an inconsistent interface with other aspects of the site. To avoid or minimize these problems, we have placed key navigation links at the top of each form (except in the case of the advertisement and the error message where we want to ensure that our user reads through the content before they click away!).

We have attached the lnkWebsrch link in Form1 to www.earthoid.com, which is a popular search engine for mobile sites.

Setting up the DataSets and Mobile Web Page took me about forty-five minutes.

## Writing the Code Behind

Switch to code behind and add the code from Listing 18.3.

**Listing 18.3**      **Code Behind for the MyTipple Application**

```
Private Sub Page_Load(ByVal sender As System.Object,
➥ ByVal e As System.EventArgs) Handles MyBase.Load
      Try
            If Not Page.IsPostBack Then
                  OleDbDataAdapter1.Fill(DataSet11,
➥ "Table1")
                  OleDbDataAdapter2.Fill(DataSet11,
➥ "Table2")
                  OleDbDataAdapter3.Fill(DataSet11,
➥ "Table3")
                  OleDbDataAdapter4.Fill(DataSet11,
➥ "Table4")
                  lstFm1.DataBind()

                  DataSet11.Tables("Table2").Columns(0).ColumnName =
➥ "Sponsor Organisation"
                  DataSet11.Tables("Table2").Columns(1).ColumnName =
➥ "Address"
                  DataSet11.Tables("Table2").Columns(2).ColumnName =
➥ "Telephone"
                  DataSet11.Tables("Table2").Columns(3).ColumnName =
➥ "Sponsor ID"
                  oblFm7.LabelField = "Sponsor
➥ Organisation"
                  oblFm7.TableFields = "Sponsor
➥ Organisation;Address;Telephone"
                  oblFm7.DataBind()

                  selFm5.DataBind()

                  DataSet11.Tables("Table4").Columns(0).ColumnName =
➥ "Date"
                  DataSet11.Tables("Table4").Columns(1).ColumnName =
➥ "Event"
                  DataSet11.Tables("Table4").Columns(2).ColumnName =
➥ "Details"
                  DataSet11.Tables("Table4").Columns(3).ColumnName =
➥ "Event ID"
                  oblFm4.LabelField = "Event"
                  oblFm4.TableFields = "Event;Date;Details"
                  oblFm4.DataBind()
            End If
      Catch
            ActiveForm = Form8
            lnkFm8.NavigateURL = "#Form1"
            lblFm8.Text = "Our server may be temporarily
➥ unavailable. Please try again."
      End Try
   End Sub
```

```vbnet
    Private Sub cmdCalendar_Click(ByVal sender As
➥ System.Object, ByVal e As System.EventArgs) Handles
➥ cmdCalendar.Click
        ActiveForm = Form3
        lnkFm3dynamic.NavigateURL = "#Form4"
    End Sub


    Private Sub cmdWinelinks_Click(ByVal sender As
➥ System.Object, ByVal e As System.EventArgs) Handles
➥ cmdWinelinks.Click
        ActiveForm = Form3
        lnkFm3dynamic.NavigateURL = "#Form5"
    End Sub


    Private Sub cmdHome_Click(ByVal sender As
➥ System.Object, ByVal e As System.EventArgs) Handles
➥ cmdHome.Click
        ActiveForm = Form1
    End Sub


    Protected Sub lstFm1_ItemCommand(ByVal source As
➥ System.Object, ByVal e As
➥ System.Web.UI.MobileControls.ListCommandEventArgs)
➥ Handles lstFm1.ItemCommand
        Session("newsid") = e.ListItem.Value
        ActiveForm = Form2
    End Sub


    Protected Sub Form2_Activate(ByVal sender As
➥ System.Object, ByVal e As System.EventArgs) Handles
➥ Form2.Activate
        Try
    OleDbDataAdapter5.SelectCommand.Parameters("news_id")
➥.Value = Session("newsid")
            OleDbDataAdapter5.Fill(DataSet11, "Table1")
            lblFm2.DataBind()
            lblFm21.DataBind()
            txtvFm2.DataBind()
        Catch
            ActiveForm = Form8
            lnkFm8.NavigateURL = "#Form1"
            lblFm8.Text = "Our server may be temporarily
➥ unavailable. Please try again."
        End Try

    End Sub

Private Sub adrFm3_AdCreated(ByVal sender As
➥ System.Object, ByVal e As
➥ System.Web.UI.WebControls.AdCreatedEventArgs) Handles
➥ adrFm3.AdCreated
```

```
        lblFm31.Text = e.AlternateText
        OleDbDataAdapter7.SelectCommand.Parameters
➥("sponsor_name").Value() = e.AlternateText
        OleDbDataAdapter7.Fill(DataSet11, "Table2")
        lblFm32.DataBind()
        cllFm3.PhoneNumber =
➥ DataSet11.Tables("Table2").Rows(0).Item(1)

    End Sub

    Private Sub selFm5_SelectedIndexChanged(ByVal sender
➥ As System.Object, ByVal e As System.EventArgs)
➥ Handles selFm5.SelectedIndexChanged
        Session("Category") = selFm5.Selection.Text

    End Sub

    Private Sub Form6_Activate(ByVal sender As
➥ System.Object, ByVal e As System.EventArgs) Handles
➥ Form6.Activate
        If Session("Category") = "" Then
➥ Session("Category") = "Fortifieds"
        txtvFm6.Text = "Our recommended suppliers for
➥ category - " & Session("Category") & " are:"
        Try
            OleDbDataAdapter6.SelectCommand.Parameters
➥("link_category").Value = Session("Category")
            OleDbDataAdapter6.Fill(DataSet21, "Table3")
            lstFm6.DataBind()
        Catch
            ActiveForm = Form8
            lnkFm8.NavigateURL = "#Form5"
            lblFm8.Text = "Our server may be temporarily
➥ unavailable. Please try again."
        End Try
    End Sub

    Private Sub cmdListing_Click(ByVal sender As
➥ System.Object, ByVal e As System.EventArgs) Handles
➥ cmdListing.Click
        ActiveForm = Form6
    End Sub

End Class
```

Working through the code from the top, we begin with the Page_Load event:

```
Private Sub Page_Load(ByVal sender As System.Object,
➥ ByVal e As System.EventArgs) Handles MyBase.Load
    Try
        If Not Page.IsPostBack Then
```

```
                OleDbDataAdapter1.Fill(DataSet11,
➥ "Table1")
                OleDbDataAdapter2.Fill(DataSet11,
➥ "Table2")
                OleDbDataAdapter3.Fill(DataSet11,
➥ "Table3")
                OleDbDataAdapter4.Fill(DataSet11,
➥ "Table4")
                lstFm1.DataBind()

                DataSet11.Tables("Table2").Columns(0).ColumnName =
➥ "Sponsor Organisation"
                DataSet11.Tables("Table2").Columns(1).ColumnName =
➥ "Address"
                DataSet11.Tables("Table2").Columns(2).ColumnName =
➥ "Telephone"
                DataSet11.Tables("Table2").Columns(3).ColumnName =
➥ "Sponsor ID"
                oblFm7.LabelField = "Sponsor
➥ Organisation"
                oblFm7.TableFields = "Sponsor
➥ Organisation;Address;Telephone"
                oblFm7.DataBind()

                selFm5.DataBind()

                DataSet11.Tables("Table4").Columns(0).ColumnName =
➥ "Date"
                DataSet11.Tables("Table4").Columns(1).ColumnName =
➥ "Event"
                DataSet11.Tables("Table4").Columns(2).ColumnName =
➥ "Details"
                DataSet11.Tables("Table4").Columns(3).ColumnName =
➥ "Event ID"
                oblFm4.LabelField = "Event"
                oblFm4.TableFields = "Event;Date;Details"
                oblFm4.DataBind()
            End If
        Catch
            ActiveForm = Form8
            lnkFm8.NavigateURL = "#Form1"
            lblFm8.Text = "Our server may be temporarily
➥ unavailable. Please try again."
        End Try
    End Sub
```

In this subroutine, we load up our DataSet with information through the DataAdapters 1 to 4. We bind the relevant controls and encase it all in a Not Page.IsPostBack to minimize the amount of work happening back at our server. If there are any difficulties with accessing the database, the error form (Form8) will be displayed with an appropriate message. Essentially, in this code we are setting up the lists for our sponsors, our calendar, the category list for wine related links, and the club calendar.

With the category list, we are after a display of the different categories that we have used in our database. We also want this to be flexible, in that it will respond to additional categories added to the database or categories being deleted. We achieve this buy using the SQL SELECT statement for OleDbDataAdapter3, which returns a single copy of each link_category data value that it can find in the database (using the DISTINCT keyword).

Because we have used ObjectList controls later in the application to display our calendar and sponsor information, we need to do a little bit of extra work here to persuade these controls to render data in a socially acceptable manner.

The control works by displaying a set of links, which when selected display the entire contents of the DataSet associated with the particular link selected. It has the unfortunate habit of using the database field headings as the data titles in the expanded data view and tends to place them into some form of order which is not what we as developers would have chosen (and then stubbornly refuse to change)!

The following code used in the Page_Load subroutine demonstrates how we can programmatically change the DataSet column headings, which in turn solves the problem of the data titles in the expanded data view of the ObjectList control:

```
        OleDbDataAdapter4.Fill(DataSet11, "Table4")
        DataSet11.Tables("Table4").Columns(0).ColumnName =
➥ "Date"
        DataSet11.Tables("Table4").Columns(1).ColumnName =
➥ "Event"
        DataSet11.Tables("Table4").Columns(2).ColumnName =
➥ "Details"
        DataSet11.Tables("Table4").Columns(3).ColumnName =
➥ "Event ID"
        oblFm4.LabelField = "Event"
        oblFm4.TableFields = "Event;Date;Details"
        oblFm4.DataBind()
```

The four highlighted lines are where we can set the DataSet column names. In this code, we have also programmatically set the TableFields property of the oblFm4 ObjectList, which determines how the data is initially displayed by the List control in browsers that can support a wider and more tabular view (such as a Web browser like Internet Explorer).

To solve the order of data displayed in the expanded data view, we need to edit the
DataSet1.xsd page. Select DataSet1.xsd from the Solution Explorer and switch to XML
View in the Designer window. Listing 18.4 illustrates the code that should then be visible.

**Listing 18.4**       *DataSet1.xsd* **in XML View**

```
<xsd:schema id="DataSet1"
➥ targetNamespace="http://www.tempuri.org/DataSet1.xsd"
➥ xmlns="http://www.tempuri.org/DataSet1.xsd"
➥ xmlns:xsd="http://www.w3.org/2001/XMLSchema"
➥ xmlns:msdata="urn:schemas-microsoft-com:xml-msdata"
➥ attributeFormDefault="qualified"
➥ elementFormDefault="qualified">
  <xsd:element name="DataSet1" msdata:IsDataSet="true">
    <xsd:complexType>
      <xsd:choice maxOccurs="unbounded">
        <xsd:element name="Table3">
          <xsd:complexType>
            <xsd:sequence>
              <xsd:element
➥ name="link_category" type="xsd:string" minOccurs="0"
➥ />
            </xsd:sequence>
          </xsd:complexType>
        </xsd:element>
        <xsd:element name="Table4">
          <xsd:complexType>
            <xsd:sequence>
              <xsd:element
➥ name="calendar_date" type="xsd:string" minOccurs="0"
➥ />
              <xsd:element
➥ name="calendar_details" type="xsd:string"
➥ minOccurs="0" />
              <xsd:element
➥ name="calendar_event" type="xsd:string" minOccurs="0"
➥ />
              <xsd:element
➥ name="calendar_id" msdata:AutoIncrement="true"
➥ type="xsd:int" />
            </xsd:sequence>
          </xsd:complexType>
        </xsd:element>
        <xsd:element name="Table1">
          <xsd:complexType>
            <xsd:sequence>
              <xsd:element
➥ name="news_date" type="xsd:dateTime" minOccurs="0" />
```

```
                    <xsd:element
➥ name="news_id" msdata:AutoIncrement="true"
➥ type="xsd:int" />
                        <xsd:element
➥ name="news_item" type="xsd:string" minOccurs="0" />
                        <xsd:element
➥ name="news_text" type="xsd:string" minOccurs="0" />
                    </xsd:sequence>
                </xsd:complexType>
            </xsd:element>
            <xsd:element name="Table2">
                <xsd:complexType>
                    <xsd:sequence>
                        <xsd:element
➥ name="sponsor_name" type="xsd:string" minOccurs="0"
➥ />
                        <xsd:element
➥ name="sponsor_tel" type="xsd:string" minOccurs="0" />
                        <xsd:element
➥ name="sponsor_id" msdata:AutoIncrement="true"
➥ type="xsd:int" />
                        <xsd:element
➥ name="sponsor_address" type="xsd:string"
➥ minOccurs="0" />
                    </xsd:sequence>
                </xsd:complexType>
            </xsd:element>
        </xsd:choice>
    </xsd:complexType>
    <xsd:unique name="Constraint1"
➥ msdata:PrimaryKey="true">
        <xsd:selector xpath=".//Table4" />
        <xsd:field xpath="calendar_id" />
    </xsd:unique>
    <xsd:unique name="Table1_Constraint1"
➥ msdata:ConstraintName="Constraint1"
➥ msdata:PrimaryKey="true">
        <xsd:selector xpath=".//Table1" />
        <xsd:field xpath="news_id" />
    </xsd:unique>
    <xsd:unique name="Table2_Constraint1"
➥ msdata:ConstraintName="Constraint1"
➥ msdata:PrimaryKey="true">
        <xsd:selector xpath=".//Table2" />
        <xsd:field xpath="sponsor_id" />
    </xsd:unique>
    </xsd:element>
</xsd:schema>
```

Of particular interest are the four `<xsd: element name="the_calendar_field_names">` tags located toward the beginning of the code. Simply rearranging the order of these four tags solves our little presentation problem for the Calendar details. We can also do the same for the Sponsor headings.

Next we have the `click` events for the cmdCalendar and cmdWinelinks Command controls. Selecting either of these controls activates the advertisement form (Form3) and sets its resident Next link to the appropriate destination from whichever Command control was selected. Here are the events:

```
Private Sub cmdCalendar_Click(ByVal sender As
➡ System.Object, ByVal e As System.EventArgs) Handles
➡ cmdCalendar.Click
      ActiveForm = Form3
      lnkFm3dynamic.NavigateURL = "#Form4"
   End Sub


   Private Sub cmdWinelinks_Click(ByVal sender As
➡ System.Object, ByVal e As System.EventArgs) Handles
➡ cmdWinelinks.Click
      ActiveForm = Form3
      lnkFm3dynamic.NavigateURL = "#Form5"
   End Sub
```

We then have a bit of code that gives the cmdHome Command control on Form2 its navigation ability:

```
Private Sub cmdHome_Click(ByVal sender As
➡ System.Object, ByVal e As System.EventArgs) Handles
➡ cmdHome.Click
      ActiveForm = Form1
   End Sub
```

The lstFm1_ItemCommand subroutine assigns the value of the selected list item (news_id) to the session variable newsid and opens Form2 (the news-details form). Here's the subroutine:

```
Protected Sub lstFm1_ItemCommand(ByVal source As
➡ System.Object, ByVal e As
➡ System.Web.UI.MobileControls.ListCommandEventArgs)
➡ Handles lstFm1.ItemCommand
      Session("newsid") = e.ListItem.Value
      ActiveForm = Form2
   End Sub
```

When a user selects a news link from Form1, they are redirected to Form2 where the details of the news item are displayed. This is taken care of in the code for Form2_Activate, as shown in the following code from this subroutine:

```
OleDbDataAdapter5.SelectCommand.Parameters("news_id")
➡.Value = Session("newsid")
```

```
OleDbDataAdapter5.Fill(DataSet11, "Table1")
lblFm2.DataBind()
lblFm21.DataBind()
txtvFm2.DataBind()
```

The first line of this code assigns the value of the session variable (newsid) to the search parameter in the SQL SELECT statement for OleDbDataAdapter5. This should load the appropriate news-item details into DataSet11 and make that information available to the relevant databound controls (lblFm2, lblFm21, and txtvFm2).

Whenever a user clicks through the Wine Related Links or Club Calendar Command controls, they are directed via Form3, which contains the AdRotator control. The idea of the advertisement form is not only to use the AdRotator control to display a different image but also to be able to access and display the stored details belonging to the organization associated with the particular advertisement being displayed. This is handled by the following code:

```
Private Sub adrFm3_AdCreated(ByVal sender As
➥ System.Object, ByVal e As
➥ System.Web.UI.WebControls.AdCreatedEventArgs) Handles
➥ adrFm3.AdCreated
        lblFm31.Text = e.AlternateText
        OleDbDataAdapter7.SelectCommand.Parameters
➥("sponsor_name").Value() = e.AlternateText
        OleDbDataAdapter7.Fill(DataSet11, "Table2")
        lblFm32.DataBind()
        cllFm3.PhoneNumber =
➥ DataSet11.Tables("Table2").Rows(0).Item(1)
    End Sub
```

This code is executed whenever the AdRotator generates a new advertisement. Given that we have already set the AlternateText property of each advertisement to the actual name of the relevant organization, we can load this directly into lblFm31 and then use it as the search parameter in the SQL SELECT statement for OleDbDataAdapter7. This enables us to retrieve other relevant information about the organization whose advertisement has been chosen by the AdRotator and to display that information in the suitably databound controls. In particular, we can use this technique to set up a PhoneCall control (cllFm3) with autodial facility for the organization's phone number. Note that we identify the DataSet column by its index number rather than its heading. The index number may vary depending on how you have configured your DataSets.

Opening Form5 displays the SelectionList control with the available categories of Links for the user to choose from. Selecting a category from the SelectionList sets the value of the Session variable (Category) to the selected category, as handled in the following event:

```
Private Sub selFm5_SelectedIndexChanged(ByVal sender
➥ As System.Object, ByVal e As System.EventArgs)
```

```
➥ Handles selFm5.SelectedIndexChanged
        Session("Category") = selFm5.Selection.Text

    End Sub
```

Selecting the cmdListing link activates Form6, as managed by the following code:

```
Private Sub cmdListing_Click(ByVal sender As
➥ System.Object, ByVal e As System.EventArgs) Handles
➥ cmdListing.Click
        ActiveForm = Form6
    End Sub
```

Activating Form6, in turn, populates the List control in Form6 with links belonging to the chosen category. This is handled by the following code:

```
Private Sub Form6_Activate(ByVal sender As
➥ System.Object, ByVal e As System.EventArgs) Handles
➥ Form6.Activate
        If Session("Category") = "" Then
➥ Session("Category") = "Fortifieds"
        txtvFm6.Text = "Our recommended suppliers for
➥ category - " & Session("Category") & " are:"
        Try
            OleDbDataAdapter6.SelectCommand.Parameters
➥("link_category").Value = Session("Category")
            OleDbDataAdapter6.Fill(DataSet21, "Table3")
            lstFm6.DataBind()
```

We set the default parameter to Fortifieds to cope with the way that many mobile browsers handle the first entry in a list—as a heading rather than an entry.

Finally, when a user chooses the OurSponsors link in Form1, they are directed to Form7, which again makes use of an ObjectList. As with the previous example of this control, we programmatically alter the column headings in DataSet11 and alter the column order in the DataSet1.xsd. The code for populating the ObjectList is handled by the Page_Load subroutine.

## Finishing Touches

As we have done with previous applications, we need to make a couple of final adjustments before deploying the application.

We need to edit our Web.config file to ensure that everything will work as it should across the various mobile device/browser/gateway combinations.

Open up Web.config from the Solution Explorer window and ensure that the <httpRuntime useFullyQualifiedRedirectUrl="true" /> tag is set in the <system.web> section, as explained in Chapter 8, "A Deeper Look at the Mobile Internet Toolkit and VB .NET."

Scroll down to the `<sessionState>` tag and set `cookieless="true"`.

Once we have tested and debugged the application, to improve runtime performance, set `debug="false"` in the `<compilation>` tag. Save the changes.

## Running the Application

As long as our typing skills were up to snuff, we should have been able to set up the project, type in the code, and test and debug it well within our three-hour limit. Of course, I am making a big assumption here that we are very familiar with the Toolkit and have already built a number of similar applications in the past!

We can manage all the information that appears in the MyTipple site directly from the database, using those data-management forms that we developed earlier. We can add and remove news items, add and remove wine-related links and alter the categories that we use, alter the details on the sponsors, and alter the calendar of events. The only aspect of site management still requiring some level of programming skill would be altering the XML file for the AdRotator.

When the user first accesses the site, they are presented with the opening form displaying key links and news-item headings, as illustrated in Figure 18.18.

The opening form for the MyTipple application

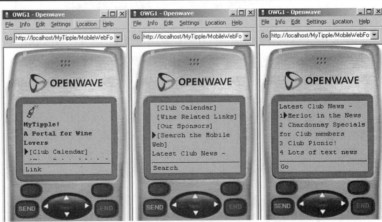

Image of UP.SDK courtesy Openwave Systems, Inc.

Selecting a news-item link takes the user to the details associated with that news item, as illustrated in Figure 18.19.

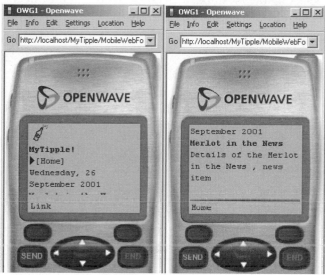

Image of UP.SDK courtesy Openwave Systems, Inc.

Note that the news item that we marked as *not current* in the database is not shown in the site.

Selecting the Calendar link initially takes us to the advertisement form featuring the AdRotator control. Refer to Figure 18.20.

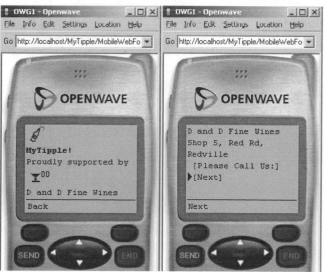

Image of UP.SDK courtesy Openwave Systems, Inc.

Selecting the Next link then takes the user to the calendar object list. Selecting an item in the calendar displays the details associated with that item. See Figure 18.21.

**FIGURE 18.21:**

The Calendar in the MyTipple application

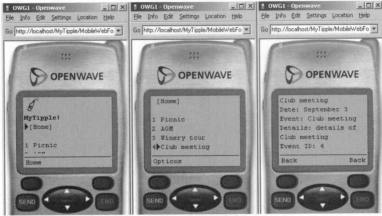

Image of UP.SDK courtesy Openwave Systems, Inc.

Returning to the Home card and selecting the Wine Related Links link again takes the user through the advertising form and to the selection list displaying the link categories. Refer to Figure 18.22.

**FIGURE 18.22:**

The Link Category selection list in the MyTipple application

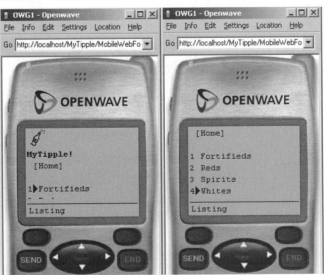

Image of UP.SDK courtesy Openwave Systems, Inc.

Choosing a category then displays the links belonging to that category. See Figure 18.23.

**FIGURE 18.23:**

The links displayed for
the Spirits category
in the MyTipple
application

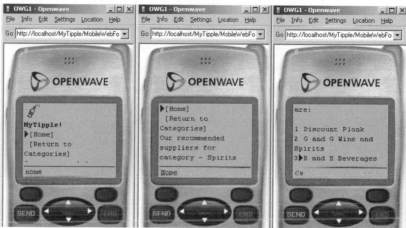

Image of UP.SDK courtesy Openwave Systems, Inc.

Again, returning to the Home card and selecting the Our Sponsors link displays the object list of sponsors. Selecting a sponsor displays the details associated with that sponsor. Refer to Figure 18.24.

**FIGURE 18.24:**

Accessing the
Sponsor section
of the MyTipple
application

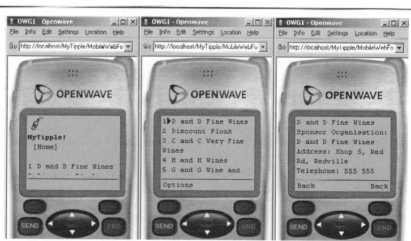

Image of UP.SDK courtesy Openwave Systems, Inc.

## Further Enhancements

In its current form, the MyTipple site is fairly rough. We could easily improve its performance by using DataReaders rather than DataSets and employing a SQL Server database.

Although we have adopted a form layout that works reasonably well for the Openwave-based browsers, the site could benefit from more attention being paid to how it renders on the Nokia-based browsers.

We also have the option of adding some device-specific elements such as color graphics for display on appropriate devices, and the exception handling in this version of the application is fairly rudimentary.

We also have a huge range of possibilities available to us for building the basic site concept. We have already mentioned having some form of user authentication and providing the opportunity for setting individual preferences. Exploiting this, we could then provide other services such as a messaging facility for club members, the capacity for online purchases, and some form of quiz or online competition.

## Full ASPX Listing

Listing 18.5 contains the full ASPX code listing for the MyTipple application.

**Listing 18.5**     **Full ASPX Code Listing for the MyTipple Application**

```
<%@ Register TagPrefix="mobile"
➥ Namespace="System.Web.UI.MobileControls"
➥ Assembly="System.Web.Mobile, Version=1.0.3300.0,
➥ Culture=neutral, PublicKeyToken=b03f5f7f11d50a3a" %>
<%@ Register TagPrefix="uc1" TagName="logo"
➥ Src="logo.ascx" %>
<%@ Page Language="vb" AutoEventWireup="false"
➥ Codebehind="MobileWebForm1.aspx.vb"
➥ Inherits="MyTipple.MobileWebForm1" %>
<meta content="Microsoft Visual Studio.NET 7.0"
➥ name="GENERATOR">
<meta content="Visual Basic 7.0" name="CODE_LANGUAGE">
<meta content="http://schemas.microsoft.com/Mobile/Page"
➥ name="vs_targetSchema">
<body Xmlns:mobile="http://schemas.microsoft.com/Mobile/
➥WebForm">
    <mobile:form id="Form1" runat="server">
<uc1:logo id="Logo1" runat="server"></uc1:logo>
<mobile:Label id="lblFm1" runat="server"
➥ Font-Size="Small" Font-Bold="True">A Portal for Wine
➥ Lovers</mobile:Label>
<mobile:Command id="cmdCalendar" runat="server">Club
➥ Calendar</mobile:Command>
<mobile:Command id="cmdWinelinks" runat="server">Wine
➥ Related Links</mobile:Command>
<mobile:Link id="lnkFm1Fm7" runat="server"
➥ NavigateURL="#Form7" SoftkeyLabel="Sponsors">Our
➥ Sponsors</mobile:Link>
```

```
<mobile:Link id="lnkWebsrch" runat="server"
➥ NavigateURL="http://www.earthoid.com"
➥ SoftkeyLabel="Search">Search the Mobile
➥ Web</mobile:Link>Latest
Club News -
<mobile:List id="lstFm1" runat="server" DataSource=
➥"<%# DataSet11 %>" DataMember="Table1"
➥ DataTextField="news_item" DataValueField="news_id"
➥ Decoration="Numbered"></mobile:List>
➥</mobile:form>
   <mobile:form id="Form2" runat="server"
➥ Paginate="True">
      <uc1:logo id="Logo2" runat="server"></uc1:logo>
      <mobile:Command id="cmdHome"
➥ runat="server">Home</mobile:Command>
      <mobile:Label id="lblFm2" runat="server"
➥ Text='<%# DataBinder.Eval(DataSet11,
➥ "Tables[Table1].DefaultView.[0].news_date", "{0:D}")
➥ %>'></mobile:Label>
      <mobile:Label id="lblFm21" runat="server"
➥ Font-Bold="True" Text='<%# DataBinder.Eval(DataSet11,
➥ "Tables[Table1].DefaultView.[0].news_item", "{0}")
➥ %>'></mobile:Label>
      <mobile:TextView id="txtvFm2" runat="server"
➥ Text='<%# DataBinder.Eval(DataSet11,
➥ "Tables[Table1].DefaultView.[0].news_text", "{0}")
➥ %>'></mobile:TextView>
   </mobile:form>
   <mobile:form id="Form3" runat="server">
<uc1:logo id="Logo3" runat="server"></uc1:logo>
      <mobile:Label id="lblFm3" runat="server">Proudly
➥ supported by</mobile:Label>
      <mobile:AdRotator id="adrFm3" runat="server"
➥ AdvertisementFile="Ads.xml"></mobile:AdRotator>
      <mobile:Label id="lblFm31"
➥ runat="server"></mobile:Label>
      <mobile:Label id="lblFm32" runat="server"
➥ Text='<%# DataBinder.Eval(DataSet11,
➥ "Tables[Table2].DefaultView.[0].sponsor_address",
➥ "{0}") %>'></mobile:Label>
<mobile:PhoneCall id="cllFm3" runat="server"
➥ PhoneNumber="0">Please Call Us:</mobile:PhoneCall>
      <mobile:Link id="lnkFm3dynamic" runat="server"
➥ SoftkeyLabel="Next">Next</mobile:Link>
   </mobile:form>
   <mobile:form id="Form4" runat="server">
<uc1:logo id="Logo4" runat="server"></uc1:logo>
      <mobile:Link id="lnkFm4Fm1" runat="server"
➥ NavigateURL="#Form1"
➥ SoftkeyLabel="Home">Home</mobile:Link>
```

```
        <mobile:ObjectList id="oblFm4" runat="server"
➡ DataSource="<%# DataSet11 %>"
➡ DataMember="Table4"></mobile:ObjectList>
    </mobile:form>
    <mobile:form id="Form5" runat="server">
<uc1:logo id="Logo5" runat="server"></uc1:logo>
        <mobile:Link id="lnkFm5Fm1" runat="server"
➡ NavigateURL="#Form1"
➡ SoftkeyLabel="Home">Home</mobile:Link>
        <mobile:SelectionList id="selFm5" runat="server"
➡ DataSource="<%# DataSet11 %>" DataMember="Table3"
➡ DataTextField="link_category"
➡ SelectType="Radio"></mobile:SelectionList>
        <mobile:Command id="cmdListing"
➡ runat="server">Listing</mobile:Command>
    </mobile:form>
    <mobile:form id="Form6" runat="server"
➡ Paginate="True">
<uc1:logo id="Logo6" runat="server"></uc1:logo>
        <mobile:Link id="lnkFm6Fm1" runat="server"
➡ NavigateURL="#Form1"
➡ SoftkeyLabel="Home">Home</mobile:Link>
        <mobile:Link id="lnkFm6Fm5" runat="server"
➡ NavigateURL="#Form5" SoftkeyLabel="Categories">Return
➡ to Categories</mobile:Link>
        <mobile:TextView id="txtvFm6"
➡ runat="server"></mobile:TextView>
        <mobile:List id="lstFm6" runat="server"
➡ DataSource="<%# DataSet21 %>" DataMember="Table3"
➡ DataTextField="link_name" DataValueField="link_URL"
➡ ItemsAsLinks="True"></mobile:List>
    </mobile:form>
    <mobile:form id="Form7" runat="server">
<uc1:logo id="Logo7" runat="server"></uc1:logo>
        <mobile:Link id="lnkFm7Fm1" runat="server"
➡ NavigateURL="#Form1"
➡ SoftkeyLabel="Home">Home</mobile:Link>
        <mobile:ObjectList id="oblFm7" runat="server"
➡ DataSource="<%# DataSet11 %>"
➡ DataMember="Table2"></mobile:ObjectList>
    </mobile:form>
    <mobile:Form id="Form8" runat="server">
<uc1:logo id="Logo8" runat="server"></uc1:logo>
        <mobile:Label id="lblFm8"
➡ runat="server"></mobile:Label>
        <mobile:Link id="lnkFm8" runat="server"
➡ SoftkeyLabel="Return">Return</mobile:Link>
    </mobile:Form>
</body>
```

## Summary

This project demonstrates how we can easily create a Mobile Website with the Mobile Internet Toolkit. We can use the Toolkit to quickly prototype prospective applications and then test them under various scenarios. The project also highlights one of the key approaches to mobile computing with the production of a fully database-driven site.

# CHAPTER 19

# Morris's Wholesale Fruit & Vege: A Mobile Intranet

- Rationale

- Planning the application

- Building the database

- Creating the Mobile Web Page

- Writing the code behind

- Finishing touches

- Expanding and enhancing the application

- Running the application

- Full ASPX code listing

**D**esigning and building a full-fledged Mobile intranet is another task that we could easily spend at least half this book on. So, to keep the application down to chapter size, we will need to make a number of concessions on which elements to include in this application and the extent to which we build them. In the section on expanding and enhancing the application, we will take a quick look at some of the further possibilities for this project.

## Rationale

Building Mobile intranets is one of the more exciting possibilities for mobile technologies. Essentially, the technology has the capacity to put a business's information flow directly into the palms of the hands of that business's representatives, wherever they may be.

The possibilities are endless, but we can begin with traditional activities such as accessing an organization's catalogs, interacting with its database, having some form of messaging system, and utilizing some form of a Personal Information Manager (PIM) system.

It is also worth pointing out that building these tools from scratch is not always the best course of action. Commercial solutions exist (such as Mobile Outlook) that are potentially the basis of a far better option than something that we might build ourselves. However, as with anything, it's a case of choosing the best option from a range of possibilities available at the time, and there will always be the situation where a simple homegrown solution may be the best course of action.

This project will also give us the opportunity to consider some of the security aspects associated with working with the Mobile Internet Toolkit and the chance to make use of one of the tools the we have so far only taken a brief look at—namely, the Calendar control.

In this example, we will build a Mobile intranet solution for a mythical greengrocer company (Morris's) that supplies wholesale quantities of produce to large organizations and smaller stores. Fruit and vegetables are products that can exhibit large price and availability swings depending on all sorts of factors such as weather and seasons. As the company's representatives are often on the road, traveling from one client to the next, they require a solution that keeps them up to date with the latest movement in prices and availability of stock. They also need to be able to leave messages for each other that they can easily access, and they need to have some sort of scheduling or calendar functionality to keep track of appointments and general movements.

Purists might argue that this type of application is not strictly an intranet, as it is delivered within the public domain of the Mobile Internet. However, the application is directed internally to company employees, gives access to company records, and is password-restricted to company personnel. Its intent, purpose, and function are that of an intranet. What it does is extend the scope of the organization's intranet beyond the boundaries of the desktop computer and out to wherever the company's representatives may be.

## Planning the Application

First, the application needs to be secure. We need to provide some form of authentication and identification process for users accessing the program.

.NET provides a range of security mechanisms for authentication, including forms-based authentication. Although security with the MIT is an area that I feel would benefit from further maturation (and it may be that this maturation will occur before the final release of the MIT—we certainly saw substantial improvements between the beta and RC releases), the option of forms-based authentication currently provides an easily managed and secure authentication mechanism. We will see how to implement forms-based authentication in Chapter 20, "*MyNewContacts*: MyContacts Revisited," but for this example we will see how to implement a slightly more downsized customized authentication process.

The solution that we will use for this particular application is a single ASPX page (and lots of forms). As a Mobile Web Page only allows access via the first form on the page, we can set this form as part of the authentication process and effectively keep unauthorized users out. For a more comprehensive level of security, we could keep everything together on the one page and apply forms-based authentication (using the cookieless option).

The best solution of all would be to break the application across multiple Mobile Web Pages (as the logical design of the application very much lends itself to this and it makes a lot of sense in terms of future expansion) and again apply forms-based authentication. I tested this form of authentication at the beta-2 stage with this application and found it a little flaky, but it should be available for you as a sensible option with the final release of the software.

In this example, we will go with the first option—a traditional login form, linked to a database of users and passwords, and a single Mobile Web Page containing all the forms making up the application. As we won't be applying any level of encryption to our password/username combination once they are sent over the Internet, we will have to assume that this will only provide our application with a moderate level of security.

The main aspects of our application will be:

- Login card
- Home card, including a list of daily specials
- Stock search/control/ordering section
- Messaging section
- Calendar section

Figure 19.1 illustrates the proposed layout for the intranet site. Although I have grouped the various aspects of the site more or less into the functional or logical areas, remember that we will place all of these cards or forms onto the one Mobile Web Page.

FIGURE 19.1:

Proposed card/form
layout for Morris's
Mobile intranet

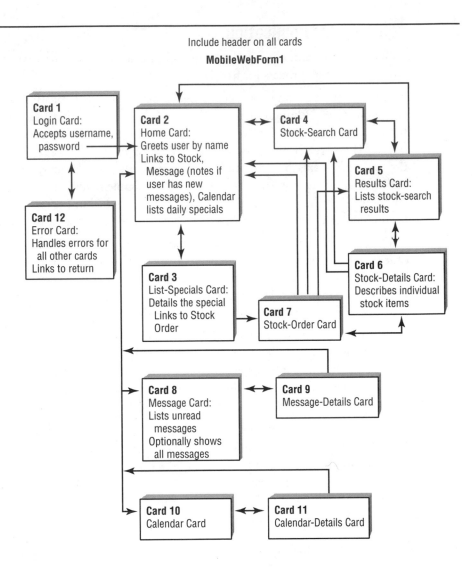

## Building the Database

We will again use Access as the backend database for this application. Create a new database
and name it morris.mdb. Open the database in Design View and create four tables: Table1,
Table2, Table3, and Table4. Set up the fields in each table as outlined in Table 19.1.

As we have covered setting up Access databases in considerable detail in previous chapters,
I will simply list the database definitions in this example.

**TABLE 19.1:** Table and Field Definitions for *morris.mdb*

| Table | Field Name | Data Type | Further Details |
|---|---|---|---|
| Table1 | user_id | AutoNumber | Primary key |
| | user_name | Text | |
| | user_pwd | Text | |
| | user_date_used | Date/Time | Format = Medium Date |
| | user_time_used | Date/Time | Format = Medium Time |
| | user_active | Text | Use the LookUp Wizard to create a Yes/No option |
| | | | Default Value = Yes |
| Table2 | stock_id | AutoNumber | Primary Key |
| | stock_item | Text | |
| | stock_cost_price | Currency | |
| | stock_sell_price | Currency | |
| | stock_quantity | Number | |
| | stock_supp_id | Number | |
| | stock_unit | Text | |
| | stock_special | Text | Use the LookUp Wizard to create a Yes/No option |
| | | | Default Value = No |
| | stock_special_price | Currency | Dafault Value = <empty> |
| | stock_reorder | Number | |
| Table3 | message_id | AutoNumber | Primary Key |
| | message_user_id | Number | Use the LookUp Wizard to create a list of available users from Table1 (Hide primary key and set it to show names) |
| | message_text | Memo | |
| | message_read | Text | Use the LookUp Wizard to create a Yes/No option |
| | | | Default Value = No |
| | message_date | Date/Time | Format = Short Date |
| | | | Default Value = date() |
| | message_time | Date/Time | Format = Medium Time |
| | | | Default Value = time() |
| Table4 | calendar_id | AutoNumber | Primary Key |
| | calendar_user_id | Number | Use the LookUp wizard to create a list of available users from Table1 (Hide primary key and set it to show names) |
| | calendar_item_date | Date/Time | Format = Short Date |
| | calendar_item_time | Text | |
| | calendar_item | Memo | |

The sample data entered into the four tables is illustrated in Figures 19.2, 19.3, 19.4, and 19.5.

FIGURE 19.2:

Data entered into Table1 of the morris .mdb database

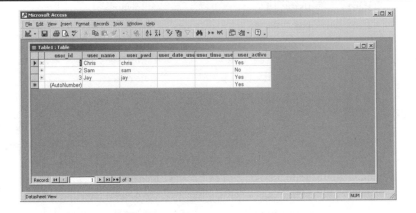

FIGURE 19.3:

Data entered into Table2 of the morris .mdb database

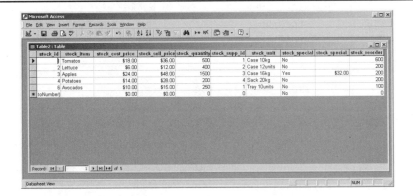

FIGURE 19.4:

Data entered into Table3 of the morris .mdb database

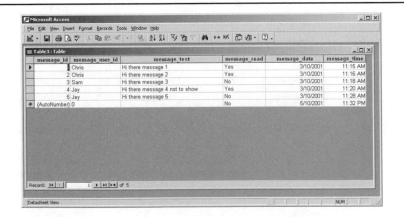

**FIGURE 19.5:**

Data entered into
Table4 of the morris
.mdb database

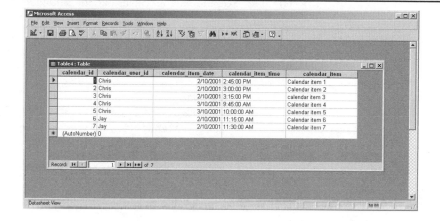

## Creating the Mobile Web Page

Create a new Mobile Web project in Visual Studio .NET and name it Morris. We will need
to set up the Mobile Web Page with twelve Form controls named Form1, Form2, Form3, ...
Form12. Set up eight OleDbdataAdapters connected to the Morris database with SQL statements as detailed in Table 19.2.

**TABLE 19.2:** SQL Statements Generated for *DataAdapters* in Mobile Intranet Application

| OleDbDataAdapter | SQL Statement |
| --- | --- |
| OleDbDataAdapter1 | SELECT user_active, user_date_used, user_id, user_name, user_time_used FROM Table1 WHERE (user_name = ?) AND (user_pwd = ?) |
| OleDbDataAdapter2 | SELECT stock_item, stock_cost_price, stock_quantity, stock_sell_price, stock_special, stock_special_ price, stock_unit, stock_id FROM Table2 WHERE (stock_special = 'Yes') |
| OleDbDataAdapter3 | SELECT stock_cost_price, stock_item, stock_quantity, stock_reorder, stock_sell_price, stock_special, stock_ special_price, stock_unit, stock_id FROM Table2 WHERE (stock_item LIKE ?) |
| OleDbDataAdapter4 | SELECT message_user_id, message_time, message_text, message_read, message_date, message_id FROM Table3 WHERE (message_user_id = ?) AND (message_read LIKE ?) |
| OleDbDataAdapter5 | SELECT message_date, message_id, message_read, message_ text, message_time, message_user_id FROM Table3 WHERE (message_id = ?) |

*Continued on next page*

**TABLE 19.2 CONTINUED:** SQL Statements Generated for *DataAdapters* in Mobile Intranet Application

| OleDbDataAdapter | SQL Statement |
| --- | --- |
| OleDbDataAdapter6 | SELECT user_id, user_name FROM Table1 |
| OleDbDataAdapter7 | SELECT calendar_item, calendar_id, calendar_item_date, calendar_item_time, calendar_user_id FROM Table4 WHERE (calendar_item_date = ?) AND (calendar_user_id = ?) |
| OleDbDataAdapter8 | SELECT calendar_id, calendar_item, calendar_item_date, calendar_item_time, calendar_user_id FROM Table4 WHERE (calendar_id = ?) |

For each DataAdapter, generate a table in DataSet1 by following the defaults. This should create the following:

- OleDbDataAdapter1 (Table1)
- OleDbDataAdapter2 (Table2)
- OleDbDataAdapter3 (Table2)
- OleDbDataAdapter4 (Table3)
- OleDbDataAdapter5 (Table3)
- OleDbDataAdapter7 (Table4)
- OleDbDataAdapter8 (Table4)

Set up the forms with the setoff controls and properties described in Table 19.3.

**TABLE 19.3:** Controls and Properties for MobileWebForm1 in the Morris's Mobile Intranet Application

| Form | Control | Property | Value |
| --- | --- | --- | --- |
| Form1 | Label | Font | |
| | | Size | Small |
| | | Bold | True |
| | | Text | Morris's Wholesale Fruit & Vege |
| | | ID | lblFm1Head |
| | Label | Text | Login Page |
| | | ID | lblFm1 |
| | Label | Text | Enter User Name: |
| | | ID | lblFm11 |
| | TextBox | Text | <empty> |

*Continued on next page*

**TABLE 19.3 CONTINUED:** Controls and Properties for MobileWebForm1 in the Morris's Mobile
Intranet Application

| Form | Control | Property | Value |
|------|---------|----------|-------|
| | | ID | txtUserName |
| | Label | Text | Enter Password: |
| | | ID | lblFm12 |
| | TextBox | Text | <empty> |
| | | MaxLength | 10 |
| | | Password | True |
| | | Size | 10 |
| | | ID | txtPassword |
| | Command | Text | Login |
| | | SoftKeyLabel | Login |
| | | ID | cmdLogin |
| Form2 | Label | Font | |
| | |   Size | Small |
| | |   Bold | True |
| | | Text | Morris's Wholesale Fruit & Vege |
| | | ID | lblFm2Head |
| | Label | Text | <empty> |
| | | ID | lblFm2 |
| | Label | Text | <empty> |
| | | Visible | False |
| | | ID | lblFm21 |
| | Link | Text | Stock |
| | | SoftKeyLabel | Stock |
| | | ID | lnkFm2Fm4 |
| | | NavigateURL | #Form4 |
| | Link | Text | Messages |
| | | SoftKeyLabel | Messages |
| | | ID | lnkFm2Fm8 |
| | | NavigateURL | #Form8 |
| | Link | Text | Calendar |
| | | SoftKeyLabel | Calendar |
| | | ID | lnkFm2Fm10 |
| | | NavigateURL | #Form10 |
| | Label | Text | Todays Specials are: |
| | | ID | lblFm22 |

*Continued on next page*

**TABLE 19.3 CONTINUED:** Controls and Properties for MobileWebForm1 in the Morris's Mobile Intranet Application

| Form | Control | Property | Value |
|------|---------|----------|-------|
| | List | DataMember | Table2 |
| | | DataSource | DataSet11 |
| | | DataTextField | stock_item |
| | | DataValueField | stock_special_price |
| | | ID | lstSpecials |
| Form3 | Label | Font | |
| | | Size | Small |
| | | Bold | True |
| | | Text | Morris's Wholesale Fruit & Vege |
| | | ID | lblFm3Head |
| | Label | Text | <empty> |
| | | ID | lblFm3 |
| | Label | Text | <empty> |
| | | ID | lblFm31 |
| | Label | Text | <empty> |
| | | ID | lblFm32 |
| | Label | Text | <empty> |
| | | ID | lblFm33 |
| | Label | Text | <empty> |
| | | ID | lblFm34 |
| | Link | Text | Purchase Order |
| | | SoftKeyLabel | Order |
| | | ID | lnkFm3Fm7 |
| | | NavigateURL | #Form7 |
| | Link | Text | Home |
| | | SoftKeyLabel | Home |
| | | ID | lnkFm3Fm2 |
| | | NavigateURL | #Form2 |
| Form4 | Label | Font | |
| | | Size | Small |
| | | Bold | True |
| | | Text | Morris's Wholesale Fruit & Vege |
| | | ID | lblFm4Head |
| | Link | Text | Home |
| | | SoftKeyLabel | Home |

*Continued on next page*

**TABLE 19.3 CONTINUED:** Controls and Properties for MobileWebForm1 in the Morris's Mobile Intranet Application

| Form | Control | Property | Value |
|---|---|---|---|
| | | ID | lnkFm4Fm2 |
| | | NavigateURL | #Form2 |
| | Label | Text | Enter Stock Item: |
| | | ID | lblFm4 |
| | TextBox | Text | <empty> |
| | | ID | txtStockSearch |
| | Label | Text | <empty> |
| | | Visible | False |
| | | ID | lblFm41 |
| | Command | Text | Search |
| | | SoftKeyLabel | Search |
| | | ID | cmdSearch |
| Form5 | Label | Font | |
| | | Size | Small |
| | | Bold | True |
| | | Text | Morris's Wholesale Fruit & Vege |
| | | ID | lblFm5Head |
| | Link | Text | Home |
| | | SoftKeyLabel | Home |
| | | ID | lnkFm5Fm2 |
| | | NavigateURL | #Form2 |
| | Link | Text | Search |
| | | SoftKeyLabel | Search |
| | | ID | lnkFm5Fm4 |
| | | NavigateURL | #Form4 |
| | Label | Text | Stock Items: |
| | | ID | lblFm5 |
| | List | DataMember | Table2 |
| | | DataSource | DataSet11 |
| | | DataTextField | stock_item |
| | | DataValueField | stock_sell_price |
| | | ID | lstStockItems |
| Form6 | Label | Font | |
| | | Size | Small |
| | | Bold | True |

*Continued on next page*

**TABLE 19.3 CONTINUED:** Controls and Properties for MobileWebForm1 in the Morris's Mobile Intranet Application

| Form | Control | Property | Value |
|------|---------|----------|-------|
| | | Text | Morris's Wholesale Fruit & Vege |
| | | ID | lblFm6Head |
| | Label | Text | <empty> |
| | | ID | lblFm6 |
| | Label | Text | <empty> |
| | | ID | lblFm61 |
| | Label | Text | <empty> |
| | | ID | lblFm62 |
| | Label | Text | <empty> |
| | | ID | lblFm63 |
| | Label | Text | <empty> |
| | | ID | lblFm64 |
| | Link | Text | Purchase Order |
| | | SoftKeyLabel | Order |
| | | ID | lnkFm6Fm7 |
| | | NavigateURL | #Form7 |
| | Link | Text | Search Results |
| | | SoftKeyLabel | Search Results |
| | | ID | lnkFm6Fm5 |
| | | NavigateURL | #Form5 |
| | Link | Text | Search |
| | | SoftKeyLabel | Search |
| | | ID | lnkFm6Fm4 |
| | | NavigateURL | #Form4 |
| | Link | Text | Home |
| | | SoftKeyLabel | Home |
| | | ID | lnkFm6Fm2 |
| | | NavigateURL | #Form2 |
| Form7 | Label | Font | |
| | | Size | Small |
| | | Bold | True |
| | | Text | Morris's Wholesale Fruit & Vege |
| | | ID | lblFm7Head |
| | Link | Text | Stock Item |

*Continued on next page*

**TABLE 19.3 CONTINUED:** Controls and Properties for MobileWebForm1 in the Morris's Mobile Intranet Application

| Form | Control | Property | Value |
|---|---|---|---|
| | | SoftKeyLabel | Item |
| | | ID | lnkFm7Fm6 |
| | | NavigateURL | #Form6 |
| | Link | Text | Search Results |
| | | SoftKeyLabel | Search Results |
| | | ID | lnkFm7Fm5 |
| | | NavigateURL | #Form5 |
| | Link | Text | Search |
| | | SoftKeyLabel | Search |
| | | ID | lnkFm7Fm4 |
| | | NavigateURL | #Form4 |
| | Link | Text | Home |
| | | SoftKeyLabel | Home |
| | | ID | lnkFm7Fm2 |
| | | NavigateURL | #Form2 |
| | Label | Text | <empty> |
| | | ID | lblFm7 |
| | Label | Text | <empty> |
| | | ID | lblFm71 |
| | Label | Text | Place an order for: |
| | | ID | lblFm72 |
| | TextBox | Text | <empty> |
| | | Numeric | True |
| | | ID | txtOrder |
| | Command | Text | Order |
| | | SoftKeyLabel | Order |
| | | ID | CmdOrder |
| Form8 | Label | Font | |
| | | Size | Small |
| | | Bold | True |
| | | Text | Morris's Wholesale Fruit & Vege |
| | | ID | lblFm8Head |
| | Link | Text | Home |
| | | SoftKeyLabel | Home |

*Continued on next page*

**TABLE 19.3 CONTINUED:** Controls and Properties for MobileWebForm1 in the Morris's Mobile Intranet Application

| Form | Control | Property | Value |
|------|---------|----------|-------|
| | | ID | lnkFm8Fm2 |
| | | NavigateURL | #Form2 |
| | Command | Text | Show All Messages |
| | | SoftKeyLabel | All_Messages |
| | | ID | cmdAllMessages |
| | List | DataMember | Table3 |
| | | DataSource | DataSet11 |
| | | DataTextField | message_date |
| | | DataValueField | message_id |
| | | ID | lstMessages |
| Form9 | | Paginate | True |
| | Label | Font | |
| | |   Size | Small |
| | |   Bold | True |
| | | Text | Morris's Wholesale Fruit & Vege |
| | | ID | lblFm9Head |
| | Link | Text | Message List |
| | | SoftKeyLabel | Messages |
| | | ID | lnkFm9Fm8 |
| | | NavigateURL | #Form8 |
| | Link | Text | Home |
| | | SoftKeyLabel | Home |
| | | ID | lnkFm9Fm2 |
| | | NavigateURL | #Form2 |
| | Label | Text | <empty> |
| | | DataBindings | Bind Text to DataBinder .Eval(DataSet11, "Tables[Table3].DefaultView .[0].message_date", "{0:D}")* |
| | | ID | lblFm9 |
| | Label | Text | <empty> |
| | | DataBindings | Bind Text to DataBinder .Eval(DataSet11, "Tables[Table3].DefaultView .[0].message_time", "{0:t}")* |
| | | ID | lblFm91 |

*Continued on next page*

**TABLE 19.3 CONTINUED:** Controls and Properties for MobileWebForm1 in the Morris's Mobile Intranet Application

| Form | Control | Property | Value |
|------|---------|----------|-------|
| | Label | Text | <empty> |
| | | ID | lblFm92 |
| | Label | Text | <empty> |
| | | ID | lblFm93 |
| | TextView | Text | <empty> |
| | | DataBindings | Bind Text to DataBinder.Eval(DataSet11, "Tables[Table3].DefaultView.[0].message_text", "{0}")[*] |
| | | ID | txtvFm0 |
| | Command | Text | Flag Message as Read |
| | | SoftKeyLabel | Flag_as_read |
| | | ID | cmdMessageRead |
| Form10 | Label | Font | |
| | |   Size | Small |
| | |   Bold | True |
| | | Text | Morris's Wholesale Fruit & Vege |
| | | ID | lblFm10Head |
| | Link | Text | Home |
| | | SoftKeyLabel | Home |
| | | ID | lnkFm10Fm2 |
| | | NavigateURL | #Form2 |
| | Calendar | ID | calrFm10 |
| | Label | Text | <empty> |
| | | Visible | False |
| | | ID | lblFm10 |
| Form11 | | Paginate | True |
| | Label | Font | |
| | |   Size | Small |
| | |   Bold | True |
| | | Text | Morris's Wholesale Fruit & Vege |
| | | ID | lblFm11Head |
| | Label | Text | <empty> |
| | | ID | lblFm111 |
| | List | DataMember | Table4 |

*Continued on next page*

**TABLE 19.3 CONTINUED:** Controls and Properties for MobileWebForm1 in the Morris's Mobile Intranet Application

| Form | Control | Property | Value |
|---|---|---|---|
| | | DataSource | DataSet11 |
| | | DataTextField | calendar_item_time |
| | | DataValueField | calendar_id |
| | | ID | lstFm11 |
| | Label | Text | <empty> |
| | | ID | lblFm112 |
| | TextView | Text | <empty> |
| | | ID | txtvFm11 |
| | Link | Text | Calendar |
| | | SoftKeyLabel | Calendar |
| | | ID | lnkFm11Fm10 |
| | | NavigateURL | #Form10 |
| | Link | Text | Home |
| | | SoftKeyLabel | Home |
| | | ID | lnkFm10Fm2 |
| | | NavigateURL | #Form2 |
| Form12 | Label | Font | |
| | |   Size | Small |
| | |   Bold | True |
| | | Text | Morris's Wholesale Fruit & Vege |
| | | ID | lblFm12Head |
| | TextView | Text | <empty> |
| | | ID | txtvFm12 |
| | Link | Text | <empty> |
| | | SoftKeyLabel | <empty> |
| | | ID | lnkFm12dynamic |
| | | NavigateURL | <empty> |

*The information here is an instruction, not a value.

Figures 19.6, 19.7, 19.8, 19.9, 19.10, and 19.11 illustrate the forms as they should appear once set up.

**FIGURE 19.6:**

Login and Home forms
for the Morris Mobile
intranet application

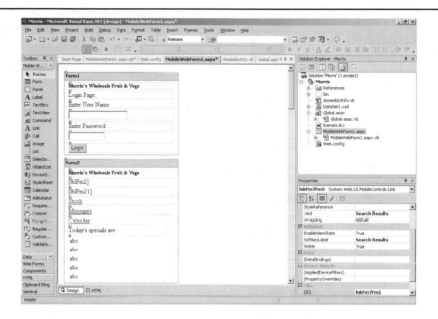

**FIGURE 19.7:**

Specials Details and
Stock Search forms
for the Morris Mobile
intranet application

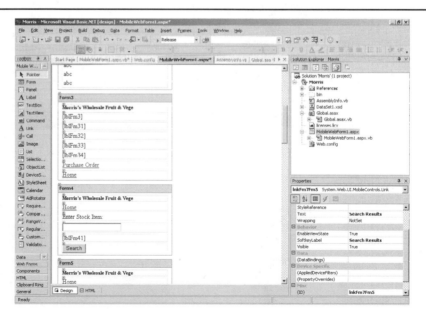

FIGURE 19.8:

Search Results and
Stock Item Detail
forms for the
Morris Mobile intranet
application

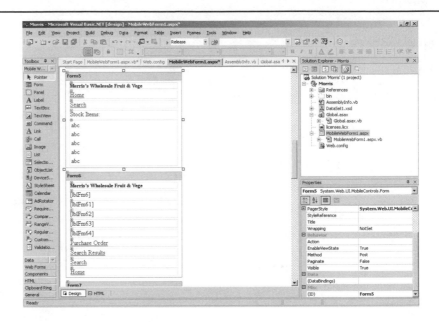

FIGURE 19.9:

Ordering and Current
Messages forms for
the Morris Mobile
intranet application

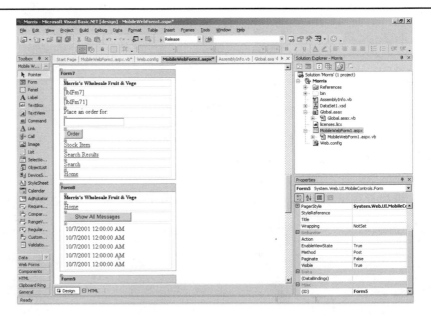

**FIGURE 19.10:**

Message Detail and
Calendar forms for the
Morris Mobile intranet
application

**FIGURE 19.10:**

Message Detail and
Calendar forms for the
Morris Mobile intranet
application

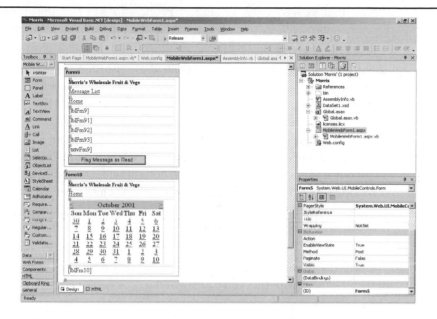

**FIGURE 19.11:**

Calendar Detail and
Error Message forms
for the Morris Mobile
intranet application

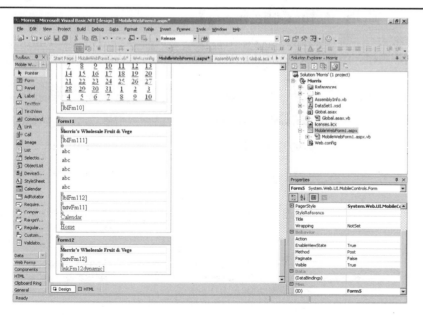

Note that we have made a number of concessions to how the application will render in the Openwave browser, by placing key links at the top of forms above items such as Lists.

However, we have struck a balance with the requirements of other browsers by placing all of our form-specific text into Label controls. In the Openwave browser, this will result in an extra line break occurring between the text and the contents of the control; however, it will render properly in other browsers such as the Nokia and MME. If we planted the text directly onto the form, we could avoid the extra line break in Openwave but would not get a line break at all in the other browsers. This would bring the first item of a list in on the same line as the list heading, which would appear a little silly. We could totally resolve the problem by making use of our device-specific capabilities to detect the device type and direct to different forms (developed specifically for the individual device). This is probably a bit excessive in this situation and does rather spoil one of the main reasons for using the MIT in the first place, which is to exploit the Toolkit's ability to render appropriate content for individual devices without having to worry too much about it ourselves.

It is also a strong possibility that Microsoft may have fixed the problem by the final release of the MIT and you, the reader, are wondering what I am talking about!

## Writing the Code Behind

Listing 19.1 contains the code behind for this project. Switch to Code View and enter the code from this listing into the project after the unused Page_Load code template.

**Listing 19.1     The Code Behind for the Morris Mobile Intranet Application**

```
Private Sub cmdLogin_Click(ByVal sender As System.Object,
➥ ByVal e As System.EventArgs) Handles cmdLogin.Click
        OleDbDataAdapter1.SelectCommand.Parameters("user_name"
➥).Value = txtUserName.Text
        OleDbDataAdapter1.SelectCommand.Parameters("user_pwd")
➥.Value = txtPassword.Text
        Try
            OleDbDataAdapter1.Fill(DataSet11, "Table1")
            If DataSet11.Tables("Table1").Rows.Count = 0
➥ Then
                ActiveForm = Form12
                txtvFm12.Text = "Sorry, either your
➥ password or user name was incorrect. Please enter
➥ your details again."
                lnkFm12dynamic.Text = "Login"
                lnkFm12dynamic.SoftkeyLabel = "Login"
                lnkFm12dynamic.NavigateURL = "#Form1"
```

```
                  ElseIf DataSet11.Tables("Table1").Rows(0).Item("user_active")
➥ = "Yes" Then
                      Session("User_name") =
➥ DataSet11.Tables("Table1").Rows(0).Item("user_name")
                      Session("User_id") =
➥ DataSet11.Tables("Table1").Rows(0).Item("user_id")
                      ActiveForm = Form2
                  Else
                      ActiveForm = Form12
                      txtvFm12.Text = "Sorry, your user account
➥ has been deactivated. Please contact the system
➥ administrator."
                      lnkFm12dynamic.Text = "Login"
                      lnkFm12dynamic.SoftkeyLabel = "Login"
                      lnkFm12dynamic.NavigateURL = "#Form1"
                  End If
          Catch
                  ActiveForm = Form12
                  txtvFm12.Text = "Sorry, the server is
➥ temporarily unavailable. Please try again."
                  lnkFm12dynamic.Text = "Login"
                  lnkFm12dynamic.SoftkeyLabel = "Login"
                  lnkFm12dynamic.NavigateURL = "#Form1"
          End Try

      End Sub

      Private Sub Form2_Activate(ByVal sender As
➥ System.Object, ByVal e As System.EventArgs) Handles
➥ Form2.Activate
          Try
                  lblFm2.Text = "Welcome " &
➥ Session("User_name")
                  OleDbDataAdapter2.Fill(DataSet11, "Table2")
                  lstSpecials.DataBind()
                  OleDbDataAdapter4.SelectCommand.Parameters
➥("message_read").Value = "No"
                  OleDbDataAdapter4.SelectCommand.Parameters
➥("message_user_id").Value = Session("User_id")
                  OleDbDataAdapter4.Fill(DataSet11, "Table3")
                  If DataSet11.Tables("Table3").Rows.Count > 0
➥ Then
                      lblFm21.Visible = True
                      lblFm21.Text = "You have new messages!"
                  Else
                      lblFm21.Visible = False
                  End If
          Catch
                  txtvFm12.Text = "The server appears to be
➥ temporarily unavailable. Please try again."
                  lnkFm12dynamic.Text = "Login"
```

```
            lnkFm12dynamic.SoftkeyLabel = "Login"
            lnkFm12dynamic.NavigateURL = "#Form1"
            ActiveForm = Form12
        End Try

    End Sub

    Private Sub lstSpecials_ItemCommand(ByVal source As
➥ System.Object, ByVal e As
➥ System.Web.UI.MobileControls.ListCommandEventArgs)
➥ Handles lstSpecials.ItemCommand
        Try
            OleDbDataAdapter2.Fill(DataSet11, "Table2")
            lblFm3.Text = e.ListItem.Text & " are on
➥ special!"
            lblFm31.Text = "At: $" & e.ListItem.Value & "
➥ per " & DataSet11.Tables("Table2").Rows(0).Item("stock_unit")
            lblFm32.Text = "We have " &
➥ DataSet11.Tables("Table2").Rows(0).Item
➥("stock_quantity") & " in stock"
            lblFm33.Text = "Our original selling price
➥ was: $" &
➥ DataSet11.Tables("Table2").Rows(0).Item
➥("stock_sell_price")
            lblFm34.Text = "Cost price was: $" &
➥ DataSet11.Tables("Table2").Rows(0).Item
➥("stock_cost_price")
            Session("Item") = e.ListItem.Text
            Session("Amount") =
➥ DataSet11.Tables("Table2").Rows(0).Item
➥("stock_quantity")
            ActiveForm = Form3
        Catch
            txtvFm12.Text = "The server appears to be
➥ temporarily unavailable. Please try again."
            lnkFm12dynamic.Text = "Home"
            lnkFm12dynamic.SoftkeyLabel = "Home"
            lnkFm12dynamic.NavigateURL = "#Form2"
            ActiveForm = Form12
        End Try
    End Sub

    Private Sub cmdSearch_Click(ByVal sender As
➥ System.Object, ByVal e As System.EventArgs) Handles
➥ cmdSearch.Click
        Try
            OleDbDataAdapter3.SelectCommand.Parameters
➥("stock_item").Value = txtStockSearch.Text & "%"
            OleDbDataAdapter3.Fill(DataSet11, "Table2")
            If DataSet11.Tables("Table2").Rows.Count > 0
➥ Then
```

```
                        lstStockItems.DataBind()
                        ActiveForm = Form5
                Else
                        lblFm41.Visible = True
                        lblFm41.Text = "There were no items in
➡ stock matching your request."
                End If
        Catch
                txtvFm12.Text = "The server appears to be
➡ temporarily unavailable. Please try again."
                lnkFm12dynamic.Text = "Stock"
                lnkFm12dynamic.SoftkeyLabel = "Stock"
                lnkFm12dynamic.NavigateURL = "#Form4"
                ActiveForm = Form12
        End Try

    End Sub

    Private Sub lstStockItems_ItemCommand(ByVal source As
➡ System.Object, ByVal e As
➡ System.Web.UI.MobileControls.ListCommandEventArgs)
➡ Handles lstStockItems.ItemCommand
        Try
                OleDbDataAdapter3.SelectCommand.Parameters
➡("stock_item").Value = e.ListItem.Text
                OleDbDataAdapter3.Fill(DataSet11, "Table2")
                lblFm6.Text = e.ListItem.Text
                Session("Item") = e.ListItem.Text
                lblFm61.Text = "$" & e.ListItem.Value
➡ & " per " & DataSet11.Tables("Table2").Rows(0).Item
➡("stock_unit")
                lblFm62.Text = "We have " &
➡ DataSet11.Tables("Table2").Rows(0).Item
➡("stock_quantity") & " in stock."
                lblFm63.Text = "Cost price was: $" &
➡ DataSet11.Tables("Table2").Rows(0).Item
➡("stock_cost_price")
                If DataSet11.Tables("Table2").Rows(0).Item
➡("stock_special") = "Yes" Then
                        lblFm64.Visible = True
                        lblFm64.Text = "Product is on special at:
➡ $" & DataSet11.Tables("Table2").Rows(0).Item
➡("stock_special_price")
                Else : lblFm64.Visible = False
                End If
                ActiveForm = Form6
        Catch
                txtvFm12.Text = "The server appears to be
➡ temporarily unavailable. Please try again."
                lnkFm12dynamic.Text = "Search Results"
                lnkFm12dynamic.SoftkeyLabel = "Search
➡ Results"
```

```
                lnkFm12dynamic.NavigateURL = "#Form5"
                ActiveForm = Form12
            End Try
        End Sub

        Private Sub Form4_Activate(ByVal sender As
➡ System.Object, ByVal e As System.EventArgs) Handles
➡ Form4.Activate
            lblFm41.Visible = False
        End Sub

    Private Sub Form7_Activate(ByVal sender As
➡ System.Object, ByVal e As System.EventArgs) Handles
➡ Form7.Activate
            txtOrder.Visible = True
            cmdOrder.Visible = True
            lblFm72.Visible = True
            Try
                OleDbDataAdapter3.SelectCommand.Parameters
➡("stock_item").Value = Session("Item")
                OleDbDataAdapter3.Fill(DataSet11, "Table2")
                lblFm7.Text = "Item: " & Session("Item")
                lblFm71.Text = "There are " &
➡ DataSet11.Tables("Table2").Rows(0).Item
➡("stock_quantity") & " in stock"
                Session("Amount") =
➡ DataSet11.Tables("Table2").Rows(0).Item
➡("stock_quantity")
            Catch
                txtvFm12.Text = "The server appears to be
➡ temporarily unavailable. Please try again."
                lnkFm12dynamic.Text = "Stock Item"
                lnkFm12dynamic.SoftkeyLabel = "Stock Item"
                lnkFm12dynamic.NavigateURL = "#Form6"
                ActiveForm = Form12
            End Try
        End Sub

    Private Sub cmdOrder_Click(ByVal sender As
➡ System.Object, ByVal e As System.EventArgs) Handles
➡ cmdOrder.Click
            Dim MyOleDbUpdateCommand1 As OleDb.OleDbCommand
            MyOleDbUpdateCommand1 = New OleDb.OleDbCommand()
            Dim intAmount As Integer = Session("Amount")
            Dim intOrderAmnt As Integer = txtOrder.Text
            Dim intStockRemaining As Integer
            If intOrderAmnt > intAmount Then
                txtvFm12.Text = "You have ordered too many of
➡ this item We do not have sufficient stock. Please try
➡ again."
                lnkFm12dynamic.Text = "Order"
                lnkFm12dynamic.SoftkeyLabel = "Order"
```

```
                lnkFm12dynamic.NavigateURL = "#Form7"
                ActiveForm = Form12
          Else
              Try
                   intStockRemaining =
    intAmount - intOrderAmnt
                   MyOleDbUpdateCommand1.CommandText =
    "UPDATE Table2 SET stock_quantity = " &
    intStockRemaining & " WHERE stock_item = '" &
    Session("Item") & "'"
                   MyOleDbUpdateCommand1.Connection =
    OleDbConnection1
                   OleDbConnection1.Open()
                   MyOleDbUpdateCommand1.ExecuteNonQuery()
                   OleDbConnection1.Close()
                   lblFm71.Text = "You have ordered " &
    intOrderAmnt & " items."
                   txtOrder.Visible = False
                   cmdOrder.Visible = False
                   lblFm72.Visible = False
              Catch
                   txtvFm12.Text = "The server appears to be
    temporarily unavailable. Please try again."
                   lnkFm12dynamic.Text = "Order"
                   lnkFm12dynamic.SoftkeyLabel = "Order"
                   lnkFm12dynamic.NavigateURL = "#Form7"
                   ActiveForm = Form12
              End Try
          End If

      End Sub

      Private Sub Form8_Activate(ByVal sender As
    System.Object, ByVal e As System.EventArgs) Handles
    Form8.Activate
          Try
              OleDbDataAdapter4.SelectCommand.Parameters
    ("message_read").Value = "No"
              OleDbDataAdapter4.SelectCommand.Parameters
    ("message_user_id").Value = Session("User_id")
              OleDbDataAdapter4.Fill(DataSet11, "Table3")
              lstMessages.DataBind()
          Catch
              txtvFm12.Text = "The server appears to be
    temporarily unavailable. Please try again."
              lnkFm12dynamic.Text = "Home"
              lnkFm12dynamic.SoftkeyLabel = "Home"
              lnkFm12dynamic.NavigateURL = "#Form2"
              ActiveForm = Form12
          End Try
      End Sub
```

```
    Private Sub lstMessages_ItemCommand(ByVal source As
➡ System.Object, ByVal e As
➡ System.Web.UI.MobileControls.ListCommandEventArgs)
➡ Handles lstMessages.ItemCommand
      Try
          Dim intMsg_sender_id As Integer
          OleDbDataAdapter5.SelectCommand.Parameters
➡("message_id").Value = e.ListItem.Value
          Session("Curr_message") = e.ListItem.Value
          OleDbDataAdapter5.Fill(DataSet11, "Table3")
          OleDbDataAdapter6.Fill(DataSet11, "Table1")
          lblFm9.DataBind()
          lblFm91.DataBind()
          intMsg_sender_id = DataSet11.Tables
➡("Table3").Rows(0).Item("message_user_id")
          lblFm92.Text = "Message from: " &
➡ DataSet11.Tables("Table1").Rows.Find
➡(intMsg_sender_id).Item("user_name")
          txtvFm9.DataBind()
          If DataSet11.Tables
➡("Table3").Rows(0).Item("message_read") = "Yes" Then
              lblFm93.Text = "This message has already
➡ been read."
              Session("Msg_read") = "Yes"
              cmdMessageRead.Text = "Flag Message as
➡ Not Read"
          Else
              lblFm93.Text = "This message has not been
➡ read."
              Session("Msg_read") = "No"
              cmdMessageRead.Text = "Flag Message as
➡ Read"
          End If
          ActiveForm = Form9
      Catch
          txtvFm12.Text = "The server appears to be
➡ temporarily unavailable. Please try again."
          lnkFm12dynamic.Text = "Messages"
          lnkFm12dynamic.SoftkeyLabel = "Messages"
          lnkFm12dynamic.NavigateURL = "#Form8"
          ActiveForm = Form12
      End Try
    End Sub


    Private Sub cmdAllMessages_Click(ByVal sender As
➡ System.Object, ByVal e As System.EventArgs) Handles
➡ cmdAllMessages.Click
      Try
          OleDbDataAdapter4.SelectCommand.Parameters
➡("message_read").Value = "%"
          OleDbDataAdapter4.SelectCommand.Parameters
➡("message_user_id").Value = Session("User_id")
```

```
                OleDbDataAdapter4.Fill(DataSet11, "Table3")
                lstMessages.DataBind()
        Catch
                txtvFm12.Text = "The server appears to be
➥ temporarily unavailable. Please try again."
                lnkFm12dynamic.Text = "Messages"
                lnkFm12dynamic.SoftkeyLabel = "Messages"
                lnkFm12dynamic.NavigateURL = "#Form8"
                ActiveForm = Form12
        End Try
    End Sub


    Private Sub cmdMessageRead_Click(ByVal sender As
➥ System.Object, ByVal e As System.EventArgs) Handles
➥ cmdMessageRead.Click
        Try
                Dim MyOleDbUpdateCommand As
➥ OleDb.OleDbCommand
                Dim intCurr_message As Integer =
➥ Session("Curr_message")
                MyOleDbUpdateCommand = New
➥ OleDb.OleDbCommand()
                If Session("Msg_read") = "No" Then
                        MyOleDbUpdateCommand.CommandText =
➥ "UPDATE Table3 SET message_read = 'Yes' WHERE
➥ message_id = " & intCurr_message
                        lblFm93.Text = "This message is now
➥ flagged as read"
                Else
                        MyOleDbUpdateCommand.CommandText =
➥ "UPDATE Table3 SET message_read = 'No' WHERE
➥ message_id = " & intCurr_message
                        lblFm93.Text = "This message is now
➥ flagged as NOT read"
                End If
                MyOleDbUpdateCommand.Connection =
➥ OleDbConnection1
                OleDbConnection1.Open()
                MyOleDbUpdateCommand.ExecuteNonQuery()
                OleDbConnection1.Close()
        Catch
                txtvFm12.Text = "The server appears to be
➥ temporarily unavailable. Please try again."
                lnkFm12dynamic.Text = "Messages"
                lnkFm12dynamic.SoftkeyLabel = "Messages"
                lnkFm12dynamic.NavigateURL = "#Form9"
                ActiveForm = Form12
        End Try

    End Sub
```

```
    Private Sub calrFm10_SelectionChanged(ByVal sender As
➥ System.Object, ByVal e As System.EventArgs) Handles
➥ calrFm10.SelectionChanged
        Try
            lblFm10.Visible = False
            lblFm111.Text = "Items listed for: " &
➥ calrFm10.SelectedDate()
            OleDbDataAdapter7.SelectCommand.Parameters
➥("calendar_user_id").Value = Session("User_id")
            OleDbDataAdapter7.SelectCommand.Parameters
➥("calendar_item_date").Value = calrFm10.SelectedDate()
            OleDbDataAdapter7.Fill(DataSet11, "Table4")
            lstFm11.DataBind()
            lblFm112.Text = "First entry for: " &
➥ calrFm10.SelectedDate()
            txtvFm11.Text =
➥ DataSet11.Tables("Table4").Rows(0).Item
➥("calendar_item")
            ActiveForm = Form11
        Catch
            lblFm10.Visible = True
            lblFm10.Text = "There are no calendar entries
➥ for this date"
        End Try
    End Sub


    Private Sub lstFm11_ItemCommand(ByVal source As
➥ System.Object, ByVal e As
➥ System.Web.UI.MobileControls.ListCommandEventArgs)
➥ Handles lstFm11.ItemCommand
        Try
            OleDbDataAdapter8.SelectCommand.Parameters
➥ ("calendar_id").Value = e.ListItem.Value
            OleDbDataAdapter8.Fill(DataSet11, "Table4")
            txtvFm11.Text =
➥ DataSet11.Tables("Table4").Rows(0).Item
➥("calendar_item")
            lblFm112.Text = "Entry for: " &
➥ e.ListItem.Text
        Catch
            txtvFm12.Text = "The server appears to be
➥ temporarily unavailable. Please try again."
            lnkFm12dynamic.Text = "Calendar List"
            lnkFm12dynamic.SoftkeyLabel = "Calendar"
            lnkFm12dynamic.NavigateURL = "#Form7"
            ActiveForm = Form11
        End Try
    End Sub
```

```
    Private Sub Form10_Activate(ByVal sender As
➡ System.Object, ByVal e As System.EventArgs) Handles
➡ Form10.Activate
        lblFm10.Visible = False
    End Sub
End Class
```

In previous chapters, we have discussed most of the code elements used in this project, so we will dispense with a detailed analysis here! There are a couple of things worth pointing out, though, and I'll give a quick rundown of the main role of each subroutine.

Selecting the Login link fires the cmdLogin_Click event, and this is where we process the user authentication. The username and password are verified with the database as well as the user's "active" status. If there are any problems, the user is directed to Form12 where an appropriate message is displayed.

On successful login, the user is directed to the Home form, where they are greeted by name and informed whether or not they have any unread messages. This is all handled by Form2_Activate. The database is also scanned for any items on special, and these are displayed.

Selecting an item on special from the list directs the user to Form3, which displays details of the item on special. This is handled by the lstSpecials_ItemCommand subroutine.

The next subroutine handles the cmdSearch_Click event and carries out a search of the database based on details entered into the TextBox control in Form4. Results of the search are displayed in Form5. If there are no items matching the search criteria, the user is held at Form4 and lblFm41 is displayed with a message to that effect. The Form4_Activate subroutine resets lblFm41.Visible to False if the user accesses the form again.

Selecting an item from the search-results list triggers the lstStockItems_ItemCommand subroutine. With this code, we display details of the item chosen in Form6. If the item is on special, then that is indicated as well.

Selecting the Purchase Order link in Form6 navigates the user to Form7. At the Form7_Activate event, Form7 is set up as an order form with information on the product selected (obtained from session variables). Selecting the Order link executes the code in cmdOrder_Click. This updates the database with the amount entered and reconfigures Form7 to act as an order confirmation form.

Form8_Activate employs the user's identity from the session variable to populate a list with any unread messages for that user. Selecting the "Show All Messages" link fires the cmdAllMessages_Click subroutine, which populates Form8's list with all the messages for the user.

Selecting a message from the list navigates the user to Form9, which displays the details for that message. This is handled by lstMessages_ItemCommand. It also sets the Flag Message as Read/Unread Command control to the appropriate setting according to the state of the message being viewed. Selecting the Flag Message As link triggers the cmdMessageRead_ Click code, which updates the database accordingly and sets its own text property value to the appropriate setting.

We use the `calrFm10_SelectionChanged` event to respond to a user selection on the calendar. In this code, we check the database for entries associated with the date selected. These entries are then displayed in Form11. If there are no entries, the user is held at Form10, and an appropriate message is displayed in `lblFm10` (which normally has its `Visible` property set to False—managed by Form10_Activate).

Selecting a calendar item from the list in Form11 triggers the code in lstFm11_Item-Command. This displays the details attached to the chosen calendar item. One weakness of this application in its current form is that this information is displayed on Form11 rather than on a separate form. We will look at this in a little more detail later in the chapter, in the section "Running the Application."

## Finishing Touches

As we have done with previous applications, we need to make a couple of final adjustments before deploying the application.

We need to edit our `Web.config` file to ensure that everything will work as it should across the various mobile device/browser/gateway combinations.

Open up `Web.config` from the Solution Explorer window and check that the `<httpRuntime useFullyQualifiedRedirectUrl="true" />` tag has been set in the `<system.web>` section, as explained in Chapter 8, "A Deeper Look at the Mobile Internet Toolkit and VB .NET."

Scroll down to the `<sessionState>` tag and set `cookieless="true"`.

Once we have tested and debugged the application, set `debug="false"` in the `<compilation>` tag, to improve runtime performance. Save the changes.

## Expanding and Enhancing the Application

In the interests of brevity, we have cut a lot of corners with the design of this application. The nature of the application also lends itself to a wide range of possible enhancements.

For example, the process of ordering simply flags a number of items as being sold. A more complete version of this application would enable the user to enter client details, negotiated price, and any other relevant details.

The Calendar section of the application only allows items to be read, and it places the text of the item on the same card as the list of returned items. A more complete version of the application would enable the user to properly manage their own records from their mobile device, including updating and deleting existing, and creating new, records. We would also direct the user to separate forms for most of these functions.

We might also wish to look at expanding the messaging function to a little more than just reading existing messages and flagging them as read or not. We could enable the user to create and post new messages as well as delete existing ones.

We could also give users the capability to change their passwords, and there are other possible features we could build into the program, such as a contacts manager or a monthly sales tracker for individual sales representatives.

As we will see, when running the application, there is some further work to be done in the order of placement of controls on the forms, as the user functionality in the Openwave environment of the calendar details form is a little less than optimal.

If our organization operated a range of mobile devices from cell phones to handheld computers, we might also look at making use of some of the device-specific capabilities to optimize user experience on the different platforms.

## Running the Application

We have created three sample users in our database. One of the users, Sam, is listed as inactive. When a user first opens the application, they are presented with the login form. If we log in using Sam's credentials, we will be presented with the message that the user account has been deactivated, and we will be returned to the login form. Logging in with one of the other users and entering an invalid password will also result in the error form with an appropriate message.

Figure 19.12 illustrates a successful login procedure for the user Jay.

**FIGURE 19.12:**

The successful login procedure for user Jay in the Morris Mobile intranet application

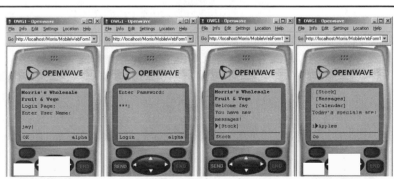

Image of UP.SDK courtesy Openwave Systems, Inc.

Once we have logged in, we are presented with the second Home form customized with Jay's name, identifying whether Jay has any new messages and giving a list of current specials.

If we select the Apple option in the list of specials, we are presented with the specific product details. From here we can select the Purchase Order link and enter a purchase quantity. See Figure 19.13.

**FIGURE 19.13:**

Product details for the Apples special, and the Purchase Order form

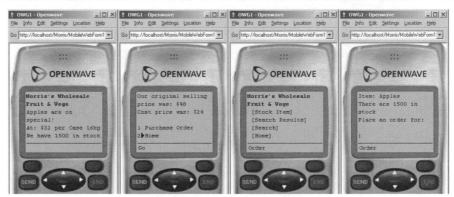

Image of UP.SDK courtesy Openwave Systems, Inc.

Figure 19.14 illustrates the outcome of entering **200** as the purchase amount. We have set this form up to dynamically represent itself as the Order Confirmation form. With some mobile devices, this is not an entirely sound approach, as it may not rerender exactly as we wish it to. It would have been safer to create a separate Confirmation form and direct the user to that.

**FIGURE 19.14:**

Ordering 200 cases of apples in the Morris Mobile intranet application

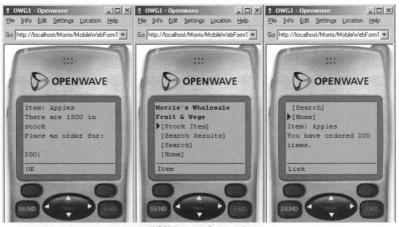

Image of UP.SDK courtesy Openwave Systems, Inc.

From the Home form, if we select the "Stock" link we are taken to the Stock Search form. If we enter the letter *a* and click OK, we are taken to a form displaying all the stock items beginning with the letter *a*. (See Figure 19.15.) In Figure 19.15, we can see the extra line break introduced by the Openwave browser between the Label and List control. (This may not be an issue for the final release of the Mobile Internet Toolkit.) We can then follow through the purchase process we illustrated in Figure 19.14.

**FIGURE 19.15:**

Searching for stock items in the Morris Mobile intranet application

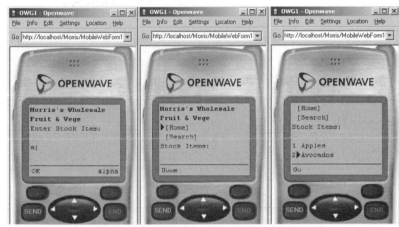

Image of UP.SDK courtesy Openwave Systems, Inc.

Selecting the Messages link from the Home form takes us into the messages section of the application. We are initially presented with any unread messages and the option to view all messages. After selecting a message to read, we are presented with its details and then given the option to mark it as read. See Figure 19.16.

**FIGURE 19.16:**

Viewing messages in the Morris Mobile intranet application

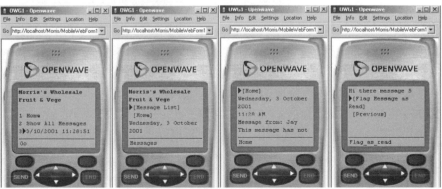

Image of UP.SDK courtesy Openwave Systems, Inc.

Selecting the Calendar link from the Home form takes us to the calendar section. We can select the current date, type a date (which I have done in the illustrated example in Figure 19.17), or select a date.

**FIGURE 19.17:**

Selecting a date to view in the calendar section of the Morris Mobile intranet application

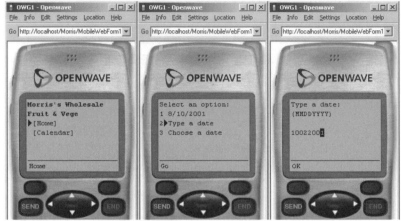

Image of UP.SDK courtesy Openwave Systems, Inc.

Once we have selected a date, we are presented with a list of entries for that date. Selecting an entry will display the details of that entry. Because we have placed the display controls on the form with the List control, it is a little awkward to view using the Openwave browser (see Figure 19.18), and we would need to remedy this for a production application by moving these controls to a separate form. It may be easier to view the application using the Nokia Toolkit, Internet Explorer, or MME (see Figure 19.19) to get some idea of how it should display.

**FIGURE 19.18:**

Viewing calendar details in the Morris Mobile intranet application, using the Openwave browser

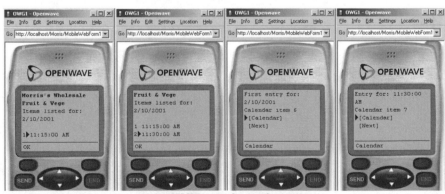

Image of UP.SDK courtesy Openwave Systems, Inc.

**FIGURE 19.19:**

Viewing calendar
details in the Morris
Mobile intranet
application, using
the MME browser

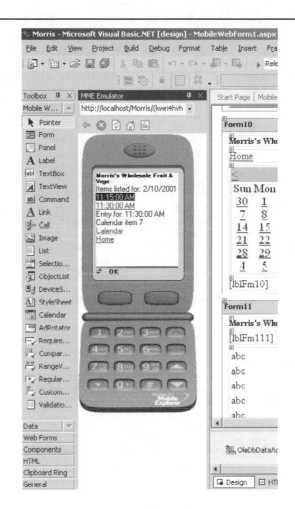

## Full ASPX Code Listing

Listing 19.2 contains the full ASPX code for this project.

**Listing 19.2     Full ASPX Code for the Morris Mobile Intranet Application**

```
<%@ Page Language="vb" AutoEventWireup="false"
➥ Codebehind="MobileWebForm1.aspx.vb"
➥ Inherits="Morris.MobileWebForm1" %>
<%@ Register TagPrefix="mobile"
➥ Namespace="System.Web.UI.MobileControls"
```

```
➥ Assembly="System.Web.Mobile, Version=1.0.3300.0,
➥ Culture=neutral, PublicKeyToken=b03f5f7f11d50a3a" %>
<meta name="GENERATOR" content="Microsoft Visual
➥ Studio.NET 7.0">
<meta name="CODE_LANGUAGE" content="Visual Basic 7.0">
<meta name="vs_targetSchema"
➥ content="http://schemas.microsoft.com/Mobile/Page">
<body Xmlns:mobile="http://schemas.microsoft.com/Mobile/
➥WebForm">
    <mobile:form id="Form1" runat="server">
        <mobile:Label id="lblFm1Head" runat="server"
➥ Font-Size="Small" Font-Bold="True">Morris's Wholesale
➥ Fruit &amp; Vege</mobile:Label>
        <mobile:Label id="lblFm1" runat="server">Login
➥ Page:</mobile:Label>
        <mobile:Label id="lblFm11" runat="server">Enter
➥ User Name:</mobile:Label>
        <mobile:TextBox id="txtUserName"
➥ runat="server"></mobile:TextBox>
        <mobile:Label id="lblFm12" runat="server">Enter
➥ Password:</mobile:Label>
        <mobile:TextBox id="txtPassword" runat="server"
➥ MaxLength="10" Size="10"
➥ Password="True"></mobile:TextBox>
        <mobile:Command id="cmdLogin" runat="server"
➥ SoftkeyLabel="Login">Login</mobile:Command>
    </mobile:form>
    <mobile:form id="Form2" runat="server">
        <mobile:Label id="lblFm2Head" runat="server"
➥ Font-Size="Small" Font-Bold="True">Morris's Wholesale
➥ Fruit &amp; Vege</mobile:Label>
        <mobile:Label id="lblFm2"
➥ runat="server"></mobile:Label>
        <mobile:Label id="lblFm21" runat="server"
➥ Visible="False"></mobile:Label>
        <mobile:Link id="lnkFm2Fm4" runat="server"
➥ SoftkeyLabel="Stock"
➥ NavigateURL="#Form4">Stock</mobile:Link>
        <mobile:Link id="lnkFm2Fm8" runat="server"
➥ SoftkeyLabel="Messages"
➥ NavigateURL="#Form8">Messages</mobile:Link>
        <mobile:Link id="lnkFm2Fm10" runat="server"
➥ SoftkeyLabel="Calendar"
➥ NavigateURL="#Form10">Calendar</mobile:Link>
        <mobile:Label id="lblFm22" runat="server">Todays
➥ Specials are:</mobile:Label>
        <mobile:List id="lstSpecials" runat="server"
➥ DataValueField="stock_special_price"
➥ DataTextField="stock_item" DataMember="Table2"
➥ DataSource="<%# DataSet11 %>"></mobile:List>
```

```
    </mobile:form>
    <mobile:form id="Form3" runat="server">
        <mobile:Label id="lblFm3Head" runat="server"
➡ Font-Size="Small" Font-Bold="True">Morris's Wholesale
➡ Fruit &amp; Vege</mobile:Label>
        <mobile:Label id="lblFm3"
➡ runat="server"></mobile:Label>
        <mobile:Label id="lblFm31"
➡ runat="server"></mobile:Label>
        <mobile:Label id="lblFm32"
➡ runat="server"></mobile:Label>
        <mobile:Label id="lblFm33"
➡ runat="server"></mobile:Label>
        <mobile:Label id="lblFm34"
➡ runat="server"></mobile:Label>
        <mobile:Link id="lnkFm3Fm7" runat="server"
➡ SoftkeyLabel="Order" NavigateURL="#Form7">Purchase
➡ Order</mobile:Link>
        <mobile:Link id="lnkFm3Fm2" runat="server"
➡ SoftkeyLabel="Home"
➡ NavigateURL="#Form2">Home</mobile:Link>
    </mobile:form>
    <mobile:form id="Form4" runat="server">
        <mobile:Label id="lblFm4Head" runat="server"
➡ Font-Size="Small" Font-Bold="True">Morris's Wholesale
➡ Fruit &amp; Vege</mobile:Label>
        <mobile:Link id="lnkFm4Fm2" runat="server"
➡ SoftkeyLabel="Home"
➡ NavigateURL="#Form2">Home</mobile:Link>
        <mobile:Label id="lblFm4" runat="server">Enter
➡ Stock Item:</mobile:Label>
        <mobile:TextBox id="txtStockSearch"
➡ runat="server"></mobile:TextBox>
        <mobile:Label id="lblFm41" runat="server"
➡ Visible="False"></mobile:Label>
        <mobile:Command id="cmdSearch" runat="server"
➡ SoftkeyLabel="Search">Search</mobile:Command>
    </mobile:form>
    <mobile:form id="Form5" runat="server">
        <mobile:Label id="lblFm5Head" runat="server"
➡ Font-Size="Small" Font-Bold="True">Morris's Wholesale
➡ Fruit &amp; Vege</mobile:Label>
        <mobile:Link id="lnkFm5Fm2" runat="server"
➡ SoftkeyLabel="Home"
➡ NavigateURL="#Form2">Home</mobile:Link>
        <mobile:Link id="lnkFm5Fm4" runat="server"
➡ SoftkeyLabel="Search"
➡ NavigateURL="#Form4">Search</mobile:Link>
        <mobile:Label id="lblFm5" runat="server">Stock
➡ Items:</mobile:Label>
```

```
        <mobile:List id="lstStockItems" runat="server"
➡ DataValueField="stock_sell_price"
➡ DataTextField="stock_item" DataMember="Table2"
➡ DataSource="<%# DataSet11 %>"></mobile:List>
    </mobile:form>
    <mobile:form id="Form6" runat="server">
        <mobile:Label id="lblFm6Head" runat="server"
➡ Font-Size="Small" Font-Bold="True">Morris's Wholesale
➡ Fruit &amp; Vege</mobile:Label>
        <mobile:Label id="lblFm6"
➡ runat="server"></mobile:Label>
        <mobile:Label id="lblFm61"
➡ runat="server"></mobile:Label>
        <mobile:Label id="lblFm62"
➡ runat="server"></mobile:Label>
        <mobile:Label id="lblFm63"
➡ runat="server"></mobile:Label>
        <mobile:Label id="lblFm64"
➡ runat="server"></mobile:Label>
        <mobile:Link id="lnkFm6Fm7" runat="server"
➡ SoftkeyLabel="Order" NavigateURL="#Form7">Purchase
➡ Order</mobile:Link>
        <mobile:Link id="lnkFm6Fm5" runat="server"
➡ SoftkeyLabel="Search Results"
➡ NavigateURL="#Form5">Search Results</mobile:Link>
        <mobile:Link id="lnkFm6Fm4" runat="server"
➡ SoftkeyLabel="Search"
➡ NavigateURL="#Form4">Search</mobile:Link>
        <mobile:Link id="lnkFm6Fm2" runat="server"
➡ SoftkeyLabel="Home"
➡ NavigateURL="#Form2">Home</mobile:Link>
    </mobile:form>
    <mobile:form id="Form7" runat="server">
        <mobile:Label id="lblFm7Head" runat="server"
➡ Font-Size="Small" Font-Bold="True">Morris's Wholesale
➡ Fruit &amp; Vege</mobile:Label>
        <mobile:Link id="lnkFm7Fm6" runat="server"
➡ SoftkeyLabel="Item" NavigateURL="#Form6">Stock
➡ Item</mobile:Link>
        <mobile:Link id="lnkFm7Fm5" runat="server"
➡ SoftkeyLabel="Search Results"
➡ NavigateURL="#Form5">Search Results</mobile:Link>
        <mobile:Link id="lnkFm7Fm4" runat="server"
➡ NavigateURL="#Form4">Search</mobile:Link>
        <mobile:Link id="lnkFm7Fm2" runat="server"
➡ NavigateURL="#Form2">Home</mobile:Link>
        <mobile:Label id="lblFm7"
➡ runat="server"></mobile:Label>
        <mobile:Label id="lblFm71"
➡ runat="server"></mobile:Label>
```

```
        <mobile:Label id="lblFm72" runat="server">Place an
➥ order for:</mobile:Label>
        <mobile:TextBox id="txtOrder" runat="server"
➥ Numeric="True"></mobile:TextBox>
        <mobile:Command id="cmdOrder" runat="server"
➥ SoftkeyLabel="Order">Order</mobile:Command>
    </mobile:form>
    <mobile:form id="Form8" runat="server">
        <mobile:Label id="lblFm8Head" runat="server"
➥ Font-Size="Small" Font-Bold="True">Morris's Wholesale
➥ Fruit &amp; Vege</mobile:Label>
        <mobile:Link id="lnkFm8Fm2" runat="server"
➥ SoftkeyLabel="Home"
➥ NavigateURL="#Form2">Home</mobile:Link>
        <mobile:Command id="cmdAllMessages" runat="server"
➥ SoftkeyLabel="All_Messages">Show All
➥ Messages</mobile:Command>
        <mobile:List id="lstMessages" runat="server"
➥ DataValueField="message_id"
➥ DataTextField="message_date" DataMember="Table3"
➥ DataSource="<%# DataSet11 %>"></mobile:List>
    </mobile:form>
    <mobile:form id="Form9" runat="server"
➥ Paginate="True">
        <mobile:Label id="lblFm9Head" runat="server"
➥ Font-Size="Small" Font-Bold="True">Morris's Wholesale
➥ Fruit &amp; Vege</mobile:Label>
        <mobile:Link id="lnkFm9Fm8" runat="server"
➥ SoftkeyLabel="Messages" NavigateURL="#Form8">Message
➥ List</mobile:Link>
        <mobile:Link id="lnkFm9Fm2" runat="server"
➥ SoftkeyLabel="Home"
➥ NavigateURL="#Form2">Home</mobile:Link>
        <mobile:Label id="lblFm9" runat="server"
➥ Text='<%# DataBinder.Eval
➥(DataSet11,
➥"Tables[Table3].DefaultView.[0].message_date",
➥"{0:D}") %>'></mobile:Label>
        <mobile:Label id="lblFm91" runat="server"
➥ Text='<%# DataBinder.Eval(DataSet11,
➥"Tables[Table3].DefaultView.[0].message_time",
➥"{0:t}") %>'></mobile:Label>
        <mobile:Label id="lblFm92"
➥ runat="server"></mobile:Label>
        <mobile:Label id="lblFm93"
➥ runat="server"></mobile:Label>
        <mobile:TextView id="txtvFm9" runat="server"
➥ Text='<%# DataBinder.Eval(DataSet11
➥, "Tables[Table3].DefaultView.[0].message_text",
➥"{0}") %>'></mobile:TextView>
```

```
        <mobile:Command id="cmdMessageRead" runat="server"
➥ SoftkeyLabel="Flag_as_read">Flag Message as
➥ Read</mobile:Command>
      </mobile:form>
      <mobile:form id="Form10" runat="server">
        <mobile:Label id="lblFm10Head" runat="server"
➥ Font-Size="Small" Font-Bold="True">Morris's Wholesale
➥ Fruit &amp; Vege</mobile:Label>
        <mobile:Link id="lnkFm10Fm2" runat="server"
➥ SoftkeyLabel="Home"
➥ NavigateURL="#Form2">Home</mobile:Link>
        <mobile:Calendar id="calrFm10"
➥ runat="server"></mobile:Calendar>
        <mobile:Label id="lblFm10" runat="server"
➥ Visible="False"></mobile:Label>
      </mobile:form>
      <mobile:form id="Form11" runat="server"
➥ Paginate="True">
        <mobile:Label id="lblFm11Head" runat="server"
➥ Font-Size="Small" Font-Bold="True">Morris's Wholesale
➥ Fruit &amp; Vege</mobile:Label>
        <mobile:Label id="lblFm111"
➥ runat="server"></mobile:Label>
        <mobile:List id="lstFm11" runat="server"
➥ DataValueField="calendar_id"
➥ DataTextField="calendar_item_time"
➥ DataMember="Table4"
➥ DataSource="<%# DataSet11 %>"></mobile:List>
        <mobile:Label id="lblFm112"
➥ runat="server"></mobile:Label>
        <mobile:TextView id="txtvFm11"
➥ runat="server"></mobile:TextView>
        <mobile:Link id="lnkFm11Fm10" runat="server"
➥ SoftkeyLabel="Calendar"
➥ NavigateURL="#Form10">Calendar</mobile:Link>
        <mobile:Link id="lnkFm11Fm2" runat="server"
➥ SoftkeyLabel="Home"
➥ NavigateURL="#Form2">Home</mobile:Link>
      </mobile:form>
      <mobile:form id="Form12" runat="server">
        <mobile:Label id="lblFm12Head" runat="server"
➥ Font-Size="Small" Font-Bold="True">Morris's Wholesale
➥ Fruit &amp; Vege</mobile:Label>
        <mobile:TextView id="txtvFm12"
➥ runat="server"></mobile:TextView>
        <mobile:Link id="lnkFm12dynamic"
➥ runat="server"></mobile:Link>
      </mobile:form>
    </body>
```

## Summary

This project is an example of one of the most likely commercial uses for mobile technologies. Businesses with highly mobile workforces have been among the early adopters of this type of technology. However, this type of application isn't just limited to the sales or company representative. For example, it could be used in a warehouse situation to manage stock, where information is entered as stock is pulled or shelved. It could also be used in an educational setting to enter absences and manage student results. In a hospital, it could be used to enter and retrieve patient records.

This particular project also highlights some of the care that we need to take when designing mobile sites, even with a tool as powerful as the MIT. It also demonstrates that despite the adaptive rendering abilities of Mobile controls, there is still a place for developing device-specific content.

# CHAPTER 20

---

# *MyNewContacts*: MyContacts Revisited

---

- Looking at the rationale

- Planning the application

- Building the database

- Creating the Login page

- Creating the Mobile Web Page

- Writing the code behind

- Adding the finishing touches

- Expanding and enhancing the application

- Running the application

- Full ASPX code listing for MobileWebForm1

Previously in Chapter 10, "Data Access with the Mobile Internet Toolkit, Part 2," we used the example of a simple contact manager program to illustrate the basics of database connectivity with the Mobile Internet Toolkit. In this version of the contact manager, we will see how to adapt it to a multi-use type environment. In particular, we will look at implementing two technologies that we have managed to avoid up until now:

- The SQL Server DataAdapters
- Forms-based authentication

Throughout this book, we have used Access when building sample databases because this is the tool that most readers are likely to have available. However, Microsoft has invested heavily in optimizing .NET for SQL Server, and this is the technology that we are likely to use in any large-scale implementation of our MIT-based mobile technologies. With this in mind, this project is designed to make use of the SQL Server connectivity objects in the MIT. As we will see, there is very little practical difference between setting up and accessing an SQL Server database and an Access database with the Mobile Internet Toolkit.

If you do not have SQL Server, don't despair! The database we will use can be just as easily built using Microsoft Access and then referenced with the `OleDbDataAdapter` and `OleDbDataConnection` objects instead.

We looked briefly at forms-based authentication in Chapter 19, "Morris's Wholesale Fruit & Vege: A Mobile Intranet," when it was flagged as an option for authentication of the application. This application demonstrates how we can make use of forms-based authentication (in cookieless mode) as the authentication model.

## Rationale

As we have previously built the MyContacts application and will be reusing a lot of the code, please refer to Part V, "Building Applications with the Mobile Internet Toolkit," for the design considerations and code discussions.

This type of application is a very typical example of the applications that are widely available on the Mobile Internet today. Despite their ubiquitous nature, contact managers are still very useful applications to attach to mobile Intranets and portal-style applications.

## Planning the Application

We will build this application using two Mobile Web Pages. This is to accommodate the forms-based authentication, which requires a separate page to handle the authentication process. Whenever a user accesses any part of the application without either the appropriate authentication cookie or "munged" URL, they are redirected back to the login page and asked to provide some credentials.

We will need the application to identify the user and then provide the user with their personalized list of contacts.

The basic structure of the application is illustrated in Figure 20.1.

Structure of the MyNewContacts application

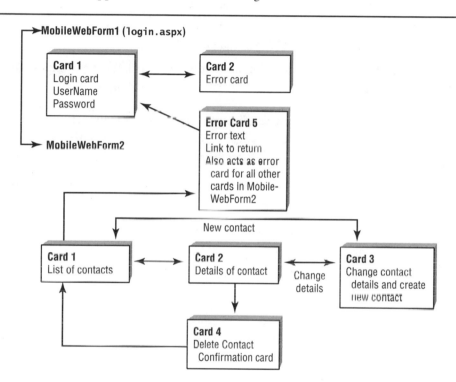

## Building the Database

As this book is not meant to be about SQL Server or SQL syntax, we will use the GUI tools to build our database in the interests of ease and simplicity. If you are new to SQL Server, be aware that this is Microsoft's industrial strength DBMS (Database Management System) and there is a lot more to it than what we will touch on here. For more about SQL Server, pick up a copy of *Mastering SQL Server 2000* by Mike Gunderloy and Joseph L. Jorden (Sybex, 2001).

We will build a simple database based on the `mobiledb1.mdb` that we created for the original MyContacts application (Chapters 9 and 10). If you do not have SQL Server, you should be familiar enough by now with the approach that we have been using in Access to adapt the code used for this project. Please note that I have used SQL Server 2000 throughout this example.

Follow these steps to build the database:

1. Open the SQL Server Enterprise Manager (Start ≻ Programs ≻ Microsoft SQL Server ≻ Enterprise Manager).

2. Expand the contents of the root node in the left pane to expose the Databases node. See Figure 20.2.

**FIGURE 20.2:**

The SQL Server Enterprise Manager

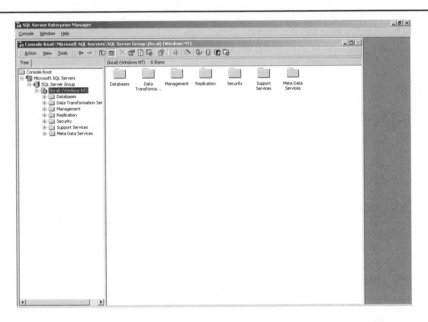

3. Right-click the Databases node and select New Database from the menu. This should open the Properties dialog box.

4. Type **mycontacts** in the Name field of the Properties dialog box, and then click OK. See Figure 20.3.

FIGURE 20.3:

The Properties dialog
box when creating a
new database in SQL
Server

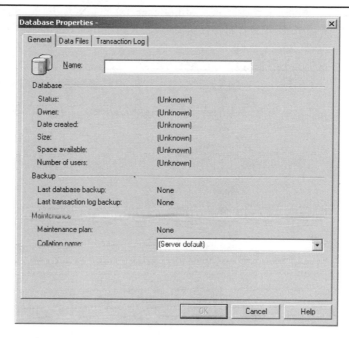

**FIGURE 20.3:**

The Properties dialog
box when creating a
new database in SQL
Server

5. Expand the Databases node in the Tree pane of the Enterprise Manager. An instance of
mycontacts should now be visible. Expand the mycontacts node (see Figure 20.4).

**FIGURE 20.4:**

The mycontacts
node exposed in the
Enterprise Manager

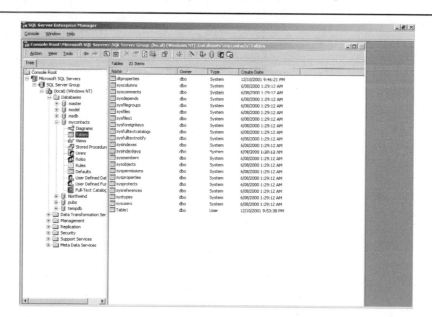

**6.** Right-click the Tables subnode, and select New Table. Set up the fields as depicted in Figure 20.5 and save it as Table1. Right-click the user_id field and set it as the primary key. Close the table.

**FIGURE 20.5:**

Field definitions for Table1 in mycontacts database

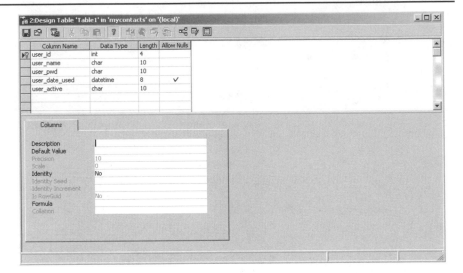

**7.** Right-click the Tables subnode again and create another new table. Set up the fields as depicted in Figure 20.6 and save it as Table2. Set the contact_id field as the primary key. Do not close Table2 yet.

**8.** Select the Relationships button on the toolbar for Table2. Click the New button in the Properties dialog box (see Figure 20.7) and set up a relationship between Table1 user_id and Table2 contact_user; stick with the default settings. Close the Properties dialog box and close Table2.

**9.** Ensuring that the Tables subnode is selected in the left Tree pane, you should have all the tables in the database listed in the right pane of the Enterprise Manager. Right-click Table1, and select Open Table ➤ Return All Rows from the menu.

**10.** Enter the sample data depicted in Figure 20.8. Close the table.

FIGURE 20.6:

Field definitions for
Table2 in mycontacts
database

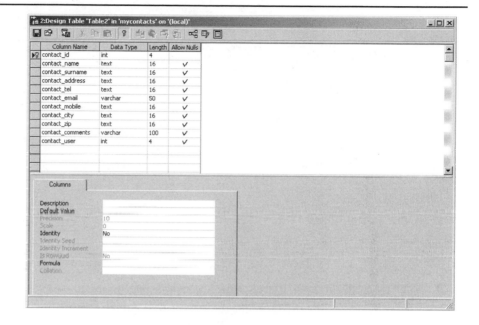

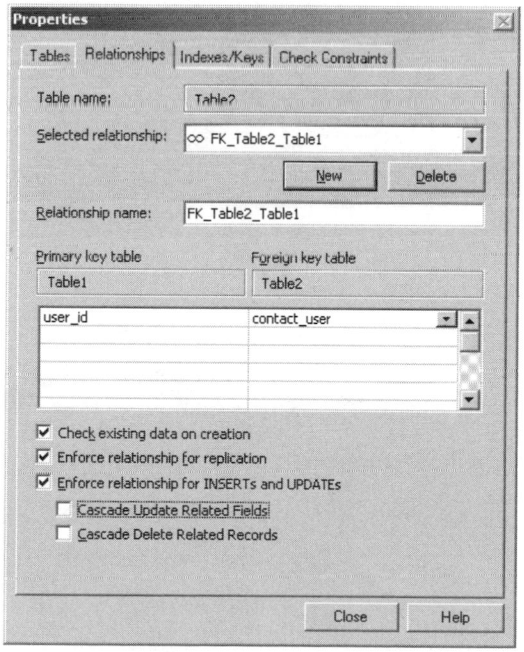

FIGURE 20.7:

Setting up a
relationship in the
Properties dialog
box for mycontacts
database

Sample data
entered in Table1 of
mycontacts database

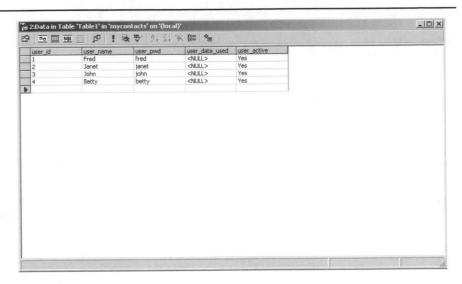

**11.** From the Enterprise Manager, right-click Table2 and select Open Table ➤ Return All
Rows from the menu. Enter the sample data depicted in Figure 20.9, and close the table.

FIGURE 20.9:

Sample data
entered in Table2 of
mycontacts database

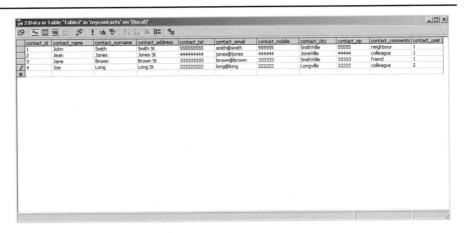

**12.** We have now completed the database. Close the Enterprise Manager.

## Creating the Login Page

We begin the project by creating the login page to which unauthenticated users will be redirected to supply their credentials. This is created as a separate MobileWebForm.

1. Open a new Mobile Web project in Visual Studio .NET (Visual Basic) and, from the Project menu, add a new Mobile Web Form and name it `login.aspx`.

2. In Design View for `login.aspx`, expose the Data tools in the Toolbox.

3. Drag an SqlDataAdapter to the MobileWebPage. This will open the Data Adapter Configuration Wizard, which is essentially the same tool that we have used for our OleDbDataAdapters.

4. Click Next and from the Choose Your Data Connection dialog box, click the New Connection button.

5. In the Data Link Properties dialog box, establish a connection to the mycontacts database. This involves three steps, which are listed on the screen (see Figure 20.11).

   A. Enter your SQL Server server name. If it is not available from the drop-down menu, open the SQL Server Service Manager by selecting Start ➢ Programs ➢ Microsoft SQL Server ➢ Service Manager (see Figure 20.10) and copy the server name from the Server field into the appropriate field in the Data Link Properties dialog box.

**FIGURE 20.10:**

The SQL Server
Service Manager

   B. You may need to select the Use Windows NT Integrated Security option.

   C. Select the mycontacts database from the drop-down menu. Check the connection by clicking the Test Connection button. If all is well, click OK (see Figure 20.11).

6. Click through the wizard until you reach the Query Builder. Set up the SQL statement as illustrated in Figure 20.12 for Table1. Note that we now use `@user_pwd` and `@user_name` as our parameters rather than the ? that we used for the OleDbDataAdapter.

7. Click through the rest of the wizard and exit.

**FIGURE 20.11:**

Completing the
Data Link Properties
dialog box

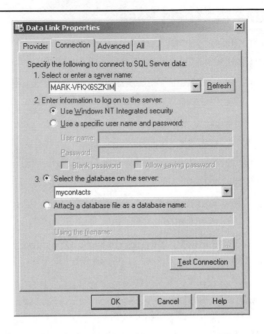

**FIGURE 20.12:**

Using the Query
Builder

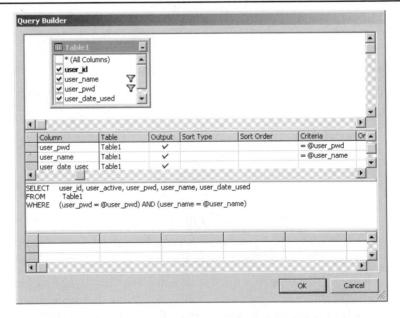

8. In Design View, right-click the SqlDataAdapter1 and select Generate DataSet from the menu. Create DataSet1, which should now appear as DatSet11 in the designer.

**9.** Drag a second Form control to the `login.aspx` MobileWebPage and set the two forms up with the controls and properties as specified in Table 20.1.

**TABLE 20.1:** Controls and Properties for *login.aspx*

| Form | Control | Property | Value |
|---|---|---|---|
| Form1 | | `Title` | MyNewContacts - Login |
| | | `ID` | loginForm1 |
| | Label | `StyleReference` | title |
| | | `Text` | MyNewContacts |
| | | `ID` | lblFm1 |
| | Label | `Text` | Login Page: |
| | | `ID` | lblFm11 |
| | Label | `Text` | Enter User Name: |
| | | `ID` | lblFm12 |
| | TextBox | `Text` | <empty> |
| | | `ID` | txtUserName |
| | Label | `Text` | Enter Password: |
| | | `ID` | lblFm13 |
| | TextBox | `Text` | <empty> |
| | | `Maxlength` | 10 |
| | | `Password` | True |
| | | `Size` | 10 |
| | | `ID` | txtPassword |
| | Command | `Text` | Login |
| | | `SoftKeyLabel` | Login |
| | | `ID` | cmdLogin |
| Form2 | | `Title` | MyNewContacts - Error |
| | | `ID` | loginForm2 |
| | Label | `StyleReference` | title |
| | | `Text` | MyNewContacts |
| | | `ID` | lblFm2 |
| | TextView | `Text` | <empty> |
| | | `ID` | txtvFm2 |
| | Link | `Text` | Login |
| | | `SoftKeyLabel` | Login |
| | | `ID` | lnkFm2Fm1 |
| | | `NavigateURL` | #loginForm1 |

The only thing of note about these settings is the use of the `Title` property at the form level. We have not previously used this property a great deal. It will only be rendered on those devices capable of supporting it. For example, we would see it rendered in Internet Explorer, but not in the Openwave browser.

We place the code for this page directly in the HTML View of the `login.aspx`. Switch to HTML View and complete the code from Listing 20.1. (Much of it will be already autogenerated.) We need to add the content between the opening and closing `<script>` tags and add `onclick="cmdLogin_Click"` to the tag for the cmdLogin control.

This code is an adaptation of the workaround for cookieless forms-based authentication provided by Microsoft in the QuickStart Tutorial for the RC1 release.

---

**Listing 20.1    Full ASPX code for *login.aspx* in the MyNewContacts Application**

```
<%@ Register TagPrefix="mobile"
➥ Namespace="System.Web.UI.MobileControls"
➥ Assembly="System.Web.Mobile, Version=1.0.3300.0, Culture=neutral,
➥ PublicKeyToken=b03f5f7f11d50a3a" %>
<%@ Page Language="vb" AutoEventWireup="false"
➥ Codebehind="login.aspx.vb" Inherits="MyNewContacts.login" %>
<%@ Import Namespace="System.Web.Security" %>
<%@ Import Namespace="System.Web.Mobile" %>
<meta name="GENERATOR" content="Microsoft Visual Studio.NET 7.0">
<meta name="CODE_LANGUAGE" content="Visual Basic 7.0">
<meta name="vs_targetSchema"
➥ content="http://schemas.microsoft.com/Mobile/Page">
<script runat="server" ID="Script1">
Private Sub cmdLogin_Click(sender As System.Object, e As
➥ System.EventArgs)
        SqlDataAdapter1.SelectCommand.Parameters("@user_name").Value =
➥ txtUserName.Text
        SqlDataAdapter1.SelectCommand.Parameters("@user_pwd").Value =
➥ txtPassword.Text
    Try
        SqlDataAdapter1.Fill(DataSet11, "Table1")
        If DataSet11.Tables("Table1").Rows.Count = 0 Then
            ActiveForm = loginForm2
            txtvFm2.Text = "Sorry, either your password or user
➥ name was incorrect. Please enter your details again."
        Else
            Dim user_id as Integer =
➥ DataSet11.Tables("Table1").Rows(0).Item("user_id")
            MobileFormsAuthentication.RedirectFromLoginPage(user_id, false)
        End If
    Catch
        ActiveForm = loginForm2
        txtvFm2.Text = "Sorry, the server is temporarily
➥ unavailable. Please try again."
    End Try
```

```
    End Sub
</script>
<body Xmlns:mobile="http://schemas.microsoft.com/Mobile/WebForm">
    <mobile:form id="loginForm1" runat="server" title="MyNewContacts -
 Login">
        <mobile:Label id="lblFm1" runat="server"
StyleReference="title">MyNewContacts</mobile:Label>
        <mobile:Label id="lblFm11" runat="server">Login
 Page:</mobile:Label>
        <mobile:Label id="lblFm12" runat="server">Enter User
 Name:</mobile:Label>
        <mobile:TextBox id="txtUserName" runat="server"></mobile:TextBox>
        <mobile:Label id="lblFm13" runat="server">Enter
 Password:</mobile:Label>
        <mobile:TextBox id="txtPassword" runat="server" Password="True"
 Size="10" MaxLength="10"></mobile:TextBox>
        <mobile:Command id="cmdLogin" onclick="cmdLogin_Click"
 runat="server" SoftkeyLabel="Login">Login</mobile:Command>
    </mobile:form>
    <mobile:form id="loginForm2" runat="server" title="MyNewContacts -
 Error">
        <mobile:Label id="lblFm2" runat="server"
 StyleReference="title">MyNewContacts</mobile:Label>
        <mobile:TextView id="txtvFm2" runat="server"></mobile:TextView>
        <mobile:Link id="lnkFm2Fm1" runat="server" SoftkeyLabel="Login"
 NavigateURL="#loginForm1">Login</mobile:Link>
    </mobile:form>
</body>
```

Apart from the addition of the code to carry out the forms authentication, this code is very similar to what we used to create our login form in Morris's Mobile Intranet in Chapter 19. We do, however, need to add two additional directives to our ASPX pages:

```
<%@ Import Namespace="System.Web.Security" %>
<%@ Import Namespace="System.Web.Mobile" %>
```

We have used the SqlDataAdapter in exactly the same fashion that we might have used an OleDbDataAdapter.

We also need to make some adjustments to the Web.config file. With these changes in place, when a user accesses the application, they are automatically directed to the login page unless they have been previously authenticated.

Open the Web.config file and locate the <authentication> and <authorization> tags. Alter the code to that contained in Listing 20.2.

---

**Listing 20.2**  **Changes to Be Made to the *Web.config* File for the MyNewContacts Application**

```
<authentication mode="Forms" />

    <authorization>
      <deny users="?" />
    </authorization>
```

---

Listing 20.2 does not include the Microsoft documentation that normally accompanies these sections of the Web.config file in Listing 20.2.

The completed forms should appear in Design View as illustrated in Figure 20.13.

---

**FIGURE 20.13:**

Form layout of login.aspx for the MyNewContacts application

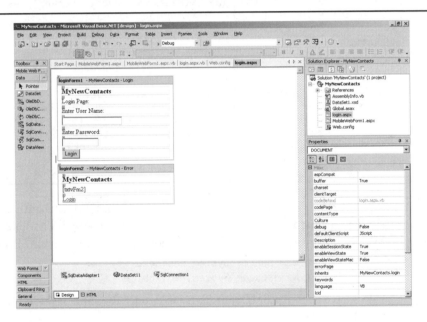

## Creating the Mobile Web Page

We will build the main part of this application on a single MobileWebForm. The idea is for users to be redirected to this page once they have been authenticated. If they attempt to access the page without valid authentication, they are redirected back to the login page.

1. Switch back to Design View for MobileWebForm.aspx. Set up the page with five forms. Drag two SqlDataAdapters to the page.

2. For the first of the SqlDataAdapters, set it up against Table2 of the mycontacts database using the SQL statement illustrated in Figure 20.14.

SQL statement for
SqlDataAdapter1 in
MobileWebForm1
of MyNewContacts
application

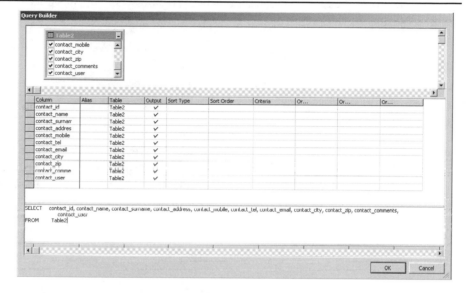

3. With the second SqlDataAdapter, set it up against Table1 of the mycontacts database using the SQL statement illustrated in Figure 20.15.

SQL statement for
SqlDataAdapter2 in
MobileWebForm1
of MyNewContacts
application

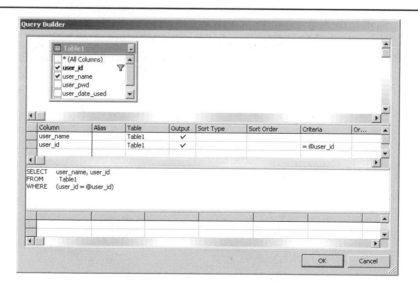

4. Once the SqlDataAdapters are set up, right-click SqlDataAdapter1 and select Generate DataSet from the menu. Choose the existing DataSet1 and Table2.

5. Right-click SqlDataAdapter2 and select Generate DataSet from the menu. Choose Table1 in the existing DataSet1.

6. From the Data Tools, drag two DataView objects to the designer.

7. Set the Table property of both DataView1 and DataView2 to DataSet11.Table2.

8. Set up the controls and properties for the MobileWebForm1 as listed in Table 20.2.

**TABLE 20.2:** Controls and Property Settings for MobileWebForm1 in the MyNewContacts Application

| Form | Control | Property | Value |
|------|---------|----------|-------|
| Form1 | | PagerStyle | |
| | | NextPageText | Go to Page {0} |
| | | PreviousPageText | Return to Page {0} |
| | | Title | MyNewContacts - List |
| | | Paginate | True |
| | | ID | Pg1Form1 |
| | Label | StyleReference | title |
| | | Text | <empty> |
| | | ID | lblFm1 |
| | List | DataMember | Table2 |
| | | DataSource | DataView2 |
| | | DataTextField | contact_name |
| | | DataValueField | contact_id |
| | | ID | lstContacts |
| | Command | Text | New Contact |
| | | SoftKeyLabel | Cntct |
| | | ID | cmdNewContact |
| | Command | Text | LogOut |
| | | SoftKeyLabel | LgOut |
| | | ID | cmdLogout |
| Form2 | | Title | MyNewContacts - Details |
| | | ID | Pg1Form2 |
| | Label | StyleReference | title |
| | | Text | <empty> |
| | | DataBindings | Custom data binding expression: String.Format ("{0} {1}", DataBinder.Eval(DataView1, "[0].contact_name"), DataBinder.Eval(DataView1, "[0].contact_surname")) |
| | | ID | lblContactName |

*Continued on next page*

**TABLE 20.2 CONTINUED:** Controls and Property Settings for MobileWebForm1 in the MyNewContacts Application

| Form | Control | Property | Value |
|------|---------|----------|-------|
| Form2 | | Type directly on form: | ID Number: |
| | Label | Font – Size | Small |
| | | Text | <empty> |
| | | DataBindings | DataBinder.Eval(DataView1, "[0].contact_id", "{0}") |
| | | ID | lblID |
| Form2 | | Type directly on form: | Address: |
| | Label | Font – Size | Small |
| | | Text | <empty> |
| | | DataBindings | DataBinder.Eval(DataView1, "[0].contact_address", "{0}") |
| | | ID | lblAddress |
| | Label | Font – Size | Small |
| | | Text | <empty> |
| | | DataBindings | DataBinder.Eval(DataView1, "[0].contact_city", "{0}") |
| | | ID | lblCity |
| | Label | Font – Size | Small |
| | | Text | <empty> |
| | | DataBindings | DataBinder.Eval(DataView1, "[0].contact_zip", "{0}") |
| | | ID | lblZip |
| Form2 | | Type directly on form: | Phone: |
| | Label | Font – Size | Small |
| | | Text | <empty> |
| | | DataBindings | DataBinder.Eval(DataView1, "[0].contact_tel", "{0}") |
| | | ID | lblTel |
| | PhoneCall | Font – Size | Small |
| | | Text | Call |
| | | AlternateFormat | {0} |
| | | SoftKeyLabel | Call |
| | | ID | pcllTel |
| | | PhoneNumber | 0 |
| Form2 | | Type directly on form: | Mobile: |
| | Label | Font – Size | Small |

*Continued on next page*

**TABLE 20.2 CONTINUED:** Controls and Property Settings for MobileWebForm1 in the MyNewContacts Application

| Form | Control | Property | Value |
|---|---|---|---|
| | | Text | <empty> |
| | | DataBindings | DataBinder.Eval(DataView1, "[0].contact_mobile", "{0}") |
| | | ID | lblMobile |
| | PhoneCall | Font - Size | Small |
| | | Text | Call |
| | | AlternateFormat | {0} |
| | | SoftKeyLabel | Call |
| | | ID | pcllMob |
| | | PhoneNumber | 0 |
| Form2 | | Type directly on form: | Email: |
| | Label | Font - Size | Small |
| | | Text | <empty> |
| | | DataBindings | DataBinder.Eval(DataView1, "[0].contact_email", "{0}") |
| | | ID | lblEmail |
| Form2 | | Type directly on form: | Comments: |
| | TextView | Font - Size | Small |
| | | Text | <empty> |
| | | DataBindings | DataBinder.Eval(DataView1, "[0].contact_comments", "{0}") |
| | | ID | txtvComments |
| | Command | Text | Delete Contact |
| | | SoftKeyLabel | Delet |
| | | ID | cmdDelete |
| | Command | Text | Change Details |
| | | SoftKeyLabel | Chnge |
| | | ID | cmdChangeDetails |
| | Command | Text | Home |
| | | SoftKeyLabel | Home |
| | | ID | cmdHomeFm2 |
| Form3 | | Title | MyNewContacts - DataEntry |
| | | ID | Pg1Form3 |
| | Label | StyleReference | title |
| | | Text | <empty> |
| | | ID | lblFm3 |

*Continued on next page*

**TABLE 20.2 CONTINUED:** Controls and Property Settings for MobileWebForm1 in the MyNewContacts Application

| Form | Control | Property | Value |
|------|---------|----------|-------|
| Form3 | | Type directly on form: | Name: |
| | TextBox | Text | <empty> |
| | | ID | txtName |
| Form3 | | Type directly on form: | Surname: |
| | TextBox | Text | <empty> |
| | | ID | txtSurname |
| Form3 | | Type directly on form: | Address: |
| | TextBox | Text | <empty> |
| | | ID | txtAddress |
| Form3 | | Type directly on form: | City: |
| | TextBox | Text | <empty> |
| | | ID | txtCity |
| Form3 | | Type directly on form: | Zip: |
| | TextBox | Text | <empty> |
| | | ID | txtZip |
| Form3 | | Type directly on form: | Telephone: |
| | TextBox | Text | <empty> |
| | | ID | txtTel |
| Form3 | | Type directly on form: | Mobile: |
| | TextBox | Text | <empty> |
| | | ID | txtMobile |
| Form3 | | Type directly on form: | Email: |
| | TextBox | Text | <empty> |
| | | ID | txtEmail |
| Form3 | | Type directly on form: | Comments: |
| | TextBox | Text | <empty> |
| | | ID | txtComments |
| | Command | Text | Create New Contact |
| | | SoftKeyLabel | Cntct |
| | | ID | cmdCreateContact |
| | Command | Text | Change Details |
| | | SoftKeyLabel | Chnge |
| | | Visible | False |
| | | ID | cmdChangeDetailsConfirm |
| | Command | Text | Home |

*Continued on next page*

**TABLE 20.2 CONTINUED:** Controls and Property Settings for MobileWebForm1 in the MyNewContacts Application

| Form | Control | Property | Value |
|------|---------|----------|-------|
| | | SoftKeyLabel | Home |
| | | ID | cmdHomeFm3 |
| Form4 | | Title | MyNewContacts - Delete |
| | | ID | Pg1Form4 |
| | Label | StyleReference | title |
| | | Text | Do you wish to delete the record for: |
| | | ID | lblFm4 |
| | Label | Text | <empty> |
| | | ID | lblFm41 |
| Form4 | | Type directly on form: | Record Number: |
| | Label | Text | <empty> |
| | | ID | lblFm42 |
| | Command | Text | Yes |
| | | SoftKeyLabel | Yes |
| | | ID | cmdDeleteConfirm |
| | Command | Text | No |
| | | SoftKeyLabel | No |
| | | ID | cmdDeleteDeny |
| Form5 | | Title | MyNewContacts - Error |
| | | ID | Pg1Form5 |
| | Label | StyleReference | title |
| | | Text | MyNewContacts |
| | | ID | lblFm5 |
| | TextView | Text | <empty> |
| | | ID | txtvFm5 |
| | Link | Text | <empty> |
| | | SoftKeyLabel | <empty> |
| | | ID | LnkFm5dynamic |
| | | NavigateURL | <empty> |
| Form6 | | Title | MyNewContacts - LogOut |
| | | ID | Pg1Form6 |
| | Label | StyleReference | title |
| | | Text | MyNewContacts |
| | | ID | lblFm6 |
| | Label | Text | Logged Out |
| | | ID | lblFm61 |

Note that in creating this application we have made use of the PhoneCall controls. This application was developed on the RC1 version of the MIT and, at the time of writing, the PhoneNumber property of the PhoneCall control required a default value at design time. For the same reason it couldn't be databound at runtime. This differed from earlier versions of the control and may be changed again by final release of the MIT.

The completed forms should appear as depicted in Figures 20.16, 20.17, and 20.18.

**FIGURE 20.16:**

Pg1Form1 and
Pg1Form2 from the
MyNewContacts
application

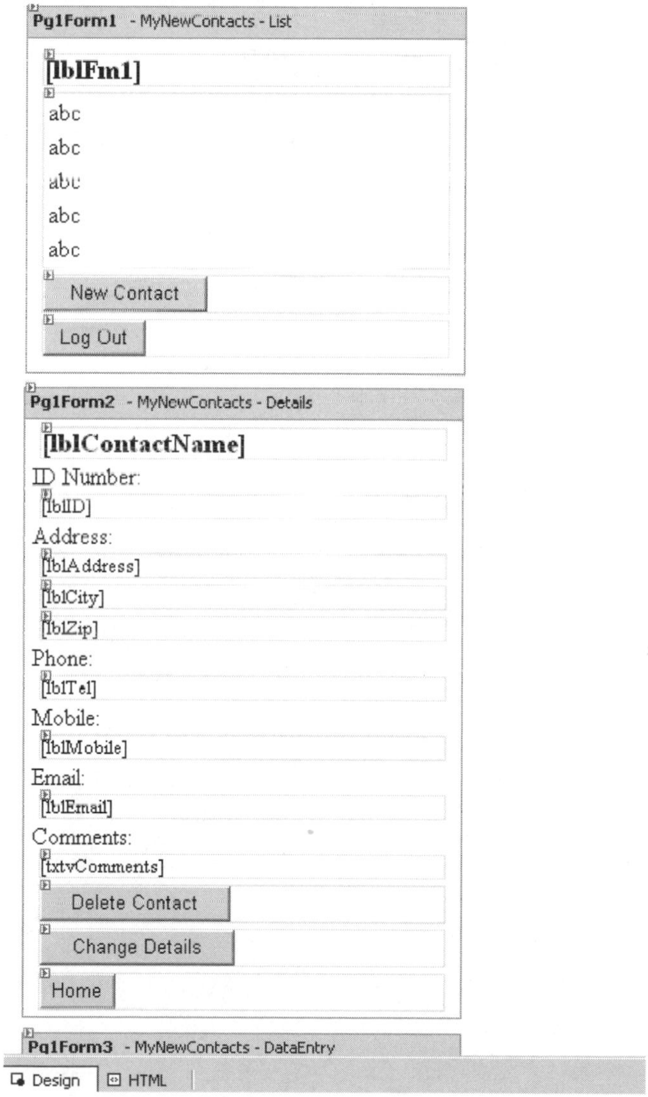

**FIGURE 20.17:**

Pg1Form3 of the MyNewContacts application

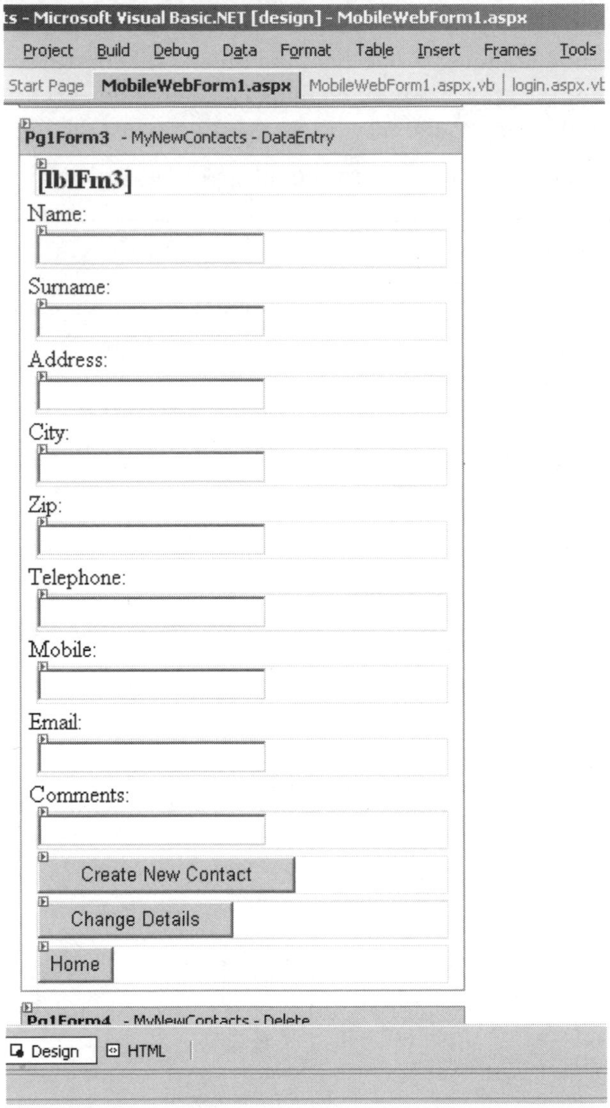

FIGURE 20.18:

Pg1Form4 and
Pg1Form5 of the
MyNewContacts
application

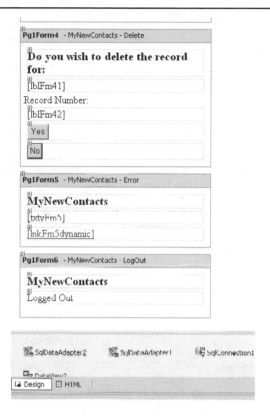

## Writing the Code Behind

To add the necessary functionality to the project, switch to Code Behind View for
the MobileWebForm1. Enter the code from Listing 20.3 into Code Behind View for
MobileWebForm1.

**Listing 20.3**     **Code Behind for MobileWebForm1 of MyNewContacts**

```
Private Sub Page_Load(ByVal sender As System.Object, ByVal e As
➡ System.EventArgs) Handles MyBase.Load
     Try
          SqlDataAdapter2.SelectCommand.Parameters("@user_id").Value
➡ = User.Identity.Name
          SqlDataAdapter2.Fill(DataSet11, "Table1")
          SqlDataAdapter1.Fill(DataSet11, "Table2")
          Session("user_name") =
➡ DataSet11.Tables("Table1").Rows(0).Item("user_name")
```

```
            Dim numRows As Integer
            numRows = DataSet11.Tables("Table2").Rows.Count - 1
            DataSet11.Tables("Table2").Columns("contact_id").AutoIncrement =
➡ True
            DataSet11.Tables("Table2").Columns("contact_id").AutoIncrementSeed =
➡ (DataSet11.Tables("Table2").Rows(numRows).Item("contact_id")) + 1
            DataSet11.Tables("Table2").Columns("contact_id").AutoIncrementStep =
➡ 1

            lblFm1.Text = Session("user_name") & "'s Contacts"
        Catch
            txtvFm5.Text = "Sorry, the server appears to be temporarily
➡ unavailable at the moment. Please try again."
            lnkFm5dynamic.Text = "Login"
            lnkFm5dynamic.SoftkeyLabel = "Login"
            lnkFm5dynamic.NavigateURL =
➡ "http://localhost/MyNewContacts/login.aspx"
            ActiveForm = Pg1Form5
        End Try
    End Sub

    Protected Sub lstContacts_ItemCommand(ByVal source As
➡ System.Object, ByVal e As
➡ System.Web.UI.MobileControls.ListCommandEventArgs) Handles
➡ lstContacts.ItemCommand
        Session("currID") = e.ListItem.Value
        ActiveForm = Pg1Form2
    End Sub

    Private Sub Pg1Form2_Activate(ByVal sender As System.Object, ByVal
➡ e As System.EventArgs) Handles Pg1Form2.Activate
        Try
            DataView1.RowFilter = "contact_id=" & Session("currID")
            lblID.DataBind()
            lblContactName.DataBind()
            lblAddress.DataBind()
            lblCity.DataBind()
            lblZip.DataBind()
            lblTel.DataBind()
            lblMobile.DataBind()
            lblEmail.DataBind()
            txtvComments.DataBind()
            pcllTel.PhoneNumber = lblTel.Text
            pcllMob.PhoneNumber = lblMobile.Text
        Catch
            txtvFm5.Text = "Sorry, the server appears to be temporarily
➡ unavailable at the moment. Please try again."
            lnkFm5dynamic.Text = "Home"
            lnkFm5dynamic.SoftkeyLabel = "Home"
            lnkFm5dynamic.NavigateURL = "#Pg1Form1"
            ActiveForm = Pg1Form5
        End Try
```

```
        End Sub

    Private Sub cmdNewContact_Click(ByVal sender As System.Object,
➥ ByVal e As System.EventArgs) Handles cmdNewContact.Click
        ActiveForm = Pg1Form3
        lblFm3.Text = "Enter Details:"
    End Sub

    Private Sub Pg1Form1_Activate(ByVal sender As System.Object, ByVal
➥ e As System.EventArgs) Handles Pg1Form1.Activate
        Try
            DataView2.RowFilter = "contact_user=" & User.Identity.Name
            lstContacts.DataBind()

            cmdCreateContact.Visible = True
            cmdChangeDetailsConfirm.Visible = False
        Catch
            txtvFm5.Text = "Sorry, the server appears to be temporarily
➥ unavailable at the moment. Please try again."
            lnkFm5dynamic.Text = "Login"
            lnkFm5dynamic.SoftkeyLabel = "Login"
            lnkFm5dynamic.NavigateURL =
➥ "http://localhost/MyNewContacts/login.aspx"
            ActiveForm = Pg1Form5
        End Try
    End Sub

    Private Sub cmdCreateContact_Click(ByVal sender As System.Object,
➥ ByVal e As System.EventArgs) Handles cmdCreateContact.Click
        Try
            Dim myContact As DataRow
            myContact = DataSet11.Tables("Table2").NewRow

            myContact("contact_name") = txtName.Text
            myContact("contact_surname") = txtSurname.Text
            myContact("contact_address") = txtAddress.Text
            myContact("contact_city") = txtCity.Text
            myContact("contact_zip") = txtZip.Text
            myContact("contact_tel") = txtTel.Text
            myContact("contact_mobile") = txtMobile.Text
            myContact("contact_email") = txtEmail.Text
            myContact("contact_comments") = txtComments.Text
            myContact("contact_user") = User.Identity.Name

            DataSet11.Tables("Table2").Rows.Add(myContact)

            SqlDataAdapter1.Update(DataSet11, "Table2")

            ActiveForm = Pg1Form1
        Catch
            txtvFm5.Text = "Sorry, the server appears to be temporarily
➥ unavailable at the moment. Please try again."
```

```
                lnkFm5dynamic.Text = "New Contact"
                lnkFm5dynamic.SoftkeyLabel = "New Contact"
                lnkFm5dynamic.NavigateURL = "#Pg1Form3"
                ActiveForm = Pg1Form5
            End Try
        End Sub

        Private Sub cmdHomeFm2_Click(ByVal sender As System.Object, ByVal e
    ➥ As System.EventArgs) Handles cmdHomeFm2.Click
            ActiveForm = Pg1Form1
        End Sub

        Private Sub cmdHomeFm3_Click(ByVal sender As System.Object, ByVal e
    ➥ As System.EventArgs) Handles cmdHomeFm3.Click
            ActiveForm = Pg1Form1
            cmdCreateContact.Visible = True
            cmdChangeDetailsConfirm.Visible = False
        End Sub

        Private Sub cmdDeleteDeny_Click(ByVal sender As System.Object,
    ➥ ByVal e As System.EventArgs) Handles cmdDeleteDeny.Click
            ActiveForm = Pg1Form1
        End Sub

        Private Sub cmdDelete_Click(ByVal sender As System.Object, ByVal e
    ➥ As System.EventArgs) Handles cmdDelete.Click
            ActiveForm = Pg1Form4
            lblFm41.Text = lblContactName.Text
            lblFm42.Text = Session("currID")
        End Sub

        Private Sub cmdDeleteConfirm_Click(ByVal sender As System.Object,
    ➥ ByVal e As System.EventArgs) Handles cmdDeleteConfirm.Click
            Try
                DataSet11.Tables("Table2").Rows.Find(lblFm42.Text).Delete()
                SqlDataAdapter1.Update(DataSet11, "Table2")
                ActiveForm = Pg1Form1
            Catch
                txtvFm5.Text = "Sorry, the server appears to be temporarily
    ➥ unavailable at the moment. Please try again."
                lnkFm5dynamic.Text = "Delete Contact"
                lnkFm5dynamic.SoftkeyLabel = "Delete"
                lnkFm5dynamic.NavigateURL = "#Pg1Form4"
                ActiveForm = Pg1Form5
            End Try
        End Sub

        Private Sub cmdChangeDetails_Click(ByVal sender As System.Object,
    ➥ ByVal e As System.EventArgs) Handles cmdChangeDetails.Click
            Try
                Dim intCurrId
                intCurrId = Session("currID")
```

```
            ActiveForm = Pg1Form3
            cmdCreateContact.Visible = False
            cmdChangeDetailsConfirm.Visible = True
            lblFm3.Text = "Enter Changes:"
            txtName.Text = DataSet11.Tables("Table2").Rows.Find
➥(Session("currID")).Item("contact_name")
            txtSurname.Text = DataSet11.Tables("Table2").Rows.Find
➥(intCurrId).Item("contact_surname")
            txtAddress.Text = DataSet11.Tables("Table2").Rows.Find
➥(intCurrId).Item("contact_address")
            txtCity.Text = DataSet11.Tables("Table2").Rows.Find
➥(intCurrId).Item("contact_city")
            txtZip.Text = DataSet11.Tables("Table2").Rows.Find
➥(intCurrId).Item("contact_zip")
            txtTel.Text = DataSet11.Tables("Table2").Rows.Find
➥(intCurrId).Item("contact_tel")
            txtMobile.Text = DataSet11.Tables("Table2").Rows.Find
➥(intCurrId).Item("contact_mobile")
            txtEmail.Text = DataSet11.Tables("Table2").Rows.Find
➥(intCurrId).Item("contact_email")
            txtComments.Text = DataSet11.Tables("Table2").Rows.Find
➥(intCurrId).Item("contact_comments")
        Catch
            txtvFm5.Text = "Sorry, the server appears to be temporarily
➥ unavailable at the moment. Please try again."
            lnkFm5dynamic.Text = "Details"
            lnkFm5dynamic.SoftkeyLabel = "Details"
            lnkFm5dynamic.NavigateURL = "#Pg1Form2"
            ActiveForm = Pg1Form5
        End Try
    End Sub

    Private Sub cmdChangeDetailsConfirm_Click(ByVal sender As
➥ System.Object, ByVal e As System.EventArgs) Handles
➥ cmdChangeDetailsConfirm.Click
        Try
            Dim intCurrId As Integer = Session("currID")
            cmdCreateContact.Visible = True
            cmdChangeDetailsConfirm.Visible = False
            DataSet11.Tables("Table2").Rows.Find(intCurrId).Item
➥("contact_name") = txtName.Text
            DataSet11.Tables("Table2").Rows.Find(intCurrId).Item
➥("contact_surname") = txtSurname.Text
            DataSet11.Tables("Table2").Rows.Find(intCurrId).Item
➥("contact_address") = txtAddress.Text
            DataSet11.Tables("Table2").Rows.Find(intCurrId).Item
➥("contact_city") = txtCity.Text
            DataSet11.Tables("Table2").Rows.Find(intCurrId).Item
➥("contact_zip") = txtZip.Text
            DataSet11.Tables("Table2").Rows.Find(intCurrId).Item
➥("contact_tel") = txtTel.Text
```

```
            DataSet11.Tables("Table2").Rows.Find(intCurrId).Item
➡("contact_mobile") = txtMobile.Text
            DataSet11.Tables("Table2").Rows.Find(intCurrId).Item
➡("contact_email") = txtEmail.Text
            DataSet11.Tables("Table2").Rows.Find(intCurrId).Item
➡("contact_comments") = txtComments.Text
            SqlDataAdapter1.Update(DataSet11, "Table2")
            ActiveForm = Pg1Form2
        Catch
            txtvFm5.Text = "Sorry, the server appears to be temporarily
➡ unavailable at the moment. Please try again."
            lnkFm5dynamic.Text = "Change Details"
            lnkFm5dynamic.SoftkeyLabel = "Change Details"
            lnkFm5dynamic.NavigateURL = "#Pg1Form3"
            ActiveForm = Pg1Form5
        End Try

    End Sub

    Private Sub Pg1Form3_Activate(ByVal sender As System.Object, ByVal
➡ e As System.EventArgs) Handles Pg1Form3.Activate
        txtName.Text = " "
        txtSurname.Text = " "
        txtAddress.Text = " "
        txtCity.Text = " "
        txtZip.Text = " "
        txtTel.Text = " "
        txtMobile.Text = " "
        txtEmail.Text = " "
        txtComments.Text = " "
    End Sub


End Class
```

Most of this code is the same as that used in the original MyContacts application. Some key differences occur in the Page_Load and Pg1Form1_Activate subroutines. We also make use of the SqlDataAdapters rather that the OleDbDataadapters throughout the application.

Unlike the original MyContacts application, in MyNewContacts we make use of two DataView objects.

As with MyContacts, we use DataView1 to provide us with a snapshot view of the details associated with a particular contact chosen from lstContacts.

We use DataView2 to provide a data snapshot of the contact records associated with the particular user. Pg1Form1_Activate handles this and the user is identified using User .Identity.Name, which contains the user ID. The records returned by the row filter in

DataView2 are used to fill lstContacts. Thus we can present the user with only those contacts listed against them in the database.

When a user creates a new contact, the record is created with that particular user's ID in the contact_user field of the database. This is handled in cmdCreateContact_Click by the myContact("contact_user") = User.Identity.Name code.

In Page_Load we use SqlDataAdapter2 with a search parameter derived from User .Identity.Name to identify the username from the database. This enables us to personalize the Pg1Form1 with the user's name.

We have also added exception handlers (Try...Catch...End Try), where appropriate, to trap likely runtime errors and navigate the user to the error form (Pg1Form5).

We then need to switch to HTML View and add some additional code directly to the ASPX page to handle the databinding for the List control and the LogOut procedure. Between the <meta> and <body> tags, add the following code:

```
<script language="vb" runat="server" ID="Script1">
protected sub List_bind(Sender as object, e as ListDataBindEventArgs)
    e.ListItem.Text = String.Format ("{0} {1}", DataBinder.Eval(e.DataItem,
➡ "contact_name"),  DataBinder.Eval(e.DataItem, "contact_surname"))
end sub
protected sub LogOut_Click(o as Object, e as EventArgs)
    FormsAuthentication.SignOut
    ActiveForm=Pg1Form6
end sub

</script>
```

Scroll down to the <mobile:List> tag in Pg1Form1 and update it to the following line of code:

```
<mobile:List id=lstContacts runat="server" DataValueField="contact_id"
➡ DataTextField="contact_name" DataMember="Table2" DataSource="<%#
➡ DataView2 %>" OnItemDataBind="List_bind">
    </mobile:List>
```

Then scroll through to the cmdLogout tag and complete it to the following:

```
<mobile:Command id="cmdLogout" onclick="LogOut_Click" runat="server"
➡ SoftkeyLabel="LgOut">Log Out</mobile:Command>
```

Listing 20.4 shows how the full ASPX code should look for this project.

## Finishing Touches

As we have done with previous applications, we need to make a couple of final adjustments before deploying the application.

We need to edit our `Web.config` file to ensure that everything will work as it should across the various mobile device/browser/gateway combinations.

Open up `Web.config` from the Solution Explorer window and ensure that the `<httpRuntime useFullyQualifiedRedirectUrl="true" />` tag is set in the `<system.web>` section as explained in Chapter 8, "A Deeper Look at the Mobile Internet Toolkit and VB .Net."

Scroll down to the `<sessionState>` tag and set it to `cookieless="true"`.

Once we have tested and debugged the application, to improve runtime performance, set `debug="false"` in the `<compilation>` tag. Save the changes.

## Expanding and Enhancing the Application

As with many of the other applications we have looked at in this book, this project is very open ended with what we might wish to do with it. Some obvious enhancements include the following:

- Rather than just presenting the user's available contacts as a list, include a search facility to locate the desired contact.

- A search facility could be further developed with a list of commonly used or preferred contacts displayed when the application opens.

- Include "call" facilities against the contacts' telephone numbers.

- Set up the database to enable users to "share" contacts.

- Create a greater range of data fields in the database, enabling more information and cross referencing of contacts.

- Identify and establish performance improvements (such as use of the SQLDataReader where appropriate and a less heavy-handed approach to exception handling).

## Running the Application

When a user accesses the MyNewContacts application, they are first directed to the `login.aspx` form as depicted in Figure 20.19.

Once the user has successfully authenticated, they are redirected to the main Mobile Web Page and presented with a personalized form containing a list of their contacts (see Figure 20.20).

FIGURE 20.19:

FIGURE 20.19:

The login card for
MyNewContacts

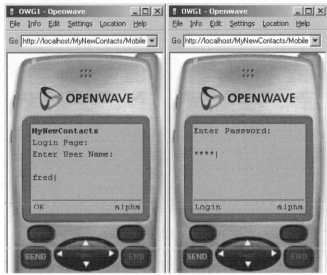

Image of UP.SDK courtesy Openwave Systems, Inc.

FIGURE 20.20:

The opening card of
the MyNewContacts
application

Image of UP.SDK courtesy Openwave Systems, Inc.

The remainder of the application operates as it did for MyContacts. We can select a contact from the list and view their details (Figure 20.21) and edit, delete, or create new contacts. We have also included an autodial facility with the PhoneCall controls for each contact's telephone and mobile numbers.

FIGURE 20.21:

Contact details as displayed in the MyNewContacts application

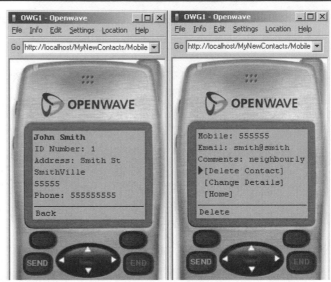

Image of UP.SDK courtesy Openwave Systems, Inc.

Any application errors that occur should be trapped by the exception handling that we have included in the code and be directed to the error form (Pg1Form5).

When a user wishes to logout, they should use the LogOut option on the first form. (A further improvement to this application may be to extend this functionality to all forms.) This ensures that their authenticated session is closed down. You can test this in Internet Explorer: Login and close off the application without clicking LogOut. Immediately run the application again and you should be given instant access to contact details without having to login again. (This will eventually expire.) If you choose the Logout option, however, you will be asked for authentication again the next time you login.

## Full ASPX Code Listing for MobileWebForm1

Listing 20.4 contains the full ASPX code for MobileWebForm1.

**Listing 20.4**    **Full ASPX Code for MobileWebForm1**

```
<%@ Import Namespace="System.Web.Mobile" %>
<%@ Import Namespace="System.Web.Security" %>
<%@ Register TagPrefix="mobile"
➥ Namespace="System.Web.UI.MobileControls"
➥ Assembly="System.Web.Mobile, Version=1.0.3300.0, Culture=neutral,
➥ PublicKeyToken=b03f5f7f11d50a3a" %>
```

```
<%@ Page Language="vb" AutoEventWireup="false"
➥ Codebehind="MobileWebForm1.aspx.vb"
➥ Inherits="MyNewContacts.MobileWebForm1" %>
<meta name="GENERATOR" content="Microsoft Visual Studio.NET 7.0">
<meta name="CODE_LANGUAGE" content="Visual Basic 7.0">
<meta name="vs_targetSchema"
➥ content="http://schemas.microsoft.com/Mobile/Page">
<script language="vb" runat="server" ID="Script1">
protected sub List_bind(Sender as object, e as ListDataBindEventArgs)
   e.ListItem.Text = String.Format ("{0} {1}",
➥ DataBinder.Eval(e.DataItem, "contact_name"),
➥ DataBinder.Eval(e.DataItem, "contact_surname"))
end sub
protected sub LogOut_Click(o as Object, e as EventArgs)
   FormsAuthentication.SignOut
   ActiveForm=Pg1Form6
end sub
</script>
<body Xmlns:mobile="http://schemas.microsoft.com/Mobile/WebForm">
   <mobile:form id="Pg1Form1" runat="server"
➥ PagerStyle-PreviousPageText="Return to Page {0}"
➥ PagerStyle-NextPageText="Go to Page {0}" Paginate="True"
➥ title="MyNewContacts - List">
      <mobile:Label id="lblFm1" runat="server"
➥ StyleReference="title"></mobile:Label>
      <mobile:List id="lstContacts" runat="server"
➥ DataValueField="contact_id" DataTextField="contact_name"
➥ DataMember="Table2" DataSource="<%# DataView2 %>"
➥ OnItemDataBind="List_bind"></mobile:List>
<mobile:Command id="cmdNewContact" runat="server"
➥ SoftkeyLabel="Cntct">New Contact</mobile:Command>
<mobile:Command id="cmdLogout" onclick="LogOut_Click" runat="server"
➥ SoftkeyLabel="LgOut">Log Out</mobile:Command>
   </mobile:form>
   <mobile:form id="Pg1Form2" title="MyNewContacts - Details"
➥ runat="server">

<mobile:Label id="lblContactName" runat="server" StyleReference="title"
➥ Text='<%# String.Format ("{0} {1}", DataBinder.Eval
➥(DataView1, "[0].contact_name"), DataBinder.Eval
➥(DataView1, "[0].contact_surname")) %>'></mobile:Label>ID
Number:
<mobile:Label id="lblID" runat="server" Font-Size="Small"
➥ Text='<%# DataBinder.Eval(DataView1, "[0].contact_id", "{0}")
➥ %>'></mobile:Label>Address:
<mobile:Label id="lblAddress" runat="server" Font-Size="Small"
➥ Text='<%# DataBinder.Eval(DataView1, "[0].contact_address", "{0}")
➥ %>'></mobile:Label>
<mobile:Label id="lblCity" runat="server" Font-Size="Small"
➥ Text='<%# DataBinder.Eval(DataView1, "[0].contact_city", "{0}")
➥ %>'></mobile:Label>
```

```
<mobile:Label id="lblZip" runat="server" Font-Size="Small"
➡ Text='<%# DataBinder.Eval(DataView1, "[0].contact_zip", "{0}")
➡ %>'></mobile:Label>Phone:
<mobile:Label id="lblTel" runat="server" Font-Size="Small"
➡ Text='<%# DataBinder.Eval(DataView1, "[0].contact_tel", "{0}")
➡ %>'></mobile:Label>
<mobile:PhoneCall id="pcllTel" runat="server" SoftkeyLabel="Call"
➡ Font-Size="Small" PhoneNumber="0"
➡ AlternateFormat="{0}">Call</mobile:PhoneCall> Mobile:
<mobile:Label id="lblMobile" runat="server" Font-Size="Small"
➡ Text='<%# DataBinder.Eval(DataView1, "[0].contact_mobile", "{0}"
➡) %>'></mobile:Label>
<mobile:PhoneCall id="pcllMob" runat="server" SoftkeyLabel="Call"
➡ Font-Size="Small" PhoneNumber="0"
➡ AlternateFormat="{0}">Call</mobile:PhoneCall> Email:
<mobile:Label id="lblEmail" runat="server" Font-Size="Small"
➡ Text='<%# DataBinder.Eval(DataView1, "[0].contact_email", "{0}")
➡ %>'></mobile:Label>Comments:
<mobile:TextView id="txtvComments" runat="server"
➡ Font-Size="Small" Text='<%# DataBinder.Eval
➡(DataView1, "[0].contact_comments", "{0}") %>'></mobile:TextView>
<mobile:Command id="cmdDelete" runat="server"
➡ SoftkeyLabel="Delet">Delete Contact</mobile:Command>
<mobile:Command id="cmdChangeDetails" runat="server"
➡ SoftkeyLabel="Chnge">Change Details</mobile:Command>
<mobile:Command id="cmdHomeFm2" runat="server"
➡ SoftkeyLabel="Home">Home</mobile:Command>
    </mobile:form>
    <mobile:form id="Pg1Form3" runat="server"
➡ title="MyNewContacts - DataEntry">

<mobile:Label id="lblFm3" runat="server"
➡ StyleReference="title"></mobile:Label>Name:
<mobile:TextBox id="txtName" runat="server"></mobile:TextBox>Surname:
<mobile:TextBox id="txtSurname"
➡ runat="server"></mobile:TextBox>Address:
<mobile:TextBox id="txtAddress" runat="server"></mobile:TextBox>City:
<mobile:TextBox id="txtCity" runat="server"></mobile:TextBox>Zip:
<mobile:TextBox id="txtZip" runat="server"></mobile:TextBox>Telephone:
<mobile:TextBox id="txtTel" runat="server"></mobile:TextBox>Mobile:
<mobile:TextBox id="txtMobile" runat="server"></mobile:TextBox>Email:
<mobile:TextBox id="txtEmail" runat="server"></mobile:TextBox>Comments:
<mobile:TextBox id="txtComments" runat="server"></mobile:TextBox>
<mobile:Command id="cmdCreateContact" runat="server"
➡ SoftkeyLabel="Cntct">Create New Contact</mobile:Command>
<mobile:Command id="cmdChangeDetailsConfirm" runat="server"
➡ SoftkeyLabel="Chnge" Visible="False">Change
➡ Details</mobile:Command>
<mobile:Command id="cmdHomeFm3" runat="server"
➡ SoftkeyLabel="Home">Home</mobile:Command>
    </mobile:form>
```

```
        <mobile:form id="Pg1Form4"
➥ title="MyNewContacts - Delete" runat="server">

<mobile:Label id="lblFm4" runat="server" StyleReference="title">Do you
➥ wish to delete the record for:</mobile:Label>
<mobile:Label id="lblFm41" runat="server"></mobile:Label>Record
➥ Number:
<mobile:Label id="lblFm42" runat="server"></mobile:Label>
<mobile:Command id="cmdDeleteConfirm" runat="server"
➥ SoftkeyLabel="Yes">Yes</mobile:Command>
<mobile:Command id="cmdDeleteDeny" runat="server"
➥ SoftkeyLabel="No">No</mobile:Command>
        </mobile:form>
        <mobile:form id="Pg1Form5" runat="server"
➥ title="MyNewContacts - Error">
            <mobile:Label id="lblFm5" runat="server"
➥ StyleReference="title">MyNewContacts</mobile:Label>
            <mobile:TextView id="txtvFm5"
➥ runat="server"></mobile:TextView>
            <mobile:Link id="lnkFm5dynamic"
➥ runat="server"></mobile:Link>
        </mobile:form>
<mobile:Form id="Pg1Form6" runat="server"
➥ title="MyNewContacts - LogOut">
            <mobile:Label id="lblFm6" runat="server"
➥ StyleReference="title">MyNewContacts</mobile:Label>
            <mobile:Label id="lblFm61" runat="server">Logged
➥ Out</mobile:Label>
        </mobile:Form>
</body>
```

## Summary

As we can see from this application, there is little practical difference from a coding point of view in implementing a solution using SqlDataAdapters or using OleDbDataAdapters. However, there is a big difference in performance between the implementations. We gain the advantage of the fact that the SqlDataConnection objects are optimized to work with SQL Server as well as the power of SQL Server itself.

Forms-based authentication offers an extra layer of security to our application, and we can also pass the user identity through to the remainder of the application from the authentication process. Additionally, other authentication options such as Passport are also becoming available, granting the developer a wider range of options for developing secure applications with the Mobile Internet Toolkit.

# CHAPTER 21

# RockPaperScissors: An Online Game

- Examining the rationale

- Planning the application

- Creating the images

- Creating the Mobile Web Page

- Writing the code behind

- Adding the finishing touches

- Running the application

- Reviewing the full ASPX code listing

In Chapter 4, "An Example of Mobile Technology: WAP and WML," we saw how to create an online game using ASP and WML (Listings 4.7 and 4.8). In this chapter, we will build the same game using the Mobile Internet Toolkit.

This will help give some practical understanding of why ASP.NET is not backward compatible with ASP, and we will see some of the steps that we need to take to port an application from ASP to ASP.NET. We will also see some of the benefits in designing and building an application using the MIT over more traditional technologies.

We can also take the opportunity to make some enhancements to the original game by adding some images and using the `MobileCapabilities` object and `HasCapabilities` method to assign different images, depending on the client device.

## Rationale

Games are proving to be the same driving force in the mobile computing industry as they continue to be for the "big screen" desktop industry. Games may be either embedded on the actual device itself or delivered through a medium such WAP. After a bit of a slow start, the second option is beginning to prove very popular as it provides a way for cell phone users to access a greater variety of games.

As mobile device and display technology improves and connection speeds increase, we will undoubtedly see an increasing demand for these types of applications. (Now, if the telephone companies would only lower their WAP rates to a level that encourages rather than discourages the average user to use the technology…)

The RockPaperScissors game will be functionally identical to the game designed in Chapter 4. The player is presented with a simple welcome screen, clicks a link to enter the game, and then chooses from "Rock," "Paper," or "Scissors." The player is then presented with the consequences of their choice and invited to play another game. A progressive score is kept along with the number of games played.

We will include a logo image and make use of rock, paper, and scissors images as part of the game play. We can use at least two levels of images to take advantage of devices capable of supporting color as well as maintaining the basic WBMP images for your more typical cell-phone browsers.

## Planning the Application

As we covered the design and build of this game in detail in Chapter 4, we will just briefly cover major elements here.

Figure 21.1 illustrates the overall structure of the game.

Form (card) structure for the revised RockPaperScissors game

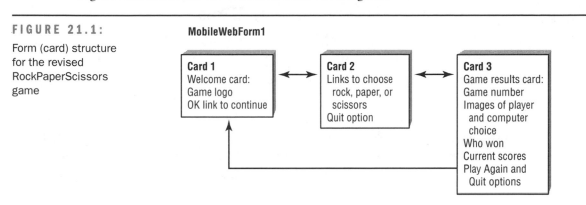

## Creating the Images

Use your favorite WBMP editor (for example, the one contained in the Nokia SDK) to create three simple images, such as the ones illustrated in Figure 21.2. (Again, I have exercised my artistic talents to their utmost!) Note that the images are shown in Figure 21.2 at 200 percent magnification. I created my images on 30 × 30 pixel canvas. Save the images as rock.wbmp, paper.wbmp, and scissors.wbmp.

Game images for the RockPaperScissors game

Combine the three images into two new images that we can use as game logos. The first image (lot.wbmp) I created for use with the UP.Browser, and the second image (lotNok.wbmp) I created for use with the slightly less tolerant Nokia Blueprint emulator screen. The lot.wbmp was set to 90 × 30 pixels (see Figure 21.3).

lot.wbmp image for use with the UP.Browser

Create the lotNok.wbmp image at a smaller 60 × 30 pixels. Refer Figure 21.4.

**FIGURE 21.4:**

lotNok.wbmp for
use with the Nokia
Blueprint emulator

Note that these images have been designed to work in the emulator screens; you may have to adjust the sizes again for "live" use.

We now need to create some color GIF images for use with browsers capable of color support. I used the images illustrated in Figure 21.5 as the game images and named them rock.gif, paper.gif, and scissors.gif. These images are shown at their normal size.

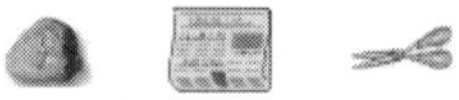

**FIGURE 21.5:**

Color game images
for use in RockPaper-
Scissors game

Figure 21.6 illustrates the combined logo of the color images (again shown at normal size), lot.gif.

**FIGURE 21.6:**

lot.gif for use
with color-capable
browsers

Save the images in a convenient place. Once the directories have been created for this application, create an Images folder in the root directory for the game default, c:\\Inetpub\ wwwroot\RockPaperScissors, and move the images into it.

## Creating the Mobile Web Page

Open a new Mobile Web Application in Visual Studio .NET and name it RockPaperScissors.

Create three Form controls on MobileWebForm1, and set the controls and properties according to Table 21.1.

**TABLE 21.1:** Control and Property Settings for RockPaperScissors

| Form | Control | Property | Value |
|------|---------|----------|-------|
| Form1 | Label | Font | True |
| | | Bold | True |
| | | ForeColor | Red |

*Continued on next page*

**TABLE 21.1 CONTINUED:**  Control and Property Settings for RockPaperScissors

| Form | Control | Property | Value |
|------|---------|----------|-------|
| | | Text | RockPaperScissors |
| | | ID | lblFm1 |
| | Image | Alternatetext | GameImage |
| | | ID | imgFm1 |
| | Label | Text | Care for a Game? |
| | | ID | lblFm11 |
| | Label | Text | Ready For a Challenge? |
| | | ID | lblFm12 |
| | Label | Text | Select OK to Continue |
| | | ID | lblFm12 |
| | Link | Text | OK |
| | | SoftKeyLabel | OK |
| | | ID | lnkFm1Fm2 |
| | | NavigateURL | #Form1 |
| Form2 | Label | Font | True |
| | | Bold | True |
| | | ForeColor | Red |
| | | Text | RockPaperScissors |
| | | ID | lblFm2 |
| | Label | Text | Which will you choose??? |
| | | ID | lbFm21 |
| | Control | Text | Rock beats Scissors |
| | | SoftKeyLabel | Rock |
| | | ID | cmdRock |
| | Control | Text | Scissors beats Paper |
| | | SoftKeyLabel | Scissors |
| | | ID | cmdScissors |
| | Control | Text | Paper beats Rock |
| | | SoftKeyLabel | Paper |
| | | ID | cmdPaper |
| | Control | Text | Quit Game |
| | | SoftKeyLabel | Quit |
| | | ID | cmdQuitFm2 |
| Form3 | Label | Font | True |
| | | Bold | True |
| | | ForeColor | Red |

*Continued on next page*

**TABLE 21.1 CONTINUED:** Control and Property Settings for RockPaperScissors

| Form | Control | Property | Value |
|------|---------|----------|-------|
| | | Text | RockPaperScissors |
| | | ID | lblFm3 |
| | Label | Text | <empty> |
| | | ID | lblGameNumber |
| | Label | Text | You Chose: |
| | | ID | lblFm31 |
| | Image | Alignment | Center |
| | | ID | imgYourChoice |
| | Label | Text | I Chose: |
| | | ID | lblFm32 |
| | Image | Alignment | Center |
| | | ID | ImgMyChoice |
| | Label | Text | <empty> |
| | | ID | lblWin |
| | Label | Text | <empty> |
| | | ID | lblYourScore |
| | Label | Text | <empty> |
| | | ID | lblMyScore |
| | Control | Text | Play again? |
| | | SoftKeyLabel | Play |
| | | ID | cmdPlayAgain |
| | Control | Text | Quit Game |
| | | SoftKeyLabel | Quit |
| | | ID | cmdQuitFm3 |

The main difference between this version of the application and the one we built back in Chapter 4 is that we only use three cards in this version, combining the function of Cards 3 and 4 from the original game.

Figures 21.7 and 21.8 illustrate how the completed forms should appear in Design View.

FIGURE 21.7:

Forms 1 and 2 of the RockPaperScissors game

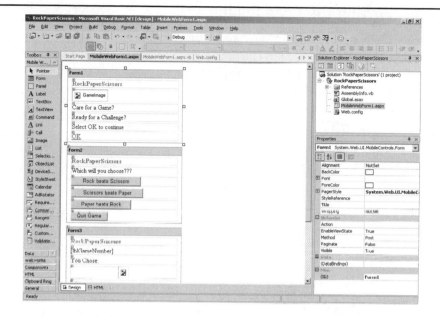

FIGURE 21.8:

Forms 2 and 3 of the RockPaperScissors game

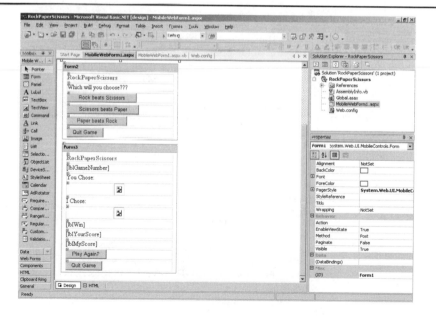

## Writing the Code Behind

Listing 21.1 contains the code behind for this application. It is essentially the same game engine that we used in Chapter 4, and if you compare the code, you will see that there are very few differences. We have added in some extra functionality to cater for different device capabilities with images.

---

**Listing 21.1**      **Code Behind for RockPaperScissors**

```
Private Sub Page_Load(ByVal sender As System.Object, ByVal e As
➡ System.EventArgs) Handles MyBase.Load
        If Not Page.IsPostBack Then
            Session("gamenum") = 0
            Session("myscore") = 0
            Session("yourscore") = 0
        End If
    End Sub

    Private Sub Form1_Activate(ByVal sender As System.Object, ByVal e
➡ As System.EventArgs) Handles Form1.Activate
        Dim imageProperties As Mobile.MobileCapabilities =
➡ Request.Browser

        If imageProperties.HasCapability("IsColor", True) Then
            imgFm1.ImageURL =
➡ "http://localhost/RockPaperScissors/images/lot.gif"
        ElseIf imageProperties.Browser() = "Nokia" Then
            imgFm1.ImageURL =
➡ "http://localhost/RockPaperScissors/images/lotNok.wbmp"
        Else
            imgFm1.ImageURL =
➡ "http://localhost/RockPaperScissors/images/lot.wbmp"
        End If
    End Sub

    Private Sub cmdRock_Click(ByVal sender As System.Object, ByVal e As
➡ System.EventArgs) Handles cmdRock.Click
        Session("choice") = "rock"
        Session("gamenum") = Session("gamenum") + 1
        ActiveForm = Form3
    End Sub

    Private Sub cmdScissors_Click(ByVal sender As System.Object, ByVal
➡ e As System.EventArgs) Handles cmdScissors.Click
        Session("choice") = "scissors"
        Session("gamenum") = Session("gamenum") + 1
        ActiveForm = Form3
    End Sub
```

```
    Private Sub cmdPaper_Click(ByVal sender As System.Object, ByVal e
➡ As System.EventArgs) Handles cmdPaper.Click
        Session("choice") = "paper"
        Session("gamenum") = Session("gamenum") + 1
        ActiveForm = Form3
    End Sub

    Private Sub cmdQuitFm2_Click(ByVal sender As System.Object, ByVal e
➡ As System.EventArgs) Handles cmdQuitFm2.Click
        Session("gamenum") = 0
        Session("myscore") = 0
        Session("yourscore") = 0
        ActiveForm = Form1
    End Sub

    Private Sub Form3_Activate(ByVal sender As System.Object, ByVal e
➡ As System.EventArgs) Handles Form3.Activate
        Dim intMyChoice As Integer
        Dim intResult As Integer
        Dim strRockURL As String
        Dim strScissorsURL As String
        Dim strPaperURL As String
        Dim imageProperties As Mobile.MobileCapabilities =
➡ Request.Browser

        If imageProperties.HasCapability("IsColor", True) Then
            strRockURL =
➡ "http://localhost/RockPaperScissors/images/rock.gif"
            strScissorsURL =
➡ "http://localhost/RockPaperScissors/images/scissors.gif"
            strPaperURL =
➡ "http://localhost/RockPaperScissors/images/paper.gif"
        Else
            strRockURL =
➡ "http://localhost/RockPaperScissors/images/rock.wbmp"
            strScissorsURL =
➡ "http://localhost/RockPaperScissors/images/scissors.wbmp"
            strPaperURL =
➡ "http://localhost/RockPaperScissors/images/paper.wbmp"
        End If

        lblGameNumber.Text = "Game Number: " & Session("gamenum")
        Select Case Session("choice")
            Case Is = "rock"
                imgYourChoice.ImageURL = strRockURL
                imgYourChoice.AlternateText = "Rock"
            Case Is = "scissors"
                imgYourChoice.ImageURL = strScissorsURL
                imgYourChoice.AlternateText = "Scissors"
            Case Is = "paper"
                imgYourChoice.ImageURL = strPaperURL
```

```
                imgYourChoice.AlternateText = "Paper"
        End Select
        intMyChoice = (Int(Rnd() * 3)) + 1
        Select Case intMyChoice
            Case Is = 1 'rock
                imgMyChoice.ImageURL = strRockURL
                imgMyChoice.AlternateText = "Rock"
                If Session("choice") = "rock" Then
                    intResult = 2 'game drawn
                ElseIf Session("choice") = "scissors" Then
                    intResult = 0 'player loses
                ElseIf Session("choice") = "paper" Then
                    intResult = 1 'player wins
                End If
            Case Is = 2 'scissors
                imgMyChoice.ImageURL = strScissorsURL
                imgMyChoice.AlternateText = "Scissors"
                If Session("choice") = "rock" Then
                    intResult = 1
                ElseIf Session("choice") = "scissors" Then
                    intResult = 2
                ElseIf Session("choice") = "paper" Then
                    intResult = 0
                End If
            Case Is = 3 'paper
                imgMyChoice.ImageURL = strPaperURL
                imgMyChoice.AlternateText = "Paper"
                If Session("choice") = "rock" Then
                    intResult = 0
                ElseIf Session("choice") = "scissors" Then
                    intResult = 1
                ElseIf Session("choice") = "paper" Then
                    intResult = 2
                End If
        End Select
        Select Case intResult
            Case Is = 0
                lblWin.Text = "I Won!!!"
                Session("myscore") = Session("myscore") + 1
            Case Is = 1
                lblWin.Text = "You Won!!!"
                Session("yourscore") = Session("yourscore") + 1
            Case Is = 2
                lblWin.Text = "We drew!!!"
        End Select
        lblYourScore.Text = "Your score is: " & Session("yourscore")
        lblMyScore.Text = "My score is: " & Session("myscore")

    End Sub
```

```
    Private Sub cmdPlayAgain_Click(ByVal sender As System.Object, ByVal
➡ e As System.EventArgs) Handles cmdPlayAgain.Click
        ActiveForm = Form2
    End Sub

    Private Sub cmdQuitFm3_Click(ByVal sender As System.Object, ByVal e
➡ As System.EventArgs) Handles cmdQuitFm3.Click
        Session("gamenum") = 0
        Session("myscore") = 0
        Session("yourscore") = 0
        ActiveForm = Form1
    End Sub

End Class
```

Examining the code, we find much that is familiar from the original Chapter 4 RockPaper-Scissors game. On Page_Load we establish the key session variables and set them to zero. This code is not executed on post-back to avoid resetting the session variables every time the player chooses to play another round.

In the Form1_Activate subroutine, we use our MobileCapabilities to determine whether the client is capable of supporting the color heading and then deliver the appropriate image to the device as illustrated in the following code snippet:

```
Private Sub Form1_Activate(ByVal sender As System.Object, ByVal e
➡ As System.EventArgs) Handles Form1.Activate
        Dim imageProperties As Mobile.MobileCapabilities =
➡ Request.Browser

        If imageProperties.HasCapability("IsColor", True) Then
            imgFm1.ImageURL =
➡ "http://localhost/RockPaperScissors/images/lot.gif"
        ElseIf imageProperties.Browser() = "Nokia" Then
            imgFm1.ImageURL =
➡ "http://localhost/RockPaperScissors/images/lotNok.wbmp"
        Else
            imgFm1.ImageURL =
➡ "http://localhost/RockPaperScissors/images/lot.wbmp"
        End If
    End Sub
```

We then have the event handlers for the click event of each of the three game-play Command controls on Form2. Selecting one of the controls increments the gamenum session variable by 1 and sets the player choice session variable (choice) to the appropriate value.

Selecting the Quit command on Form2 returns the player to Form1 and resets the appropriate session variables to zero. This is handled by the cmdQuitFm2_Click subroutine.

```
Private Sub cmdQuitFm2_Click(ByVal sender As System.Object, ByVal e
➡ As System.EventArgs) Handles cmdQuitFm2.Click
      Session("gamenum") = 0
      Session("myscore") = 0
      Session("yourscore") = 0
      ActiveForm = Form1
   End Sub
```

The main game engine is found in the code for Form3_Activate. This is largely unchanged from the original game except that we display the results as images rather than text and use the `MobileCapabilities` object to determine the appropriate image to display on the client device being used.

We then finish with a simple navigation option to play another game or another option to quit the game.

We also need to add some device-specific behavior to the image tags on Form3. We can do this using Property Overrides in Design View or by adding the following device-specific code to the image tags in Form3. (You will need to add this snippet to both sets of image tags.)

```
<mobile:Image id="imgYourChoice" runat="server" Alignment="Center">
        <DeviceSpecific>
            <Choice Filter="isHTML32" Alignment="Left"></Choice>
        </DeviceSpecific>
</mobile:Image>
```

The code ensures that the images stay with the rest of the application when viewed in a large browser, such as Internet Explorer. (Otherwise, they are centered on the page and the whole thing looks faintly ridiculous!) Refer to Listing 21.1 for the full ASPX listing for this application.

## Finishing Touches

As we have done with previous applications, we need to make a couple of final adjustments before deploying the application. We need to edit our `Web.config` file to ensure that everything will work as it should across the various mobile device/browser/gateway combinations.

Open up `Web.config` from the Solution Explorer window and check that the `<httpRuntime useFullyQualifiedRedirectUrl="true" />` tag is set in the `<system.web>` section as explained in Chapter 8, "A Deeper Look at the Mobile Internet Toolkit and VB .NET." Scroll down to the `<sessionState>` tag and set `cookieless="true"`.

Once we have tested and debugged the application, to improve runtime performance, set `debug="false"` in the `<compilation>` tag. Save the changes.

## Running the Application

Figures 21.9 through to 21.14 illustrate the RockPaperScissors game running in both the Openwave browser and MME.

Opening form of
RockPaperscissors
in Openwave

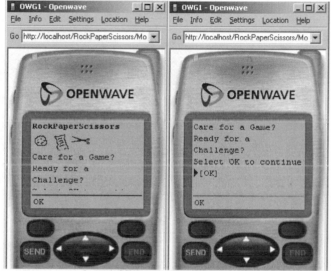

Image of UP.SDK courtesy Openwave Systems, Inc.

Opening form of
RockPaperScissors
in MME

Form2 of
RockPaperScissors
in Openwave

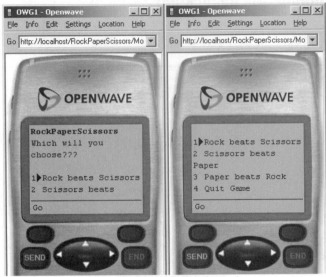

Image of UP.SDK courtesy Openwave Systems, Inc.

Form2 of
RockPaperScissors
in MME

**FIGURE 21.13:**

Form3 of
RockPaperScissors
in Openwave

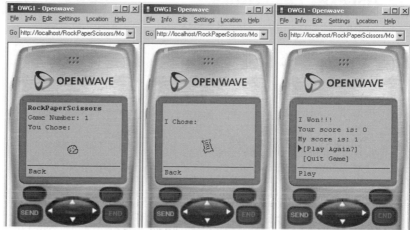

Image of UP.SDK courtesy Openwave Systems, Inc.

**FIGURE 21.14:**

Form3 of
RockPaperScissors
in MME

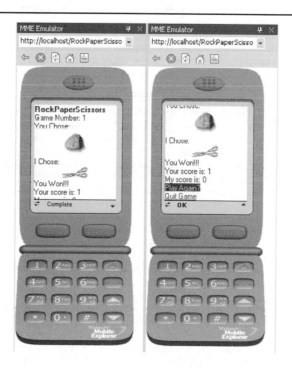

## Full ASPX Code Listing

Listing 21.2 contains the full ASPX code for this application.

**Listing 21.2**      **ASPX Code for RockpaperSeissors Game**

```
<%@ Register TagPrefix="mobile"
➥ Namespace="System.Web.UI.MobileControls"
➥ Assembly="System.Web.Mobile, Version=1.0.3300.0, Culture=neutral,
➥ PublicKeyToken=b03f5f7f11d50a3a" %>
<%@ Page Language="vb" AutoEventWireup="false"
➥ Codebehind="MobileWebForm1.aspx.vb"
➥ Inherits="RockPaperScissors.MobileWebForm1" %>
<meta name="GENERATOR" content="Microsoft Visual Studio.NET 7.0">
<meta name="CODE_LANGUAGE" content="Visual Basic 7.0">
<meta name="vs_targetSchema"
➥ content="http://schemas.microsoft.com/Mobile/Page">
<body Xmlns:mobile="http://schemas.microsoft.com/Mobile/WebForm">
    <mobile:form id="Form1" runat="server">
        <mobile:Label id="lblFm1" runat="server"
➥ ForeColor="Red"
➥ Font-Bold="True">RockPaperScissors</mobile:Label>
        <mobile:Image id="imgFm1" runat="server"
➥ AlternateText="GameImage"></mobile:Image>
        <mobile:Label id="lblFm11" runat="server">Care for a
➥ Game?</mobile:Label>
        <mobile:Label id="lblFm12" runat="server">Ready for a
➥ Challenge?</mobile:Label>
        <mobile:Label id="lblFm13" runat="server">Select OK
➥ to
➥ continue</mobile:Label>
        <mobile:Link id="lnkFm1Fm2" runat="server"
➥ NavigateURL="#Form2"
➥ SoftkeyLabel="OK">OK</mobile:Link>
    </mobile:form>
    <mobile:form id="Form2" runat="server">
        <mobile:Label id="lblFm2" runat="server"
➥ ForeColor="Red"
➥ Font-Bold="True">RockPaperScissors</mobile:Label>
        <mobile:Label id="lblFm21" runat="server">Which will
➥ you
➥ choose???</mobile:Label>
        <mobile:Command id="cmdRock" runat="server"
➥ SoftkeyLabel="Rock">Rock beats Scissors</mobile:Command>
        <mobile:Command id="cmdScissors" runat="server"
➥ SoftkeyLabel="Scissors">Scissors beats Paper</mobile:Command>
        <mobile:Command id="cmdPaper" runat="server"
➥ SoftkeyLabel="Paper">Paper beats Rock</mobile:Command>
        <mobile:Command id="cmdQuitFm2" runat="server"
➥ SoftkeyLabel="Quit">Quit Game</mobile:Command>
    </mobile:form>
```

```
        <mobile:form id="Form3" runat="server">
            <mobile:Label id="lblFm3" runat="server"
➡ ForeColor="Red"
➡ Font-Bold="True">RockPaperScissors</mobile:Label>
            <mobile:Label id="lblGameNumber"
➡ runat="server"></mobile:Label>
            <mobile:Label id="lblFm31" runat="server">You
➡ Chose:</mobile:Label>
            <mobile:Image id="imgYourChoice" runat="server"
➡ Alignment="Center">
                <DeviceSpecific>
                    <Choice Filter="isHTML32" Alignment="Left"></Choice>
                </DeviceSpecific>
</mobile:Image>
            <mobile:Label id="lblFm32" runat="server">I Chose:</mobile:Label>
            <mobile:Image id="imgMyChoice" runat="server"
➡ Alignment="Center">
                <DeviceSpecific>
                    <Choice Filter="isHTML32" Alignment="Left"></Choice>
                </DeviceSpecific>
</mobile:Image>
            <mobile:Label id="lblWin"
➡ runat="server"></mobile:Label>
            <mobile:Label id="lblYourScore"
➡ runat="server"></mobile:Label>
            <mobile:Label id="lblMyScore"
➡ runat="server"></mobile:Label>
            <mobile:Command id="cmdPlayAgain" runat="server"
➡ SoftkeyLabel="Play">Play Again?</mobile:Command>
            <mobile:Command id="cmdQuitFm3" runat="server"
➡ SoftkeyLabel="Quit">Quit Game</mobile:Command>
    </mobile:form>
</body>
```

## Summary

This application is a good demonstration of some of the issues involved in porting applications from ASP to ASP.NET. It is not that our algorithms (or even much of our basic code) are different, but the basic framework of the application is altered. As this process is as much intuitive as it is logical, it makes it almost impossible to create some automated process (within the bounds of current technology!) that could reliably do the job.

We have also seen the practical use of some of the device-specific capabilities of the Mobile Internet Toolkit in this application. Although the MIT allows us to conveniently forget the individual device needs for much of programming, there are still going to be circumstances that warrant catering to these needs. It is reassuring to know that the MIT includes a powerful and flexible range of device-specific options that we can exploit where necessary.

## Conclusion

Well, that's it! Well, not quite exactly. This book has focused on working with beta versions of first generation products of a whole a new technology. I'll go completely out on a limb here and make the bold prediction that we can probably expect at least a few changes somewhere down the track! In fact, it's fair to say that we have only scratched the surface of what is to come.

There will undoubtedly be differences between the beta and release versions of MIT and VS .NET. Mobile technologies are in a period of rapid growth and development. From the time that I began writing this book until now, there have been complete generational jumps in mobile products that have been released to market. Promising technologies have fizzled and apparent duds have blossomed.

We stand at the pointy end of something new and exciting. If you are like me and love the latest gadgets, new technologies, and finding ways to use them meaningfully and productively in our home, social, and working lives, then you'll be in your element with the mobile revolution. Good luck!

# Class Listing for the Mobile Internet Toolkit

Table A.1 contains a listing of the available classes as found in the RC1 version of the Mobile Internet Toolkit. Note that these classes each contain (where relevant) their own constructors, methods, properties, and elements.

This appendix is designed as a quick reference. For more detailed information on the respective classes, please refer to the relevant Microsoft documentation.

**TABLE A.1:** Class Descriptions for the Mobile Internet Toolkit

| Class | Description |
| --- | --- |
| AdRotator | Displays randomly selected advertisements. |
| ArrayListCollectionBase | Implements functionality of Icollection interface to inheriting classes by using a Web Forms System.Collection .ArrayList object for storage. |
| BaseValidator | Is the base class for the validation controls. |
| Calendar | Displays a calendar based on the Web Forms Calendar control. Has limited functionality, but it is possible to access underlying Web Forms control. |
| ChtmlCalendarAdapter | Displays a calendar control across multiple pages for the CHTML adapter set. |
| ChtmlCommandAdapter | Provides adapter for Command control for CHTML adapter set. |
| ChtmlFormAdapter | Provides adapter for the Form control for CHTML adapter set. |
| ChtmlLinkAdapter | Provides adapter for Link control for CHTML adapter set. |
| ChtmlMobileTextWriter | Provides text writer functionality for CHTML adapter set. |
| ChtmlPageAdapter | Provides a page adapter for CHTML adapter set. |
| ChtmlPhoneCallAdapter | Provides adapter for PhoneCall control for CHTML adapter set. |
| Command | Is an element that enables users to invoke an event. |
| CompareValidator | Performs validation by comparing field of one control with the field of another control. |
| ControlAdapter | General abstract, base class that control adapters can inherit from; cannot be instantiated. |
| ControlPager | Used to determine page index for a control. |
| CustomValidation | Is used for custom validation against another control. |
| DeviceSpecific | Is used for making distinctions between devices. |
| DeviceSpecificChoice | Provides a single choice within a DeviceSpecific/Choice construct. |
| DeviceSpecificChoiceCollection | Is used to hold a set of choices. |
| DeviceSpecificControlBuilder | Provides parsing support for DeviceSpecific/Choice constructs. |
| ErrorFormatterPage | Specifies page to handle error information. |

*Continued on next page*

**TABLE A.1 CONTINUED:** Class Descriptions for the Mobile Internet Toolkit

| Class | Description |
|---|---|
| FontInfo | Provides all relevant font information concerning a mobile control. |
| Form | Is a form container. |
| FormControlBuilder | Provides parsing support for Form controls. |
| HtmlCalendarAdapter | Provides adapter for the Calendar control for HTML adapter set. |
| HtmlCommandAdapter | Provides adapter for the Command control for HTML adapter set. |
| HtmlControlAdapter | Provides the control adapter base class for the HTML adapter set. |
| HtmlFormAdapter | Provides adapter for the Form control for HTML adapter set. |
| HtmlImageAdapter | Provides adapter for the Image control for HTML adapter set. |
| HtmlLabelAdapter | Provides adapter for the Label control for HTML adapter set. |
| HtmlLinkAdapter | Provides adapter for the Link control for HTML adapter set. |
| HtmlListAdapter | Provides adapter for the List control for HTML adapter set. |
| HtmlLiteralTextAdapter | Provides a literal text adapter class for the HTML adapter set. |
| HtmlMobileTextWriter | Provides text writer functionality for HTML adapter set. |
| HtmlObjectListAdapter | Provides adapter for the ObjectList control for HTML adapter set. |
| HtmlPageAdapter | Provides a page adapter for the HTML adapter set. |
| HtmlPanelAdapter | Provides adapter for the Panel control for HTML adapter set. |
| HtmlPhoneCallAdapter | Provides adapter for the PhoneCall control for HTML adapter set. |
| HtmlSelectionListAdapter | Provides adapter for the SelectionList control for HTML adapter set. |
| HtmlTextBoxAdapter | Provides adapter for the TextBox control for HTML adapter set. |
| HtmlTextViewAdapter | Provides adapter for the TextView control for HTML adapter set. |
| HtmlValidationSummaryAdapter | Provides adapter for the ValidationSummary control for HTML adapter set. |
| HtmlValidatorAdapter | Provides a validator adapter class for the HTML adapter set. |
| Image | Displays an image. |
| ItemPager | Used to paginate contents of a control. |
| Label | Displays text. |
| Link | Is used for creating links. |
| List | Renders a list of items. |
| ListCommandEventArgs | Provides data for ItemCommand event of a List control. |
| ListCommandEventHandler Delegate | Represents method that handles the ItemCommand event of a List control. |
| ListControlBuilder | Provides parsing support for List and SelectionList controls. |
| ListDataBindEventArgs | Provides parameters for ItemDataBind event. |

*Continued on next page*

**TABLE A.1 CONTINUED:** Class Descriptions for the Mobile Internet Toolkit

| Class | Description |
|---|---|
| LiteralText | Provides instantiation of literal text in a form. |
| LoadItemsEventArgs | Provides data for controls that support custom pagination. |
| MobileCapabilities | Used to access information about a client device. |
| MobileControl | Base class for all mobile control classes (except MobilePage). |
| MobileControlBuilder | Provides parsing support for all Mobile Web Form controls; is internally created. |
| MobileFormsAuthentication | Appends authentication information to URLs when device in cookieless mode. |
| MobileListItem | Individual items within List and SelectionList controls. |
| MobileListItemCollection` | Used to hold the items from a SelectionList or List control. |
| MobilePage | Base class for all Mobile Web Forms pages. |
| MobileTextWriter | Base class for all TextWriter objects used when rendering mobile controls. |
| MobileUserControl | Base class for mobile user controls. |
| ObjectList | Enables multiple fields to be specified for display in an ObjectList. |
| ObjectListCommand | Is a command of an ObjectList. |
| ObjectListCommandCollection | Container for the controls of an ObjectList control. |
| ObjectListCommandEventArgs | Provides data for the ItemCommand event of an ObjectList control. |
| ObjectListControlBuilder | Provides parsing support for ObjectList control. |
| ObjectListDataBindEventArgs | Provides data for the ItemDataBind event of an ObjectList control. |
| ObjectListField | The field of an ObjectList control. |
| ObjectListFieldCollection | Container for the fields of an ObjectList control. |
| ObjectListItem | Individual item within ObjectList control. |
| ObjectListItemCollection | Container for the items from an ObjectList control. |
| ObjectListSelectEventArgs | Provides the data for ItemSelect event of the ObjectList control. |
| ObjectListShowCommandsEventArgs | Provides data for ShowItemCommands for an ObjectList control. |
| ObjectListTitleAttribute | Provides title of ObjectList. |
| PagedControl | Base class for controls supporting pagination. |
| PagerStyle | Provides style capability to the pagination of a form. |
| Panel | Is used for creating and manipulating Panels. |
| PanelControlBuilder | Provides parsing support for the Panel control. |
| PhoneCall | Enables user to autodial specified telephone numbers. |

*Continued on next page*

**TABLE A.1 CONTINUED:** Class Descriptions for the Mobile Internet Toolkit

| Class | Description |
| --- | --- |
| RangeValidator | Validates that a control's contents fall within a specified range. |
| RegularExpressionValidator | Validates that a control's contents matches a specified regular expression. |
| RequiredFieldValidator | Validates that a control has had a value entered or changed. |
| SelectionList | Adds selection capability for a list. |
| Style | Sets style characteristics for a control. |
| Stylesheet | Contains styles that can be applied to other controls. |
| StyleSheetControlBuilder | Provides parsing support for the StyleSheet control. |
| TemplateContainer | Inherits direct from Panel class and enables templates to be instantiated within a control. |
| TextBox | User input text control. |
| TextBoxControlBuilder | Provides parsing support for the TextBox control. |
| TextControl | Base class for text-based controls. |
| TextView | Provides TextView control for handling large quantities of text. |
| TextViewElement | Provides text for TextView control. |
| UpWmlMobileTextWriter | Provides text writer adapter class specific to Openwave browser. |
| UpWmlPageAdapter | Provides page adapter class specific to Openwave browser. |
| ValidationSummary | Provides a summary of any validation errors that may have happened. |
| WmlCalendarAdapter | Provides adapter for the Calendar control for WML adapter set. |
| WmlCommandAdapter | Provides adapter for the Command control for WML adapter set. |
| WmlControlAdapter | Provides the control adapter base class for the WML adapter set. |
| WmlFormAdapter | Provides adapter for the Form control for WML adapter set. |
| WmlImageAdapter | Provides adapter for the Image control for WML adapter set. |
| WmlLabelAdapter | Provides adapter for the Label control for WML adapter set. |
| WmlLinkAdapter | Provides adapter for the Link control for WML adapter set. |
| WmlListAdapter | Provides adapter for the List control for WML adapter set. |
| WmlLiteralTextAdapter | Provides a literal text adapter class for the WML adapter set. |
| WmlMobileTextWriter | Provides text writer functionality for WML adapter set. |
| WmlObjectListAdapter | Provides adapter for the ObjectList control for WML adapter set. |
| WmlPageAdapter | Provides a page adapter for the WML adapter set. |
| WmlPanelAdapter | Provides adapter for the Panel control for WML adapter set. |
| WmlPhoneCallAdapter | Provides adapter for the PhoneCall control for WML adapter set. |
| WmlSelectionListAdapter | Provides adapter for the SelectionList control for WML adapter set. |

*Continued on next page*

**TABLE A.1 CONTINUED:** Class Descriptions for the Mobile Internet Toolkit

| Class | Description |
| --- | --- |
| WmlTextBoxAdapter | Provides adapter for the TextBox control for WML adapter set. |
| WmlTextViewAdapter | Provides adapter for the TextView control for WML adapter set. |
| WmlValidationSummaryAdapter | Provides adapter for the ValidationSummary control for WML adapter set. |
| WmlValidatorAdapter | Provides a validator adapter class for the WML adapter set. |

# Appendix B

# WML Language Reference

Table B.1 is a brief overview of the some of the WML tags and their respective attributes that are commonly used in mobile site design. I have followed the version 1.1 specification in this list. (The 1.1 specification is met by the Beta 2 release of the Mobile Internet Toolkit and remains the most commonly implemented WAP specification at the time of publication.)

For a more extensive WML reference, please refer to either the Nokia (`http://forum.nokia.com`) or Openwave (`www.openwave.com`) Websites.

The following conventions have been observed:

- **Boldface** is used for required attributes.

- *Italic* is used for default values.

**TABLE B.1:** WML Tags and Their Attributes

| Tag | Attributes | Description | Can nest the following tags | Is valid when nested in the following tags |
|-----|-----------|-------------|----------------------------|-------------------------------------------|
| `<a>` | | Link. | `<br>`, `<img>` | `<p>`, `<fieldset>`, `<td>` |
| | **href** | Address of the link. | | |
| `<access>` | | Controls access to the deck. | | `<head>` |
| | `domain` | Domain suffix of allowed pages. | | |
| | `path` | Path prefix of allowed pages. | | |
| `<anchor>` | | Defines a link associated with a task. For example, go, prev, or refresh. | `<br>`, `<img>`, `<go>`, `<prev>`, `<refresh>` | |
| `<b>` | | Renders text in bold where possible. | `<em>`, `<strong>`, `<i>`, `<u>`, `<big>`, `<small>` | `<p>`, `<td>`, `<fieldset>`, `<br>`, `<em>`, `<strong>`, `<i>`, `<u>`, `<big>`, `<small>` |
| `<big>` | | Renders text in large font where possible. | `<em>`, `<strong>`, `<i>`, `<u>`, `<b>`, `<small>` | `<p>`, `<td>`, `<fieldset>`, `<br>`, `<em>`, `<strong>`, `<i>`, `<u>`, `<b>`, `<small>` |
| `<br>` | | Break tag to start a new line. | | `<p>`, `<anchor>`, `<a>`, `<fieldset>`, `<td>` |
| `<card>` | | Defines a card element of a deck. | `<do>`, `<onevent>`, `<timer>`, `<p>` | `<wml>` |
| | `title` | Browser may display title in any one of a variety of ways. | | |

*Continued on next page*

**TABLE B.1 CONTINUED:** WML Tags and Their Attributes

| Tag | Attributes | Description | Can nest the following tags | Is valid when nested in the following tags |
|---|---|---|---|---|
| | newcontext | Indicates current browser context needs to be reinitialized on entry to card. Can be either *False* or True. | | |
| | ordered | Helps card order content. Can be either *False* or True. | | |
| | onenterforward | Specifies URL to load when user enters card using a forward go task. | | |
| | onenterbackward | Specifies URL to load when user enters card via backward navigation. | | |
| | ontimer | Specifies URL to load when timer expires. | | |
| <do> | | Enables user to perform some task on a card. | <go>, <prev>, <noop>, <refresh> | <template>, <card>, <p>, <fieldset> |
| | **type** | Specifies particular binding to execute: accept, prev, help, reset, options, delete, unknown. | | |
| | label | Enables a label to be specified for the task. | | |
| | name | The name of the do event binding. | | |
| | optional | Can be either *False* or True. If True, then browser may ignore this binding. | | |
| <em> | | Renders text with emphasis. | <b>, <strong>, <i>, <u>, <big>, <small> | <p>, <td>, <fieldset>, <br>, <big>, <strong>, <i>, <u>, <b>, <small> |
| <fieldset> | | Defines a group of related fields and text. | <a>, <anchor>, <br>, <do>, <img>, <input>, <select>, <table> | <fieldset>, <p> |
| <go> | | Defines forward navigation to new URL. | <postfield>, <setvar> | <anchor>, <do>, <setvar> |

*Continued on next page*

**TABLE B.1 CONTINUED:** WML Tags and Their Attributes

| Tag | Attributes | Description | Can nest the following tags | Is valid when nested in the following tags |
|-----|-----------|-------------|---------------------------|------------------------------------------|
| | href | The URL to load. | | |
| | sendreferer | Determines whether URL of referring deck should be transmitted. | | |
| | method | get, post. | | |
| | accept-charset | Specifies list of character encodings that the server must accept. | | |
| | cache-control | "no-cache" forces browser to ignore local cache. | | |
| \<head\> | | Defines information specific to the deck (such as meta-data). | \<access\>, \<meta\> | \<wml\> |
| \<i\> | | Renders text in italic where possible. | \<b\>, \<strong\>, \<em\>, \<u\>, \<big\>, \<small\> | \<p\>, \<td\>, \<fieldset\>, \<br\>, \<big\>, \<strong\>, \<em\>, \<u\>, \<b\>, \<small\> |
| \<img\> | | Image tag. | | \<fieldset\>, \<p\>, \<td\> |
| | **alt** | Text to display when image cannot be shown. | | |
| | **src** | Identifies URL of image. | | |
| | localsrc | Alternative local representation of image if available. | | |
| | vspace | Specifies the amount of white space to appear above and below image. | | |
| | hspace | Specifies the amount of white space to appear to the left and right of the image. | | |
| | align | Specifies alignment of image with respect to text (*bottom*, middle, top). | | |
| | height | Vertical size of image. | | |

*Continued on next page*

**TABLE B.1 CONTINUED:** WML Tags and Their Attributes

| Tag | Attributes | Description | Can nest the following tags | Is valid when nested in the following tags |
|---|---|---|---|---|
| | width | Horizontal size of image. | | |
| `<input>` | | Data entry field. | | `<fieldset>`, `<p>` |
| | name | Specifies WML variable to hold result of user's input. | | |
| | value | Default value to be used. | | |
| | format | Format mask for user's input. | | |
| | emptyok | Indicates that an empty input string is acceptable. | | |
| | size | Width in characters of input field. | | |
| | maxlength | Maximum number of characters allowed. | | |
| | tabindex | Specifies tabbing position of the control. | | |
| | title | Specifies a title for the element. | | |
| `<meta>` | | Contains meta-information related to the deck. | | `<head>` |
| | **http-equiv** | May be used instead of name attribute. Indicates how the meta-data should be interpreted. | | |
| | **name** | Specifies property name. | | |
| | forua | Can be either *False* or True. Specifies whether property is intended to reach the browser. | | |
| | **content** | Specifies property value. | | |
| | scheme | Conveys information about structure of data (property value). | | |
| `<noop>` | | Specifies that no task is to be done. | | `<do>`, `<onevent>` |
| `<onevent>` | | Binds a task to an intrinsic event. | `<go>`, `<noop>`, `<prev>`, `<refresh>` | `<card>`, `<template>`, `<option>` (onpick type only) |

*Continued on next page*

**TABLE B.1 CONTINUED:** WML Tags and Their Attributes

| Tag | Attributes | Description | Can nest the following tags | Is valid when nested in the following tags |
|---|---|---|---|---|
| | **type** | Specifies the particular event: onenterforward, onenterbackward, ontimer, onpick. | | |
| `<optgroup>` | | Identifies group of related elements in a selection list. | `<option>` | `<select>` |
| | `title` | Title for the element. | | |
| `<option>` | | Specifies a single element within a selection list. | `<onevent>` (onpick only) | `<optgroup>`, `<select>` |
| | `value` | A value associated with this option. | | |
| | `onpick` | URL loaded when user selects this option. | | |
| | `title` | Specifies a title for the element. | | |
| `<p>` | | Paragraph tag. | `<a>`, `<anchor>`, `<br>`, `<do>`, `<fieldset>`, `<img>`, `<input>`, `<select>`, `<table>`, `<big>`, `<strong>`, `<i>`, `<u>`, `<b>`, `<small>`, `<em>` | `<card>` |
| | `align` | Alignment attribute (*left*, center, right). | | |
| | `mode` | Wrapping attribute (wrap, nowrap). | | |
| `<post`➡`field>` | | Specifies field name and value for transmission to application server. | | `<go>` |
| | **name** | Specifies variable name. | | |
| | **value** | Specifies value of data. | | |
| `<prev>` | | Defines backward navigation task. | `<setvar>` | `<anchor>`, `<do>`, `<onevent>` |
| `<refresh>` | | Defines screen refresh. | `<setvar>` | `<anchor>`, `<do>`, `<onevent>` |
| `<select>` | | Defines selection list. | `<option>`, `<optgroup>` | `<fieldset>`, `<p>` |

*Continued on next page*

**TABLE B.1 CONTINUED:**  WML Tags and Their Attributes

| Tag | Attributes | Description | Can nest the following tags | Is valid when nested in the following tags |
|---|---|---|---|---|
| | multiple | Can be either False or True. Specifies whether list is multiselect or single select. | | |
| | tabindex | Tabbing position of control. | | |
| | name | WML variable to receive user's selection. | | |
| | value | Determines default value of variable in name attribute. | | |
| | iname | Specifies WML variable to hold index value of selection. | | |
| | ivalue | Specifies default, selected element. | | |
| | title | Title of control. | | |
| \<setvar\> | | Assigns a value to a variable. | | \<go\>, \<prev\>, \<refresh\> |
| | **name** | Specifies variable name. | | |
| | **value** | Specifies value to be assigned to variable. | | |
| \<small\> | | Specifies text to be rendered in small font (if possible). | \<b\>, \<strong\>, \<em\>, \<u\>, \<big\>, \<i\> | \<p\>, \<td\>, \<fieldset\>, \<br\>, \<big\>, \<strong\>, \<em\>, \<u\>, \<b\>, \<i\> |
| \<strong\> | | Specifies text to be rendered with strong emphasis (if possible). | \<b\>, \<i\>, \<em\>, \<u\>, \<big\>, \<small\> | \<p\>, \<td\>, \<fieldset\>, \<br\>, \<big\>, \<i\>, \<em\>, \<u\>, \<b\>, \<small\> |
| \<table\> | | Table specifying tag. | \<tr\> | \<p\>, \<fieldset\> |
| | **columns** | Specifies non-zero number of columns in table. | | |
| | title | Title of table. | | |
| | align | Sequence of characters L, C, R (one for each column), specifying alignment of each column. | | |

*Continued on next page*

**TABLE B.1 CONTINUED:** WML Tags and Their Attributes

| Tag | Attributes | Description | Can nest the following tags | Is valid when nested in the following tags |
|-----|-----------|-------------|----------------------------|-------------------------------------------|
| `<td>` | | Specifies a cell within a table. | `<a>`, `<anchor>`, `<img>`, `<br>`, `<big>`, `<i>`, `<em>`, `<u>`, `<b>`, `<small>`, `<strong>` | `<tr>` |
| `<template>` | | Specifies event bindings that apply to all cards within a deck. | `<do>`, `<onevent>` | `<wml>` |
| | onenterforward | Specifies URL to load when user enters card using a forward go task. | | |
| | onenterbackward | Specifies URL to load when user enters card via backward navigation. | | |
| | ontimer | Specifies URL to load when timer expires. | | |
| `<timer>` | | Specifies an event to occur after a period of time. | | `<select>`, `<optgroup>` |
| | name | WML variable to control timer value. | | |
| | value | Default value of variable identified in name attribute. | | |
| `<tr>` | | Specifies a row in a table. | `<td>` | `<table>` |
| `<u>` | | Specifies text to be underlined (if possible). | `<b>`, `<i>`, `<em>`, `<strong>`, `<big>`, `<small>` | `<p>`, `<td>`, `<fieldset>`, `<br>`, `<big>`, `<i>`, `<em>`, `<strong>`, `<b>`, `<small>` |
| `<wml>` | | Defines a WML deck. | `<card>`, `<head>`, `<template>` (deck must contain at least one card; head and template are optional) | |

**WARNING** Note that WML is an XML-based language and is, therefore, a lot less forgiving than HTML. It is case sensitive and does not tolerate errors (such as mistakes in syntax or missing close tags).

# Appendix C

# Internet References

Tables C.1 and C.2 are lists of useful Internet references related to both .NET and Mobile technologies and are by no means definitive.

**TABLE C.1:** .NET and Microsoft Technologies-Related Websites

| Website | URL |
| --- | --- |
| **Microsoft** | |
| Microsoft | www.microsoft.com |
| Microsoft Downloads | http://msdn.microsoft.com/downloads |
| Microsoft .Net | www.microsoft.com/net |
| Microsoft XML Web Services | http://msdn.microsoft.com/vstudio/nextgen/technology/webdefault.asp |
| Microsoft MSDN Library | http://msdn.microsoft.com/library/default.asp? |
| **.NET** | |
| GotDotNet | www.gotdotnet.com |
| Nothin' But .NET User Group | www.nothinbutdotnet.com |
| C# Corner | www.c-sharpcorner.com |
| **General** | |
| DevX | www.devx.com |
| IT White Papers | www.itpapers.com |
| **ASP** | |
| ASP 101 | www.asp101.com |
| ASPToday | www.asptoday.com |
| ASP Resource Index | www.aspin.com |
| DevASP for ASP Developers | www.devasp.com |
| ASP Toolbox | www.tcp-ip.com |
| **XML** | |
| XML Today | www.xmltoday.com |
| **Visual Basic** | |
| Carl & Gary's Visual Basic Home Page | www.cgvb.com |
| MSDN Visual Basic Tips and Tricks | http://msdn.microsoft.com/vbasic/technical/tips.asp |
| Visual Basic Code | www.vbcode.com |
| Visual Studio Magazine | www.vbpj.com |
| VB-World | www.vbworld.com |

**TABLE C.2:**  Mobile Technologies–Related Websites

| Website | URL |
| --- | --- |
| **Microsoft** | |
| Microsoft Mobile | www.microsoft.com/mobile |
| Microsoft MIT Newsgroup | microsoft.public.dotnet.framework.aspnet.mobile accessed through http://msdn.microsoft.com/newsgroups |
| **News, Views & Support** | |
| Wap Forum | www.wapforum.com |
| AnyWhereYouGo | www.anywhereyougo.com |
| allNetDevices | http://allnetdevices.com |
| WAPsites.com.au | www.wapsites.com.au |
| Gelon | www.gelon.net |
| WMLScript | www.wmlscript.com |
| WAPnet | www.wap.net |
| **Tools and Development** | |
| DotWAP | www.dotwap.com |
| Openwave | http://developer.phone.com |
| Nokia | http://forum.nokia.com/main.html |
| Ericsson | www.ericsson.com/mobilityworld |

# Index

Note to reader: **bolded** page numbers refer to definitions and main discussions of a topic. *Italicized* page number refer to illustrations.

# TELL US WHAT YOU THINK!

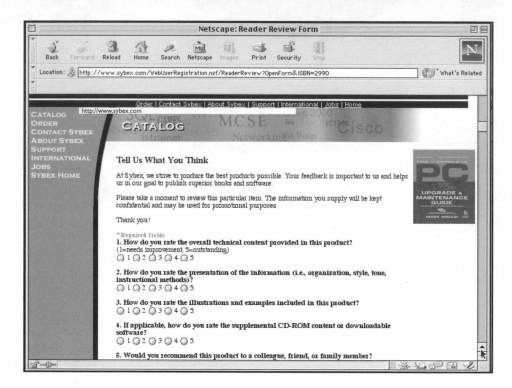

Your feedback is critical to our efforts to provide you with the best books and software on the market. Tell us what you think about the products you've purchased. It's simple:

1. Visit the Sybex website
2. Go to the product page
3. Click on **Submit a Review**
4. Fill out the questionnaire and comments
5. Click **Submit**

With your feedback, we can continue to publish the highest quality computer books and software products that today's busy IT professionals deserve.

## www.sybex.com

SYBEX Inc. • 1151 Marina Village Parkway, Alameda, CA  94501 • 510-523-8233

*The quotation on the bottom of the front cover is taken from the twenty-seventh chapter of Lao Tzu's* Tao Te Ching, *the classic work of Taoist philosophy. These particular verses are from the translation by D. C. Lau (copyright 1963) and are part of a larger exploration of the nature of the Tao, sometimes translated as "the way."*

*It is traditionally held that Lao Tzu lived in the fifth century B.C. in China, but it is unclear whether he was actually a historical figure. The concepts embodied in the* Tao Te Ching *influenced religious thinking in the Far East, including Zen Buddhism in Japan. Many in the West, however, have wrongly understood the* Tao Te Ching *to be primarily a mystical work; in fact, much of the advice in the book is grounded in a practical moral philosophy governing personal conduct.*